Punk Ethnography

Edited by Michael E. Veal and E. Tammy Kim

PUNK ETHNOGRAPHY

Artists and Scholars Listen

to Sublime Frequencies

Wesleyan University Press   Middletown, Connecticut

Wesleyan University Press
Middletown, CT 06459
www.wesleyan.edu/wespress
© 2016 Wesleyan University Press
All rights reserved
Manufactured in the United States of America
Designed by Mindy Basinger Hill
Typeset in Minion Pro

Library of Congress Cataloging-in-Publication Data

Names: Veal, Michael E., 1963– editor. | Kim, E. Tammy, editor.
Title: Punk ethnography: Artists and Scholars
Listen to Sublime Frequencies /
edited by Michael E. Veal and E. Tammy Kim.
Description: Middletown, Connecticut: Wesleyan University Press,
[2016] | Series: Music/culture | Includes bibliographical
references, discography, videography, and index.
Identifiers: LCCN 2016006282 (print) | LCCN 2016016928 (ebook) |
ISBN 9780819576521 (cloth: alk. paper) | ISBN 9780819576538
(pbk.: alk. paper) | ISBN 9780819576545 (ebook)
Subjects: LCSH: Sublime Frequencies (Firm) | Ethnography. |
World music—History and criticism. | Sound recordings—
Social aspects. | Sound recording executives and producers—
Interviews. | Motion picture producers and directors—Interviews.
Classification: LCC ML3792.S83 P86 2016 (print) |
LCC ML3792.S83 (ebook) | DDC 780.9—dc23
LC record available at https://lccn.loc.gov/2016006282

5   4   3   2   1

CONTENTS

PART ONE

Background Context

MICHAEL E. VEAL AND E. TAMMY KIM

Introduction

AN INTRIGUING NEW LABEL

Around 2003, a peculiar batch of sound and video recordings began to appear on the "world music" racks of specialty music stores like Other Music in New York and now-defunct Twisted Village in Boston. These CDs, LPs, and DVDs, adorned with comic-style cutouts, film stills, and advertisements, seemed out of place alongside traditional, ethnographic recordings. Their titles ranged from prosaic to eccentric and evocative: *Radio Morocco, I Remember Syria, Thai Pop Spectacular, The World Is Unreal Like a Snake in a Rope, The Pierced Heart and the Machete,* and *Princess Nicotine,* just to name a few.[1] The contents appeared to span folk, classical, and popular styles, but the liner notes provided little context or information—in general, much less on genre, instrumentation, performers, or translated lyrics than your typical world-music recording. While transparency of presentation in an academic sense was not the label's priority, Sublime Frequencies' releases were surreal, fascinating objects of sound art tackling a diverse range of world music.

Radio Thailand, for example, is a two-disc collection of regional Thai broadcasts compiled over a 15-year period, encompassing court-based "gong-chime" orchestras, *molam* pop music, "shadow pop" (Thai adaptations of American surf rock), songs played on the *khaen* mouth organ, random radio excerpts of news bulletins, Buddhist devotional chanting, and pure signal noise.[2] The arrangement of these sounds departs from the traditionally ethnographic and makes explicit the creative hand of the producers. Most tracks, with fanciful titles such as "21st Century Perspiration" and "Rubber of High Quality," are collagist in nature, providing a wild ride across genres and traditions that recalls the frantic sensuality of Stan Brakhage's experimental films. The release belongs

Radio Java (SF002) established the visual and audio trajectory
of Sublime Frequencies' flagship *Radio* series.

to Sublime Frequencies' *Radio* series, a distinctive strand of the label's oeuvre.[3] Each disc is a sound collage scavenged from the airways of the world; together, they constitute Sublime Frequencies' flagship endeavor and most clearly embody its aesthetic philosophy: a fragmentary, anarchic approach to sound and graphic design and the belief in collage as a medium of cultural representation. Over time, this style has earned the label a dedicated and, in some cases, fanatically devoted following, particularly among "hipster" audiences in the United States and United Kingdom. The recordings have been plugged by taste-making radio stations like KEXP in Seattle, and Sublime Frequencies' founders have appeared in prominent pop cultural outlets and venues like the *Believer* magazine (see Andy Beta's contribution), the Barbican in London, and the Brooklyn Academy of Music.[4] Meanwhile, Sublime Frequencies has courted an equal amount of controversy through its renegade capture of world music traditions, its unconventional approach to documentation, and its founders' explicit criticisms of the field of ethnomusicology.

For all these reasons, Sublime Frequencies is more than a label or esoteric cult project. It represents an indie turn in global pop; a rebellious, at times neocolonial streak in ethnography; and an occasion to talk about globalized cultural consumption. There are many reasons to celebrate, vilify, critique, and/or ponder the label's activities. This book—created without the involvement or endorsement of Sublime Frequencies—attempts to make sense of them all, or, at the very least, to begin asking the right questions.

AGAINST TRADITION

Sublime Frequencies was founded in 2003 by brothers Richard and Alan Bishop— two-thirds of the art-punk band Sun City Girls—and their friend Hisham Mayet. The label naturally grew out of its founders' artistic projects, which encompassed dozens of self-released cassettes, 7-inch singles, and CD/LP albums by the Sun City Girls (whose third member, Charles Gocher, died in 2007). The Bishops, Mayet, and their close collaborator Mark Gergis loved to travel and collect, and had amassed a huge archive of the world's music. Indeed, many Sublime Frequencies releases are curated from their personal troves. Other releases employ a network of "recordists"—including indie-rock producer Tucker Martine (interviewed herein by Julie Strand), ethnomusicologist Laurent Jeanneau (interviewed by Gonçalo Cardoso) and filmmaker Olivia Wyatt (interviewed by Jonathan Andrews)—who travel the world capturing local sounds (and sights) and transforming their semi-refined field recordings into deftly packaged CDs, LPS, and DVDs. Since its initial releases in 2003, Sublime Frequencies has issued a truly stunning range of the world's musical traditions—folk, classical, popular, experimental, and everything in between.

As explained on its website, and as contributor David Novak elaborates, Sublime Frequencies positions itself as a new-media successor to hallowed ethnographic recording labels such as Bärenreiter-Musicaphon, Folkways, Smithsonian Folkways, Chant du Monde, Playasound, Lyrichord, Ocora, and Nonesuch:

> SUBLIME FREQUENCIES is a collective of explorers dedicated to acquiring and exposing obscure sights and sounds from modern and traditional urban and rural frontiers via film and video, field recordings, radio and short wave transmissions, international folk and pop music, sound anomalies, and other forms of human and natural expression not documented sufficiently through all channels of academic research, the modern recording industry, media, or corporate foundations. SUBLIME FREQUENCIES is focused on an aesthetic of

extra-geography and soulful experience inspired by music and culture, world travel, research, and the pioneering recording labels of the past including OCORA, SMITHSONIAN FOLKWAYS, ETHNIC FOLKWAYS, LYRICHORD, NONE-SUCH EXPLORER, MUSICAPHONE [sic], BARONREITER [sic], UNESCO, PLAYA-SOUND, MUSICAL ATLAS, CHANT DU MONDE, B.A.M., TANGENT, and TOPIC.[5]

This informal "mission statement" places Sublime Frequencies in a tradition of "sound ethnography" historically associated with the field of ethnomusicology and, to a lesser extent, cultural anthropology—not surprising given that most canonical field recordings of the world's music have been the products of academic research.[6] But while "ethnography" is obviously a central term in ethnomusicology and cultural anthropology, "sound ethnography" is less common. We use this term to indicate the *writing of culture*, with the important distinction that, in sound ethnography, culture is written via the technologies of sound recording. Field recordings, in this light, become more than *presentations of the sounds* of music cultures; they become *representations* of music cultures. In addition to raising all the issues that we typically associate with ethnography (the writing of culture), phonography (writing via sound), and the idea of sound recordings as art objects in and of themselves, field recordings dramatize the more basic fact that different ethnographic recordings frame their sounds in different ways, each painting a different—and by definition, partial and subjective—portrait of a music culture.

Like the older ethnographic labels, Sublime Frequencies' releases tend to use sound to present cultures in a certain way. But despite their professed admiration for their predecessors, Sublime Frequencies' founders have expressed strongly ambivalent feelings about bringing the label's products into critical dialogue with ethnomusicology (the field that traditionally has been the main conduit of Western knowledge about non-Western music cultures). In their interviews reprinted here, Alan Bishop and Hisham Mayet express suspicion of the academic ethnomusicological tradition.

On closer examination, the Sublime Frequencies crew has often invoked ethnomusicology as a straight man, as it were, in order to carve out the label's own space in the world-music market. The founders have presented themselves as ethnographic Robin Hoods, redressing the power imbalance between the Euro-American sphere and other areas of the world through musical advocacy. Bishop told the music blog *Made Like a Tree*: "Western export culture is a one-way highway shoving itself down the throats of the entire world. The developing nations do not have a reciprocal avenue to fire back at the West, to promote their culture. Hopefully the Sublime Frequencies releases can provide a stray bullet seeping through the holes in reverse to inspire others to create larger weaponry to make greater inroads in the future."[7]

But how accurate or genuine are these sentiments? Sublime Frequencies seems quick to elide the involvement of post–World War II ethnomusicology in implicitly and explicitly contesting Western musical hegemony. While it is true that the discipline has historical roots in the colonizing project and relies largely on Western modes of inquiry and analysis, it could also be argued that, with scholars working in the context of nationalism and de-colonization, post-war ethnomusicology has fundamentally contested the pervasive influence of Western musical culture. Sublime Frequencies' commitment to the same is less clear. On the one hand, the label has produced albums from George W. Bush and Dick Cheney's so-called Axis of Evil—including Iraq and North Korea (see E. Tammy Kim's chapter, "*Noraebang* with the Dear Leader")—and other majority-Muslim countries demonized by the United States, such as Syria, Palestine, Pakistan, Mali, and Indonesia.[8] On the other hand, the label's releases are strongly shaped by their founders' own idiosyncratic sensibilities and in most cases lack input from and fail to credit the original creators (see André Redwood's essay on copyright). This type of decontextualization arguably reaches its height in the substantial liberties that Sublime Frequencies takes in matters of cultural representation, forcibly reframing a variety of local musics to suit Western punk/indie rock/experimental sensibilities. The reframing lies in direct opposition to ethnomusicology's emphasis on accurate contextualization as a primary means of understanding musical styles and traditions. After all, if the presence of a cello or organ in Western rock does not automatically resignify that music as "classical," neither does the presence of electric guitars and keyboards automatically qualify non-Western folk or vernacular musics as "rock."

The same can be said for Sublime Frequencies' treatment and selection of world music genres that conform to its stylistic criteria for a musical avant-garde or its experimental construction of the *Radio* albums discussed later in this introduction. Non-Western concepts of sound, meter, pitch, and structure, for example, do not qualify as "experimental" on the mere basis of their stylistic unfamiliarity. We might also ask whether the avant-garde always represents an inherently progressive stance in a given society or whether, as Kay Dickinson suggests, it can just as easily align with reactionary, conservative, and imperialist ideologies and practices.[9] And despite Sublime Frequencies' advocacy claims, to what extent does its brand of avant-gardism adhere to the (neo-) colonial agendas of revitalizing American culture by "mining" the musical traditions of the wider world and exoticizing unfamiliar sounds through lack of adequate explanation? Matters of discretion and creative license are understandable, but all this begs the question of how effectively the label's releases function as the antihegemonic "weaponry" of Alan Bishop's claims.

Bishop has also taken aim at one of ethnomusicology's core values: so-called "bi-musicality," or the emphasis on acquiring hands-on competence in a given tradition in order to represent and teach it more effectively. "Tradition is not about slavish imitation," he said. "The last thing I want to see is a bunch of fucking white guys playing Javanese gamelon [sic] proper... They are being disrespectful because they are not evolving the situation. They are not rolling the dice. They are copying, just following somebody else's rules."[10]

The concept of bi-musicality was first articulated by ethnomusicologist Mantle Hood in 1960, as a corrective to decades of Western distortion and misrepresentation of world-music traditions.[11] The concept contained both practical and political overtones. Most immediately, it strengthened the rigor of non-Western musical instruction in Western institutions. But it also justified bringing non-Western musicians and scholars to Western schools and performance venues, thereby challenging the balance of power between the West and its former colonial (and current neo-colonial) subjects. This produced a literal, concrete example of the "firing back" to which Bishop alludes above, and it has had long-term consequences: By now, several generations of students, scholars, and musicians have been profoundly influenced by their exposure to the musical traditions of the wider world, and have carried those traditions into previously untouched social and musical spaces in America.

If Bishop and Mayet intend to specifically condemn a conservative, preservationist streak in ethnomusicology, this, too, was prefigured within the discipline. Since the 1980s, large numbers of ethnomusicologists have turned their attention to popular styles of the non-Western world and other practices reflecting cross-cultural mixing and borrowing. Today, the field is well aware of its pitfalls, and self-critique has become a fundamental component of its ongoing internal dialogue.[12] More significant (and ironic), however, is the fact that the Sublime Frequencies' founders and artists often have subscribed to a preservationist agenda, seeing themselves as documenting cultures and media endangered by the processes of modernization, migration, and globalization. In this sense, Sublime Frequencies conforms, in spite of itself, to one of the founding agendas of ethnomusicology.

Ethnography can be a fraught undertaking, but Bishop's criticisms don't stand up to historical scrutiny; nor do they justify the label's cavalier approach to crediting and compensating musicians. (It is, at least, equally hands-off in defending the pirating of its own releases, many of which are available for streaming on YouTube.) Time will tell whether Sublime Frequencies' transgressive model can be reconciled with the hard-won ethical battles previously fought by ethnomusicologists and the large-scale attempts to redefine intellectual property as it relates to artistic traditions of the non-Western world. For the moment, however, we believe there is another way of understanding the label's mission. Sublime Frequencies is rejecting something much larger than the norms of ethnographic practice: It is an enterprise that rejects rules altogether—essentially asserting punk and experimental impulses as valid prisms for viewing the world's music.

PUNK-INDIE ETHNOGRAPHERS

To understand Sublime Frequencies is to ground it in the history and philosophy of punk, one of the most significant, transformative developments in 1970s' music and culture and, a generation later, the driving force behind America's 1990s' indie-rock revolution.[13] Both punk and indie rock, as Marc Masters chronicles in his essay, heavily influenced the Bishops' avant-garde trio, Sun City Girls, and in turn shaped the sensibility of Sublime Frequencies. The very naming of their band after Sun City—an Arizona retirement community but also the name of a controversial entertainment complex that symbolized apartheid South Africa—places them in the tradition of rebellious, irreverent band monikers such as the Dead Kennedys, Circle Jerks, the 4-Skins, and Butthole Surfers.

Sublime Frequencies' brand of musical ethnography is governed by punk: a do-it-yourself, take-what-you-want ethos; a reaction against homogeneity, insularity, and centralized narratives; and, most important for Sublime Frequencies, a flair for the deliberately outrageous gesture and embrace of contradiction. How else can we square Bishop's excoriating comments about ethnomusicology with co-founder Mayet's admission that: "I was just a nut for geography and ethnography and anthropology. I studied all that stuff in school. It was informal—I have an art history degree and a history degree. But I just love anthropology and history, music, film. So it just organically happened."[14]

What might the philosophies and procedures of punk mean for the practice of ethnography? In the context of rock music history, punk unfolded in categorical opposition to the normative rock practices of the time. As shaped by groups like the Sex Pistols, Crass, the Exploited, and the Ramones, it relied more on rhetorical irony and brash simplicity than finely wrought reasoning or methodical musical construction. Later, as punk gave way to New Wave, its techniques were used to gradually modulate mainstream practices, injecting edge and energy into more traditional conceptions of rock and pop song-craft, as exemplified by musicians like Elvis Costello, Squeeze, and Joe Jackson. The underlying idea here—whether musical or ethnographic—is that, in the end, all traditions are eventually transformed through the influence of radical, formerly outsider impulses. By extension to the academic sphere, Sublime Frequencies represents its own new wave: a refreshing, at times provocative, and ultimately necessary critique of established ethnographic practices. As much as the label has decontextualized "other" musics, it has also implicitly re-contextualized them. Some releases accomplish this by presenting a fuller range of various societies' musical expression (for example, Thai surf and soul music, Indian country-and-western, and Saharan guitar rock) than the West typically has been aware of via traditional world-music or ethnomusicological channels. Other releases accomplish this by radically resignifying sounds. *Broken Hearted Dragonflies*, for example, takes the ostensibly most austere, "non-musical" aspect of traditional field recordings—ambient sounds of chirping insects, in this case from Indonesia—and rebrands them for the listener as "insect electronica"—a witty resignification that simultaneously works as a marketing strategy, a readjustment of the terms of listening, and a political assertion (see David Font-Navarrete's chapter). Each strategy serves, in its own way, to lift these cultures out of the historical ghetto of "tradition" within the enforced binary of tradition versus modernity. After all, if the mating sounds of insects can be resignified for human ears as not only music but as *electronic* music (with all of the latter's technologically advanced associations), this automatically renders moot the uneven classification of *human* music cultures.

Most significant here is Sublime Frequencies' indictment of academic insularity. The discourses of the humanities, including music, have become alienating and excessively inward looking, even to highly educated people. While specialized, technical languages are central to all disciplines, this exclusivity seems especially upsetting in the case of music, which, although not the "universal language" that the romanticized term suggests, contains a sonic-affective power capable of surviving the transition across cultural borders. Narrowing the scholarly discourse around music subverts this power and reduces its potential to the province of a select and elite few. Viewed from another angle, this rhetorical insularity is as much a byproduct of the increasing corporatization of the academy and the excessive specialization it demands as it is a marker of scientific rigor. Academics have a responsibility as society's paid thinkers, but too often seem only interested in talking to each other. Sublime Frequencies aims to break this hermetic seal. Its fun, populist, post-punk, garage-band ethnography not only documents outlying musical traditions but also makes them accessible to listeners who, for reasons of age, taste, or background, fall outside the traditional audience categories for world music.

This sensibility extends to Sublime Frequencies' visual presentation. Just as punk music later morphed into the smooth artistry of New Wave rock, so did the shocking irreverence of punk fashion and style evolve into indie design.[15] (Today's DIY aesthetic can be seen as a less irreverent, less transgressive version of the punk design impulse.) Sublime Frequencies has a penchant for this smoothed-out version of punk style. While a far cry from the Sex Pistols' jagged, "ransom note" album covers or Sid Vicious's dingy, hand-marked tee-shirts, Sublime Frequencies' graphics do recall the zine, punk's paper analog. As defined by Stephen Duncombe, zines are handmade, cheaply reproduced, pamphlet-like publications made through rough, provocative combinations of original and appropriated image and text—via layering, cut-ups, collage, bricolage, and pastiche—that reject "professional standards of argument and design."[16] The album art of Sublime Frequencies combines canny, ironic, popular, and found photographs, ornament, illustrations, maps, and typed and handwritten text, in contrast to the straight, documentary photography that graced old ethnographic LPs. Images of rural musicians and traditional symbols compete with those of low-cost dwellings, blurred streets, repurposed posters, bright colors, and pulp. The label "exposes [world music's] colorful inner workings rather than slapping a coat of waxy polyurethane to cover up the knotholes and askew grains."[17]

On Sublime Frequencies' radio-collage releases—by nature fragmentary and literally "edgy"—design mirrors sound. The album art for *Radio Morocco* and *Radio Palestine*, for example, feature postage stamps and cut-up Arabic text alongside local symbols. Other albums reference elements of modern chaos: those of bird's eye photographs (*Radio Palestine*), maps (*Radio India*), and streetscapes (*Radio Java*), as well as pop-cultural motifs like movie stills, manipulated symbols (a Hindu god or pharaonic head), subversively treated traditional images (a female Thai dancer collaged onto a fluorescent checkered background), and psychedelic comic book scraps (prominent on *Radio Thailand*).

Zine-style collage even finds its way onto Sublime Frequencies' retro-pop compilations and de facto field recordings. The cover of *1970's Algerian Proto-Rai*

Underground CD/LP features a crude pastiche of text and photocopied images. The black-outlined graphics include an antique handgun, a mustachioed man in a bad period suit, a sultry blonde staring at the camera, and another woman, cropped at the neck à la Baudelaire, in bra and underwear, straddling an ornate armchair. The compilation *Leaf Music, Drunks, Distant Drums*, presented by the label as "an impressionistic ride from 21st century Thailand to the medieval corners of Myanmar," features an abstract cover collage of Indian and Southeast Asian iconography, text, money, and ticket stubs.

The arty, avant-garde look of Sublime Frequencies finds distant company with Luaka Bop, the world-pop label run by David Byrne and Yale Evelev. Luaka Bop—with acts like Tom Zé, Susana Baca, Os Mutantes, and Zap Mama—has comfortably occupied the hip, contemporary edge of the genre since 1989, focusing exclusively on popular musics, in contrast to Sublime Frequencies.[18] As Evelev told us in an interview, Luaka Bop is not "a pure world music label" but "where world music is now. . . . We are a pop label, 'cause it could come from somewhere else and be in another language, but still be pop."[19] Luaka Bop's album art is sleeker and more polished than Sublime Frequencies': bright colors, photography, professional illustration, and well-chosen typefaces on par with the design at major commercial labels. Sublime Frequencies, on the other hand, is "an arty music label . . . They're trying to be somewhat provocative and not particularly informational," Evelev said.

Both labels' visual aesthetic is far removed from the sanitized bohemia of "World Music 1.0" label Putumayo, known as much for its compilation CDs geared toward uninitiated listeners—*World Sing-Along, Arabic Beat, African Dreamland, Brazilian Café*—as its unmistakable artwork: whimsical, childlike illustrations by artist Nicola Heindl. "Luaka Bop and Sublime Frequencies have in common that hipster look. There's something about it that appeals to people that's maybe 'art scene' or 'alternative,'" said ethnomusicologist Jacob Edgar, former director of music research and product development at Putumayo and current head of Cumbancha (which signed Tuareg guitarist Bombino, previously on Sublime Frequencies).[20] "Meanwhile labels like Putumayo go for cartoony, 'we are the world,' happy-go-lucky accessible artwork. You can get it at Whole Foods," Edgar said, adding that the music on Putumayo is every bit as good as that on top world music labels.

Sublime Frequencies' boutique, post-punk style, a rebuke to the austere, realist presentation of the old labels such as Folkways and Ocora, proclaims a broad critique of ethnomusicology and, more important, a specific critique of the representation of cultures via recorded sound. Whether or not Sublime Frequencies conforms to the ethics and aesthetics of field recordings as fashioned by ethnomusicologists (one of the key issues that this volume was conceived to address), it is beyond question that the label can be situated at the intersection of phonography and ethnography, albeit in unequal proportions. But the amount of creative license Sublime Frequencies exercises—using techniques of (sonic and visual) collage, sound processing, and creative editing, particularly in its *Radio* series—brings its releases as close to *musique concrète* as it does to traditional field recording.

To draw out this central contribution of the label, developed in the early years of Sublime Frequencies (and still strongly evocative of its aesthetic and operational philosophy), the present essay collection gives considerable attention to the *Radio* albums.[21] Radio, a medium disembodied from fixed points in space and time, serves multiple purposes: communication, surveillance, sound-capture, and musical composition. As a fieldwork tool, radio could, in theory, allow sounds to be captured without the recordist ever even leaving the airport of the country in question. Using radio as an ethnographic and creative tool, Sublime Frequencies' producer-recordists do not concern themselves with orthodox approaches to fieldwork. Some of the *Radio* recordings were in fact captured extraterritorially, in whole or in part (see, for example, *Radio Palestine* and *Radio Pyongyang*). However troubling this may be from the standpoint of conventional ethnomusicology, scholars recently have begun to acknowledge the utility of radio as a de facto ethnographic site.[22] And Sublime Frequencies' fragmentary impressions provide a resonant cultural experience (albeit one tailored to short attention spans).

The ease with which the label has collected, lifted, decontextualized, and recontextualized its musical source materials points beyond radio to the larger technological environment in which the Bishop brothers, Mayet, and Gergis developed as connoisseurs and artists. Many Sublime Frequencies compilations hark back to the 1970s' and 1980s' cassette culture of bootlegs and mixtapes. As compared to its vinyl predecessor, the cassette allowed studio, homemade, and copied recordings to circulate widely, and, because of its small size and accessibility, was highly conducive to the collecting impulse.[23] Some Sublime Frequencies releases are relatively straightforward format transfers, including Gergis's *Cambodian Cassette Archives*, a mixtape built from deteriorating tapes found in the Oakland Public Library; and *Choubi Choubi!*, Iraqi dance tracks compiled from cassettes found in Detroit-area immigrant neighborhoods. The radio-collage releases, too, are tape byproducts with the feel of basement recordings made straight from the FM dial.

The sonic technologies of the digital era, even more susceptible to reconfiguration, have further inspired the label's recordists to repurpose archival and found materials. This is as true for the label's DVDs as for its CDs and LPs. The Sublime Frequencies "film" releases are digital productions in form but reach far back in style and feel, beyond the 1970s' cassette era, to the early decades of travelogue filming, when such recordings were pursued mainly as creative endeavors and not yet formalized as a component of academic ethnography.

Most of Sublime Frequencies' DVD output, like its sonic repertoire, is a deliberate departure from the academy. The film titles reference magical and supernatural themes—*Burma's Carnival of Spirit Soul*, *Morocco's Rendezvous of the Dead*, *Magic and Ecstasy in the Sahel*, *Staring into the Sun*, etc.—and sheer, seductive, audio/visual pleasure is an important aspect of the Sublime Frequencies project, reminiscent of novelist-collector Pierre Loti's mantra: "*J'arrive, j'aime, je m'en vais.*" There is no sin in making recordings for purely aesthetic purposes or in seeking magic above analytical rigor; after all, that is how the vast majority of humanity experiences music and visual art. Nevertheless, as intentional works of assemblage, each Sublime Frequencies work implies an ethical point of view. The chapter by Lynda Paul examines Sublime Frequencies' visual oeuvre in the context of film and video practices and ponders its implications as visual representations of culture.

NEW WORLD WAVE

We would like to make clear that this collection is not conceived as an *ethnography of a music label*, but rather as *a set of critical essays about* an ethnographic music label. This is an important distinction: Some of the articles make overtly theoretical observations on the ethnographic process; others do not. The goal is to provide (cultural, political, historical, intellectual) context for the releases, through a multiplicity of voices and narrative/rhetorical styles. The Sublime Frequencies founders and recordists are creative artists appealing to like-minded fans, and the contributors to this volume understand Sublime Frequencies' oeuvre as being equally significant outside the confines of academic ethnography as it is within. It might be, in fact, that the label's most substantive impact has been felt among a particular subculture of creative artists in the major cultural centers of the United States, for whom Sublime Frequencies' "neo-frontier" narratives of world music adventurism strike a resonant chord. (See the "reception" interviews with composers Chris Becker and Robert Hardin, musician Ethan Holtzman, and DJ and archivist Brian Shimkovitz.) For the most part, these fans are young men: cool-hunting musicians, artists, writers, and curators who keep clubs and record shops in business, surf music websites, collect LPs, download obscure up-and-comers, and memorize biographical details of their favorite artists. Will Straw describes this crowd as a "largely white bohemia" united by "specific forms of connoisseurship."[24]

Sublime Frequencies' new slice of the world-music audience, what one might call "underground cosmopolitans," has paid growing attention to foreign styles and sounds. Judging from mentions of the label on music blogs, online reviews, curated talks, concerts, screenings, and media coverage, the worldviews of its audience are marked by an open-ended stance toward culture and citizenship, identity and belonging. As they dance to Omar Souleyman, exchange Group Inerane tracks, and groove to Hayvanlar Alemi, they vicariously participate in the liminal lives and aesthetics of refugees and immigrants. For these consumers, "Meaningful options may come . . . as items or fragments from a variety of cultural sources. . . . materials are simply available, from all corners of the world, as more or less meaningful fragments, images, and snatches of stories . . ."[25]

It was once said of the highly influential rock group the Velvet Underground that they barely sold any records, but that everyone who bought one of their records went out and started a band of their own.[26] It is not inconceivable that, in the very near future, American rock bands and electronic artists will refract the influences of Southeast Asian folk traditions, guitar rock from the West African Sahel, North Korean pop-propaganda, the music of Brazilian drug gangs, or any of the other traditions that have found their way via Sublime Frequencies onto CD shelves in Berkeley and Brooklyn.

Of course, there have been previous phases of American popular interest in the music of the wider world. In the mid-twentieth century, jazz composers from Duke Ellington to Tadd Dameron to Sun Ra explored the sphere of jazz exotica as a way of evoking far-away locales. In the 1960s, the Beatles' interest in Indian classical traditions, as well as patterns of post–World War II immigration, helped catalyze the American interest in South Asian classical music. With hits like "Pata Pata" and "Grazing in the Grass," South African singers Miriam Makeba and Hugh Masekela became household names in America during the 1960s. The major turning points, however, were the rise of Jamaican reggae singer Bob Marley in the 1970s' context of African and Caribbean decolonization (which created a template for the global popularity of political singers from the developing world), and the 1985 release of Paul Simon's record *Graceland*, a collaboration with South African musicians in the midst of apartheid's collapse. Simon became the first in a long line of Western megastars to collaborate with locally or regionally popular artists from the developing world—a genre that would soon be dubbed "world beat."

It is safe to say, then, that until the present era of globalization and information, American interest in world music typically has carried political inflections. But new models of musical consumption have enabled Sublime Frequencies fans to enjoy sounds detached from their contexts as never before. Contemporary listeners are "'free' (to choose), 'single' (that is, 'individual'), and 'disengaged' (from the influence of dominant ideology), by virtue of [our] access to a seemingly limitless variety of musical objects and a corresponding multiplicity of readings," wrote John Corbett, presciently, in 1990.[27] As discussed in Rachel Lears's essay, contemporary modes of collecting hold the potential for both new (liberatory) and old (neocolonial) ways of understanding the world. These new collectors, worldlier yet more destabilized, often lack an appreciation of the social and political background of cultural products, necessitating that labels provide their audiences more context, not less. The liner notes to recent Sublime Frequencies releases such as *1970's Algerian Folk & Pop* and *Folk Music of the Sahel, Vol. 1* hint that the label may be gradually changing its attitude toward documentation and attribution.

Sublime Frequencies' target audience has grown up in a confusing world of "posts" in which historical metanarratives are to be passed by, viewed with suspicion, or transcended. In these circumstances, compounded by easy manipulation and reconfiguration of cultural materials, translation is a tricky undertaking. If "ethnographic realism," per Clifford and Marcus's ideas of reflexivity, is ultimately a mere fiction, what is the ethical, authentic way to represent a culture for the eyes and ears of outsiders?[28] If Sublime Frequencies' goal is to help the developing world "fire back" at the West, what role should its fans play? Does being antihegemonic simply involve partaking of foreign music, or can deeper affective alliances be formed?

For its own part, do the Sublime Frequencies founders—and, more generally, American world-music impresarios—bear ethical responsibilities? One might argue that Sublime Frequencies' reluctance to engage critically with the wider world while partaking freely of its cultural products smacks of a particular brand of American insularity and isolationism. While talking a good, antihegemonic game, the Sublime Frequencies founders demur from the expressly political and have few qualms about "finding," taking, and selling—often without citing. In the end, Sublime Frequencies' business model betrays an undeniable exercise of cultural, financial, and technological privilege.

Given the rarefied nature of their market niche, most of the identified artists on Sublime Frequencies releases would seem to be consigned to eternal indie-hipster status. But Sublime Frequencies has brought pop-ethnography to all kinds of indie luminaries. Acclaimed producer Tucker Martine (see Julie Strand's interview) is among their recordists; Sublime Frequencies and Group Doueh played a festival curated by the well-known experimental/psych outfit Animal Collective; former act Bombino had his most recent album produced by the Black Keys' Dan Auerbach, followed by a high-profile concert at New York's Carnegie Hall; and another former act, Omar Souleyman (see Wills Glasspiegel's and Shayna Silverstein's contributions), did his own remix for Björk.[29] And however much the Sublime Frequencies founders have portrayed themselves as naively curious, glorified hobbyists, they have, at the same time, vertically consolidated their activities in the music industry, grooming star artists to tour internationally under the label's aegis. Their constructed outsider stance and casual self-presentation as "music explorers" obscures the reality that the label has more or less conformed to the typical evolutionary structure of the music industry: moving from indie status (boutique releases and vintage reissues) to a gradual consolidation of production, visual media, concert promotion, and the cultivation of solo recording artists, all of this in the context of a collapsing music industry that has rendered outsider approaches uniquely viable. At the same time, the approach also exposes the tension inherent in the process of converting the collecting impulse into a commercial one. The fact that celebrated acts like Bombino and Omar Souleyman eventually left Sublime Frequencies for more established companies also places the label in the tradition of intrepid indie labels who function as de facto "farm" operations, cultivating unique and lesser-known talent until they are snatched up.

These are important considerations, but this volume is not conceived as an academic dressing down or dismissal of Sublime Frequencies' work. Instead, ours is a collection of critically conceived liner notes, a filling-in of the proverbial blanks. The essays are written by area specialists as well as by authors with a broader cultural or thematic focus. Many are academics; others are journalists, curators, filmmakers, musicians, and visual artists. We all share an appreciation for Sublime Frequencies' work and simultaneously believe that our critical contributions can enhance the aesthetic experience of the label's products while providing deeper context.

GLOBALIZED DISCONTENT AND MUSIC MARKETS

In many respects, we are living through dark times. The United States–led military interventions in Iraq, Afghanistan, Egypt, and more recently, Syria, are coextensive with "foreign" policy at home, namely the blunt demonization of American Muslims post-9/11 and a broader, rightward political shift since the 1980s. Our bellicosity abroad is also a direct cause of austerity in our own neighborhoods and cities, famously illustrated by post-bankruptcy Detroit, the Bishop brothers' hometown and a major hub for immigrants from the Middle East. The worlds of conflict underlying Sublime Frequencies releases such as *Choubi Choubi!, I Remember Syria,* and *Radio Palestine* find their local parallel in the increasing militarization of American police forces and the pervasiveness of deadly confrontation between police and unarmed citizens.

Music from the Middle East happens to be Sublime Frequencies' specialty, with disproportionate representation of the Muslim world. (See the chapters on Mali [Strand], Palestine [Joseph Salem], Syria [Silverstein], and Niger [Michael E. Veal].) But even as the world chronicled in its oeuvre has experienced violent upheaval (Syria), false starts at democracy (Egypt), civil war (Mali), bewildering provocations (North Korea), and to-be-determined political openings (Burma), Sublime Frequencies and its founders—each with familial roots in the Middle East—have remained aloof, keeping a cool distance from turmoil abroad. There has been no measurable change in their liner notes, no politicization of their work, even as they tour films and acts and curate events centered on the region, again raising ethical questions. Is there a principled way to import and sell cultural products in times of conflict?

Our current geopolitics seem overwhelming, yet in these troubled times, culture—how it's represented, made and marketed, bought and sold—matters. Given the present state of U.S. global intervention, world-music entrepreneurs have the choice of representing and marketing foreign cultural products in their full complexity.

Since the 1980s, scholars have tended to approach ethnography as a highly literary discourse that ultimately holds no exclusive claims on truth, accuracy, or objectivity. The idea of ethnography as a writing practice with inviolable standards has been problematized for several decades, as the ethnographic fields (i.e., cultural anthropology and ethnomusicology) have opened themselves up to various influences from cultural studies, literary criticism, journalism, and other academic and nonacademic discourses. Ethnography as a practice is in fact an empty vessel that is shaped according to the priorities of the author. It can be radical or it can be reactionary, depending on the perspective of the ethnographer. It can be used to reveal, to distort, or to project. If we suspend judgment and enjoy Sublime Frequencies' sound ethnographies as cultural documents, we nevertheless do so with the understanding that they present not only *what was heard* in the world but also, in their design and presentation, *a particular way of hearing and seeing.* The question of how closely their releases conform to academic field recordings becomes "What kind of understanding of the world's musics do they present?"

Situated between the spaces of Clifford and Marcus's crisis of ethnographic representation and the digital deluge of the information age, the label struggles with its own contradictions.[30] On one level, Sublime Frequencies engages in the cultural titillation of exoticism by presenting a sonic and visual world of scratchy radio transmissions, advertisements, insect sounds, comic books, and surrealist expression of wildly indeterminate meaning. This aesthetic, the Sublime Frequencies team contends, flows from the rejection of political ideologies and academic metanarratives, in favor of the purely sensual aspects of world music. Their claim holds some truth: While ripe for criticism on Orientalist grounds, Sublime Frequencies' approach can sometimes foster a type of cross-cultural understanding, in its own, idiosyncratic way. In a tense, repressed American climate in which the sensual has given way to pervasive fear and anxiety, the voluptuary, magical aspects of music can sometimes provide an antidote to indifference and xenophobia. The Sublime Frequencies releases embrace the world of feeling, injecting mystery and sensuality—the qualities that drew us all to music and film in the first place—back into "ethnography." We propose a middle path: to celebrate the awe of new music and sights, appreciating the complexities of the cultures that birthed them and remaining critical of our own interactions with them. That is the ultimate goal of this collection.

NOTES

The authors would like to thank their families and friends, the diligent team at Wesleyan University Press, Parker Smathers, Eliot Bates, Chris Dodge, Wills Glasspiegel, and all the talented authors in this volume.

1. See Various Artists, *Radio Morocco,* Sublime Frequencies SF007, CD, 2004; Various Artists, *Radio Palestine*, Sublime Frequencies SF008, CD, 2004; Various Artists, *I Remember Syria*, Sublime Frequencies SF009, CD, 2004; Various Artists, *Thai Pop Spectacular: 1960's–1980's*, Sublime Frequencies SF032, CD, 2007; *This World Is Unreal Like a Snake in a Rope,* directed by Robert Millis (Seattle, WA: Sublime Frequencies, 2012), DVD; *The Pierced Heart and the Machete,* directed by Olivia Wyatt (Seattle, WA: Sublime Frequencies, 2013), DVD; Various Artists, *Eat the Dream: Gnawa Music from Essaouira*, Sublime Frequencies SF071, LP, 2012; Princess Nicotine, *Princess Nicotine: Folk and Pop Sounds of Myanmar (Burma), Vol. 1,* Sublime Frequencies SF006, CD, 2004; *Staring into the Sun,* directed by Wyatt (Seattle, WA: Sublime Frequencies, 2011), DVD.

2. Various Artists, *Radio Thailand: Transmissions from the Tropical Kingdom*, Sublime Frequencies SF028, two-CD set, 2006.

3. The *Radio* series includes the releases: Various Artists, *Radio Java*, Sublime Frequencies SF002, CD, 2003; Various Artists, *Radio Morocco*; Various Artists, *Radio Palestine*; Various Artists, *Radio India: The Eternal Dream of Sound*, Sublime Frequencies SF014, two-CD set, 2004; Various Artists, *Radio Phnom Penh*, Sublime Frequencies SF020, CD, 2005; Various Artists, *Radio Sumatra: The Indonesian FM Experience*, Sublime Frequencies SF021, CD, 2005; Various Artists, *Radio Thailand*; Various Artists, *Radio Algeria*, Sublime Frequencies SF029, CD, 2006; and Various Artists, *Radio Myanmar (Burma)*, Sublime Frequencies SF044, CD, 2008.

4. Justin Spicer, "Agitated Atmosphere: Alvarius B—*Baroque Primitiva*," KEXP (blog), June 24, 2011, blog.kexp.org/2011/06/24/agitated-atmosphere-alvarius-b-baroque-primitiva/; Andy Beta's chapter in this volume.

5. Sublime Frequencies' website; sublimefrequencies.com.

6. For example, see Kay Kaufman Shelemay, "Recording Technology, the Record Industry, and Ethnomusicological Scholarship," in *Comparative Musicology and the Anthropology of Music*, ed. Bruno Nettl and Philip Bohlman (Chicago: University of Chicago Press, 1991), 277–92.

7. Alan Bishop, as quoted in Dave Segal, "mlat85: Sublime Frequencies," *Made Like a Tree* (blog), March 25, 2013, madelikeatree.com/mlat85-Sublime-Frequencies.

8. Andrew R. Tonry's and Beta's chapters in this volume; Beta, "Sublime Frequencies," *Spin.com*, September 6, 2012, www.spin.com/articles/sublime-frequencies/; Douglas Wolk, "Heard on the Streets (of the Axis of Evil)," *New York Times*, November 20, 2005, www.nytimes.com/2005/11/20/arts/music/20wolk.html.

9. See the introduction to *The Arab Avant-Garde: Music, Politics, Modernity*, ed. Thomas Burkhalter, Kay Dickinson, and Benjamin J. Harbert (Middletown, Conn.: Wesleyan University Press, 2013).

10. See Marc Master's chapter in this volume.

11. Mantle Hood, "The Challenge of Bi-Musicality," *Ethnomusicology* 4, no. 2 (May 1960): 55–59.

12. This ongoing critique is even apparent in an introductory text such as Bruno Nettl, *The Study of Ethnomusicology: Thirty-One Issues and Concepts* (Champaign: University of Illinois Press, 2005), in which the central practices and concepts of the discipline are presented not as inviolable tenets, but as questions to be explored and critiqued.

13. See Jon Savage, *England's Dreaming: Anarchy, Sex Pistols, Punk Rock and Beyond* (New York: St. Martin's Press, 1992), which surveys punk in the British context. Clinton Heylin's *From the Velvets to the Voidoids* (New York: Penguin, 1993) and Bernard Gendron's *Between Montmartre and the Mudd Club* (University of Chicago Press, 2002) are good introductions to punk in the American context.

14. See Tonry's chapter in this volume.

15. In 2013, punk couture, alongside a replicated CBGB toilet, went on display at the Metropolitan Museum of Art.

16. Stephen Duncombe, *Notes from Underground: Zines and the Politics of Alternative Culture* (London: Verso, 1997), 33.

17. Spicer, "Agitated Atmosphere: Group Doueh—*Treeg Salaam*," *KEXP* (blog), June 19, 2009, blog.kexp.org/2009/06/19/agitated-atmosphere-group-doueh-treeg-salaam/.

18. Luaka Bop, "The First Ten Years," *Luaka Bop* (website), luakabop.com/history/.

19. Yale Evelev, interview by E. Tammy Kim, September 8, 2011.

20. Jacob Edgar, interview by E. Tammy Kim, June 24, 2011.

21. At the time of writing, the most recent Sublime Frequencies release is Baba Commandant and The Mandingo Band, *Juguya*, Sublime Frequencies SF097, LP, 2015.

22. For an extended discussion of this theme, consult *Radio Fields: Anthropology and Wireless Sound in the 21st Century*, ed. Daniel Fisher, Lucas Bessire, and Faye Ginsburg (New York: New York University Press, 2012).

23. Although Peter Manuel's *Cassette Culture: Popular Music and Technology in North India* (Chicago: University of Chicago Press, 1993) is mainly concerned with North India, many of the issues raised are broadly applicable to the impact of cassettes worldwide.

24. Will Straw, "Systems of Articulation, Logics of Change: Communities and Scenes in Popular Music," *Cultural Studies* 5, no. 3 (October 1991): 361–75, 377–78.

25. Jeremy Waldron, "Minority Cultures and the Cosmopolitan Alternative," *University of Michigan Journal of Law Reform* 25, no. 751 (1992): 783, 785.

26. For example, see Albin Zak's preface to *The Velvet Underground Companion: Four Decades of Commentary* (New York: Schirmer Trade Books, 1997).

27. John Corbett, "Free, Single, and Disengaged: Listening Pleasure and the Popular Music Object," *October* 54: (Autumn 1990): 99.

28. See *Writing Culture: The Poetics and Politics of Ethnography*, ed. James Clifford and George Marcus (Berkeley: University of California Press, 1986).

29. Souleyman even showed up in the Style section of the *New York Times*: His remix was recommended by a DJ playing parties at Fashion Week. John Ortved, "Music to Strut the Collection By," *New York Times*, September 15, 2011, www.nytimes.com/2011/09/15 /fashion/djs-make-the-music-to-move-fashion-shows.html.

30. See Clifford and Marcus, *Writing Culture*.

BIBLIOGRAPHY

Beta, Andy. "Sublime Frequencies." *Spin.com,* September 6, 2012. www.spin.com/articles /sublime-frequencies/.

Burkhalter, Thomas, Kay Dickinson, and Benjamin J. Harbert, eds. *The Arab Avant-Garde: Music, Politics, Modernity.* Middletown, Conn.: Wesleyan University Press, 2013.

Clifford, James, and George Marcus, eds. *Writing Culture: The Poetics and Politics of Ethnography.* Berkeley: University of California Press, 1986.

Corbett, John. "Free, Single, and Disengaged: Listening Pleasure and the Popular Music Object." *October* 54 (Autumn 1990): 79–101.

Duncombe, Stephen. *Notes from Underground: Zines and the Politics of Alternative Culture.* London: Verso, 1997.

Edgar, Jacob. Interview by E. Tammy Kim. June 24, 2011.

Evelev, Yale. Interview by E. Tammy Kim. September 8, 2011.

Fisher, Daniel, Lucas Bessire, and Faye Ginsburg, eds. *Radio Fields: Anthropology and Wireless Sound in the 21st Century.* New York: New York University Press, 2012.

Gendron, Bernard. *Between Montmartre and the Mudd Club.* Chicago: University of Chicago Press, 2002.

Heylin, Clinton. *From the Velvets to the Voidoids.* New York: Penguin, 1993.

Hood, Mantle. "The Challenge of Bi-Musicality." *Ethnomusicology* 4, no. 2 (May 1960): 55–59.

Luaka Bop. "The First Ten Years." *Luaka Bop* (website). luakabop.com/history/.

Manuel, Peter. *Cassette Culture: Popular Music and Technology in North India.* Chicago: University of Chicago Press, 1993.

Nettl, Bruno. *The Study of Ethnomusicology: Thirty-One Issues and Concepts.* Champaign: University of Illinois Press, 2005.

Ortved, John. "Music to Strut the Collection By." *New York Times.* September 15, 2011. www. nytimes.com/2011/09/15/fashion/djs-make-the-music-to-move-fashion-shows.html.

Savage, Jon. *England's Dreaming: Anarchy, Sex Pistols, Punk Rock and Beyond*. New York: St. Martin's Press, 1992.

Segal, Dave. "mlat85: Sublime Frequencies." *Made Like a Tree* (blog), March 25, 2013. madelikeatree.com/mlat85-Sublime-Frequencies.

Shelemay, Kay Kaufman. "Recording Technology, the Record Industry, and Ethnomusicological Scholarship." In *Comparative Musicology and the Anthropology of Music*, ed. Bruno Nettl and Philip Bohlman. Chicago: University of Chicago Press, 1991, 277–92.

Spicer, Justin. "Agitated Atmosphere: Alvarius B—*Baroque Primitiva*." *KEXP* (blog), June 24, 2011. blog.kexp.org/2011/06/24/agitated-atmosphere-alvarius-b-baroque-primitiva/.

———. "Agitated Atmosphere: Group Doueh—*Treeg Salaam*." *KEXP* (blog), June 19, 2009. blog.kexp.org/2009/06/19/agitated-atmosphere-group-doueh-treeg-salaam/.

Straw, Will. "Systems of Articulation, Logics of Change: Communities and Scenes in Popular Music." *Cultural Studies* 5, no. 3 (October 1991): 361–75, 377–78.

Sublime Frequencies. Website. sublimefrequencies.com.

Waldron, Jeremy. "Minority Cultures and the Cosmopolitan Alternative." *University of Michigan Journal of Law Reform* 25 (1992): 783, 785.

Wolk, Douglas. "Heard on the Streets (of the Axis of Evil)." *New York Times*, November 20, 2005. www.nytimes.com/2005/11/20/arts/music/20wolk.html.

Zak, Albin. *The Velvet Underground Companion: Four Decades of Commentary*. New York: Schirmer Trade Books, 1997.

DAVID NOVAK

The Sublime Frequencies
of New Old Media

A new world of world music was built on *Cambodian Rocks*. The CD was released on the New York City–based Parallel World label in 1996, and for most listeners, it was hard to find anything else like it. The compilation collected tracks from a number of legendary 1960s' Phnom Penh bar bands, most of whose members were executed by the Khmer Rouge soon after the recordings were made. Their brief reinventions of garage rock powerfully echo the impact of the U.S. presence in Southeast Asia and the global spread of recording and broadcast technologies during this period. On *Cambodian Rocks*, the Western listener hears the psychedelic sounds of Santana, James Brown, and the Animals anew through the ears of seemingly anonymous Cambodian musicians. The mystery of the music was amplified by the opaque presentation of its origins. The compiler, Paul Wheeler, an American English teacher in Japan who had collected cassettes on a brief tour of Cambodia in 1994, provided no biographical detail for the material, neglecting even track titles or artist names. Although several of these songs are beloved classics for Cambodians, the backgrounds and artistic intentions of the musicians were unknown to Western listeners. For those cognizant of Cambodian folk music styles, the mix of sounds might suggest the continuity of traditional vocal techniques and local song forms beneath the novel rhythms, reverb, and twang of imported rock music. But most North Americans, who heard this music for the first time in the 1990s, were surprised and intrigued to encounter the transformation of familiar music in an unknown cultural context. The effect was less like hearing a documentary presentation of a recognizable musical culture than tuning a radio to the staticky, somehow familiar sounds of a fuzzed-out, reverb-soaked Khmer version of "Gloria."

Sublime Frequencies co-founder Alan Bishop, right, was one-third of the long-running experimental trio Sun City Girls, with his brother, Richard Bishop, left, and Charles Gocher (center). Photo by Toby Dodds, 2003.

In this essay, I describe a recent intervention into the circulation of "world music," which has been associated since the 1950s with the academic field of ethnomusicology and since the 1980s with the music industry categories of "world music" and "world beat." I argue that both contexts have been transformed substantially in recent years by the redistribution networks represented by Sublime Frequencies and a host of other independent labels, websites, and blogs. As world music becomes part of online culture, its new listenership has realigned against hegemonic frameworks of intellectual property. This new world music, sometimes called "World Music 2.0," disengages from earlier collaborations and hybridized genres of world music in the 1980s and 1990s, which provoked a broad scholarly critique of its production and marketing as a thinly veiled form of musical imperialism.[1] Many of these reactions focused on the unauthorized use of specific song or sound material, as appropriated by Western authors via imitation, and/or quasi-coercive collaborations (Paul Simon, Peter Gabriel, and

David Byrne are typical examples, but there are many others). The charge of appropriation was exacerbated by industrial procedures of technological sampling and rerecording, which were said to detach cultural materials from their original contexts. A well-known example was documented in Steven Feld's 2000 *Public Culture* essay "A Sweet Lullaby for World Music." Feld traces the charged ethical and legal situation involved in the circulation of "Rorogwela," a song by the Solomon Island singer Afunakwa recorded in 1970 by the Swiss ethnomusicologist Hugo Zemp. In 1992, the track was licensed from the United Nations Educational, Scientific and Cultural Organization (UNESCO) and sampled by the Belgian electronic group Deep Forest for their track "Sweet Lullaby," which was subsequently reworked by the Norwegian saxophonist Jan Garbarek as "Pygmy Lullaby." Among other consequences, Feld shows how Afunakwa's voice was slowly drowned out in the remediated telephone games and sampled shuffles that marked the "triumphant industrialization of global sonic representation" in world music.[2]

But World Music 2.0 does not originate in the appropriation of global sounds in popular works by Western authors, who impose technological mediation on traditional forms. Rather, it is based in the redistribution of existing recordings of regional popular music—most of which already bear a strong formal and technological relationship with Western popular culture—as "new old" media. Its largely North American listenership came to world music from earlier contexts of analog exchange in an "independent" musical underground of the 1980s and 1990s, which began to circulate familiar-sounding pop music from Southeast Asia and Africa. Much of this is period-specific material, often contemporaneous with 1960s' psychedelic and garage rock, but sung in local languages and incorporating regional musical influences. Releases compile different tracks under titles like *Love, Peace and Poetry: Asian Psychedelic Music*, *Analog Africa*, *Thai Beat A-Go-Go*, and *Hava Narghile: Turkish Rock Music, 1966–1975*. A range of small independent labels circulates these "lost" recordings of Afrofunk and Asian surf guitar to a new transnational listenership. Redistributors stress their discovery of unknown gems (one "accidental world music" label is called Finders Keepers) in the hidden confluence between strange marginal forms and a familiar homeland of pop nostalgia.

If the first problem I want to bring out in this essay is the contemporary form of world music, the second is the relationship between old and new media. I put stress on the redistribution of world music as a process of "remediation," in which content is transferred from one media context to another to create new media, but also new subjects of mediated culture.³ Remediation shows us that new media always incorporate "experiences of older media, as well as the hopes and anxieties around the introduction of new media technologies themselves."⁴ In online networks, earlier imaginaries of local production and musical independence are juxtaposed with technical platforms that offer unprecedented accessibility to cultural material. World Music 2.0, then, is more than just the end point of a chain of misbegotten appropriations. It is the subject of an emergent open source culture of global media.

What are the ethical and ideological goals of constructing "new old" media in the present confluence of digital, analog, physical, and virtual forms? As redistributors argue for an open access circulation of world music, they wear their ambivalent relationship to its cultural representation on their sleeves. Their musical sources are both raw and technological; they are derivative of Western mass media but deeply transformed by local interpretations. For most North American listeners, the mix evokes surrealist collage as much as intercultural hybridity. Many labels champion the obscurity of their recorded sources, to appeal to their audience's desire for direct access to raw, uncirculated material. They reissue CD mixes of out-of-print (or never-printed) recordings, drawing sounds from bootleg cassette tapes, amateur home recordings, regional radio and television broadcasts, and field recordings not otherwise "released" into global circulation. MP3 blogs have proliferated, posting recordings of obscure recordings for free download. Bloggers like Brian Shimkovitz (aka thursdayborn, who posts MP3s of African cassette tapes on his *Awesome Tapes from Africa* site) describe their crate-digging search for recordings as an "aural ethnography" of lost and disappearing regional media, previously locked away in the vaults of academic research. But even when labels continue to produce obsolescent physical media in the form of CDs (and also, importantly, on vinyl LPs and cassettes), they reorient world music from an analog past toward the free exchanges of a global digital commons.

Many remediators consider their work as a corrective to the limited scope of academic field recordings. Ethnomusicology, they claim, has focused on revivalist projects and ethnonationalist folk genres that cut out the noise of the street and the technologically driven beats of popular music. They describe their own releases, however, as a way of opening access to the distorted reality of global pop beyond the academic frame. World Music 2.0 is celebrated for its impure mixes of imitative sounds, which bring global popular music into a contemporary realm of ethnographic surrealism "that values fragments, curious collections, [and] unexpected juxtapositions."[5] But if this is aural ethnography, it documents the distortions of North American underground reception as much as the cultures that created the music. Even when cultural histories are not perceived as totally irrelevant, many bloggers post their strange media discoveries first and ask questions later.[6] A recent post from Shimkovitz's blog is titled "What's the Name of This Band/Album?" immediately followed by a note that begins, "I have no idea, but this tape from Guelmim, a town in Southern Morocco, is INSANE."

World music, with all of its fascinated culturalist desires, anticorporate tones of collaborative resistance, and uneasy debates of appropriation, is back—but a new online public has recast its circulation as an open access project of redistribution. Listeners do not discover the borders of these musical worlds through copious explanatory notes providing details of sociocultural backgrounds. Instead, regional music cultures are filtered through the wow and flutter of an unlabeled cassette, the obscuring static of an ephemeral radio signal, or the chains of quasi-anonymous speculations about sources in the comments of a YouTube video. These ripped files chart out a new galaxy of golden hits from unknown stars, whose distant light is filtered through time and space, reaching us only after its sources have changed or disappeared. So what happens when we begin to hear, and really listen to, the distortions of World Music 2.0—not just as an Orientalist appropriation of local culture but as part and parcel of an emergent ethics of new media circulation? We join this broadcast already in progress.

REMEDIATING THE MYSTERIES OF WORLD MUSIC

I turn first to the Seattle-based independent label Sublime Frequencies, whose popularity has crystallized the recent shift in the circulation of world music. Sublime Frequencies' mission statement describes the label as a collective of explorers dedicated to acquiring and exposing obscure sights and sounds from modern and traditional urban and rural frontiers via film and video, field recordings, radio and short wave transmissions, international folk and pop music, sound anomalies, and other forms of human and natural expression not documented sufficiently through all channels of academic research, the modern recording industry, media, or corporate foundations.[7]

The label founders, Alan Bishop and Hisham Mayet, cite the inspiration of Ocora, Smithsonian Folkways, Nonesuch, Unesco, Lyrichord, and other foundational world music labels that informed their broad aesthetic of "extra-geography and soulful experience."[8] It might seem strange that Sublime Frequencies would champion these midcentury projects of musical preservation initiated by folklorists and ethnomusicologists, who often considered their field recordings of traditional music as auxiliary research material inseparable from extended projects of cultural documentation.[9] But these recordings were far more influential than the ethnographic texts they were meant to accompany. Consumer guides to world music (e.g., the Rough Guide series) describe the contributions of ethnomusicology as a lineage of great field recordings, essential to the historical roster of alternative media. The fluid category of world music, then, was neither a purely commercial invention nor the supplemental byproduct of an emerging academic discipline. It has also been an exemplary production of independent media, which was distributed successfully on the fringes of the music industry.

But if Sublime Frequencies embraces the media productions of ethnomusicology, it rejects its mission of cultural exegesis. Instead, the label stresses its own ethical ambivalence about cultural preservation in ways that align with the self-conscious skepticism of its North American underground audience. Listeners revisit familiar themes of cultural loss and modernization, but with a crucial change in protocol. For Sublime Frequencies, the core of world music's difference does not lie in disappearing performance traditions or premodern musical survivals that mandate preservation for their own sake. Rather, its material is sieved from a global media mix that has become a conduit for new experimental channels of listening.

There is no question that Sublime Frequencies provides access to an enormous range of rare and uncanny sounds. From its earliest releases in 2003, the label took as its mission the redistribution of "decaying documents and eccentric artifacts" drawn from "unknown" public media circulations in Southeast Asia and North Africa.[10] Over the past several years, it has released an astonishing amount of unique material. *Guitars of the Golden Triangle* presents previously undiscovered 1970s' garage and psychedelic rock from the Shan state in eastern Myanmar, while *Radio Pyongyang: Commie Funk and Agit Pop from the Hermit Kingdom* presents the "now NOW sound of North Korea . . . Schmaltzy synthpop, Revolutionary rock, Cheeky child rap, and a healthy dose of hagiography for Dear Leader Kim Jong-il."[11] Sublime Frequencies also has released several films (including *Niger: Magic and Ecstasy in the Sahel*, *Phi Ta Khon: Ghosts of Isan*, and the "mindblowing in your face document" *Folk Music of the Sahara: Among the Tuareg of Libya*), which consist of unnarrated and minimally edited raw footage of isolated cultural performances. Recent recordings focus on individual artists and groups, such as the synthesizer-driven "street-level folk-pop" of the Syrian musician Omar Souleyman or the Moroccan ensemble Group Doueh, whose virtuosic guitarist weaves the melismatic melodies and quarter-tone scales of Mauritanian folk song into a Hendrixian warp of phasers and distortion. But most often, the label redistributes existing products of regional media, by compiling and reissuing recordings that have already been distributed in local networks.

Sublime Frequencies is well known for its *Radio* compilations, which juxtapose a huge variety of sound materials from decades of personal field recordings. Ethnographic field recordings typically document live on-site performances, while most industrial world music CDs are produced in studios controlled by foreign producers or their local agents. In the *Radio* series, Sublime Frequencies breaks from both modes. Its recordists occasionally make field recordings of their own, capturing unidentified amplified street performances or public soundscapes, but most sounds are gleaned from informal circulations of local media. Songs are taken from cassette recordings in local markets or recorded straight from local radio, television, or other site-specific broadcasts. Music and other sounds are presented in montages that do not distinguish between live and mediated, historical and contemporary, local and foreign styles. Instead, they conjure the mystery of an immeasurable, unknowable mix of sounds beyond the reach of archival documentation and scholarly concern.

In deference to the "impossibility" of identifying its sources, the label discourages curious listeners from being distracted by such details. "To the veteran international sound collector," state the liner notes for *Radio Java* (2003), "Javanese music is no secret. For the uninitiated, rather than going through an introductory outline of Javanese music history, I will wish you away to the Internet, a library, or bookstore where you can find plenty of information on the subject." But it is left to the ironic reader to note the extreme unlikelihood of finding resources from a title like "Music Collage w/Imam/Sunda/JPG" or "Miscellaneous Music Collage." Other titles for individual tracks surrealistically displace the sounds they name (e.g., "Shiny Radio in a Blind Man's Wallet"). The sound objects on many Sublime Frequencies releases, too—fuzzy broadcasts of local AM, FM, and shortwave radio; truncated recordings of television ads and public address announcements; noisy soundscapes of public markets and streets; and distorted home-cassette recordings—reinforce the sensory displacement valued by the label's underground listenership. "What's happening now on Indonesian Radio from the FM airwaves of Sumatra?" "A completely mystifying Universe of Sound swirling in an explosive musical kaleidoscope, that's what!"[12]

Where is this world of music? The scene of local cultural production is a relentlessly obscure collage of different sources, joined by their strangeness and irreconcilable difference from any sort of musical mainstream. The form of the regional compilation here—*Radio Java*, *Shadow Music of Thailand*, and so forth—is a common rubric for conjoining disparate material. North American music scenes, for example, are often introduced with compilation recordings that map out the "Seattle sound" or the "San Francisco underground." The context of radio broadcast further downgrades the obligation to document local authors, as the distant listener tunes in to an imaginary media landscape through the flowing mix of sounds from "various artists." The lo-fi qualities of distortion in these analog recordings, too, echo underground music's sonic distance from institutional product. In these and other ways, new world music circulations are strongly derivative of "old media" aesthetics developed in the American musical underground of the 1980s and 1990s.

FROM WEIRD MUSIC TO WORLD MUSIC

The experimental aesthetics of Sublime Frequencies were influenced by the social and musical background of its primary organizers, brothers Alan and Richard Bishop, who were mystical stars of American underground music in their group Sun City Girls. Formed in Arizona in 1981 with drummer Charles Gocher, the trio toured extensively in North America over the next two and a half decades. Sun City Girls released more than one hundred recordings on vinyl, cassette, and CD. Most were self-released in limited editions and distributed by mail and person-to-person barter exchange in the burgeoning independent music scenes of North America and Europe. The obscurity and rarity of their recorded output helped generate a cult audience for their famously unpredictable live performances, in which the band would present an entire set of droning Middle Eastern–influenced guitar improvisation dressed in masks and robes or taunt the audience interminably between blasts of angular hardcore punk.

By embodying an untraceable mix of mysterious musical styles, Sun City Girls had an almost magical influence on an experimental listenership in North America during the 1980s and 1990s. The band's musical and cultural references were unclear to most underground music fans in this period, though its travels in the East had become legendary gossip among their fans. The lack of background information on its album covers (sometimes adorned with surreally decontextualized images of foreign lands and people) added to the band's inscrutability. Underground music "zines" occasionally published missives from the Bishop brothers that reported the mystical fruits of their travels. In one essay, Richard Bishop expounded on the "magic of the fourth world" and its effects:

> Once you've tasted the third world, you realize the possibility of a fourth. It grows on you and in you like the sweetest of cancers, and when you return, if you decide to . . . there can be even greater experiences that you won't dare share with anybody! Nobody would get it! . . . When you are traveling in a remote area and you come to the realization that you don't know who, where, or what you are anymore, that's when the magic of the fourth world begins. The senses explode on a grand scale, and the unknown, or at least the "unheard of," presents itself . . . whether you're ready for it or not.[13]

Sun City Girls fans passed along cassette mixes of the group's output in a mail exchange network that incorporated all sorts of mixed "weird music," which by the 1980s and 1990s began to include carefully selected examples of world music. A listener connected to this underground "cassette culture" might receive a tape from a fellow trader compiling North American experimental groups juxtaposed with tracks of Tuvan throat singing, Bollywood film music, or Inuit versions of Rolling Stones hits. This informal distribution mixed old and new content—from lo-fi tapes by an up-and-coming Noise band to out-of-print LPs of Filipino *kulintang* percussion borrowed from a local library—anything, as long as it was surprising and unknown. By the time Sun City Girls disbanded in 2007 (after Gocher's death), North American fans of independent music had developed a new interest in strange sounds from the global margins.

Not the least important legacy of this circulation is Sublime Frequencies, whose approach to world music strongly echoes the analog values of the 1980s' underground. Like most punk and experimental recordings of this era, its releases are distributed in limited quantities (often one thousand copies) on CD, and the most in-demand recordings are also pressed in an especially limited run of LPs. The physical media become collectible almost immediately, especially the vinyl records, which have become concentrated objects of cultural capital for underground music fans. But LPs and CDs are transferred rapidly into digital file formats, and the content is usually redistributed online through a variety of free file-sharing programs and MP3 blogs within a few days of each release. As its base of underground barter networks extends into a new context of circulation, Sublime Frequencies scales the boundless digital distribution of the Internet back down to the social models inspired by the label's punk roots, which insist on a "DIY approach to everything."[14] This has meant subverting official histories of popular music with unfamiliar material that cannot be slotted into older categories, so that the sounds of "world music" can be heard as "experimental."

Both Sun City Girls and the Sublime Frequencies label became invested in the radical transformation of mass media through their discovery of the "psychedelic" difference and "raw punk spirit" in world music. Some have argued that Sublime Frequencies' ambivalence about cultural documentation is an effect of its founders' own ethnic positions. The Bishop brothers are both Lebanese Americans, Hisham Mayet was born in Tripoli, and Alan Bishop is married to a Burmese woman who helped gather a three-volume collection of folk and pop music from Myanmar. But the label owners reject celebratory multiculturalism and do not represent their catalog as a project of global hybridity. On the contrary, the mix here is a blind encounter with pure mystery, a punk transcendence of negotiable meaning, "an encyclopedia without an index," and a "strange mystical surround-sound that is very open to atmospheric interpretation."[15] In the context of world music, where, as Michael C. Vazquez points out, "most 'song-catchers' today go to great lengths to demonstrate that they, in [Mickey] Hart's words, 'understand that music belongs to the people who make it,' the Sublime Frequencies crew are equally interested in the idea that music belongs to the people who hear it."[16]

But to experience this self-conscious audition, one must abandon objectivity and listen beyond cultural context. When standard modes of representation become suspect, listeners tune in to culture as a realm of experimental possibility, where "the test of a work's resonance is precisely its irreducibility, its resistance to interpretation."[17] Experimental listeners refuse translation, in order to embrace the strangeness of their unprecedented encounters with a raw and unfiltered musical difference. This perspective has a particularly powerful effect on the recognition of cultural ownership. Any attempts to clarify the mystery of the sounds with further information—the pretense of cultural knowledge condensed into liner notes, recordists' interpretations, biographies, and record company blurbs—would only get in the way of an authentically remediated experience. To receive the true message, listeners must unlearn official modes of explanation. And as the real experience of musical media is ripped from its false industrial curation, it is only well and good if peripheral information ends up being left by the side of the road.[18]

The ethical challenge of "new old" world music is thus to recognize the transformational distortions of another musical world without adhering to institutional logics that remake culture as property. For Alan Bishop, listening means experiencing unknown sounds without "giving in to respect." "Tradition," Bishop says, "is not about slavish imitation. The last thing I want to see is a bunch of fucking white guys playing Javanese gamelon [sic] proper. It's disrespectful . . . they are not evolving the situation. They are not rolling the dice."[19] Against this failed attempt to reproduce musical tradition, Bishop considers Sublime Frequencies as a kind of avant-garde channel surfing, a creative act of tuning into the "fourth world" that bears out his claim that "the radio is the most underappreciated electronic instrument ever created."[20] He cites the extreme difficulty of documenting his sources and is frustrated by accusations regarding compensation. Bishop argues that independent labels rarely make money in an era of online file sharing and that the uncommercial nature of the material ensures that making a profit is impossible. "When it starts selling like fucking Outkast," he claims, "I'll fly to Medan and start handing out Benjamins [U.S. $100 bills] to anyone who looks like these guys."[21]

Those sympathetic to the label usually defend as part of a progressive modern cosmopolitanism the value of this "lost-in-translation" encounter with the extremes of cultural difference. One writer argues that while Sublime Frequencies' confrontational approach can be "coarse, even prurient . . . theirs is an ethnographic surrealism that stalks the marvelous."[22] Others value the label as an intervention that disrupts commercial world music productions and deflates ethnomusicology's aura of "superiority, exclusivity, expertise and analytical spin."[23] An early review on the website of the San Francisco experimental record store Aquarius Records fluently sums up this perspective: "While much of the post-Explorer purveyors of 'world music' shamelessly produce an endless slough of slick garbage that sounds like the crap you can hear on any U.S. top 40 radio station merely sung in another language, the recordings you'll hear presented by Sublime Frequencies come from the cracks in the pavement of the culture makers. . . . Balls to fidelity, none of the artists here would be allowed within 10 miles of a Putumayo A&R executive, this is the punk rock of field recordings!"[24]

But in a later take, the same reviewer admits to a creeping ambivalence, writing that "it seems somehow disingenuous to travel to another country, turn on the radio, record several hours worth of music and sound, come home, put those recordings on a CD and then sell them."[25]

Despite his rhetorical stance, Alan Bishop says that Sublime Frequencies does compensate artists in many cases. When I presented an early version of this article in Seattle at the Experience Music Project Conference in April 2008, Bishop and

Sublime Frequencies filmmaker Mayet were in attendance to correct and critique this point (among others). Over the course of a conversation following the talk and a phone interview a few weeks later, Bishop told me that, although Sublime Frequencies operates "outside the moneymaking machine," he had in fact made attempts to compensate authors when possible.[26] For some later releases, Sublime Frequencies reached agreements directly with artists, in contracts that conform to common standards for the release of original music.[27] But when Bishop could not easily locate or identify musicians—as in the mixes constructed from radio broadcasts—he decided the sounds were fair game.

There are many reasons to dismiss Sublime Frequencies as a punk-rock re-iteration of Orientalist procedures of appropriation and exploitation. Bishop's invocation of the *mondo bizarro* of cultural difference is blithely provocative. His anachronistic critique of academic ethnography reduces its complex history to a straw-man caricature of cultural imperialism. And in light of a rapidly changing discourse about cultural rights, his indifference to issues of ownership and compensation may seem disingenuously naive. But in several important ways, Sublime Frequencies' approach is rooted in an emergent public ethics of new media.[28] Bishop argues for an approach to media circulation that is already in place in informal economies worldwide: one that recognizes that media are limited by their own structures of reproduction, that appropriation is multidi-rectional, and that any attempt to regulate access is an attempt to control public consciousness. In the remainder of this article, I examine the following questions: What do redistributions of world music tell us about changing frameworks of intellectual property? How have informal economies of redistribution, especially online circulations, influenced contemporary representations of local music cultures? And what is the relationship between the aesthetics of distortion formed by this Northern listenership and the conditions of technological reproduction in the global South?

WORLD MUSIC WANTS TO BE FREE

As legal interpretations of intellectual property have tightened in the past decade, listeners broadly refuse to accept the terms of copyright law, which expand the power of media industries to control artistic content and limit creativity, even as they fail to fairly compensate original authors. And on a global scale, consumers do not attribute authorship to recorded media in the ways demanded by insti-tutional logics of ownership. Increasingly, a shared commons of information is viewed as a global democratic ideal of open source culture, and any attempt to regulate its flow is characterized as the corporate censorship of instrumental capitalism. In the United States, this argument has been associated with a cluster of overlapping policy groups: the "free culture" movement of Lawrence Lessig's Creative Commons project, the legal advocacy of the Electronic Frontier Foundation, and communities of free software developers such as the Free Software foundation, all of which gather under the oft-cited slogan "Information wants to be free" (attributed initially to Stewart Brand and repoliticized by the "copyleft" free software pioneer Richard Stallman).[29]

This notion of informational freedom could only emerge in a U.S.–based social context that historically has foregrounded the legal rights of independent liberal subjects.[30] Freedom to access information is presented first as an individual right and then extended into an ideological mandate for an open society. But this notion of individual freedom was redoubled by the alternative consumption imagined by populist countercultures, for whom freeing music from commodity systems of distribution required that they also must be free of monetary value ("Free, as in beer," to paraphrase Stallman, as well as "free, as in speech"). Alternative media imposed the goals of an earlier project of independence, which demanded new and participatory modes of distribution that would liberate popular culture from commodity markets. Contemporary open source movements have brought these long-standing countercultural binaries—of utopian alternative systems opposed to the corporate regulation of culture—into the sphere of digital circulations and productions of "new media."

The current resistance to musical copyright fuses the oppositional politics of popular music with ethical codes that have filtered up from 1980s cyberpunks and hackers, who developed the multiple-access user systems and Bulletin Board Systems (BBSS) that informed the later structure of the Internet. The hacker ethic challenged the use of technology to form elites: Hackers demanded that information technologies be decentralized, proposing that all "users had a basic right to free access to all information."[31] In the 1990s, the nascent politics of online society drew heavily on the romantic libertarianism of North American countercultures, combining values of underground popular culture with new systems for disseminating information. But as the Internet became realized on a mass scale in the 2000s, online publics began to project the underground populism of open source culture against the backdrop of a mass-mediated consumption that could "rip" music away from its corporate curation. In other words, they developed an ethical position that demanded that consumers free musical culture from its industrial context by forming an independent network of individual redistributors.

The populist demand for free media joined voices with policy groups outraged by legal reinterpretations of intellectual property law that favored corporate industry. Several high-profile legislative battles (most notoriously the Sonny Bono Copyright Term Extension Act and the Digital Millennium Copyright Act, which were both signed into law in 1998 and enabled the technology of Digital Rights Management) fueled a groundswell of antagonism toward "permission culture." Among online freedom advocates, ownership of content was characterized as a top-down control system that disregards artistic compensation and locks culture away from disenfranchised citizens. As a result, industrial media distribution was associated with state projects of exploitation and censorship, as opposed to practices of creative sharing and free information exchange that take place on the level of the individual subject.[32]

Music has become the terrain on which this battle has been fought in the starkest terms. Widespread use of digital file-sharing services, and the legal repercussions that followed, have inspired far-reaching projections of global musical communities as well as paranoid visions of social control. Against desperate, late corporate attempts to control online media circulation and stem the flow of piracy, music redistributors validate their project through the demands of a changing public sphere. We, they claim, can get the job of media circulation done better, faster, and more democratically than either industry or academe. Because of the label's historical relationship to DIY projects of independent music, then, Sublime Frequencies is easily mapped onto new media discourses about the participatory ethics of open access, despite having formed in old media networks based in analog cassettes and LPs. Music redistributors, like hackers, view their activity as a corrective to the failures of industry. If creative expression is bound by untenable copyright protection laws or falsified cultural revivals, they claim that people will naturally bypass these controls to appropriate content for liberatory purposes.

But the legacy of independent music also helps listeners to envision a decentralized and egalitarian public for world music. If listeners develop the ability to tune in to the experimentalism of marginal cultural forms, the argument goes, then world music could escape industrial mediation in ways that aid its producers as well as distant consumers.[33] For instance, although the music on Parallel World's *Cambodian Rocks* compilation has long been important in Cambodia, its overseas success affects the local population in several ways. American reissues of classic Khmer pop music by artists such as Sinn Sisamouth and Ros Sereysothea are embraced, both as a homage to the cosmopolitan public lost during the destructive regime of Pol Pot and as a boon to tourism that has brought much-needed economic stimulus to the region.[34] The recirculation of this material has inspired new connections with the diaspora as well, most significantly by the Los Angeles–based group Dengue Fever, which performs classic 1960s Cambodian garage rock mixed with some original songs.[35] Founding member Ethan Holtzman was inspired by *Cambodian Rocks* to travel to Cambodia as a tourist. On his return, he organized a band to perform Khmer rock music, eventually convincing recent emigrant Chhom Nimol to join the group. Although Nimol initially was reluctant to sing such dated material, the group found great success in North America with indie rock audiences and Cambodians alike, and Dengue Fever went on to perform in Cambodia in 2005 (the tour is documented in the 2007 film *Sleepwalking through the Mekong* [dir. John Pirozzi, Film 101 Productions]).[36]

Proponents of an open access network of media redistribution argue that music would be kept from its present and future publics—and that these publics could not even begin to be formed—if circulation were forced to comply with purified perspectives of intellectual property. Mack Hagood, on the blog *The Far Eastern Audio Review*, chastised Parallel World for neglecting proper credits even in its second reissue of *Cambodian Rocks*—by which time the artists and tracks had been identified properly by listeners—but admitted that the compilation "is a perfect example of something great that couldn't have existed if our Draconian copyright laws had been followed."[37] Most redistributors describe themselves as selfless amateurs dedicated to providing access to uncommercial music without achieving personal gain (the logo of Mississippi Records reads "Always—Love Over Gold"). This is small-scale material, they say, that could never enter circulation without breaking the rules; to become known, it requires the determined work of an underresourced independent agent. "If I didn't release this music," Alan Bishop told me, "people would never get to hear it."[38]

This approach invokes a reverse architecture of online documentation. Redistributors leave it to the network to fill in the blanks, retroactively assembling a body of knowledge that trails after the recording after it has already been released. Information constantly develops around content through its public circulation. Authentication follows access: First make the material available and then wait for its history to accumulate through a cloud of references, links, and associations. A blog post, for example, usually develops through constant updating and expansion of posted materials. It is not uncommon for bloggers to post a downloadable file of an undocumented LP recording alongside an image of its worn sleeve and ask, "What's the name of this album? Does anyone know anything about this?" Commentators sometimes follow up by providing background on the content or links to other online resources. For instance, although the physical CD release of *Cambodian Rocks* neglected liner notes and song and artist data, many bloggers have discovered and posted the track information, often with brief explanations of the historical context and biographies of the musicians. So although the Parallel World label never redressed the initial lack of documentation, the album is now redistributed online with the corrected track information provided by knowledgeable fans.[39]

Cultural preservation, in the logic of open source culture, demands that content be backed up collectively through a continuous process of redistribution. In order to keep hold of an original, as many copies as possible must be circulated to the widest possible spectrum of recipients. Existing archives are criticized, however, for the narrowness of their scope, as well as for their unethical de facto ownership of usurped materials.[40] Institutional policies make important collections inaccessible to public circulation, and libraries fail their stated mission by allowing materials to disappear through negligence or deaccession. This loss is most egregious for underpreserved artifacts of popular culture. Mark Gergis, for example, spent six years copying materials from the Oakland Public Library to collect the tracks for the Sublime Frequencies release *Cambodian Cassette Archives: Khmer Folk and Pop, Volume 1*. Gergis claims to have saved the archive from its ongoing demise at the hands of its would-be preservers, the library employees who unwittingly erased the cassettes by passing them through the magnetic security system. "Even with the best intentions of the public library as a repository for culture," as one reviewer put it, "Cambodian music was being erased, one cassette at a time."[41]

PIRACY, INDEPENDENCE, AND CONTROL

The redistribution of new old media I have described here draws from technologies that have been transformed in the digital era. But it nostalgically extends the independence of analog media networks, like the 1980s cassette culture, which represented participatory musical exchange at an earlier technological stage. Brian Larkin proposes that analog infrastructures of piracy corrupt the official logics of media distribution by exploiting the discontinuities and breakdowns of technological systems. This corruption is especially apparent in informal economies, which are necessarily "underground" and detached from centers of media production and legal frameworks of cultural ownership. In contexts like the Nigerian bootleg video market, the cultural effects of piracy are woven into a circulation "marked by poor transmission, interference, and noise."[42] Distortion, miscommunication, loss of information—the byproducts and accidental effects of analog media exchange have themselves become aesthetic icons of fair use and open access.[43] My point here is that projects of redistribution like Sublime Frequencies are rooted not just in ideologies of access and control but also in the technological limitations of media. As a result, overlapping categories of piracy, appropriation, sharing, and bootlegging have become crucial to the participatory ethics of World Music 2.0.

The criminality of piracy proposed by copyright law is not just defused or ignored, it is reversed. Redistributors insist that freedom of access always trumps the controls of ownership; in fact, it would be criminal to allow these recordings to remain uncirculated. Further, they argue that existing industrial setups for authorial compensation are practically dysfunctional anyway, especially in the informal economies of regional music scenes. For example, Jack Carneal, who releases Malian popular music on his Yaala Yaala label, claims to have made efforts to set up contractual terms for a release by the *ngoni* lute player Yoro Sidibé, only to discover that a corrupt producer had stolen the advance money.[44] Subsistence-level distributions are the only sensible channels for compensation, Carneal argues, especially in the face of piracy and online circulation. Recordings essentially serve as calling cards for musicians to drum up an audience for their live performances.[45] Carneal has since set up a fund called the Yaala Yaala Rural Musicians Collective that would distribute any profits from his releases, but he makes it clear that his small-scale productions are designed to cover costs only. As the music recording collapses as an exchangeable commodity, "people around the world have recognized that the old paradigm of ensuring that people hear your music is broken. . . . Bootlegging and other sub-industry means of distributing music will eradicate any semblance of the industry as we know it before too long."[46] But since musicians in the North American underground have been giving away their recordings for decades, the shift toward open access appears in many ways to vindicate an existing project of DIY circulation.

In bringing this subsistence model into a digital network, redistributors fuse two very different contexts of access, one from the online realm of crowdsourced open culture and the other from an earlier model of underground media exchange. They write their open access manifesto on a page taken from analog music scenes, limited to an alternative circle operating beyond the mainstream. Music recordings are presented in a purist, amateur realm, whose possibilities for profit are naturally restricted by the aesthetic challenges of the musical material itself. The priority is that "people hear your music," whether in a live or mediated context. Of course, this scenario also requires world music to stay in the scene—in the frame of an independent musical world created through local infrastructures—when, in the participatory context of online exchange, it is bound to do just the opposite.

Craig Calhoun argues that the social development of the Internet tends to tamp down public scrutiny over privacy concerns (and, as I am arguing, problems of cultural ownership and compensation) until after the network is already constructed and operational. Users "think mainly in terms of new information being gathered rather than recognizing the immense quantity of information already produced as by-products of computer use. . . . The issues involve not just 'exposure' but control."[47] In the face of this uncontrollable proliferation of material, the Internet finds its balance through an endless self-correction that provokes paranoid dialectics of freedom and control.[48] For the publics formed in this context, anything documented by an acknowledged institutional source must necessarily be incomplete, and possibly also biased beyond authentication. This means that the thing you haven't heard before quickly becomes the next version of the truth. Anything outside the loop becomes new archival material for the constituents of Reality 2.0, who must mash up structures of the past to match the beat of an alternative future.

New media publics are created through an endless reiteration of their own possibilities within the fluid boundaries of online networks. Christopher Kelty describes how the creation and exchange of free software helped programmers conceptualize themselves as a "recursive public," that is, a public "concerned with the ability to build, control, modify, and maintain the infrastructure that allows [it] to come into being in the first place."[49] In the context of free software development, the ability to distribute new cultural materials carries with it an ethical mandate to maximize access. But access is always invoked with a purpose; its production of knowledge is aimed toward a certain set of limits. A recursive public remediates the construction of knowledge toward its own formation. Its ability to transform culture depends on defining the center of cultural participation within its own collaborative projects.

To remain independent in a participatory online context, musical undergrounds must generate similar limits on circulation, which will allow listeners to recognize specific transformations of content. The vinyl LP, then, remains a frontline standard of independent media, and some contemporary labels release cassettes as well. Unlike a digital file, an analog music recording is inherently limited by the transience and noise that accrues in its reproduction. As they are copied and redistributed, physical media inevitably are changed by their handlers; their content bears the marks of their circulation. The underground listenership of world music is distinguished by its recognition of these obscure analog traces, even as they are extended into a parallel world of digital exchange.

In this context, Sublime Frequencies comes to represent an untimely logic of authority and control: We circulate it, they don't, and if we didn't find it and reproduce it for you, you'd never hear it. At the very moment when all music will, it seems, be available to anyone at any time—when the very idea of a unique, undiscovered sound seems impossible—Sublime Frequencies revitalizes the limitations of an analog form. Its listenership replaces the industrial claim to mastery with its own circuitry of access, projecting the ghostly distortions of the underground into the limitless realms of digital media.

I have argued that the cultural appropriations of labels like Sublime Frequencies are neither a mere vestige of historical Orientalism nor a function of new media that somehow clashes with earlier analog networks. Rather, these "new old" media are formed in a feedback loop, in which the political formations of online culture are used to highlight the distortions of world music. Central to this process of remediation are aesthetics derived from analog technology. I conclude by discussing how the sound of distortion has become emblematic of cultural representation in World Music 2.0. Distortion is important because it embodies the noisy, "lossy," discontinuous experiences of media circulation. While official distribution attempts to make reproduction disappear into the background—"bringing the music to you" in a "lossless" repetition of the original—experimental listeners bring the noise to the surface. World Music 2.0 aestheticizes the distortions of a conflicted musical imaginary and in so doing attempts to return to listeners through reproduction the "capacity for experience which technological production threatens to take away."[50]

AUTHENTICATING DISTORTION

Distortion is a crucial proof of world music's authenticity. Because it is formed in the context of limitations, distortion authenticates world music in two ways.

First, it verifies that regional popular music is still "raw" and therefore unintegrated into the fidelities of the music industry. But second, and equally important, distortion echoes the local sonic aesthetics of the North American underground. Distorted source materials emphasize direct access to cultural sources that overload the imagination of a distant listener. For example, *Dimanche à Bamako*, the 2004 release by the Malian (but Paris-dwelling) duo Amadou and Mariam, blends studio-recorded guitar and drum tracks with noisy field recordings of public gatherings, conversations, and police cars recorded by the French-Spanish producer Manu Chao in the streets of Bamako. The contrasting mix of sound sources makes it difficult to know where the original musicians stand in relation to the end result.[51] But in many ways, this is the point: distortion mediates the gaps of intentionality and accident between Southern cultural production and Northern media consumption.

Distortion has become a sonic emblem of local creativity under conditions of limited technological access. One of the clearest examples is Konono No 1, a Congolese *likembe* (an African instrument also known as the thumb piano) group whose 2005 album *Congotronics* became a smash hit among experimental listeners worldwide. A great part of the music's appeal to its overseas audience derives from the distorted electronic sounds of the group's makeshift amplifiers, which transform a locally recognized music style ("Bazombo trance music") that might otherwise have been circulated as a classic ethnomusicological field recording of village music.[52] In marketing Konono No 1 as an "electrotraditional" group, the Belgian label Crammed Discs explains that this distortion is the product of local conditions and not aesthetic intention. Because they had no access to standard sound equipment, the musicians "had to incorporate the originally unwanted distortions of their sound system. This has made them develop a unique style which, from a sonic viewpoint, has accidentally connected them with the aesthetics of the most experimental forms of rock and electronic music, as much through their sounds than through their sheer volume."[53]

These accidental connections are the material parallel of the listening aesthetics that have allowed Konono No 1 to slip somewhere between underground and world music. Distortion represents the real sound of regional music. But it also makes audible the technological differences that disrupt the possibility of a global media commons.[54] To aestheticize these ruptures is to connect with new creativities based in limitations and liminality, which stress technocultural feedback over transcultural connections. Konono No 1 amplifies its unique sounds through failed, jerry-rigged systems that echo half-forgotten moments of earlier

Western musical technology. It was no surprise, then, that the Icelandic indie star Björk asked the band to record rhythm tracks on her 2007 album *Volta*, claiming that the group's wild sound was both futuristic and somehow nostalgic of 1980s' drum machines.[55] Experimental music listeners return to their own local world of magic in the icon of analog noise, which makes world music sensible as underground media. But this also means that there can be no authentic reproduction of world music that could carry this original context forward; "the very act of recording Konono's music," as one writer puts it, "breaks it out of the mold its history has cast for it."[56]

Debates about musical locality—which have been strongly influential in public representations of cultural authenticity—often presume coterminous relationships between sounds and sources, particularly those of the body and the voice. Sonic representations of social "presence" put listeners back in the space of an original musical context, projecting their dislocated audition back onto unique scenarios of immediacy, "liveness," and local authorship.[57] But the desire for embodied local presence is undermined by increasing global access to sounds, which leads to the constitutive participation of broader listening publics. The process appears to strip musicians of their cultural voices; at worst, they are ventriloquized by foreign agents through "schizophonic" techniques of recording, distribution, sampling, and remixing.[58]

Yet the deconstruction of world music's presence also has uncovered layers of productive distortion, which challenge consumers to "own" the problems of global media circulation. Remediation, technological manipulation, distance, and the mashups and remixes of cosmopolitan listening are more than the effects of distant reception: They reframe the conditions of musical creativity and participation on a global scale. The historical and social differences of circulation hit home in the noisy hardcore crunch of a synthesizer in Angolan *kuduro*, the looped horns of northern Mexican *banda* resampled in electronic *Nortec*, or the endlessly repetitive drum machines of Puerto Rican *reggaeton*. In the search for gritty cultural realities that characterize World Music 2.0, distortion is a crucial part of the sound—not a bug but a feature of global media.

At the threshold of technological access, distortion becomes world music's creativity-by-accident. It allows listeners to distinguish agency somewhere between the unintended (but uniquely creative) limitations of local voices and the global transformations of sound. For the creators of lo-fi world music, distortion may have a very different provenance. Far from being a marker of local limitations, distortion can represent entry into a global sphere of modern production. Among contemporary Javanese listeners, as R. Anderson Sutton tells us, distorted timbres fluidly integrate regional aesthetics with technological power. "If a 'poorly tuned gong' serves as an effective icon for nature," he asks, "might not an electronically distorted singing voice serve as an icon for the condition of progress and modernity?"[59] But in circulation, these distorted voices are folded into new layers of distortion, feeding back into one another.

A NOISY WAKE-UP CALL FOR GLOBAL MEDIA

In the Sublime Frequencies DVD *Jemaa El Fna: Morocco's Rendezvous of the Dead*, shot among folk performers in a Marrakesh night market, the camera lingers at a small stall that plays 7-inch 45 rpm records for spare change. The records are almost unplayable, half-destroyed by dirt, age, and abuse. For several minutes, the camera holds on a badly focused shot of various records spinning on the platter, alternating with blurry shots of the battered cardboard sleeve. At one point, the proprietor attempts to play a record that originally was recorded at a slower format. But because the tiny plastic record player cannot switch speeds, the proprietor attempts to slow down the record by hand. He presses his finger against the side of the disc and then directly on the grooves, causing the recording to fluctuate and warble on top of the already distorted sound issuing scratchily from the tinny speaker. Although we witness the image of the record spinning around the turntable next to its dusty slipcover, our focus is on the noise of the medium itself.

World Music 2.0 signals a sea change in the way we document the world of music. This is a world formed in the margins of global exchange, which takes shape in our recognition of its limits. Sublime Frequencies mediates the loss of analog underground culture for North American listeners by discovering its own nostalgic distortions elsewhere in the world. But this does not simply reduce to a polemic of gonzo ethnography against the artificiality of corporate and academic production. And although World Music 2.0 stresses the effects of disappearance and loss, this is not a Lomaxian moment of cultural preservation. If it documents a shifting world of music, it also records its mashups and overlaps, degraded sources and untraceable short-circuits. This sound, to revise Feld's phrase, is less a sweet lullaby for world music than a noisy wake-up call for global media.

Distortion has become part of how world music should sound. It marks the limits of a free media circulation, but also promises the creative possibilities that unfold at its anonymous thresholds. "Sound fidelity," Jonathan Sterne reminds us, is "more about faith in the social function and organization of machines than it is about the relation of a sound to its 'source.' "[60] For experimental listeners, the presence of original sound is proven by the *in*fidelity of the machine: in its partiality, imbalance, and lack of ability to faithfully represent the original. Recognizing the failure of recordings to transmit the sources of musical culture, they tune in to distortion as a new cultural form.

To appreciate distortion, of course, means recognizing that there may be, somewhere, something different from what we hear. Distortion evokes the transformations of sound in circulation. It conjures the survival of an undistorted expression separate from the technological context of mediation. But we can't begin to imagine that magical unreproducible original until we have learned to recognize the differences of distortion—to perceive its qualities and thereby remediate its effects. If we listen to a distorted sound, a world of music may lie beneath. The way in, though, is a mystery, and all we have to guide us is the noise.

NOTES

This chapter originally appeared in *Public Culture* 23, no. 3 (2011): 603–34, published by Duke University Press. Multimedia links and audiovisual illustrations for this article are accessible on the Public Culture website at www.publicculture.org/news/view/supplemental-media-for -david-novaks-the-sublime-frequencies-of-new-old-media-fall-2011. I would like to acknowledge the Society of Fellows in the Humanities at Columbia University for support in writing this article, and my gratitude to *Public Culture*'s editorial board and all respondents and readers, including Dilip Parameshwar Gaonkar, Marilyn Ivy, Wayne Marshall, Brian Karl, and Alan Bishop. Thanks also to Tammy Kim, Mike Veal, and all at Duke and Wesleyan University Presses for enabling reproduction in this volume.

1. The 1990s literature in ethnomusicology and anthropology was particularly thick in the critique of world music; see in particular Feld 1994, 1996, 2000, as well as Meintjes 1990, 2003; Guilbault 1993; Erlmann 1996; Zemp 1996; Taylor 1997; Frith 2000; Hutnyk 2000; Brennan 2001; and Stokes 2004.

2. Steven Feld, "From Schizophonia to Schizmogenesis: The Discourses and Practices of World Music and World Beat," in *Music Grooves*, ed. Charles Keil and Steven Feld (Chicago: University of Chicago Press, 1994), 146.

3. The term "remediation" here draws from Jay David Bolter and Richard Grusin, who use the term to describe how forms of older media are incorporated into new technologies in an interdependent media environment, as well as from a recent literature that extends the concept further into cultural identities and socioeconomic networks (Bolter and Grusin 1999; Acland 2007; Silvio 2007; Novak 2010).

4. Teri Silvio, "Remediation and Local Globalizations: How Taiwan's 'Digital Video

Knights-Errant Puppetry' Writes the History of the New Media in Chinese," *Cultural Anthropology* 22, no. 2 (2007): 286.

5. James Clifford, "On Ethnographic Surrealism," *Comparative Studies in Society and History* 23 (1981): 540.

6. Many MP3 blogs advertise an "opt-out" policy to address possible disputes over unauthorized distribution of posted content. A blurb on the front page of the MP3 blog *Holy Warbles*, for example, read: "we strongly believe in the free flow of artistic inspiration & kultural awareness. if you got beef because yer recording is featured in this realm, simply leave a comment & we'll happily remove the offending comment with the quickness." holywarbles.blogspot.com (accessed January 29, 2011).

7. Sublime Frequencies website: sublimefrequencies.com.

8. Ibid. Unmentioned here is perhaps the most obvious precedent for Sublime Frequencies: Harry Smith's 1952 *Anthology of American Folk Music* (Folkway Records, New York), an unauthorized compilation mix of commercial recordings that became the touchstone for the burgeoning 1960s' folk revival movement (Boon 2006). Partly to avoid the problem of copyright violation for redistributing commercial material, Smith's notes for each track deliberately misspelled names and omitted information about the artists' musical histories, regional locations, and race, and instead used a mysterious set of narrative and cosmological categories to arrange the anthology's complex mix of sources.

9. The ethnomusicologist John Bailey, in "*Modi Operandi* in the Making of 'World Music' Recordings," *Recorded Music: Performance, Culture, and Technology*, ed. Amanda Bayley (Cambridge: Cambridge University Press, 2010), remembers that his early fieldwork recordings in 1970s Afghanistan were uncompensated productions "made as research documents, without thought as to their eventual publication as world music records." In recent decades, ethnomusicologists have turned their attention to issues of intellectual property, cultural rights, and repatriation of historical sound collections, as well as the popular recirculation of ethnomusicological field recordings (Feld 1996; Seeger 1996; Zemp 1996).

10. Sublime Frequencies website; Sublime Frequencies, *Radio Pyongyang: Commie Funk and Agit Pop from the Hermit Kingdom*, SF023, CD, 2005, www.sublimefrequencies.com/item.asp?Item_id=26.

11. Ibid.

12. Sublime Frequencies, *Radio Sumatra: The Indonesian FM Experience*, SF021, CD, 2005, www.sublimefrequencies.com/item.asp?Item_id=24 (accessed October 3, 2007; NB: the text on this page has been altered since the original date of access).

13. Richard Bishop, "Travels," *Halana* 1, no. 4 (1999): 7–16.

14. Brandon Stosuy, "No Sleep Till Beirut: A Conversation with Alan Bishop," *Arthur* 18 (2005), archived at www.arthurmag.com/2010/10/25/no-sleep-till-beirut-a-conversation-with-alan-bishop-by-brandon-stosuy.

15. Tim Bugbee, "Third Eye Staring Contest," *Popwatch* 10 (1999), www.furious.com/perfect/suncitygirlsinterview.html.

16. Michael C. Vazquez, "Disorientalism," *Bidoun* (2007), www.bidoun.org/magazine/10 -technology/disorientalism-by-michael-c-vazquez.

17. Barbara Kirshenblatt-Gimblett, "Confusing Pleasures," in *The Traffic in Culture: Refiguring Art and Anthropology,* ed. George E. Marcus and Fred R. Myers (Berkeley: University of California Press, 1995), 240. Kirshenblatt-Gimblett goes on to identify a process of "unlearning" at the heart of these "confusing pleasures," through which "aficionados of avant-garde and experimental performance can sit and watch something they don't 'understand' because of what they have unlearned—namely, the expectations, attitudes, values, and sensibility associated with establishment art forms."

18. Alan Bishop, ironically, complained to me that writers who accuse Sublime Frequencies releases of lacking liner notes often have downloaded ripped MP3s rather than purchase the physical CDs or LPs that include track descriptions.

19. Erik Davis, "Cameo Demons: Hanging with the Sun City Girls," 2004, www .techgnosis.com/scg.html.

20. Douglas Wolk, "Heard on the Streets (of the Axis of Evil)," *New York Times*. November 20, 2005, www.nytimes.com/2005/11/20/arts/music/20wolk.html.

21. Davis, "Cameo Demons."

22. Ibid.

23. Wolk, "Heard on the Streets."

24. Aquarius Records, www.aquariusrecords.org (accessed January 31, 2008).

25. Ibid. Many underground writers are dismissive of the Orientalist critique of Sublime Frequencies. In his eulogy for the Sun City Girls, the critic and underground music archivist Byron Coley describes "sniping in some quarters regarding the band's purported heisting of ethnic musical traditions," but says that "we had a good laugh about the idea of them as cultural imperialists," in "Sun City Girls: God, How They Sucked, 1981–2007," *Arthur*, no. 26 (2007): 5.

26. Bishop, telephone interview with author, April 30, 2009.

27. Bishop claims to be endorsed by local broadcast institutions, and he has visited Radio Republic Indonesia with copies of his Indonesian radio compilations for special programs. He told me that no one at the national radio station mentioned issues of compensation: "They just want the music to be promoted—they see it that way, and I see it that way." Ibid.

28. My approach to media ethics in this article is descriptive of the social contexts within which moral positions about media are developed and exercised. Rather than evaluating possible good or bad outcomes of ethical behavior or prescribing normative solutions for the moral problems of appropriation and open access in relation to autho-

rial rights, I consider the ever-shifting ethics of media exchange in relation to the ways that standards of right and wrong are applied to music recordings in their social and technological circulations.

29. Lawrence Lessig, *Free Culture: How Big Media Uses Technology and the Law to Lock Down Culture and Control Creativity* (New York: Penguin, 2004); Lessig, *Remix: Making Art and Commerce Thrive in the Hybrid Economy* (New York: Penguin, 2008). See also www.eff.org, www.fsf.org, www.free-culture.cc, and creativecommons.org for more on copyleft licensing as a less-restrictive alternative to existing copyright law.

30. E. Gabriella Coleman and Alex Golub, "Hacker Practice: Moral Genres and the Cultural Articulation of Liberalism," *Anthropological Theory* 8 (2008): 255–77.

31. Andrew Ross, "Hacking Away at the Counterculture," in *Technoculture*, ed. Constance Penley and Andrew Ross (Minneapolis: University of Minnesota Press, 1991), 116.

32. Coleman points out that the common binaries of "open and closed" and "proprietary and free" foreclose other possibilities in the complex field of digital circulations, which is reduced to a clash between capitalist proprietorship and liberal access, in "Ethnographic Approaches to Digital Media," *Annual Review of Anthropology* 39 (2010): 487–505.

33. The recent experimental turn in world music extends earlier projects of musical recovery. In the late 1990s, Brazilian rock "nuggets"—first recirculated on bootlegs, then on the small indie label Omplatten, and eventually on David Byrne's "major indie" label, Luaka Bop—sparked a cult fandom of the late 1960s' *Tropicália* movement led by artists such as Caetano Veloso, Tom Zé, and Os Mutantes. *Tropicália* offered a potential nexus of global affinities that previously had been unlinked in existing histories of rock music, as "cannibalistic hipsters" excavated global undergrounds in hopes of finding common aesthetic ground. See John Harvey, "Cannibals, Mutants, and Hipsters: The Tropicalist Revival," in *Brazilian Popular Music and Globalization,* ed. Charles Perrone and Christopher Dunn (Gainesville: University Press of Florida, 2001), 117.

34. Stephen Mamula, "Starting from Nowhere? Popular Music in Cambodia after the Khmer Rouge," *Asian Music* 39 (2008): 26–41.

35. Dengue Fever is also praised for creating a new kind of underground world music fan. As the bassist Senon Williams puts it, "The underground people are getting hip to world music, and the world music side is getting hip to how you don't have to have a dreadlock wig and Guatemalan pants to be cool." Quoted in R. J. Smith, " They've Got those Mekong Blues Again." *New York Times.* January 20, 2008. www.nytimes.com/2008/01/20/arts/music/20smit.html.

36. Several recent U.S.-released films focus on the cultural history of Cambodian rock music. *The Golden Voice* (dir. Greg Cahill, Rising Falcon Cinema, 2006) is a short biopic on Ros Sereysothea, and a documentary on 1960s Cambodian garage rock, *Don't Think I've Forgotten* (dir. John Pirozzi, 2014), was released in 2014 to critical acclaim

(www.dtifcambodia.com, accessed November 16, 2015). Other films use Cambodian rock prominently in their soundtracks, notably *City of Ghosts* (Mainline Productions), a 2002 independent feature shot in Cambodia by the writer, director, and star Matt Dillon.

37. Mack Hagood, "Review of *Cambodian Rocks* Reissue," *Far Eastern Audio Review*, April 26, 2004, www.fareastaudio.com.

38. Bishop, telephone interview with author.

39. See, for example, the detailed commentary on the post of *Cambodian Rocks* MP3s on the blog of the freeform radio station WFMU, December 9, 2007, blog.wfmu.org /freeform/2007/12/cambodian-rocks.html (accessed May 7, 2008). Commenters added significant discographic information as well as some cultural and biographical background on the recordings. Critiques of redistribution practices are also strongly evidenced in online forums and blog commentaries, with redistributors posting in their own self-defense. For a complex and productive example, see the extensive commentary that followed Chief Boima's post "The Scramble for Vinyl" on the blog *Africa Is a Country*, http://africasacountry.com/2010/09/the-scramble-for-vinyl/ (accessed November 16, 2015).

40. Ross Simonini, for example, credits Frank "Conakry" Gossner (aka DJ Soulpusher) with making the musical findings of his "crate-digging" expeditions to West Africa available to online publics on his *Voodoo Funk* blog. Under "academic circumstances," Ross Simonini writes, "you could picture Conakry's findings remaining deep in the stacks at a university library," in "Mining African Blog Riches: A Fresh Wave of Globally Minded Music Websites Will Broaden Your Horizons," *Village Voice*, August 19, 2008.

41. Aquarius Records website (accessed January 5, 2009).

42. Brian Larkin, "Degraded Images, Distorted Sounds: Nigerian Video and the Infrastructure of Piracy," *Public Culture* 16 (2004): 291.

43. For an in-depth discussion of the technological context of "fair use" legislation and its influence on the aesthetics of bootleg video circulation, see Hilderbrand 2009.

44. Max Goldberg, "Jack Carneal's Yaala Yaala Records Pipelines the Sounds of Mali," *San Francisco Bay Guardian,* June 11, 2008.

45. Sublime Frequencies, for example, arranged European and North American tours for Syrian singer Omar Souleyman and the Moroccan guitar ensemble Group Doueh in 2009 and 2010. "The only reason we're doing it," Alan Bishop told *Wire* reporter Clive Bell, "is so these guys can make some real money. That's the inspiration here, 'cause albums don't cut it" (Bell 2009: 28).

46. Jack Carneal, interview by Nick Storring, posted October 29, 2008, endofworldmusic .blogspot.com.

47. Craig Calhoun, "Information Technology and the International Public Sphere," in *Shaping the Network Society: The New Role of Civil Society in Cyberspace,* ed. Douglas Schuler and Peter Day (Cambridge, Mass.: MIT Press, 2004), 241.

48. See Wendy Chun, *Control and Freedom: Power and Paranoia in the Age of Fiber*

Optics (Cambridge, Mass.: MIT Press, 2006) on the constitutive relationship between freedom and control in Internet ideologies.

49. Christopher Kelty, *Two Bits: The Cultural Significance of Free Software* (Durham, N.C.: Duke University Press, 2008), 7.

50. Susan Buck-Morss, *The Dialectics of Seeing: Walter Benjamin and the Arcades Project* (Cambridge, Mass.: MIT Press, 1989), 268.

51. Ryan Skinner, "Civil Taxis and Wild Trucks: The Dialectics of Social Space and Subjectivity in *Diamanche* à *Bamako*," *Popular Music* 29, no. 1 (2010): 17–39.

52. For more on the representations of Konono No 1's distortion as a discourse of authenticity among Western media sources, see Font-Navarrette 2011.

53. Crammed Discs web page for Konono No 1, www.crammed.be/konono (accessed May 29, 2009).

54. Lo-fi recording quality has been a long-standing sonic hallmark of ethnomusicological fieldwork. This lack of attention to marketplace standards of sound production can be seen as a purifying move, which attempts to disarticulate scholarly projects of field recordings from industrial curation and the traffic of musical commodities (Feld 1994; Turino 2008).

55. Konono No 1 continues to be a primary source for World Music 2.0's diverse remediations and remixes (and an inspiration for ethnomusicologists—see Font-Navarrette 2011). In 2010, Crammed Discs released *Tradi-Mods vs Rockers*, a two-CD set of "alternative takes" on Congotronics by prominent U.S. indie bands such as Deerhoof, Animal Collective, and Oneida. The same year, the Belgian-Congolese rapper Baloji used Konono No 1 tracks on his single from *Kinshasa Succursale*, "Karibu ya Bintou" ("Welcome to Limbo"), the video for which was filmed through hazy, polluted air on the streets of Kinshasa. Baloji went "back to the future" to improvise tracks with other Kinshasa musicians, praising the "unique patina" of their "patched-up" instruments; "even the distortions of the guitars," he claims, "were natural." "'Kinshasa Succursale': The Sorcerer of Words Returns," listed under "Bio" on www.baloji.com/index2.html#.

56. Pieter Hugo, "Electrifying Fetishism," *Wire*, no. 314 (2010): 40.

57. Louise Meintjes, "Paul Simon's *Graceland*, South Africa, and the Mediation of Music," *Ethnomusicology* 34 (1990): 37–73; Philip Auslander, *Liveness: Performance in a Mediatized Culture* (London: Routledge, 1999).

58. Feld, "From Schizophonia to Schizmogenesis"; Feld, "A Sweet Lullaby for World Music," *Public Culture* 12 (2000): 145–71.

59. R. Anderson Sutton, "Interpreting Electronic Sound Technology in the Contemporary Javanese Soundscape," *Ethnomusicology* 40 (1996), 255.

60. Jonathan Sterne, *The Audible Past: Cultural Origins of Sound Reproduction* (Durham, N.C.: Duke University Press, 2003), 219.

BIBLIOGRAPHY

Acland, Charles R., ed. *Residual Media*. Minneapolis: University of Minnesota Press, 2007.

Auslander, Philip. *Liveness: Performance in a Mediatized Culture*. London: Routledge, 1999.

Bailey, John. "*Modi Operandi* in the Making of "World Music" Recordings." In *Recorded Music: Performance, Culture, and Technology*. Amanda Bayley, ed. Cambridge: Cambridge University Press, 2010.

Bell, Clive. "Sublime Frequencies: The Secret Life." *Wire* 303 (2009): 28–33.

Bishop, Alan. Telephone interview with author. April 30, 2009.

Bishop, Richard. "Travels." *Halana* 1, no. 4 (1999): 7–16.

Bolter, Jay David, and Richard Grusin. *Remediation: Understanding New Media*. Cambridge, Mass.: MIT Press, 1999.

Boon, Marcus. "Sublime Frequencies' Ethnopsychedelic Montages." *Electronic Book Review*. 2006. www.electronicbookreview.com/thread/musicsoundnoise/ethnopsyche.

Brennan, Timothy. "World Music Does Not Exist." *Discourse* 23, no. 1 (2001): 44–62.

Buck-Morss, Susan. *The Dialectics of Seeing: Walter Benjamin and the Arcades Project*. Cambridge, Mass.: MIT Press, 1989.

Bugbee, Tim. "Third Eye Staring Contest." *Popwatch* 10 (1999). www.furious.com/perfect/suncitygirlsinterview.html.

Calhoun, Craig. "Information Technology and the International Public Sphere." In *Shaping the Network Society: The New Role of Civil Society in Cyberspace*. Douglas Schuler and Peter Day, eds. Cambridge, Mass.: MIT Press, 2004.

Carneal, Jack. Interview by Nick Storring. Posted October 29, 2008. endofworldmusic.blogspot.com.

Chief Boima. "The Scramble for Vinyl." *Africa Is a Country* (blog), September 14, 2010. http://africasacountry.com/2010/09/the-scramble-for-vinyl/ (accessed October 6, 2010).

Chun, Wendy. *Control and Freedom: Power and Paranoia in the Age of Fiber Optics*. Cambridge, Mass.: MIT Press, 2006.

Clifford, James. "On Ethnographic Surrealism." *Comparative Studies in Society and History* 23 (1981): 539–64.

Coleman, E. Gabriella. "Ethnographic Approaches to Digital Media." *Annual Review of Anthropology* 39 (2010): 487–505.

Coleman, E. Gabriella, and Alex Golub. "Hacker Practice: Moral Genres and the Cultural Articulation of Liberalism." *Anthropological Theory* 8 (2008): 255–77.

Coley, Byron. "Sun City Girls: God, How They Sucked, 1981–2007." *Arthur*, no. 26 (2007): 5.

Davis, Erik. "Cameo Demons: Hanging with the Sun City Girls," 2004. www.techgnosis.com/scg.html.

———. "Speaking in Tongues." *Wire* 240 (2004): 25–29.

Erlmann, Veit. "The Aesthetics of the Global Imagination: Reflections on World Music in the 1990s." *Public Culture* 8 (1996): 467–87.

Feld, Steven. "From Schizophonia to Schizmogenesis: The Discourses and Practices of World Music and World Beat." In *Music Grooves*, ed. Charles Keil and Steven Feld. Chicago: University of Chicago Press, 1994.

———. "Pygmy POP: A Genealogy of Schizophonic Mimesis." *Yearbook for Traditional Music* 28 (1996): 1–35.

———. "A Sweet Lullaby for World Music." *Public Culture* 12 (2000): 145–71.

Font-Navarrette, David. "File Under 'Import': Musical Distortion, Exoticism, and Authenticité in Congotronics." *Ethnomusicology Review* Vol. 16 (2011). http://ethnomusicology review.ucla.edu/journal/volume/16/piece/460.

Frith, Simon. "The Discourse of World Music." In *Western Music and Its Others: Difference, Representation, and Appropriation in Music,* ed. Georgina Born and David Hesmondhalgh. Berkeley: University of California Press, 2000.

Goldberg, Max. "Jack Carneal's Yaala Yaala Records Pipelines the Sounds of Mali." *San Francisco Bay Guardian,* June 11, 2008.

Guilbault, Jocelyn. "On Redefining the 'Local' through World Music." *World of Music* 35, no. 2 (1993): 33–47.

Hagood, Mack. "Review of *Cambodian Rocks* Reissue." *Far Eastern Audio Review*, April 26, 2004. www.fareastaudio.com.

Harvey, John. "Cannibals, Mutants, and Hipsters: The Tropicalist Revival." In *Brazilian Popular Music and Globalization,* ed. Charles Perrone and Christopher Dunn. Gainesville: University Press of Florida, 2001.

Hilderbrand, Lucas. *Inherent Vice: Bootleg Histories of Videotape and Copyright.* Durham, N.C.: Duke University Press, 2009.

Hugo, Pieter. "Electrifying Fetishism." *Wire*, no. 314 (2010): 36–43.

Hutnyk, John. *Critique of Exotica.* London: Pluto, 2000.

Kelty, Christopher. *Two Bits: The Cultural Significance of Free Software.* Durham, N.C.: Duke University Press, 2008.

Kirshenblatt-Gimblett, Barbara. "Confusing Pleasures." In *The Traffic in Culture: Refiguring Art and Anthropology,* ed. George E. Marcus and Fred R. Myers. Berkeley: University of California Press, 1995.

Larkin, Brian. "Degraded Images, Distorted Sounds: Nigerian Video and the Infrastructure of Piracy." *Public Culture* 16 (2004): 289–314.

Lessig, Lawrence. *Free Culture: How Big Media Uses Technology and the Law to Lock Down Culture and Control Creativity.* New York: Penguin, 2004.

———. *Remix: Making Art and Ccommerce Thrive in the Hybrid Economy.* New York: Penguin, 2008.

Mamula, Stephen. "Starting from Nowhere? Popular Music in Cambodia after the Khmer Rouge." *Asian Music* 39 (2008): 26–41.

Meintjes, Louise. "Paul Simon's *Graceland*, South Africa, and the Mediation of Music." *Ethnomusicology* 34 (1990): 37–73.

———. *Sound of Africa! Making Music Zulu in a South African Recording Studio*. Durham, N.C.: Duke University Press, 2003.

Novak, David. "Cosmopolitanism, Remediation, and the Ghost World of Bollywood." *Cultural Anthropology* 25 (2010): 40–72.

Ross, Andrew. "Hacking away at the Counterculture." In *Technoculture*, ed. Constance Penley and Andrew Ross. Minneapolis: University of Minnesota Press, 1991.

Seeger, Anthony. "Ethnomusicologists, Archives, Professional Organizations, and the Shifting Ethics of Intellectual Property." *Yearbook for Traditional Music* 28 (1996): 87–105.

Silvio, Teri. "Remediation and Local Globalizations: How Taiwan's 'Digital Video Knights-Errant Puppetry' Writes the History of the New Media in Chinese." *Cultural Anthropology* 22, no. 2 (2007): 285–313.

Simonini, Ross. "Mining African Blog Riches: A Fresh Wave of Globally Minded Music Websites Will Broaden Your Horizons." *Village Voice*, August 19, 2008.

Skinner, Ryan. "Civil Taxis and Wild Trucks: The Dialectics of Social Space and Subjectivity in *Diamanche à Bamako*." *Popular Music* 29, no. 1 (2010): 17–39.

Smith, R. J. "They've Got those Mekong Blues Again." *New York Times*, January 20, 2008. www.nytimes.com/2008/01/20/arts/music/20smit.html.

Sterne, Jonathan. *The Audible Past: Cultural Origins of Sound Reproduction*. Durham, N.C.: Duke University Press, 2003.

Stokes, Martin. "Music and the Global Order." *Annual Review of Anthropology* 33 (2004): 47–72.

Stosuy, Brandon. "No Sleep Till Beirut: A Conversation with Alan Bishop." *Arthur* 18 (2005). Archived at www.arthurmag.com/2010/10/25/no-sleep-till-beirut-a-conversation-with-alan-bishop-by-brandon-stosuy.

Sublime Frequencies website, sublimefrequencies.com.

Sutton, R. Anderson. "Interpreting Electronic Sound Technology in the Contemporary Javanese Soundscape." *Ethnomusicology* 40 (1996): 249–68.

Taylor, Timothy D. *Global Pop: World Music, World Markets*. New York: Routledge, 1997.

Turino, Thomas. *Music as Social Life: The Politics of Participation*. Chicago: University of Chicago Press, 2008.

Vazquez, Michael C. "Disorientalism." *Bidoun,* 2007. www.bidoun.org/magazine/10-technology/disorientalism-by-michael-c-vazquez.

Wolk, Douglas. "Heard on the Streets (of the Axis of Evil)." *New York Times*, November 20, 2005. www.nytimes.com/2005/11/20/arts/music/20wolk.html.

Zemp, Hugo. "The/An Ethnomusicologist and the Record Business." *Yearbook for Traditional Music* 28 (1996): 36–56.

MARC MASTERS

Meet the

Sun City Girls

One of the most exciting aspects of Sublime Frequencies is also one of the simplest: the huge volume of its catalog. In just over a decade, the label has created upwards of 100 CDS, LPS, and DVDS. All the global hunting and gathering required to build such a wide discography has taken some obsessive effort from Alan Bishop and company. But for those tracking the label's every move, the effect is less that of diligent construction work than a wrecking crew blasting holes in a dam. With each detonation, another wave of sounds and images comes tumbling from an endless trove of international art and culture.

It's tempting to chalk up Sublime Frequencies' prolific output to stereotypical record-collector enthusiasm. After all, releasing everything you can find is a logical product of seeking and devouring it. And it's fair to say that Bishop approached his project with a collector's mentality even before he knew exactly what it would be, since some of the source recordings for the *Radio* entries in the Sublime Frequencies catalog were made before the label existed.

But Bishop's penchant for prolificacy has another, more significant precedent: the even more vast, hard-to-chart discography of his pioneering avant-garde rock trio Sun City Girls. From 1981 to 2007, the trio built a catalog so dauntingly large, it's doubtful that anyone outside the band owns it all. According to their official website, the group generated 50 albums, 23 cassettes, 12 7-inch singles, 12 soundtracks, 25 compilation appearances, 6 feature-length videos, and an undetermined number of other curios and oddities. And the volume of sounds and ideas they injected into those releases—fractured rock, twisted ragas, creepy ballads, surf-riding jams, tightly wound Asian-inflected pop, blabbering poetry, and so much more—seemed even larger than the discography's sheer size.

The album *Torch of the Mystics*, from 1990, is often cited
as Sun City Girls' highest achievement.

Sun City Girls' dizzying productivity reflected an attitude summed up by Alan's bandmate and brother Rick, in a 2009 interview with Mark Prindle. "We just thought, 'What the hell, get it out there, who cares what people think—let's be done with it and start on the next one,'" he said. "That's how we worked. We released stuff that no band in their right mind would ever consider releasing. It was a beautiful thing" (www.markprindle.com/bishop-i.htm).

This insistence on finding beauty in sprawl is what set Sun City Girls' high-volume approach apart. And it matched the music, which itself sprawled at every turn, barreling through genres, ethnicities, and languages, and trashing notions of spiritual, political, and cultural taste. Always happy to err on the side of abandon, courting bemusement, embarrassment, and critical punishment, Sun City Girls stretched a take-the-bad-with-the-good philosophy to a place where the distinction between good and bad eventually broke down altogether. "We make hard decisions and we make 'em quickly, and we move on," Alan told *The Wire* in 2004. "The downside of that approach is that there is too much for people to digest. The upside is that it's fearless . . . So we leave a few diamonds by the roadside and we leave a few heaps of pterodactyl shit as well" (Issue 240, February 2004).

The diamonds emerged because, ironically, Sun City Girls were unafraid to be ugly. They loved to wander through shambling songs, confounding rants, untamed improvisations, and goofball theatrics, in search of some unknown truth that even they might not understand. Often when it seemed they might have drowned in the deep end, they'd resurface with artistic gold, hitting epiphanies that only made sense because of all the diving it took to find them. That's also a fair description of how Alan approaches Sublime Frequencies. Digging through what might seem like cultural detritus, he champions the "ugly"—or at least what the unfamiliar might find discomforting or baffling—and in doing so casts light on its beauty.

This drive to baffle, to see the ugliness in beauty and the beauty in ugliness, goes back to Sun City Girls' earliest days. Formed in 1981 by the Bishop brothers in Phoenix, Arizona (home of a retirement community known as "Sun City"), they briefly went through a few lineups before becoming a trio with drummer Charlie Gocher. Soon after, they entered the hostile territory of the hardcore punk scene. Their first gig was an opening slot for California hardcore-punk pioneer Black Flag (in front of "a bunch of skinheads [who] absolutely hated us," Rick told *Forced Exposure* (Issue 15, Summer 1989), and their first American tour supported skate-punks JFA, aka Jodie Foster's Army. That may have been a deal with the devil—Alan played bass in JFA in exchange for Sun City Girls tagging along—but it actually helped cement the trio's resolve.

"It was easy to develop sort of an anti-audience attitude," Rick told *Popwatch* in 1999 (Issue 10, May 1999). "Much of the time it was us against the crowd, and the more they hated us the more we relished the fact that we were controlling their evening by purposefully putting them in an environment they were uncomfortable with." Taking naturally to the role of contrarian villains, they found power in eschewing automatic acceptance. As Gocher put it to *Forced Exposure* (same issue as above), "It takes a certain kind of person to understand the joy of being rejected."

Why did punk crowds reject Sun City Girls? Perhaps because, ironically, their music was so open. More than any other underground American rock band in the previous three decades, they used the entire world for artistic inspiration and sonic miscegenation. In the span of one album—sometimes even one song—they could switch between Bollywood soundtrack appropriation, classic jazz improvisation, absurd anticomedy, precisely rendered Western rock, and moving street-bard balladry, just to name a few of their modes. It's no wonder the music sprawled: When every sound made in every far corner of the earth is fair game, things can get messy.

The group's worldly influences were acquired firsthand. Since the mid-1980s, the Bishops frequently have traveled the globe, playing and recording everywhere from India to Morocco to Indonesia. But the seeds of their non-Western obsessions were planted even earlier, when the brothers grew up in a Michigan family with close ties to its Lebanese ancestry. Especially vital was their grandfather who lived nearby. He was a master musician who regularly riffled off Arabic tunes during basement jam sessions as the brothers watched in awe. His home was also a gathering place for friends versed in Freemasonry, fueling the Bishops' later interest in rituals and the occult. "There was a weird *Arabian Nights* type of magic in that house, both light and dark," Rick told *Popwatch* (same issue as above). "My most vivid childhood dreams and experiences took place there and they were dark indeed. By the age of 10, I had an entire pantheon of different spirits catalogued in my head."

Those spirits persisted throughout Sun City Girls' career, which was a kind of roller-coaster ride through a secret, bastardized history of the global underground. Even some of their farthest-out jams hinted at tunes uncovered in dusty foreign cassette bins or torn from trebly soundtracks of salvaged Bollywood classics. Just as often, the trio would quickly learn those melodies and rip them out in sharp, masterful form between looser improvisations.

Such discoveries guided 1990's *Torch of the Mystics*, an enchanting record often cited as the group's finest achievement. It showcases Rick's versatile guitar playing, capable of conjuring sonic specters from thin air; Gocher's limitless drumming, rooted in jazz but hard enough to chisel rock; and Alan's mesmerizing voice, darting from hypnotic moans to spirit-channeling warble. But even though *Torch of the Mystics* can get wild, it's mostly pretty focused (the longest song lasts merely seven minutes), making it a bit of an anomaly in the group's discography.

More typical were albums mixing Sun City Girls' non-Western interests with distended explorations of power-trio rock. Take 1996's *330,003 Crossdressers from Beyond the Rig Veda*, 130 minutes of electrifying sound stretched across two CDs. Absorbing its 23 songs is an immersive experience, like waking up inside an experimental film where catchy Hindi surf snuggles with spooky street-folk, rattling experiments frame surreal skits, and a 35-minute live odyssey called "Ghost Ghat Trespass/Sussmeier" conjures demons.

If that sounds too daunting, try 1993's *Kaliflower,* a midpoint between *Torch*-style precision and the outer realms of *Crossdressers*. (It was also the first studio album released on Abduction, after years spent with JFA's label Placebo and the stellar Seattle label Majora). It offers the loping séance "Dead Chick in the River," the eerie prayer "And So the Dead Tongue Sang," the "Monster Mash"-on-acid "I Knew a Jew Named Frankenstein," and a 17-minute storm called "The Venerable Uncle Tompa" (a variation on the even-longer "Venerable Song (The Meaning of Which Is No Longer Known)" from 1993's *Bright Surroundings, Dark Beginnings*).

Kaliflower opens with one of the band's most potent tracks, "X+Y = Fuck You." Here, Alan raps punning beat-poetry in the mode of a character he dubbed "Uncle Jim," while Charlie spills rolling beats and Rick unleashes radio-static feedback. Uncle Jim closes with a command that sums up the Sun City Girls attitude: "If you can comprehend polyrhythmic murder to the tune of 'Ignorance is Bliss' / You know there will never be a critic who will be qualified to critique this."

Plenty of critics ignored that dictum, particularly when discussing Sun City Girls' use of sights and sounds absorbed from their global travels. Confronted by their masks, costumes, and other borrowed iconography, some branded them cultural imperialists. For aficionados, such pageantry was more about mystery; the creepiness of their garb matched the weird amalgams in the music. But others saw disrespectful appropriation with a dose of ugly American privilege.

One such objection came from Chris Bohn of *The Wire* after he saw the trio perform in late 2005 (Issue 262, December 2005). "Their Tourette-like tirades in an indeterminate language, cyberdelic exotica visuals, alarmingly poor skits, and palm-wine drunkard storytelling are all so poorly executed that you can only conclude that a trio of loutish fools rather than jesters are inhabiting their carnival costumes," he wrote. "Their satire . . . ends up trampling all over the sensibilities of the places and folklores they romp through."

It's doubtful that Sun City Girls agreed, but I bet they were amused. After all, they had long enjoyed rejection. Besides, Alan had already answered those charges in *The Wire* itself, a year before Bohn's reaction. "Tradition is not about slavish imitation," he told the magazine (Issue 240, February 2004). "The last thing I want to see is a bunch of fucking white guys playing Javanese gamelon [*sic*] proper . . . They are being disrespectful because they are not evolving the situation. They are not rolling the dice. They are copying, just following somebody else's rules."

Similar accusations of misappropriation and exploitation have been leveled at Sublime Frequencies. Critics have particularly questioned whether the label fairly treats and compensates the artists whose works they disseminate. Alan, Rick, and everyone else involved in the label have never been shy about answering and rebutting those charges, and these issues are covered in depth elsewhere in

this book. But I would argue that the label is ultimately an achievement in preservation, albeit a thorny one that perhaps raises more questions than it answers.
For me, the value lies in the Bishops' unique approach to sprawl; many of the
best Sublime Frequencies releases say as much about their knack for grabbing
sounds and images quickly, freezing them and recycling them, as it does about
the sounds and images themselves. In turn, Sublime Frequencies serves as a kind
of living musical bibliography of the influences behind Sun City Girls' own work.

Additionally, the label has exposed the Western world to some great current
artists, leading to global renown for excellent Syrian musician Omar Souleyman.
"If the source material wasn't documented beyond the context of its specific locales, the material would be deprived of its full power and magnificence," he told
the website *Artist Advocacy* in 2010 (www.artistadvocacy.com/music/interviews/
sun-city-girls/). "And many others who could actually benefit from these powers
would never get the opportunity to experience it otherwise."

Sun City Girls' music offered a similar kind of education, but anyone showing
up to their concerts hoping for a musicology lesson would have been disappointed. They actually didn't tour that much, but their rare appearances proved
perplexing. At one of their biggest shows, at the Great American Music Hall in
San Francisco, they abandoned instruments altogether, offering what long-time
Sun City Girls producer Scott Colburn described to *The Wire* as "a skit about
three hobos waiting for a train." (Issue 240, February 2004). Added Rick, "A lot
of people were upset with it, but that's just the breaks . . . we thought, if there's
going to be 600 people there, let's do something they'll remember." Even more
baffling was a Seattle show billed as "Sun City Girls play John Coltrane's *Live
in Seattle*," which featured the original Coltrane album playing on the club's PA
with the band nowhere to be found.

As prankish as Sun City Girls' performances could be, the group could also
approach shows with surprising forethought. According to Colburn, the trio
prepared for one tour by combing through old set lists to avoid song repeats.
That story matches my own personal experience. In 2004, my brother and I followed the band during a short East Coast tour, filming each show along the way
(with the group's approval). It was the only time I've ever trailed a band, but I
was amazed by how different each performance was. The trio consistently pulled
out obscure compilation contributions or odd B-sides from 7-inch singles that
were over a decade old. And they jumped from sharp rock jams to free-form
blare with an exactitude that would require years of rehearsal for most bands.

If you're looking for a single Sun City Girls release that captures that kind of head-rushing range . . . well, there are a lot of them. The brave could start with the neck-breaking triple-CD *Box of Chameleons*, a vault-clearing compilation spanning the time between their first home recordings and its 1996 release. It's like a space-based radio station picking up the band's beamed transmissions, but it's probably too schizophrenic for the uninitiated.

Instead I recommend the group's most successful extended project, the Carnival Folklore Resurrection Series. Volumes in this series came out so quickly—14 between 2000 and 2006—that it was tempting to assume it was another vault dump. But each one showed a different, integral side of the band. There are the hypnotizing séances of *Cameo Demons and Their Manifestations*; the high-level free-jazz of *A Bullet through the Last Temple*; the ritualistic creep of *Sumatran Electric Chair*; and the best-of blasts of *Libyan Dream*, which supposedly was "originally released as 50 cassette copies dropped in cassette vendors racks in various cities throughout SE Asia in 1993" (www.suncitygirls.com/discography/ LibyanDream.php). The series also includes the requisite bafflement, this time courtesy of two volumes made for radio broadcasts, and one called *The Handsome Stranger* featuring Gocher's growling, oft-unbearable tales.

It's that kind of release where Sun City Girls' risky approach most openly courted failure. Their absurd storytelling was like stand-up comedy without punchlines, and it could turn tedious—take Gocher's weird yarns on the double-CD *Dante's Disneyland Inferno*, or an early LP of painful covers and interludes called *Midnight Cowboys from Ipanema*, which even Rick admitted to *The Wire* was "pretty bad stuff" (Issue 240, February 2004). Perhaps the best way to reconcile these more maddening moments is to watch Sun City Girls' feature-length videos, especially the legendary 1994 VHS tape *Cloaven Theater* (an extension of their early self-released cassettes from the late 1980s). Seeing them get a kick out of flirting with disaster and threatening to kill you with boredom is somehow more thrilling when it's all hacked together in a manic kaleidoscope.

Boredom was less of a danger when Sun City Girls targeted politics. Take the bizarre early LP *Horse Cock Phepner*, with its vulgar paeans to Nancy Reagan and the CIA, or the juvenile, Fugs-like "Prick of the World," a psycho-sexual tribute to the Washington Monument. Rick downplayed the former record's topical bent to *Popwatch*: "We looked at it as a chance to catch up with our obscenity quota. I don't think we had any intention of doing anything that resembled a political album. I think it was more of a documentation of the American nightmare in all its incestuous beauty." But there's something hilarious about the way the group applied absurdist humor to serious subjects.

Maybe that's why Sun City Girls meshed so well with experimental guitarist Eugene Chadbourne, who also has baffled audiences by conflating the sublime and the silly. In 1989, Sun City Girls collaborated with him on *Country Music in the World of Islam Volume XV* (featuring cover art by Simpsons creator Matt Groening), a miniature classic of wry ditties and frayed improv. The humor level may not rise past titles like "Don't Burn the Flag, Let's Burn the Bush," but the songs are consistently interesting, upending notions of whether novelty music can also offer something of substance.

But to me, the best Sun City Girls moments came when they leavened the humor and theatrics by simply hammering out improvised rock music. This often resulted in long pieces that seem to fly by, like "Distorted Views," a cinematic 34-minute track from 2002's *Wah* that in other hands might be interminable. Elsewhere, they chopped their rock into heavy chunks, such as on 1993's *Valentines from Matahari* and 2006's *Djinn Funnel*, both masterpieces of raw, primal jamming. It's a sound that may seem harsh to some, but for a certain sect of Sun City Girls fanatics, it was the molten core of their musical earth.

That core felt strong enough to last forever. But in 2007, Gocher passed away after a long fight with cancer, and the Bishops decided they couldn't continue Sun City Girls without him. They subsequently toured as the Brothers Unconnected, playing a handful of classics and screening Gocher's films beforehand. Both also have forged evolving solo careers—Rick with his fast-handed guitar missives under the name Sir Richard Bishop, and Alan with his creepy bedroom folk as Alvarius B as well as his Egyptian quartet the Invisible Hands, formed in 2011. Sun City Girls' legacy is also evolving. Their prolific activity and affinity for sprawl were picked up by acts such as No-Neck Blues Band, Jackie-O Motherfucker, Bardo Pond, Sunburned Hand of the Man, and Animal Collective (who hired Scott Colburn to record *Feels* because of his work with Sun City Girls, and have tapped Sir Richard Bishop to open for them).

Yet there's something illogical about anyone even attempting to approximate what this unique band accomplished, much as it would be futile to mimic Sublime Frequencies' idiosyncratic approach to collecting and disseminating art. The Bishops sometimes speak of Sun City Girls as a phenomenon that occurred when they were in a room with Charlie Gocher—something beyond their control that even they couldn't replicate. And the point was always to move forward rather than look back. Maybe the title of the final track on one of their best live records, *Live from Planet Boomerang*, says it best: "You Could Be Making History and We're Already Forgetting You."

In a sense, Sublime Frequencies has furthered that idea by inverting it. Alan Bishop is now preserving (or reframing, or remixing, or even shattering) history, to make sure what's worth remembering isn't forgotten. And it's history preserved through enthusiastic saturation rather than guarded selectivity. Certainly Alan and company put thought into every release, and it's likely that many more audiovisual artifacts are stowed away in their vaults. But if the project were to live forever, it seems just as likely that those vaults would eventually empty.

Ultimately, the label's impulsive, keep-getting-it-out-there approach is an extension of the heads-down, mega-prolific attitude of Sun City Girls. From the moment they first began making music, the Bishop brothers seemed to race against time, bent on exploring every idea that came to them while they still had the chance, without wasting much time on justifications or consequences. It turns out the band's demise was no finish line: with Sublime Frequencies, the race continues.

NOTE

This chapter originally appeared, in shorter form, on September 11, 2012, in *Pitchfork*, http://pitchfork.com/features/underscore/8935-sun-city-girls/. Minor edits and corrections have been made to the text.

ANDY BETA

Interview with Alan Bishop

Sun City Girls Member and Co-Founder of Sublime Frequencies

In terms of perceptions of the culture, most people
don't think about music. They're not concerned with it.
They don't take their musical legacy seriously.

WESTERN INFLUENCES ON THAI MUSIC
A surf band named the Shadows
The guitar riff from "Jumpin' Jack Flash"

THAI INFLUENCES ON WESTERN MUSIC
The Butthole Surfers' "Kuntz"

Alan Bishop

In 1981, in the golf course purgatory that is Phoenix, Arizona, a pair of half-
Lebanese brothers from Detroit and a So-Cal transplant formed Sun City Girls
(named after a nearby retirement community). Unclassifiable from the start,
guitarist Richard and bassist Alan Bishop, along with drummer Charles Gocher
Jr., were cacti in the hardcore punk scene: prickly, unapproachable, yet strangely
beautiful. These "girls" understood that punk at its purest meant total negation
of the genre, and for decades they confronted their audiences with the detritus
of the music world: Dada, Kabuki, prog, hobo monologues, puppetry, unfettered
noise, surf instrumentals, guerrilla street theater, and so on and so forth. Their
official discography wavers between fifty and a hundred releases, no two lists
quite alike, but the sounds within provided mutant genetic code for much of

the current American underground: bands like Animal Collective, Deerhoof, No-Neck Blues Band, Six Organs of Admittance, Devendra Banhart, and Dengue Fever took the Sun City Girls' cue to elucidate international noise through their own local muse.

At the height of Thrillermania in 1983, the Bishop brothers voyaged to Morocco. Rick stayed for three weeks, whereas Alan immersed himself for two months. By day Alan jammed on sax and guitar with local musicians; by night he captured snippets of shortwave broadcasts. Twenty years on, he would weave these audio artifacts into *Radio Morocco,* the seventh release on Sublime Frequencies, the "world music" label/collective he co-founded with Hisham Mayet and his brother (with frequent contributions from Mark Gergis, Robert Millis, and others).

Eschewing the rubber gloves of elevator world-music labels and the ivory towers of academic ethnomusicology, Sublime Frequencies' recordings and videos dunk listeners and viewers headfirst into the cultures they document. Following the example of Smithsonian Folkways and Ocora, each Sublime Frequencies release reveals music and sights that are at once workaday and bewildering to Western ears. From Iraq's *choubi* music to Syrian *dabke* to North Korean pop and opera, the label determinedly showcases the uncanny beauty from purported "axes of evil" and other non-tourist destinations.

Cantankerous, chain-smoking, and obsessive, Alan Bishop is hell-bent on undermining Western hegemony and exalting the cultural contributions of the downtrodden. This interview took place on the phone, with Bishop in his garage office where he was hard at work on the next batch of Sublime Frequencies releases and preparing for the final Sun City Girls tour, a tribute to Gocher, who passed away from cancer in early 2007.

I. OBSESSED LIKE ME

THE BELIEVER: In the liner notes for your *Radio Morocco* sound collage, which you recorded there on your first trip in the early eighties, you mention how you came across *Thriller* being shoved down the peoples' throats half a world away and how you hope that the mix can help unbrainwash people. In collaging this stuff, does the radio mix become a cultural jammer?

ALAN BISHOP: Yes, I suppose it does. I have always been inspired by the Burroughs/Gysin cut-up technique, yet I never needed to put it on paper and actually cut and rearrange words. I've always just done it in my head—sometimes I write as I listen to a language I don't understand and reinterpret the language into English—and also with radio and sound. Sound collage has always been one of my favorite mediums to work in, and with a shortwave radio, it's the perfect tool to create audio collage endlessly, spontaneously, on the spot, anytime and anywhere. The source material just happens to be better and more inspiring to me in the areas I've roamed—North Africa, the Mideast, South Asia, etc.

You hear Police songs or modern R&B or Outkast on the radio. It's so common now, there's not much you can do. You expect to hear it—it's going to be everywhere. There are colonial stations run by American companies, European, UK, or Japanese, or whatever powerful entities are in all these countries, pushing this culture and its export. In some instances, they don't even have to push it—it comes in through osmosis, this middle management that works on its own to keep the world going in the social engineering direction that it's being pushed to go, without anyone having to manage it. It's already alive, it's got this life of its own, it takes off to where these people get into it and then propagate it themselves, and the local cultures and people in those cities and towns that are playing songs on the radio are going to like that stuff.

BLVR: Like, do you *really* have to sell Coca-Cola anymore?

AB: Right. Same thing.

BLVR: Traveling as frequently as you do, I'm curious as to how many languages you speak.

AB: I don't speak anything very well. The longer that you travel, you find out that you really don't even need to speak the language to get around and get things done, to live in those places. If you're somewhat resourceful and perceptive, you're pretty much going to know what's going on because human nature is human nature: They understand it, you understand it, and it works.

BLVR: So how often do you understand what you're dealing with then? When I think about my favorite moments on these discs, I conjure the sound first, be it the guitar tone on those *Cambodian Cassette Archives* or the sounds of chickens and crying babies in the background of this stunning vocal/guitar duet from northeast Cambodia. I almost never remember names and never know what they're singing about.

AB: The lyrics are not an important thing to me. In fact, it can be a distraction. If I knew the language enough to know it was a horrible love song with stupid lyrics—like most of the popular songs are today in the English language that I hear—then it would be much more of a turnoff than if it would allow me to interpret it from the expressive capabilities of the vocalizing or of the sound itself, which allows me to create my own meaning for it, which elevates it into a higher piece of work for me. So it's the same way about a Thai song, the Thai language does that to me because I don't understand exactly what's going on in the song. I can read it into my own way of formulating what it means to me. For the same reason that the guy singing that Thai song may even listen to Western music, but he's not going to know what's going on with the Western music either. He doesn't know the fine points. He doesn't speak English. Let's say that all the Thais are listening to all this Western pop music and they don't understand what they're saying either. But they love it because it's doing the exact same thing to them as their songs do to me. That's the similarity here. That's what is much more interesting than knowing what the songs are about.

BLVR: And each side thinks the other is crazy for liking the other culture's pop music.

AB: Correct. They think that I'm crazy for liking their music. I think they're crazy for liking ours.

BLVR: When you're seeking out music, do you find most countries have scant regard for preserving their culture?

AB: It's a matter of economy and standard of living—it dictates how much of a cultural legacy that can be not just preserved but promoted, and it's sort of perpetuated through history. And [most countries] just don't have the resources. You have storerooms of old tapes and old films in hundred-degree heat rooms, just baking. Records are warping or developing mold and insects. I've had records come over via cargo and there's still millipedes running around inside them. The culture is left to rot, just like the buildings and the infrastructure. Roads are getting worse. No money is going back into preserving things. The corruption is so obvious there, where it's not as obvious here.

BLVR: Mentioning the cargo of records, how much time do you spend just in terms of processing stuff?

AB: Most of my spare time is spent doing that. There are seventy-five Sublime projects in production right now. Some may not get done for two to three years. Some of them may never get released, many probably will. But when I go overseas, I'm firing on all cylinders: Doing radio recordings, looking to record musicians live that I encounter, and sometimes I will find them as I go or performing at a club. I record wherever I can. I'll ask people to perform.

BLVR: Having spent so much time with the Sublime Frequencies catalog, to where I am able to vicariously live through the music and pretend that I am in these far-flung regions, I developed this illusion that this stuff is easy to come by, that there's some sort of Tower Records in other countries where all this music is just waiting for you. Once I was over to Southeast Asia, though, it wasn't like that at all.

AB: That's a *big* mistake for people to assume. There's a lot of people that say that: "Oh, you just turn on the radio and bring it back." To which I respond: "Let's see what you come up with! How much patience do you have? How long are you going to spend on that radio?" You have to put in a hundred hours on the radio for one CD. You've got to work for it.

Sure, you can do searches and hear who's cool online, but [over there] everything's written in Thai. Even if you can say it in English, to sit there and pronounce the name of an artist you think you know how to pronounce, the Thai, even if they know the context, even if they know what you're trying to say, they may just pretend not to know. Just to fuck with you. You don't know how many people go overseas looking for music and they come back and they're just amazed how we do it. They can't find shit. You got to work. We're over there working every day. I've been to Thailand thirty times.

BLVR: Returning each time, do you find things disappearing out from under you due to encroaching globalization and the homogenizing effects of monoculture?

AB: Going back year after year, you can see it's getting harder and harder to find stuff going on live or find stuff on tape. I've watched it dissipate through time. And it's going to continue to do that. There's no apparatus set up to preserve it yet. There will be at some point. People will get to developing a sense of pride in their own musical legacy—to back it up, document it, store it. That will happen.

In terms of perceptions of the culture, most people don't think about music. They're not concerned with it. They don't take their musical legacy seriously. They look at it as signposts of their life: "I remember that old song. You like that? That's funny." Are they thinking about how great that was? Do they know who played guitar, the singer's name? Do they know what year it's from? Probably not. They're not paying attention to it like someone who is obsessed, like me.

BLVR: When I read the criticism about Sublime Frequencies, it almost invariably comes down to the same thing, that you're just taking this music from other cultures and not paying royalties on it.

AB: It's not true. We do pay some royalties. We have contracts with some artists, the ones that we can find or the ones that we can film or that we're in direct contact with. But in terms of archival recordings, it's a lot trickier. It's just not easy to find the original owner of the material, and so we sometimes just go and pay the artist if we can find them, knowing that they don't have the rights, but we feel better about it. Or we don't pay anyone because we can't find anyone to pay. We throw it out there.

II. THANKS TO KARAOKE

BLVR: Coming from that Western viewpoint, where you know about Hendrix and the Rolling Stones, you can hear that even overseas they heard these people as well, from the visiting American G.I.s and stuff during the Vietnam War. It's an odd reflection back on us about our own culture. I think of this one *molam* song [Thai folk music] that uses the "Jumpin' Jack Flash" riff that just sounds off. Not to deem it as being "lost in translation," but how they reappropriate our pop music is striking. On the *Bollywood Steel Guitar* and *Shadow Music of Thailand,* you hear how in India they came under the sway of Merle Travis and Chet Atkins's guitar-picking records, or in the case of the latter, an inconsequential surf band like the Shadows.

AB: When I first heard that Stones' riff [on "Lam Plern Chawiwan" from *Molam: Thai Country Groove from Isan, Vol. 2*], it was killing me. And then it goes into the traditional *molam* vibe and it always comes back to that break and there's a screeching violin in there. Not only the influence of Vietnam and the G.I.s and the American military bases being there, but also through their own culture. There would be children in school in the States coming back with this music. All those American kids interested in foreign rock are not any different than today's young Thai kids interested in modern R&B and hip-hop and pop music like Green Day and blink-182.

BLVR: It seemed that everywhere I went, be it Thailand, Laos, or Cambodia, karaoke lorded over all. It was on the bus, in the clubs. There are no audio CDs, every single one is a VCD that you use to sing karaoke. The audio portion is just an afterthought. It's cheesy and a bit frightening, but at the same time, pop music was something that people could actually interact with now.

AB: I've had to adjust to karaoke as a modern reality that obscures our hunt for what we're truly after. Karaoke and the workstation keyboard setup eliminates the need for a live band and any further evolution of the ensemble in the club circuit. Almost all the bars in Southeast Asia are lady bars. The listener and participants who interact and frequent the clubs are exclusively male who become actively involved with the ladies, not the music. Coming to them to listen only to the music is not what people do—so we [Sublime Frequencies] are either laughed at for doing so or confusing to the locals by being interested in the music.

But in people's homes, at parties, and at certain other public functions, restaurants, outdoor shows, etc.—that's where the society actively becomes engaged with the music by singing or being encouraged to sing. Everyone's a singer now, thanks to karaoke, for better and for much worse. But the live band is now becoming ancient history in Thailand, Cambodia, and Burma.

BLVR: In compiling stuff like the *Thai Pop Spectacular, Molam: Thai Country Groove,* and *Cambodian Cassette Archives,* I've always wondered if their equivalent here is more like a K-Tel comp, meaning ubiquitous pop radio hits or something more obscure, like *Nuggets.*

AB: We probably listened to over a thousand *molam* songs that we deemed "good tracks," meaning another thousand that were shitty. Of the thousand deemed good, the ones that are on that disc are from a hundred songs as our final cut. They are all highly unique and interesting rhythmically, vocally, or arrangement-wise, and they don't take the usual approach to what the majority of period tracks do. A lot sound regular and normal. We're choosing the most unusual and interesting ones that have the most appealing and unique way of going about the genre of all the pool we had to choose from.

The Thai pop stuff is a different animal. We're covering *luk thung* and *luk krung* stuff. It's a loose term that can mean almost anything: rock and roll, traditional beat pop, slow ballad, or something kind of folky. You familiar with the Butthole Surfers' tune "Kuntz"? That's a *luk thung.* A Thai would make the argument that every song on our comp is a *luk thung.* There hasn't been a true breakdown or effort to break Thai music into genres. They're not into dicing and slicing everything up.

BLVR: Not that you can catch the lyrics yourself, but *molam* are generally raunchy songs, are they not? The one concert performance I caught on TV in Roi Et featured lots of hip-thrusting and bared belly buttons, which was weird for such a modest people as the Thai.

AB: They can be. Especially today, the new style is completely raunchy. It was more suggestive back then. Modern *lam sing,* the fast *molam* style, covers a wide variety of topics. It's storytelling and social commentary, running the gamut from lost love and falling in love to very bitter attacks against a neighbor for sleeping with their wife, or crying in your beer and shooting up the place. A lot of the *molam* and *luk thung* stars of the past had really crazy high-profile lives and would get shot and killed on stage. There's some really interesting stuff in the history of *luk thung* and *molam* artists, even the Khmer Surin stuff. Darkie, the king of Khmer Surin music in the 1990s, was supposedly gunned down in Bangkok, or else died of a drug overdose—no one seems to have the same story.

BLVR: You mentioned in the liner notes to *Radio Phnom Penh* about how the Cambodians go back to their old music and re-record instruments and "remix" it, obliterating the old versions from the public record, and ultimately from the public consciousness.

AB: It's not unusual for them to want to spruce up the old recordings to attract the younger culture to maintain and preserve their musical legacy. There is a conscious effort by a select few, operating out of the States in Long Beach and Oakland, that are into preserving their old music. What's curious to me is why they want to take the originals off the shelf and think no one will know the difference. They're spruced up with new drum tracks, with modern MIDI keyboard that sounds horrible, like a fine shit mist hovering atop the music—and you can still hear the original vocals happening in the background. That's taken over the market. If you want to buy oldies, that's what you're going to find. In our culture, that would not be acceptable: You can get the new remixed *Rubber Soul*, but you can't find the original?

BLVR: Do you think their view of the past and their not holding on to it is a facet of Buddhism?

AB: It probably has something to do with it. It's a different mental approach to their lifestyle. There's a thing about "new is everything." Old is unwanted. You don't find Thais going to the thrift store. They want new clothes. They want the newest cell phone. There's a status system even crazier than here. America went through that years ago. It's all about out with the old, especially with music: "Let's hear something new."

NOTE

This interview was originally published in the July/August 2008 issue of the *Believer* magazine. Minor edits and corrections have been made to the text.

ANDREW R. TONRY

Interview with Hisham Mayet

Co-Founder of Sublime Frequencies

ANDREW TONRY: Group Doueh just arrived in the States from the Western Sahara and you flew out to meet them. Are you often the guy shepherding bands on tours for the label?

HISHAM MAYET: Every tour that they've been on I've managed the tour and kind of been the utility guy—translator, tour manager, recorder, logistics, you name it, even prepping the visas from the get go. It's pretty extensive.

AT: I want to get a little background on the label before we talk about Doueh. How did you come to be a part of this thing?

HM: The label was started officially in 2003 by myself, Alan and Rick Bishop. It was a loose collection of friends who gathered on weekends to show our films and generally have a good time. We all traveled a lot, sort of collecting recordings and shooting video and documenting this stuff for ourselves. One thing led to another, we had some really successful film screenings in Seattle back in 2002 and 2003. The response was kind of overwhelming and so we just decided to give it a go. Me and Alan and Rick officially started it. And about a year later Rick pursued his solo art career. So ever since then it's been a two-man company. We have a solid crew of contributors that include Rob Millis, Mark Gergis, Laurent Jeanneau, and many others that have made contributions over the years . . .

AT: So you started coming across bands that interested you on personal travels?

HM: Essentially. The early stuff was just me out doing field recordings. Just kind of weird video and running into stuff that seemed to find me more than anything else.

AT: Well, what spurred the idea of even doing field recordings?

HM: Ever since I was a kid I've been interested in ethnic music. I've been collecting that stuff for a long time. I was born overseas in North Africa and did quite a bit of traveling when I was a kid. I was always really fascinated by foreign and exotic cultures, their music and art and the landscape that they are from.

AT: Where were you born?

HM: I was born in Tripoli, Libya, and lived there until I was about seven years old. Then the family moved to the UK and I lived in London, England, for about four years in the late 1970s and moved to the States in about 1980. I've been living here ever since.

AT: Okay, so back to the field recordings . . . What inspired you to start doing them?

HM: When I was a kid I would make whole entire atlases with tracing paper on maps. I was just a nut for geography and ethnography and anthropology. I studied all that stuff in school. It was informal—I have an art history degree and a history degree. But I just love anthropology and history, music, film. So it just organically happened that I would travel and record this stuff and look for music at the same time.

AT: When you go out looking for music and bands do you start by doing research or simply see what you see?

HM: It's a little bit of both. It's gotten much more refined, now that it's a full-time job.

AT: Can you take me through what one of those trips might be like?

HM: I just took a trip over the winter. I've been going to a lot of the same locations because I've developed a lot of relationships with these musicians. So I'm checking back in with them, making new recordings.

This time I visited Doueh again. We cut a couple albums. Then I flew to Niger to check in on Group Inerane. I've been doing a lot of work in Niger beyond the guitar bands. I've been extensively documenting trance possession ceremonies of the animist minorities there for the last eight or nine years. I've been stockpiling all that kind of footage.

A lot of it is just me dealing with ongoing projects, finishing up projects that have been started. And this trip I decided to go to Benin because there is an annual voodoo festival happening early in January and I'd never been. I've got a really great contact in Niger who's got a car and we were able to drive from Niger through Burkina Faso, down to Benin. We didn't know what we would find. We knew there was a festival, and it was celebrated all over the country, so we presumed we'd find something . . . and boy did we!

And so we just drove. We just went there. We showed up to these villages and sort of asked around, told 'em what we were up to, that we were into experiencing some of the celebrations and ceremonies and that we'd like to film or record some of it. One thing leads to another and suddenly you're in the middle of this crazy ceremony filming, documenting, and trying to get as much footage as we can.

AT: How do these villages and musicians greet you when you show up wanting to film and record? And also when you want to go into business together—are they happy? Weary?

HM: It's a combination of a lot of stuff. Early on I was kind of maverick with the approach, I would show up with cameras rolling, recording street scenes, street noises, street musicians. It was really informal. Now we've become more patient and organized about it. Now I show up, find out where the musicians are, we have a talk over a few days, we tell 'em what I do and what I'm up to. Sometimes bands find out that I'm in town—because I try to get the word out that I'm there to record music and I pay good money. It's a combination of musicians coming to me because they know they're going to get paid really well and/or musicians I've heard of and we're chasing them down. I record so much material and really only the tip of the iceberg is released and marketed. All of it's not phenomenal, although a lot of it is.

AT: It sounds like this started more as a video project. Is there a big repository for all this stuff? Is it something you're currently working on?

HM: We've done seven films for the label. We've got 11 DVDs out there. The film angle is definitely a big part of the label. We've done releases on DVD. A lot of the footage gets released sometime, though a lot doesn't.

For me, we started on that angle, in the sense that I was filming stuff. But I also recorded a lot of audio. It's a combination of both. With a video camera you're able to capture audio and video.

AT: Has the Arab Spring affected any of your bands or your travels or business in general? Relationships? Motivations?

HM: Yeah. I don't want to get too much into the political angle of it—that's a whole other book that needs to be written.

But we have friends in all of these countries. Libya is going through an intense revolution. I was born there and have a lot of close relatives that are in the middle of it. My dad is exiled now to Egypt now because of it.

Syria is just completely falling apart. Omar is from there. Although he's still able to get out and travel, it's really difficult to negotiate him leaving for these tours. Egypt was insane. We've got friends there as well.

It's definitely created a more extreme environment for us to be around. We're into it and we're not. We're happy when it's an organic process, like Egypt. We're kind of unhappy when we realize that a lot of these revolutions, be it in Syria or Libya, are really being orchestrated by the West. That's a situation where we know there are malevolent forces creating chaos for their own greed and thirst for destruction.

AT: That is a totally different conversation, and another time, when you're not in a rush, I'd love to have it. Anyway, moving on. I feel like Sublime Frequencies has become a huge tastemaker. It's a widely respected imprint. Do you have any feelings about that?

HM: We're incredibly proud of the label. We're incredibly proud of what we've done. We work hard, man. It's intense. It's become our lives. It hopefully shows in the way we present things and the quality of the material. The whole collective is entirely obsessed and driven and hopefully these recordings manifest all of that passion.

I don't think about that stuff. I just keep working. I don't pay attention to how it's being received. We've been doing it long enough now—it's coming up on ten years—and it's really been an organic process where it wasn't an overnight thing. There's been a slow build and we've been able to manage it that way. And we've been able to keep it small, too, keep it manageable. We don't want it to get so big that we can't do what we want to do because of the machinery of it.

AT: Western taste for world music and African music in particular has definitely grown in the last couple years. Can you attribute that to anything? Is it a matter of finally just being able to access it? Or has something changed in people's taste?

HM: I think it's probably a combination of a lot of different factors. The Internet certainly has exposed people to an insane amount of material. There's not a single country or genre that isn't being thrown up on YouTube for consumption.

As a matter of fact, in the last few years a label like Sublime Frequencies has really shed light on styles that were never really marketed to the West. We were able to kind of expose that and show audiences that there's a really intense, homegrown music that was being made that wasn't pandering to Western taste. And I think once people found out about that a lot of people started digging much further. It's just snowballed. Now you've got all kinds of labels following suit, whoever they may be, I don't want to mention names. But they're out there.

AT: On the converse, do you see bands in these countries being more influenced by Western styles? Is it opening both ways?

HM: The Internet is definitely the portal that goes both ways. A lot of rural parts of the world are connected now. You go to these Internet cafés when you're out traveling and there's kids huddled around all kinds of videos. So it's definitely bringing to light a cross-cultural exchange that's unparalleled and unprecedented.

Back in the early days it was radio—radio did the same thing. There was a lot of Western music that was being heard over the airwaves all over, be it Southeast Asia, North Africa or even central Africa.

In the 1950s, rumba was huge in central Africa. And rumba came to Cuba via the African diaspora. Then it created its own beats and came back to Africa and totally revolutionized the music again. There's all this cross-pollination and crossbreeding and that's been happening (forever). Caravans carried musical styles from one geographic area to the other. There's this idea of cross-cultural pollination that has been happening organically for hundreds and hundreds of years. And now the Internet is just the latest technology to be facilitating that exchange.

AT: With Group Doueh, how did you come across them? Can you take me through the trip?

HM: Alan Bishop and I were traveling in Morocco and Algeria in 2005, just kind of on another one of these expeditions, gathering as much data and recordings as we could.

AT: How often do you make these trips?

HM: I go at least once a year. I'll try to go for a couple months each year and I've been able to do that for the last seven or eight years.

AT: Okay, now back to Doueh.

HM: We were in Morocco and I was recording radio and just kind of hanging out, writing. Chillin' out in our room. Alan was surfing the radio and we heard this amazing song come on. It was just unbelievable. We'd never heard anything that unhinged and raw and blasted.

On the radio, the broadcast was lacking information. We just caught the tail end of it. We were just utterly blown away and we recorded it. Then we hit the streets for the next two weeks asking anybody who would help us who this might be and if they had any more information. Nobody really knew. They just kept saying it was music from the south. Hassaniya music, Saharawi music.

We heard some of that stuff before, Mauritanian stuff and whatnot. But nothing that unhinged. We had no luck and never did find out anything because we weren't there for that much longer. It was just three weeks. And then we went to Algeria and sort of got caught up dealing with that scene and the logistics of being in Algeria, which is another whole interview's worth of material.

Then we came home and we just kind of became obsessed. I went crazy and decided to go back and try to find this group. I started at the very north of the country in Morocco, and just went to every city, every village along the coast, playing that recording off the radio.

AT: Have they played in the States before?

HM: This is their first U.S. tour. They toured Europe in 2009 with Omar Souleyman. And we finished an extensive tour of Europe. It was a great tour.

AT: Is that their first time really touring outside of Africa?

HM: In the early to mid-1990s they did a few one-off festival gigs in Portugal and France . . . But 2009 was the most extensive touring they've done.

AT: What's it like playing tour guide to a band that's never been to the States before?

HM: It's kind of intense. I think they got indoctrinated to Western culture in an intense way when we did the European tour in 2009. There's cultural hurdles. They come from the desert. A small desert town in the middle of nowhere. It's not like they've never seen TVs. They've got radios and the Internet. It's not like they're living in a cave or anything. But when you're in London or the UK and there's a couple hundred people getting totally wasted in front of them then it can be intimidating. It's always fascinating when you're in Europe and the United States and you get to see things through their eyes you have a different perspective of what the West is. I'm not judging it. I'm just saying for a cultural shock value it's gotta be totally intense for them—the way people dress, the booze, the wealth, just the general modern Western culture. It's kind of a mind-fuck if you've been living in the desert all your life.

NOTE

This interview was originally published in full on June 30, 2011 on the website of alt-weekly, *Portland Mercury* (www.portlandmercury.com/endhits/archives/2011/06/30/interview-sublime-frequencies-co-founder-hisham-mayet). Minor edits and corrections have been made to the text.

ANDRÉ REDWOOD

Collage, Creativity, and Copyright
Sublime Frequencies and the Ethics
of Intellectual Property

Sublime Frequencies' co-founder Alan Bishop, responding to a question about the absence of credit and compensation for the original performers on the album *Folk and Pop Sounds of Sumatra Vol. I*, once said: "When it starts selling like fucking Outkast I'll fly to Medan and start handing out Benjamins to anyone who looks like these guys."[1] To anyone with an opinion about Sublime Frequencies' practices, this now decade-old quotation continues to provoke. For those inclined to be critical, Bishop's rhetoric reads as a hypocritical and disrespectful statement about the individuals and cultures that Sublime Frequencies professes to admire, even as the label enjoys the benefits of appropriation with impunity. This is arguably of a piece with the oft-expressed view of Sublime Frequencies as peddlers of "mere orientalist exotica" rather than contextually sensitive ethnographer-artists.[2] Certainly, there is little doubt that Sublime Frequencies' practices have left them vulnerable to the charge that "from critical and anthropological perspectives . . . what [they] do is regressive, even repugnant."[3] Sympathizers, by contrast, may see in Bishop's retort a willingness to shake up the proprieties of a world obsessed with political correctness and point out that the label provides an exposure many of these performers would not otherwise have. Bishop himself has addressed the issue of compensation, noting, "We do pay some royalties. We have contracts with some artists, the ones that we can find or the ones that we can film or that we're in direct contact with. But in terms of archival recordings. . . . we sometimes just go and pay the artist if we can find them, knowing that they don't have the rights, but we feel better about it."[4]

Controversies persist over Sublime Frequencies' crediting
and compensation of original artists, such as those on *Folk and Pop
Sounds of Sumatra Vol. 1* (SF001).

Leaving aside the polemical character of Bishop's Outkast comment, what do we make of his underlying point? The financial stakes of the Sublime Frequencies project are perhaps low, at least compared to the money made by the famed hip-hop duo or other high-profile mainstream acts. As mentioned in Douglas Wolk's *New York Times* piece about the label, Sublime Frequencies' Robert Millis acknowledged, "we've all struggled with" the challenges of finding the musicians, but also asserted, "it's not like I've made any money off of this or anything. Believe me, if I could find these people and record them again or give them money, I would."[5] Moreover, the nature of Sublime Frequencies' work—particularly in the earlier, collagist *Radio* releases for which the label became famous—has raised logistical barriers to compensating artists, even if this were a priority. For the *Radio* releases, whose source sounds are varied and potentially difficult to track, an earnest effort to surmount problems of documentation would require considerable time and resources that, fans might argue, Sublime Frequencies could better spend searching out music.

Yet the label arguably does its work from a secure vantage point, for it seems unlikely that many of the musicians featured on its releases would be in a position to negotiate for compensation. Marcus Boon, for example, writes, "if those recorded on Sublime Frequencies disks had access to Western legal representation, it's doubtful that they would wait around for Bishop to show up with a pile of cash in order to establish their ownership of their musical performances." A few lines earlier, he makes the passing observation that, "interestingly, none of the Sublime Frequencies discs is copyrighted."[6] His implication seems to be that the Sublime Frequencies team shows little interest in taking a strongly proprietary stance toward their releases. Indeed, a visual inspection of the label's CDs and CD jackets confirms this supposition: They bear none of the familiar tokens of intellectual property ownership—no copyright notices, no trademark symbols, no evidence of any kind of registration.

But just how clear-cut are the intellectual property issues that a label such as Sublime Frequencies presents? And more importantly, what would we, as consumers of cultural products, want our intellectual property regime to be? To help frame these questions for readers, this chapter looks to the history and practice of U.S. intellectual property, and to copyright law in particular.[7] It is not the goal of this chapter to stake out a position on Sublime Frequencies' appropriation practices; those have long been the subject of robust and energetic debate. Rather, I want to ask basic questions of our copyright regime: Why it operates as it does, and whether it represents a satisfactory solution to the challenges of music production in a globalized and digital age. Of particular interest are Sublime Frequencies' *Radio* releases, in part because of what they have in common with (but also critically differ from) digital sampling—namely, the copying of music off a pre-existing sound recording—the practice of which has been extensively litigated, critiqued, and otherwise commented upon. Inasmuch as the *Radio* collections create something new from existing materials, would we prefer a system that permits this kind of work whole cloth or, instead, one that confers legal legitimacy only in exceptional cases? More broadly, we may cautiously use the Sublime Frequencies team as a test case for our own preferences: Would we like a system in which work such as theirs is encouraged, discouraged, or neither? How would we like the law to balance the interests of the label, the musicians it records, and the audiences who enjoy its music? Does the mediation of radio broadcast, as opposed to direct copying from a recording, change our view of what Sublime Frequencies does or what we believe it ought to do?

This chapter gives an overview of the principal mechanisms by which copyright operates in the United States, with reference to relevant case law, and offers an historical account of how the system evolved from its initial codification in U.S. law. Since Sublime Frequencies is an American label, the primary focus is on copyright law as it has evolved historically and currently exists in the United States; however, the discussion necessarily refers to international dimensions of intellectual property. I draw particular attention to areas in which typical perceptions of the law differ from the specific details of the mechanisms that are in place. Most important among these is the notion that, under the present system, the absence of a visible copyright notice is not equivalent to the absence of a copyright. I suggest that confusion about this distinction—perhaps an unintended consequence of historical changes in the law's formulation—allows for ambiguity in how Sublime Frequencies communicates its own implied stance toward intellectual property, an ambiguity that is itself an element of the label's presentation of its values to its audience.

———

Over the past few decades, as digital technology and the associated ease of near-perfect reproduction have become commonplace, copyright law has seemed increasingly outmoded and come into focus as a site of public and academic debate. In principle and in practice, copyright provides owners (who may or may not be the author or authors of a work) with a potent and wide-ranging means of exerting control over content. As stated in the U.S. Copyright Act of 1976, which provides the current legal framework, owners are granted "the exclusive rights to do and to authorize" the reproduction, distribution, performance, display, and digital audio transmission (in the case of sound recordings) of a protected work.[8] Importantly, the law also grants an exclusive right over the preparation of derivative works (those "based upon one or more preexisting works . . . in any . . . form in which a work may be recast, transformed, or adapted").[9] Copyrights are designed explicitly to outlive authors. As of the implementation of the Copyright Term Extension Act (CTEA) of 1998, copyright terms generally extend seventy years beyond an author's life.[10] The law provides harsh penalties for infringers; a single instance of willful infringement can result in damages of up to $150,000.[11] If an infringing work contains multiple infringements (as might occur in a hip-hop track based on sampling), that initial figure can easily rise into the millions.[12] In the case of sound recordings, moreover, at least two separate copyrights are involved: that protecting the "composition" and that protecting the recording. The burden typically falls on the would-be user of copyrighted material to acquire permission from the copyright owner. When a work is under copyright but no copyright owner can be found, it is considered an "orphan work," a status that creates a risk for would-be users, especially since copyrights are so long-lasting: One's failure to locate a copyright owner does not prevent an owner from appearing and claiming infringement.[13]

Despite the all-encompassing definition of copyright in the federal statute, the law sets certain limitations, most of which are designed to accommodate specific uses of protected material. For example, works may be reproduced (within tight limits) by a library or archive, and musical works are subject to compulsory licensing (by which a user of copyrighted music can pay a royalty to use the work).[14] But perhaps the best-known limitation on the exclusivity of a copyright—and one that is arguably especially relevant to the collagistic approach of the *Radio* releases—is also among the most controversial: fair use.

Courts understand fair use as a way of making the copyright system compatible with the First Amendment.[15] In theory, fair use guards against the abuse and monopolization of copyright—its potential use as a tool of censorship. According to the statute, "the fair use of a copyrighted work . . . for purposes such as criticism, comment, news reporting, teaching . . . scholarship, or research, is not an infringement of copyright."[16] The law does not specifically define when a use is fair and when it is not. Instead, it offers four factors that courts may consider:

> the purpose and character of the use, including whether such use is of a
>   commercial nature or is for nonprofit educational purposes;
> the nature of the copyrighted work;
> the amount and substantiality of the portion used in relation to the work
>   as a whole; and
> the effect of the use upon the potential market for or value of the
>   copyrighted work.[17]

This four-factor "test" does not provide definitive criteria for determining whether a use is fair, nor are decisions about fair use limited to a consideration of these factors—the text simply states that determinations "shall include" them.[18] In practice, it is not difficult to see why the notion of fair use as a free-speech safeguard lends itself to criticism: the language is open-ended, the criteria are nonspecific, and the clause operates on a case-by-case basis. What constitutes fair use is decided—through litigation—by a court, not by the copyright user or copyright owner. But given how expensive and time-consuming lawsuits are, the threat of being sued for infringement is an obstacle to fair use of copyrighted material. Fair use also has been criticized for the zero-sum outcomes to which it leads: either a use is found to be fair and the author is entitled to no compensation (regardless of whether that use creates additional financial value), or a use is found to infringe and is enjoined, thus restricting the user's "speech."[19]

Fair use, then, is by no means immune from overreach by copyright owners. Nevertheless, many artists have succeeded in defending their uses as fair. Two famous examples are especially relevant to discussion of Sublime Frequencies. First, in *Blanch v. Koons*, fashion photographer Andrea Blanch sued collage artist Jeff Koons for using a portion of one of her photographs in one of his pieces. Although Koons had been on the losing end of previous copyright-infringement suits, here he succeeded in persuading the courts (at trial and on appeal) that his appropriation was sufficiently transformative to count as a fair use.[20] Also relevant is the most well-known fair-use case involving music: hip-hop group 2 Live Crew's blatant, extensive copying of Roy Orbison's "Oh, Pretty Woman," which the Supreme Court implied could be a legitimate fair use in the context of 2 Live Crew's parody of the original.[21]

An open question concerns the extent to which fair-use arguments can be applied to cases involving the copyright in the sound recording itself (as distinct from the copyright in the work). In 2005, the U.S. Court of Appeals for the Sixth Circuit created a controversial rule that prohibited even the most minuscule instance of unlicensed sampling.[22] In that case, *Bridgeport Music, Inc. v. Dimension Films*, the court rejected a *de minimis* defense to the unlicensed use of a sound recording, thereby taking a hard line against any unlicensed digital sampling.[23] Fair use was never raised as a defense in that case, however, so it is not clear how such an argument would have affected the court's bright-line rule. Nor does *Bridgeport* represent the final word on *de minimis* defense: In 2013, a district court in California (in a different federal circuit and thus not bound by the *Bridgeport* decision) rejected the application of *Bridgeport*'s bright-line rule to the appropriation alleged in that case.[24]

Little, if anything, about the present-day copyright system is inevitable. Indeed, the scheme that has been in place since the late 1970s represents a departure from its predecessors. U.S. copyright law began as a brief, narrow grant of a small number of exclusive rights. Its fundamental rationale, as articulated in the Constitution, was "[t]o promote the Progress of Science and useful Arts, by securing for limited Times to Authors and Inventors the exclusive Right to their respective Writings and Discoveries."[25] The first American copyright law, established in 1790, contemplated copyrights for printed material only: maps, navigational charts, and books. For a work to be registered and protected, the author was required to deposit a copy with the local district court. A notice of that registration was to be printed in any U.S. newspaper for a length of four weeks, with an additional copy deposited with the secretary of state within six months after the work's publication.[26] The original term of protection extended fourteen years from the date of publication—a term that could be renewed should the author take the necessary steps to do so. After fourteen (or twenty-eight, if renewed) years from publication, the work would fall into the public domain, for all to use as they wished. Copyright granted the owner the right to "print, reprint, publish or vend," maps, charts or books.[27] The owner was not granted control over adaptations, translations, quotations, or performance. The nineteenth century saw copyright expand: The baseline term became twenty-eight years, renewable for another twenty-eight; and new kinds of works could be copyrighted, including musical compositions.[28] Still, copyright protection largely continued to be the exception rather than the rule, and owners did not always take full advantage.[29]

Copyright law was significantly transformed in the twentieth century due to the invention and proliferation of new media technologies that the laws were ill-suited to regulate. With each new technology, from piano rolls to the Internet, new conflicts arose between copyright owners—who wished to gain the greatest possible financial benefit from their works—and newcomers, who stood to benefit from new technologies using pre-existing (and often copyrighted) material. Technological change far outpaced legislative change, which is slow by design. As legal scholar Jessica Litman has detailed, the solution to this problem was to let the laws evolve through negotiations between affected industries, that is, interest groups. These groups would reach compromises, draft laws, then present bills to Congress—lobbying, in other words.[30] Historically, as with so much legislation, groups not involved in these backdoor negotiations were in no position to receive any benefit at all. As Litman points out, ordinary people—the intended beneficiaries of copyright law—had little if any say in these negotiations.[31]

The Copyright Act of 1976 went well beyond extending the scope and duration of copyright; it made significant changes to the law's fundamental operation. Under the preceding scheme, set forth by the Copyright Act of 1909, a work had to be published, and required a copyright notice, in order to receive federal copyright protection.[32]

The 1976 law changed this considerably: Copyright protection went into effect the moment a work was "fixed in a tangible medium of expression"—that is, from the moment it came into existence as a legally cognizable work.[33] In essence, a work now became copyrighted at the moment of its fixation.[34] Copyright protection no longer required additional steps beyond the creation of the work. Moreover, although the requirement for a copyright notice initially was retained in the 1976 law, it was later eliminated by the Berne Convention Implementation Act of 1988.[35]

Yes, one must still register a work to be able to sue for infringement—some states allow lawsuits to proceed against copyrights in the application stage—and the presence of a copyright notice prevents a defendant from claiming that his or her use of a copyrighted work was innocent. But the presence or absence of a copyright notice does not fundamentally alter the copyright itself.[36] In short, the law has shifted from requiring that the copyright in a new work be claimed to one in which the existence of a copyright is essentially assumed.

Matters become still more complicated when the international dimension of copyright is considered. One key difference among legal systems is the status of so-called moral rights (*droit moral*): a mostly irrelevant category in common law countries such as the United States but one important to the civil law systems of France and its former colonies, for instance. Moral rights describe a set of personal and reputational rights that belong solely to the author and that exist independently of the economic rights connected to copyright ownership.[37] In general, moral rights include the right of attribution of a work to its author (and conversely, protection against false attribution); the right to the integrity of a work (that is, the right not to have one's work altered in a manner that is derogatory or distortive); and in some countries, the rights of publication and withdrawal of a work.[38] Although the laws of some countries allow moral rights to be waived, these rights cannot be assigned to another party.

The notion of moral rights is perhaps an intuitively appealing one, in that it recognizes the interest of the creator of a work as something deserving of protection, independent of who owns the mechanical rights of reproduction and economic use. Moral rights frameworks vary considerably by country, however, and are practically nonexistent in the U.S. Copyright Act.[39] Indeed, the United States was long reluctant to include moral rights in its copyright scheme, and it is partly for this reason that it did not adopt the Berne Convention (of 1886) until 102 years after its original signing. The Berne Convention requires nations to recognize and enforce the copyrights of citizens from other signatory countries, but the only moral-rights protection offered by the U.S. copyright law applies to visual artworks. A foreign musician would have no recourse under the Copyright Act to seek protection of his or her moral rights within the United States. If, for example, a foreign musician believed that Sublime Frequencies had infringed his or her moral rights and wished to bring a lawsuit in the United States, the only possible avenues would be to make a case under other federal laws or state law (such as defamation, privacy and publicity, and trademark and unfair competition).[40]

———

It is not difficult to see why the Sublime Frequencies project invites a discussion of these issues. Consider again, for example, Boon's suggestion that "none of the Sublime Frequencies discs is copyrighted."[41] As discussed above, the revised language of the 1976 statute means that a copyright "subsists" in a work from the moment it becomes "fixed in a tangible medium of expression" and that the mere absence of a copyright notice cannot be taken to indicate the absence of an existing copyright. So what meaning can actually be derived from the omission of copyright notices on many Sublime Frequencies CDs and LPs? Does the label, perhaps in keeping with its countercultural ethos, wish to dissociate itself from the proprietary implications of staking claim to a copyright? It is no stretch to speculate that the Bishops and company would find the copyright regime un-congenial—all the more so as the rise of digital media has turned up stories of copyright owners and their advocates against file-sharing teenagers and hip-hop artists. To the extent that Sublime Frequencies has retained its loyalties to values of anti-authoritarianism, anti-establishment, and a DIY approach to making and distributing music—all components of the team's artistic persona—it is unsur-prising that it would disavow any copyright claim that the law might grant. Yet it could also be argued that Sublime Frequencies enjoys the best of both worlds: Omitting copyright notices allows a nonproprietary disposition to be inferred by commentators without in fact having to sacrifice copyright ownership.

It is not difficult to suppose that Sublime Frequencies would willingly partake in a give-and-take ethic with respect to its music and the music of others. But it is perhaps appropriate to wonder what the label would do if, to borrow Siva Vaidhyanathan's phrasing, they went from being a "copyright poor" operation to a "copyright rich" one.[42] As we have seen, however, the ambiguity surrounding our perceptions of Sublime Frequencies' copyrights is at least partially a consequence of the law itself. Given that the label's "mission statement" (as found on its website) projects the image of a group operating outside the mainstream, profit-driven avenues of cultural production and exchange, it may be a relatively simple matter for Sublime Frequencies to clarify its position on copyright, if it felt any need to do so.[43]

Matters are somewhat more complicated when we look to other examples of its output. A brief examination of Sublime Frequencies' DVD releases, for example, shows that it does place copyright notices on some of its material, but not in a manner that is altogether consistent. Some of the DVDs look fully proprietary. The DVDs *Sumatran Folk Cinema* and *Musical Brotherhoods from the Trans-Saharan Highway* include prominent copyright notices on the liner notes and again at the end of the credits. Others, such as *Nat Pwe: Burma's Carnival of Spirit Soul*, *Niger: Magic and Ecstasy in the Sahel*, *Phi Ta Khon: Ghosts of Isan*, and *Isan: Folk and Pop Music of Northeast Thailand* do not include notices anywhere on the external packaging, but do include them at the end credits. Those notices usually name Sublime Frequencies as the copyright holder, but this is not universally the case: The notice on *Phi Ta Khon: Ghosts of Isan* names cameraman Robert Millis as the copyright owner.

In other cases, such as those involving the wholesale reproduction of a single artist or group, the label has indicated explicitly that it obtained permission. Take, for instance, the liner notes to *Group Doueh: Guitar Music from the Western Sahara*, in which Hisham Mayet trumpets the fact that "[f]or the first time ever, [Doueh] has given his permission and material from his archives to facilitate the release of his recordings!" Elsewhere is an explicit indication that "all photos [are] courtesy of Doueh's personal archive." The Group Doueh recording, of course, focuses on a single, living artist rather than a collage, so the source is obviously known (in arguable contrast to other releases of more ephemeral material), so the issue of getting permission is considerably simpler. Moreover, it might also evince a greater degree of intervention from Doueh himself. Indeed, the website advertisement for the LP states that "Doueh has turned down countless offers from Morocco and Europe to release his music but he decided to offer us access to his homemade recordings and photo archive for this amazing debut LP."[44]

Although this chapter takes the collagist principle of the *Radio* releases as its point of departure, even a cursory look at other releases (such as the Group Doueh disc and DVDs described above) seems to indicate multiple approaches to copyright by the Sublime Frequencies team. Copyright has a long and complex history, and like all areas of law, continues to evolve. As has long been the case, intellectual property tends to be the province of experts. As such, whatever the legal merits of a particular copyright dispute may be, the parties that find their way to trial almost always involve moneyed interests on at least one side—and often on both. In this respect, at least, Alan Bishop's point that Sublime Frequencies does not sell like Outkast may be more than merely rhetorical.

NOTES

1. Erik Davis, "Cameo Demons: Hanging with the Sun City Girls," February 2004, www.techgnosis.com/scg.html. Bishop backpedaled in a later interview, claiming that the statement was "obviously" not meant to be taken seriously, and that Sublime Frequencies would compensate the performers if circumstances enabled them to do so. See Andy Beta's chapter in this volume. It also must be acknowledged, of course, that not all of Sublime Frequencies' output consists of this sort of appropriation.

2. Peter Margasak, "Music Without a Map," *Chicago Reader,* May 13, 2004, www .chicagoreader.com/chicago/music-without-a-map/Content?oid=915472.

3. Mike Powell, "Sublime Frequencies," *Stylus,* June 4, 2007, www.stylusmagazine.com/ articles/hi/sublime-frequencies.htm.

4. See Beta's chapter in this volume.

5. Douglas Wolk, "Heard on the Streets (of the Axis of Evil)," *New York Times,* November 20, 2005, www.nytimes.com/2005/11/20/arts/music/20wolk.html. Wolk goes on to note that "According to Mr. Bishop, a typical Sublime Frequencies release sells about 1,000 copies: 'If sales and money were an issue, we'd not waste our time with the label.'"

6. Marcus Boon, "Sublime Frequencies' Ethnopsychedelic Montages," *Electronic Book Review,* December 12, 2006, www.electronicbookreview.com/thread/musicsoundnoise/ ethnopsyche.

7. The broad term "intellectual property" typically refers to three legal areas: copyright, trademark, and patent law. (Trade secret is sometimes counted as a fourth.) Of these, copyright deals with creative works such as songs, novels, plays, and so on.

8. U.S. Copyright Act of 1976, 17 U.S.C. §106.

9. 17 U.S.C. §101.

10. 17 U.S.C. §302(a). Term limits vary depending on the circumstances of authorship and the status of the works created prior to the enactment of the 1976 Act; see §§302–304. The extension provided by the CTEA added twenty years to the fifty-year term initially provided for by the Copyright Act of 1976. The CTEA provoked constitutional objections, which ultimately were argued before the U.S. Supreme Court. In *Eldred v. Ashcroft*, the CTEA was challenged in part on the basis that its retroactive extension of copyright terms for works already in existence created a perpetual copyright, and that this violated the constitutional language stating that such rights would be granted for "limited times."

Despite the challenge, the Court upheld the constitutionality of the extension by a 7–2 majority. *Eldred v. Ashcroft*, 537 US 186 (2003).

11. §504(c)(2).

12. In one such example, recounted by vocal copyright critic Lawrence Lessig, information technology student Jesse Jordan was threatened with a lawsuit by the Recording Industry Association of America (RIAA) because he had modified his school's search engine such that it became easier to locate files on other users' computers, including music files. The RIAA initially demanded $15,000,000 in damages (the $150,000 maximum amount specified in the copyright statute, times one hundred alleged instances of infringement), demanded that he admit to wrongdoing, and demanded that he forego many future careers working in technology. The case was settled for $12,000—Jordan's total savings. See Lawrence Lessig, *Free Culture: The Nature and Future of Creativity* (New York: Penguin Books, 2004), 48–52.

13. For an instructive illustration of the problems created by orphan works, see James Boyle, *The Public Domain: Enclosing the Commons of the Mind* (New Haven, Conn.: Yale University Press, 2008), 9–16. In cases involving orphan works, it is the burden of the would-be user of the material to seek out the copyright owner as diligently as possible in order to defend him or herself from any potential future claim of willful infringement.

14. On the library and archive exceptions, see U.S. Copyright Act of 1976, §108; on compulsory licenses for musical works, see §115. As the name suggests, compulsory licensing requires that certain uses of a copyrighted work (such as a cover performance of a song, certain digital transmissions of audio recordings, cable transmissions, and so on) be permitted in exchange for a royalty payment.

15. For clear articulations of this view, see *Suntrust Bank v. Houghton Mifflin Co.* 268 F.3d 1257 (11th Cir. 2001) at 1263–65, and *Eldred v. Ashcroft*, 537 US 186 (2003) at 29.

16. U.S. Copyright Act of 1976, §107.

17. §107.

18. §107.

19. See Alex Kozinski and Christopher Newman, "What's So Fair about Fair Use?" *Journal of the Copyright Society of the USA* 46/4 (1999): 530–31.

20. *Blanch v. Koons*, 467 F.3d 244 (2d Cir. 2006).

21. *Campbell v. Aucuff-Rose Music, Inc.*, 510 US 569 (1994).

22. *Bridgeport Music, Inc. v. Dimension Films*, 410 F.3d 792 (6th Cir. 2005). The decision was read by many commentators as a deeply problematic one, particularly with respect to the way in which the court interpreted the meaning of the relevant statute. See, for example, "Copyright Law—Sound Recording Act—Sixth Circuit Rejects De Minimis Defense to the Infringement of a Sound Recording Copyright," *Harvard Law Review* 118 (2005): 1355–62; M. Leah Somoano, "Intellectual Property: Copyright: Note: *Bridgeport Music, Inc. v. Dimension Films*: Has Unlicensed Digital Sampling of Copyrighted Sound

Recordings Come to an End?" *Berkeley Technology Law Journal* 21, no. 1 (2006): 289–309; and Joshua Crum, "The Day the (Digital) Music Died: *Bridgeport*, Sampling Infringement, and a Proposed Middle Ground," *Brigham Young University Law Review* 943, no. 3 (2008): 943–69. For a viewpoint endorsing the court's decision, see Tracy L. Reilly, "Debunking the Top Three Myths of Digital Sampling: An Endorsement of the Bridgeport Music Court's Attempt to Afford 'Sound' Copyright Protection to Sound Recordings," *Columbia Journal of Law and the Arts* 355, no. 31 (Spring 2008): 356–407.

23. *De minimis* refers to the common law principle of *de minimis non curat lex*, by which courts may dismiss extremely minor violations.

24. *VMG Salsoul LLC v. Madonna Louise Ciccone, et al.,* Case No. CV 12–05967 BRO (CWx) (C.D. California). www.scribd.com/doc/185237664/VMG-Salsoul-v-Madonna#scribd.

25. U.S. Constitution. Article I. Section 8.

26. Copyright Act of 1790 §§3–4. For a fuller account, see Neil Weinstock Netanel, *Copyright's Paradox* (Oxford: Oxford University Press, 2007), 54–55. The original text can be found at http://copyright.gov/history/1790act.pdf.

27. Copyright Act of 1790 §1.

28. Ibid., 55.

29. According to legal scholar James Boyle, 85 percent of 28-year copyrights were not renewed for a second term. Boyle, *The Public Domain*, 9.

30. Some of these exceptions, born of industry compromises, were outpaced by new technologies and thus rendered irrelevant even before they came into effect. See Jessica Litman, *Digital Copyright: Protecting Intellectual Property on the Internet* (Amherst, N.Y.: Prometheus Books, 2001), 58–59.

31. See Litman, *Digital Copyright*, 35–69. An even more detailed version of her excellent historical account can be found in Litman, "Copyright Legislation and Historical Change," *Oregon Law Review* 68 (1989): 275–361. For a perspective somewhat more favorable to copyright's expansion, see Paul Goldstein, *Copyright's Highway: From Gutenberg to the Celestial Jukebox* 2nd ed., (Stanford, Calif.: Stanford University Press, 2003).

32. According to the law, "Any person entitled" to a copyright could "secure copyright for his work by publication thereof with the notice of copyright required by this title; and such notice shall be affixed to each copy thereof published or offered for sale in the United States by authority of the copyright proprietor[.]" The Act indicated that the notice should "consist either of the word 'copyright' or the abbreviation 'Copr.,' accompanied by the name of the copyright proprietor, and if the work be a printed literary, musical, or dramatic work, the notice [should] include also the year in which copyright was secured by publication." Copyright Act of 1909, §10. Certain other cases also allowed for "the letter C inclosed [*sic*] within a circle, thus: ©, accompanied by the initials, monogram

mark, or symbol of the copyright proprietor: *Provided,* That on some on some accessible portion. . . . his name shall appear." §18.

33. U.S. Copyright Act of 1976, 17 USC. §101: "A work is 'fixed' in a tangible medium of expression when its embodiment in a copy or phonorecord, by or under the authority of the author, is sufficiently permanent or stable to permit it to be perceived, reproduced, or otherwise communicated for a period of more than transitory duration. A work consisting of sounds, images, or both, that are being transmitted, is 'fixed' for purposes of this title if a fixation of the work is being made simultaneously with its transmission."

34. "Copyright protection subsists . . . in original works of authorship fixed in any tangible medium of expression, now known or later developed, from which they can be perceived, reproduced, or otherwise communicated, either directly or with the aid of a machine or device." §102(a).

35. The earlier language specifying that "a notice of copyright . . . *shall* be placed on all publicly distributed copies from which the work can be visually perceived[,]" was changed to "*may* be placed." §401(a). Italics added.

36. See §§401(3)(d), 402(3)(d), and 411(a).

37. The United States has virtually no explicit moral rights provisions in its copyright code, with the only exception being the Visual Artists Rights Act (VARA), which, as the name suggests, applies exclusively to visual artists. (See 17 USC. §106A.) On the evolving status of moral rights in common law countries, see Cyril P. Rigamonti, "Deconstructing Moral Rights," *Harvard International Law Journal* 47, no. 2 (2006): 353–412.

38. Although the scope of moral rights differs by country, the general principles are stated in the Berne Convention, which currently has 168 member countries. See Berne Convention for the Protection of Literary and Artistic Works, Paris Text Art. 6*bis*(1). For a full discussion, see Paul Goldstein and Bernt Hugenholtz, *International Copyright: Principles, Law, and Practice,* 2nd ed. (Oxford: Oxford University Press, 2010), 345–57.

39. The only moral rights explicitly granted under U.S. law are limited to a small category of visual artworks. The Visual Artists Rights Act (VARA) was not initially part of the Copyright Act of 1976. It was added in 1990 as part of the United States' move in 1988 to sign on to the Berne Convention. See 17 USC. §106A for the full text of VARA.

40. As of this writing, Sublime Frequencies is not trademarked. I am grateful to Jason Koransky, Esq., for researching this question.

41. Boon, "Sublime Frequencies' Ethnopsychedelic Montages."

42. See Siva Vaidhyanathan, *Copyrights and Copywrongs: The Rise of Intellectual Property and How It Threatens Creativity* (New York: New York University Press, 2001), 82.

43. See Sublime Frequencies website, www.sublimefrequencies.com.

44. Sublime Frequencies, *Group Doueh: Guitar Music from the Western Sahara,* LP SF030, www.sublimefrequencies.com/item.asp?Item_id=33.

BIBLIOGRAPHY

Berne Convention for the Protection of Literary and Artistic Works, Paris Text.

Blanch v. Koons, 467 F.3d 244 (2d Cir. 2006).

Boon, Marcus. "Sublime Frequencies' Ethnopsychedelic Montages." *Electronic Book Review*. December 12, 2006. www.electronicbookreview.com/thread/musicsoundnoise/ethnopsyche.

Boyle, James. *The Public Domain: Enclosing the Commons of the Mind* (New Haven, Conn.: Yale University Press, 2008).

Bridgeport Music, Inc. v. Dimension Films, 410 F.3d 792 (6th Cir. 2005).

Campbell v. Aucuff-Rose Music, Inc., 510 U.S. 569 (1994).

"Copyright Law—Sound Recording Act—Sixth Circuit Rejects De Minimis Defense to the Infringement of a Sound Recording Copyright. *Bridgeport Music, Inc. v. Dimension Films*, 383 F.3d 390 (6th Cir. 2004)." *Harvard Law Review* 118 (2005): 1355–62.

Crum, Joshua. "The Day the (Digital) Music Died: *Bridgeport*, Sampling Infringement, and a Proposed Middle Ground." *Brigham Young University Law Review* 943, no. 3 (2008): 943–69.

Davis, Erik. "Cameo Demons: Hanging with the Sun City Girls." February 2004. www.techgnosis.com/scg.html.

Eldred v. Ashcroft, 537 U.S. 186 (2003).

Goldstein, Paul. *Copyright's Highway: From Gutenberg to the Celestial Jukebox*, 2nd ed. (Stanford, Calif.: Stanford University Press, 2003).

Goldstein, Paul, and Bernt Hugenholtz. *International Copyright: Principles, Law, and Practice*, 2nd ed. (Oxford: Oxford University Press, 2010).

Kozinski, Alex, and Christopher Newman. "What's So Fair about Fair Use?" *Journal of the Copyright Society of the USA* 46, no. 4 (1999): 530–31.

Lessig, Lawrence. *Free Culture: The Nature and Future of Creativity* (New York: Penguin Books, 2004).

Litman, Jessica. "Copyright Legislation and Historical Change." *Oregon Law Review* 68 (1989): 275–361.

——— . *Digital Copyright: Protecting Intellectual Property on the Internet* (Amherst, N.Y.: Prometheus Books, 2001).

Margasak, Peter. "Music Without a Map." *Chicago Reader.* May 13, 2004. chicagoreader.com/chicago/music-without-a-map/Content?oid=915472.

Netanel, Neil Weinstock. *Copyright's Paradox* (Oxford: Oxford University Press, 2007).

Powell, Mike. "Sublime Frequencies." *Stylus,* June 4, 2007. www.stylusmagazine.com/articles/hi/sublime-frequencies.htm.

Reilly, Tracy L. "Debunking the Top Three Myths of Digital Sampling: An Endorsement of the Bridgeport Music Court's Attempt to Afford 'Sound' Copyright Protection to

Sound Recordings." *Columbia Journal of Law and the Arts* 355, no. 31 (Spring 2008): 356–407.

Rigamonti, Cyril P. "Deconstructing Moral Rights." *Harvard International Law Journal* 47, no. 2 (2006): 353–412.

Somoano, M. Leah. "Intellectual Property: Copyright: Note: *Bridgeport Music, Inc. v. Dimension Films*: Has Unlicensed Digital Sampling of Copyrighted Sound Recordings Come to an End?" *Berkeley Technology Law Journal* 21, no. 1 (2006): 289–309.

Sublime Frequencies website. www.sublimefrequencies.com.

Suntrust Bank v. Houghton Mifflin Co. 268 F.3d 1257 (11th Cir. 2001)

U.S. Constitution. Article I. Section 8.

U.S. Copyright Act of 1790.

U.S. Copyright Act of 1909.

U.S. Copyright Act of 1976. 17 U.S.C. §101 *et seq.*

Vaidhyanathan, Siva. *Copyrights and Copywrongs: The Rise of Intellectual Property and How It Threatens Creativity* (New York: New York University Press, 2001).

VMG Salsoul LLC v. Madonna Louise Ciccone, et al., Case No. CV 12–05967 BRO (CWx) (C.D. Cal.). www.scribd.com/doc/185237664/VMG-Salsoul-v-Madonna#scribd.

Wolk, Douglas. "Heard on the Streets (of the Axis of Evil)." *New York Times.* November 20, 2005. www.nytimes.com/2005/11/20/arts/music/20wolk.html.

INTERLUDE

Sublime Frequencies

Listener Interviews

Interview with Brian Shimkovitz

DJ and Head of *Awesome Tapes from Africa*

JANUARY 21, 2015

E. TAMMY KIM: How did you come to know about Sublime Frequencies?

BRIAN SHIMKOVITZ: When I found out about them, it was like they're doing exactly what I want to be doing. I studied ethnomusicology for a bachelor's degree, and then I did fieldwork for a year and tried to imagine myself as an academic doing work in the field. And then coming to New York, I was like, "I'm more interested in reaching more people outside the insular world." I started *Awesome Tapes from Africa* in part as a reaction to all that but also to keep in mind the stuff that I learned. The first tape I posted I knew nothing about. And previously, as an ethnomusicologist, I wouldn't do that before getting primary and secondary sources. I see that with Sublime Frequencies, just from reading the interviews and meeting the gentlemen once or twice, there is a preoccupation with exploring the traditional ethnomusicological realm, but for me it's the opposite: I follow it privately, but I see myself as a public ethnomusicologist.

ETK: What were your musical interests leading up to *Awesome Tapes*?

BS: It has always been popular music in an urban setting. My research was in hip-hop and I was just interested in music in cities. I'd heard about Sublime Frequencies and was also inspired by Smithsonian Folkways. I'd done an internship there between college and buying a one-way ticket to Thailand and spending a year there, where I went to stores and bought a shit ton of music.

ETK: How would you compare labels like Sublime Frequencies and Smithsonian Folkways, and what you're doing with *Awesome Tapes*?

BS: [Smithsonian Folkways] is a staff of brilliant people who all have masters and PhDs, and they're quasi-governmental. To do a 13-CD series of Indonesian street music, you have to be. Their liner notes are extensive and always written by people I read in college who've spent their entire lives focused on this. But I know from the meetings there they don't make much money. The amount of releases Sublime Frequencies has done over these years is amazing. In terms of *Awesome Tapes'* output, I've been doing these remix-y things that are digital-only—there are eight or nine—but I've got a lot more stuff that I want to do. The blog has a couple hundred posts, maybe 250, but it's just scratching the surface. There's so much music out there, it's just blowing my mind. You could devote an entire life to this.

ETK: Who follows *Awesome Tapes*?

BS: I came back from Ghana in 2005, and people were talking to me about Myspace, M.I.A., Animal Collective. I was really inspired by this whole thing, where suddenly the normal indie rock types were checking out something different. I noticed in 2006, when I started the blog, there were people from places I didn't expect that were checking out the music. There was a change from the ponytail, tie-dye, and bookish [world music fans]. When I started, my audience was just me and my buddies, in theory—music people you'd sit around and listen with. I was thinking about what kind of music I want to show my buddies that I came back with from West Africa, and [show] strangers what "African music" sounds like in Africa. And the other part was getting it out there. The people I met in Ghana had no hope of getting this music heard outside the Ghanaian community. That's what every [musician] wants: They all want people to dance to it, to rock out. So I thought to myself, "I guess I'm just putting up free music . . . but there'd be no [other] way for anyone to hear this." [The audience] is more male than female, definitely 18 to 34 years old, and it's all over the world. I'm seeing traffic from every single place in the world.

ETK: Why do you think this new world-music audience cropped up in the mid-2000s?

BS: I think part of it has to do with the Internet; part of it is everything's been done with bass drums and two guitars. So much interesting music has been available to us on records and CDs, but we get pushed by hegemonic culture. But as the Internet began to blossom and people started to realize how easy it was to go outside the Top 40, it kind of just exploded. There were also a lot of blogs similar to mine that were doing specialized things—and a lot of them are gone now. I stayed [in New York] for seven years, running into all kinds of musicians: people making singer-songwriter, jazz, or hardcore, and everyone being like, "Oh, yeah,

Fela Kuti! *Mbira* music!" People I knew from punk shows in D.C. were emailing me about South African Kwaito CDs. Just like with Sublime Frequencies, people look at a white dude messing with African music and they're worried about the issues that pile up, which are totally relevant. But I'm mostly on this enthusiastic trip that's taken several pages from my work and research experience.

ETK: It looks like you're making actual albums now, too. Tell me about that.

BS: A few years ago Secretly Canadian contacted me. They have a distribution company and said, "If you want to ruin your life and start a record label, we'd love to help you." They gave me the backing to put out releases. I'm stalking musicians to find licensing agreements, a 50–50 split, so I can put stuff out on vinyl and CD. It's not losing money, and I'm trying to help the artists who are able to get booking agents. I spent all my time in New York working in public relations for musicians like Peter Frampton, Philip Glass, Nonesuch-y jazz, and I got a sense of how the music industry can work for some people with regard to booking agents and record deals. So I thought about if I can actually help people I talked to back in Ghana.

ETK: Do you deal with musicians directly?

BS: I'm trying to with all of them. For example, there's an artist from northern Ghana named Bola. I set up a thirteen-day tour for him but at the last minute, the embassy denied him his visa. I ran into Hisham [Mayet] right after that, and he was like, "You have to physically be there." But I didn't have the time or money—this artist lived twelve hours away from the capital. So all this bad shit happened because of that. Another was Penny Penny, a singer from South Africa who has a brilliant story and makes house music. He played at the Sydney Opera House last [spring]. That was cool, to get ten South Africans over for a single show. That's the dream-come-true scenario.

ETK: On your website, you have a statement telling people to get in touch if they want their music taken down. Has anyone ever contacted you?

BS: Recently the descendant of somebody who had a record label in West Africa came up to me and was like, "Take these down." [Until that], nobody had [contacted me] except for a single person who had one song on a Burkina Faso compilation. I'm not trying to steal people's shit. If somebody said "I'm losing money because of your downloads," I'll take it down. But I've had more of the other, many more, where labels or management have tried to grease the wheels for some sort of promotional opportunity.

ETK: How much do you learn about the albums you post?

BS: It all varies. The lyrics have never been a big focus of mine, unless it's in

Twi, which is the only thing I can kind of speak. The crucial thing about the blog structure is that people are able to comment. Often times I'm like, "I have no idea what this is. Please help." And sometimes people will come in and give full or minor translations and give guidance about biographical information. There's a lot more info on blogs, a lot more from Africans posting in a YouTube format. That's quite impressive about Sublime Frequencies—they actually get a lot of the details. [But] it's just me alone doing this stuff. I don't have the time or money to visit the folks where they are.

ETK: Is there a sociopolitical dimension to your project?

BS: I don't separate politics from music or activism from music, but my main enthusiasm has to do with music, so I just focus on that. And I do believe that when people get exposed and get more excited about culture, that makes them an advocate for an entire community. Clearly our government and the other governments of the world don't give a fuck. When I started the label side, my idea was also to start, in addition to the blog and the label, an information service—a BBC-type aggregator, a Buzzfeed of smart, positive information about Africa, from African perspectives. Some people have talked shit about what I'm doing and characterized me as clueless, but I'm someone who's spent a lot of time with this stuff.

MICHAEL E. VEAL

Interview with Robert Hardin

Artist and Musician

JANUARY 24, 2015

MICHAEL E. VEAL: How did you become familiar with Sublime Frequencies?

ROBERT HARDIN: I knew about the Sun City Girls, and I knew of the Bishop brothers. When I first heard Sublime Frequencies, one thing that struck me was the idea of treating the sounds of distant places, let's say, from a less objective viewpoint . . . The older labels, like Smithsonian Folkways, and the traditional ethnomusicological standard was to go in and start recording songs that were traditional in the areas. You always come with your viewpoint, but what those older recordings tried to do was erase that viewpoint. But in some ways, because of what they chose, and how long they chose to record, or whatever, the framing device became the viewpoint. So I thought it was refreshing to hear a label that went about recording just random sounds, the sounds of the environment, not mediated by them.

MEV: Do you think it's possible to document without mediating?

RH: No, I don't—and that's what I thought was good about Sublime Frequencies, that they were not pretending that they weren't mediating . . .

MEV: How accurate do you think it is to place Sublime Frequencies directly in the tradition of the older ethnographic labels? Or do you tend to consider them as more artistic?

RH: Have you ever heard of the Egyptian composer Halim El-Dabh?[1] In the mid-1940s, this guy took an old wire recorder, a really bulky piece of equipment. He went out into the desert, and there was a sect of female chorus musicians. And they had a sort of traditional repertoire that they would do, but they wouldn't allow men to listen to it. And so he and his friend disguised themselves as women and took this recording device out there. And halfway through it he was discovered, beaten within an inch of his life, and then somehow managed to persuade them to let him record them anyway! And what he ended up doing was taking this recording into a studio that had large echo chambers, and he created what could be called the first piece of *musique concrète*—maybe about four years before [Pierre] Schaeffer and [Pierre] Henry came out with their experiments. So it's one of those things where it turns the ideas of *musique concrète* and of "world music" on their heads a little bit. Because the history is not as "concrete" (no pun intended) as it's told by most historians of electronic music.

MEV: Do we position the Sublime Frequencies producers as creative artists, using recordings of world music as their source material? Do we position them as field music documentarians? How would you position them?

RH: When I hear the recordings, I respond to them as if they are field recordings. And the one that I listen to most of the time is probably *Radio Morocco*. That one was basically recorded off the radio, and they were listening to whatever was being broadcast. And so that, as a recording, is sort of open to chance. If you're gonna go for a walk with your recorder, you're gonna basically capture any random sound that happens in your environment. That was sort of what they did with *Radio Morocco*, and I thought it was an interesting idea, because you don't know what's gonna be playing.

MEV: It kind of problematizes the concept of a field recording because, even if the visitor is holed up in their hotel room, they've arguably still done some fieldwork, of a sort [laughs]!

RH: It's pretty much [consistent] with how today's journalism works. There are gonna be correspondents who are stationed in various areas—Morocco would be a fairly good example of this. What you do is, you stay in your hotel room and you listen to reports of what's going on, and then you transmit what you've learned back to your news source.

MEV: So this almost positions the Sublime Frequencies recordists as musical correspondents . . .

RH: I was almost thinking of it as an updating of the idea of field recordings . . . I think a lot of people think of the old field recordings as presenting the "natural environment." But how much "natural environment" is really left to us these days?

MEV: There's an assumption that the field recording is something that must be made on site. And your "correspondent" idea kind of challenges that assumption.

RH: I just think that technology, and the way that it's captured the environment, is altering the way that we go about it. Using a source like the radio is another form of media, but who's to say that radio is not the "natural environment" as experienced by one of the recordists in a hotel room out in Morocco?

MEV: What about the way that these recordings may have affected your creative process in particular?

RH: I'm more aware of using sampled sounds, for instance. I have some pieces where I've taken an old portable television that has the old dial tuning. And somewhere up in the UHF sphere, it actually captures a local cable channel. I'm in an area where that could [be] anything. There's a channel that I picked up that has Indian music—Bollywood film music, basically. And I transformed that for a piece that I did for a large-scale performance. In some sense it was intentionally sampling a sound but by manipulating it, really turning it into something that was about the *sound*, and not necessarily about the cultural reference. I mean there were a few people who could actually recognize that it was a sample, which— considering how sophisticated most of the Bollywood music is—I was flattered that anybody thought that I could actually *play* that well [laughs]!

But as far as the cultural exchange goes, it was pretty empty. I grabbed a sound from the ether, basically, and its [cultural] origin really had nothing to do with what I was trying to get across. So, it was an appropriation that didn't really have much to do with any involvement with Indian music.

MEV: It was just source material.

RH: So in some sense, it wasn't as politically correct as the approach of going out into remote places and recording. But in a sense, it was also perhaps honest in the way that we as composers and sound artists gather our material.

NOTE

1. For information on Halim El-Dabh, consult: Denise Seachrist, *The Musical World of Halim El-Dabh* (Kent: Kent State University Press, 2003).

PART TWO

Visual and
Sonic Culture

LYNDA PAUL

"Just Pure Sound and Vision"

Rawness as Aesthetic-Ideological Fulcrum
in Sublime Frequencies' Videos

When Sublime Frequencies describes its work in terms such as "pure" and "raw," it may be tempting for scholars to be dismissive; any thoughtful observer can see that the output of Sublime Frequencies is—in spite of the company's claims to have no spin or agenda—carefully edited to create particular affective responses in the receiver. On the one hand, the label's insistence on its works' purity might be seen as evidence of the team's carelessness in how they speak about what they are doing; perhaps the group does not realize the contradictions inherent to the concept or the dubious political implications of such a stance.[1] On the other hand, the label has made itself known as a provocative group; the often problematic claims made by its creative collaborators could at any time be geared toward raising hackles. Or alternatively, the company could be using excessive language simply to market its wares. On the whole, one might wonder what analytical use the company's self-produced publicity materials could have for a scholar.

Yet, there is much to be gained by taking the creators' words seriously. Indeed, when we examine their publicity prose in detail, many of the inconsistencies that seem to plague the team's polemical interviews are put into deeper context, and the aesthetic decisions that these recording artists have made relate more clearly to their self-professed ideals. By viewing Sublime Frequencies' various verbal proclamations as legitimate and valuable entryways into understanding its oeuvre, we are able much more thoroughly to unpack the aesthetics and ideologies underlying the work. A close analysis of the label's videos in light of

The DVD *Niger: Magic and Ecstasy in the Sahel* (SF022) exemplifies the sense of danger and transgression that pervades Sublime Frequencies' visual oeuvre.

the filmmakers' more problematic claims illuminates much about the relationship between experimental art and cultural representation in the late twentieth and early twenty-first centuries, and helps us better comprehend the tangled intersections of visual culture, alternative media, and popular ethnography in a globalized world fraught with uncertainties about how to represent cultural others.

This essay argues that the concept of rawness, found throughout Sublime Frequencies' publicity materials and interviews, can serve as a useful, multidimensional key to understanding the label's videos. I do not argue that the videos themselves are raw in some essential way, but rather, that an examination of the concept of rawness in Sublime Frequencies' words and videos offers us a useful way to come to grips with first, the label's formal and aesthetic decisions; second, the group's opposition to normative ethnographic and documentary video techniques; and third, the team's seeming antagonism toward critical thought and interpretation in general. Because of the particular constellation of meanings embedded within it, rawness helps explain what Sublime Frequencies is striving for, what the group is resisting, and how it is doing so. Ultimately, rawness links the aesthetic objects with the company's stated ideological goals, giving researchers a valuable paradigm with which to further interrogate the videos without dismissing their creators' positions.

I begin by defining the term "rawness" and then move to an overview of the polemics surrounding the label's output. I next discuss the videos themselves, offering a general description of the DVDs' content and style and a more detailed appraisal of their engagement with the raw aesthetic. Finally, I connect the aesthetics of rawness to the group's implicit ideological agendas.

DEFINITIONS

The Sublime Frequencies website features blurbs describing the material on every recording. The language of these blurbs frequently evokes tropes of travel or adventure literature (along the lines of Rudyard Kipling or Joseph Conrad) and calls to mind exotic safaris and spectacles (e.g., the "hot and dusty [. . .] sand swept dunes of the Western Sahara").[2] But the exceptional frequency of the word "raw" is telling. "Raw" is used to describe the "blazing street music" of Jemaa el Fnaa, to convey the quality of TV excerpts recorded in Sumatra, to characterize the "cultural heritage of the Mekong interior," and to define the "folk stylings of Moroccan music." It is thus used by Sublime Frequencies to suggest something ineffable and thrilling about a variety of phenomena, from specific musical performances and general musical styles to television excerpts and even entire cultures.

The term "rawness" has a long history in the English language, and can refer to many objects and situations. Some of its typical definitions are summarized in the following list (emphases mine):[3]

Uncooked; unprocessed, unrefined.

Undigested, unassimilated; not fully digested.

Of the taste or flavour of tea: harsh, bitter.

Of sinew: untreated. Of leather or hide: untanned; undressed

Of fabric or cloth: unfinished, *spec.* unfulled, untucked, or undyed.

Of a fibre used in the manufacture of cloth: unprocessed, *spec.* (of cotton) that has been ginned . . . but otherwise processed no further.

Ceramics. Designating a glaze made from materials which need no preparation

Of land: undeveloped, not cleared or otherwise prepared for cultivation or building.

fig. Of a quality or faculty: pure, unmitigated; sheer.

Of a person (also occas. of an animal): inexperienced; unskilled, untrained; naive.

Of a thing, quality, action, etc.: indicative or characteristic of inexperience.

Crude in form or quality; lacking finish or polish.

Uncivilized, coarse; brutal.

Of flesh, a part of the body, etc.: exposed by having the skin removed; inflamed and painful, esp. as a result of skin abrasion; excoriated, lacerated; (of a wound) bloody

Of an emotion: deeply felt, undisguised; strong, palpable.

in the raw: (*a*) in a natural or untreated state; (*b*) bare, naked; in a starkly realistic way (*colloq.*).

While the various uses of "raw" do not all signify precisely the same thing, the majority do have one underlying concept in common: a sense of *unprocessed essence*—and this concept both grounds the aesthetic principle shaping the Sublime Frequencies videos and links the videos' aesthetic qualities to the team's stated positions regarding art, culture, and mainstream commercial and educational enterprises.

CRITICISMS AND CONTEXTS

Sublime Frequencies' videos comprise a complex segment of the company's output.[4] They are "ethnographic" in the broadest sense: While they may not follow all of the conventions traditionally ascribed to ethnographic film (as laid out, for example, in classic texts on the subject such as those by Karl Heider), they do involve a filmmaker's foray into a "field" where musical performances from "real life" are documented.[5] But although the videos use images and sounds taken from so-called real life, they do not represent the cultures they record so much as transform those cultures into the raw material for elaborate experimental art. With their experimental approach to "real life" material, the videos enter into artistic traditions in which materials from everyday life are reframed as aesthetic objects (for example, "found art" à la Duchamp, or the multitude of musical practices in which sounds made by the natural environment or utilitarian objects are reframed as "music").[6] The videos also call to mind what film theorist Catherine Russell calls "experimental ethnography," a mode of cinema that "circumvents the empiricism and objectivity conventionally linked to ethnography" by "dismantling the universalist impulse of realist aesthetics into a clash of voices, cultures, bodies, and languages."[7] In other words, unlike conventional ethnographic film, which purports to offer a window into an objective or complete "reality," cinematically experimental ethnographies disorient their viewers, offering not so much a monolithic depiction of "truth" as a multivalent reality that shifts with the perspective of the camera.

Such an experimental approach resists those who would unify into a seemingly comprehensive narrative the disparate and sometimes contradictory stories within individuals, cultures, and societies. In challenging the idea that reality could ever be fully unified or truly knowable, experimental ethnographies illuminate the fragmentary condition of human subjectivity and knowledge. But in spite of the Sublime Frequencies videos' aesthetic and philosophical power, and their potential to disrupt in a positive way the dominant norms of cultural representation, the team's experimental treatment of ethnographic material has led to much criticism.

Some commentators have raised questions about the label's financial compensation of performers (or lack thereof).[8] Others have taken issue with the label's stance *vis-à-vis* intellectual property regulations.[9] Yet others have found fault with the label for its cultural "othering."[10] Such issues—compensation, attribution, and exoticization—comprise the main concerns in a critical discourse that has grown to surround Sublime Frequencies. The different strands of this discourse are connected by a sense on the part of the critics that the label has exhibited a kind of careless disregard for its subjects—this, in spite of the company's oft-stated admiration and respect for both the music and the people of the cultures it has recorded.

Ultimately, most of the criticism directed at Sublime Frequencies' videos implies that, because the videos are in some sense ethnographic records, they call for a particular kind of precision and care in their treatment—the kind of approach, for example, demanded of professional anthropologists and ethnomusicologists today. For although the American disciplines of anthropology and ethnomusicology may never be able to escape fully the colonialist implications that accompanied their rise in the early twentieth century (and that, arguably, are inextricable from any discipline founded upon representing cultural others), current researchers acknowledge the imperialistic history of their fields as an important problem with which they must grapple, and generally work hard to create ethically responsible documentation.[11] In pursuit of this goal, many scholars develop thoughtful plans to combat "the pitfalls of objectification, faulty cultural assumptions, and cultural projection that can occur when viewers are not made privy to the successive degrees of cultural translation involved in these cross-cultural endeavors."[12] It is for this reason that academic ethnographers who work with cinematic media tend to disclose the reasons for their aesthetic and representational choices, providing detailed explication of their videos in an attempt to prevent the objectification of a culture and its people that can come from the mystification of its practices.

But to what extent can explanation truly prevent cultural objectification? Does any Western explication of a non-Western culture in itself represent a type of discourse control, reifying imbalanced power relationships and reinforcing colonialist ideology? If so, might "experimental ethnography," with its dynamic subjectivity, and its refusal to present a "universalist" aesthetics of realism, actually help combat this problem?

The various members of the Sublime Frequencies video team seem to argue for this latter point of view.[13] In public interviews, they have said that they "present a sense of wonderment that is sometimes lacking within the confines of a purely academic approach" and "sidestep [. . .] traditional ethnomusicology, academic protocol and corporate funding, documenting the sound and images of ignored cultural phenomenon [sic] rich in expressive ideas."[14] The Sublime Frequencies filmmakers also implicitly argue that because of the fact that their videos are largely devoid of explanatory materials (liner notes, narrative voice-overs, and so on), they are more politically and ethically sound than the institutionally legitimate recordings that have received the imprimatur of academia and commercial enterprises across the world. Alan Bishop has stated, for example, that "[a] narrator is a distraction [. . .] which 'guides' the viewer [. . .] I'm not an idiot. I can figure out what's going on most of the time. Other people are not idiots. They can make up their own mind about how to interpret non-narrated film.'"[15] The label thus seems to want to combat academia, commerce, and Western hegemony by infusing its films with excitement, avoiding corporate funding, drawing attention to unnoticed cultural forms, and presenting footage without the imposition of the filmmaker's perspective.

In an attempt to allow the cultures to "speak for themselves," then, Sublime Frequencies aims to create a sense of unfiltered, uninterpreted immediacy in the videos—a sense of rawness. Intersecting with this cultural agenda is the label's commitment to negation in a more general sense, a value that is surely related to the musical background of Sublime Frequencies' founders. Alan and Richard Bishop, who started Sublime Frequencies in 2003 with Hisham Mayet, performed for nearly three decades (from 1979 to 2007) in a three-man experimental band, the Sun City Girls, which produced socially critical, multimedia musical extravaganzas informed by punk.[16] Anti-establishment at its core, the punk perspective is iconoclastic, its adherents fighting against any and all established organizations or orthodoxies. Punk's insistent avoidance of traditional institutions allowed it to function as a medium for the expression of diverse (often contradictory) ideologies, and although the political agendas of various punks might diverge, they have in common a general suspicion of any cultural forms that have won the approval of the mainstream. Instead, punk culture celebrates radical individualism, free thought, and the authenticity that comes with turning away from standard authorities.[17]

In this spirit, Sublime Frequencies has worked outside of (and even against) the more widely accepted norms and conventions of ethnographic film and commercial recording industries. As musical performance artists up to the present, the Bishops have had a history of shocking the public in the name of anticapitalist, anti-establishment, independently produced art, and, as noted above, have expressed deep suspicion of the agendas of mainstream institutions.[18] Most importantly, a goal of general negation—*not*-this, *not*-that, *un*-this, *un*-that—serves as a crucial context for the label's output, connecting the punk origins of the group to their emphatically independent approach to production and dissemination, and ultimately to the aesthetics of rawness (*un*processed, *un*filtered, etc.) that can be seen and heard in their recordings.

VIDEO CONTENT I: GENERAL FEATURES

Before one can appreciate the ways in which an ideal of rawness is manifested stylistically in the videos, it is necessary to understand the videos' basic content. The videos of Sublime Frequencies encompass a broad range of subjects and use diverse cinematic and audiovisual techniques, but a few general statements may be made about the collection. On the broadest level, each of the videos makes a point of playing with the subjectivity of the viewer. In line with Russell's idea that experimental ethnographic film "dismantl[es] the universalist impulse of realistic aesthetics," Sublime Frequencies' videos often are shot with a dizzying variety of camera angles.[19] In one scene from *Musical Brotherhoods of the Trans-Saharan Highway*, for example, the viewer is made to feel as if she were immersed in a crowd.[20] During this scene, we begin with the close-to-the-ground perspective of a small child ensconced in a mob of adults. Then, the camera shifts location, hovering just slightly above a group of chattering, dancing, musical participants, much as an especially tall adult—or perhaps an otherworldly spirit—might. Later, the camera peers out from among the instruments being played by a group of musicians, giving the viewer an odd sense of being a "part" of the band—although not from a perspective usually experienced. With such a variety of angles, the viewer's sense of location is made to shift frequently and dynamically, destabilizing the spectatorial gaze, and subsequently preventing the viewer from feeling any singular, decided sense of "insider" or "outsider" perspective on the events or people being filmed.[21]

In terms of narrative, tight cinematic "coherence" does not seem to be the point of Sublime Frequencies' videos: Complementing the shifting camera angles and their sense of destabilization is the videos' typical vignette-based structure. Sometimes different "scenes" are transitioned into with the abruptness of a sudden cut, emphasizing disjunction and disrupting any potential sense of wholeness that a viewer might begin to impose. Other times, distinct scenes are tied to each other with more recognizably transitional footage, often involving the camera moving rapidly down some form of passageway—for example, a dirt road in the countryside, down which a camera bumps swiftly along as if the viewer were riding on a motorcycle or in the back of a truck—while some form of music (not necessarily synchronized to the images) plays in the background.[22] Moments in which the camera tracks a passage down some kind of road occur in nearly all of Sublime Frequencies' videos to date. These scenes evoke a sense of movement suggestive of the vast expanse that beckons the global traveler, while simultaneously engendering an affect of stagnation in the road's seeming infinitude. This creates the feeling that one is fated to journey down a road that does not lead anywhere in particular: Although the spectator "moves" quickly along these roads in Sublime Frequencies' videos, she rarely "arrives" at an endpoint, more frequently being abruptly cut off and led immediately into some new setting. Such a vignette-like, seemingly random structure does not preclude Sublime Frequencies' filmmakers from juxtaposing scenes whose proximity invites provocative contrastive or continuous relationships. Although a viewer theoretically could leave the room for a period while one of these videos is playing, come back to the room, and not necessarily feel "lost" in terms of the video's whole, something is nonetheless gained by watching the scenes progress in the order in which they have been put together—a sense of potential relationships, implicit comparisons, strangely serendipitous mixtures. The videos thus create for the spectator a journey with a meaningful order, if not of a rigidly linearized kind.

More specifically in terms of content, Sublime Frequencies' videos, although focused on musical performances of various kinds throughout the non-Western world, combine diverse types of sounds taken from music, machines, and the natural world with equally diverse images. They frequently capture mesmerizing shots of landscapes (some stationary, while others, as mentioned above, whiz by); playful and humorous interactions (children and adults joking with each other, musicians grinning and dancing for the video camera); and vaguely unsettling footage, often with violent or illicit implications (predatory animals eating raw flesh, young women gyrating their hips for male audiences at nightclubs, rebel armies constructing what appear to be explosives).[23] These images might be accompanied by sounds that did or did not accompany them in "real life." For example, while watching a bird fly across the sky, the viewer might hear the strumming and singing of local musicians, the chirping or barking of other animals, the chatter of television and radio personalities, the electronic bass-thumping of a local nightclub, or the roaring of motorcycles along a gravel road. The videos use a range of tones, running the gamut from joy and warmth to mystic solemnity, each affect created through a particular moment's precise amalgamation of image and sound.

Language is treated with almost as much diversity in Sublime Frequencies' videos as sound and image. Some of the videos display written texts between scenes in order to explain the meaning of, say, a non-Western ceremony; others simply cut from one moment to the next with no annotation.[24] Some videos feature spoken dialogue. When this is the case, the conversation occasionally takes place in English, but in most cases is in other languages. When the viewer hears non-English conversation, she may be treated to subtitles or not. As a whole, most of the videos employ very little dialogue, featuring mainly audio tracks comprised of nonlinguistic sound.

One last subtle but persistent trait pervades the audiovisual collages of Sublime Frequencies: a provocative treatment of nonhuman animals. In *Niger: Magic and Ecstasy in the Sahel*, for example, the viewer is shown numerous animals—cows, camels, donkeys—walking around, eating, and generally living in the environment with the musicians whose lives and music are on display.[25] The roaming animals impart an authenticity, or naturalness, to the videos. In part, this is because of their seeming lack of interest or ability to "perform" for the camera, and in part it is because working animals are associated with more agriculturally based, less-industrialized societies (a frequent trope in exoticist, primitivist imagery), and their casual presence among the humans indicates a harmonious relationship between humankind and the natural world. One sees similar footage in other Sublime Frequencies videos. Birds are shown flying or walking the streets next to people in a marketplace. Dogs meander along pathways. In the extra footage on *Sumatran Folk Cinema*, a sun bear lies on its back on a dirt road, playing with a plastic bottle and lounging around.[26]

This type of animal footage—nonchalant and casually harmonious—is only one way in which animals are treated in the group's oeuvre; in many of the videos, the shots of animals are intensified. Sometimes this intensification is achieved through extreme close-ups (of, for example, fat, hairy green caterpillars inching along in *Phi Ta Khon: Ghosts of Isan* or of what appears to be a large water monitor darting its forked tongue into a body of water in the bonus footage to *Sumatran Folk Cinema*).[27] Other times, intensification is accomplished through violent imagery. In *Nat Pwe*, the viewer watches scores of dead fish being gutted and scraped of their scales by an elderly woman in a marketplace; in *Musical Brotherhoods from the Trans-Saharan Highway*, we see a large chicken in a cage, picking at (and possibly eating) the decapitated head of a smaller chicken; and in *Sumatran Folk Cinema* (one of the more violent videos in general), we watch bloody, wounded fish being pulled in from the ocean, some gasping for air and flopping around on the sand, others simply lying in a slimy, blubbery pile.[28]

The animal footage seems designed to offer a continual gloss on the shots of humans throughout the videos. When violent images of dead fish are juxtaposed with footage of humans engaged in violent acts, the viewer is asked implicitly to compare or contrast these types of destruction. When animals are shown immediately before or after young children, the transition between the two invites the viewer to ponder potential similarities between the groups.

Overall, the animal footage calls to mind the film genre of animal documentary, in which naturalist-cinematographers aim to capture their nonhuman subjects in their "natural habitat," without the interference of outsiders.[29] This raises the possibility that Sublime Frequencies is entering into dialogue not only with ethnographic and experimental film genres, but also with naturalist ones. Does Sublime Frequencies aim (intentionally or not) to treat these videos—with their human subjects, musical-performance objects, and non-Western cultures—in a naturalist manner, analogous to an animal documentary? If so, this might add a new dimension to the ethical and cultural questions that have thus far concerned critics, complicating further the already murky questions about the treatment of human subjects.

In sum, Sublime Frequencies' videos can be characterized by a tendency to play with the viewer's subjectivity through destabilizing camera angles; a structure based on vignettes and notably transitional material (often either abrupt or including motion that feels like "driving" somewhere); a sense of experimentation with the synchronicity (or lack thereof) between visuals and audio tracks; a seeming ambivalence toward language and its explanatory uses; and a provocative treatment of nonhuman animals. Most importantly, each of these points can be seen as the outcome of specific techniques and aesthetic goals based on the idea of rawness.

VIDEO CONTENT II:
AESTHETICS OF RAWNESS

Rawness is manifested aesthetically in Sublime Frequencies' videos in multiple ways. In terms of cinematic features, the videos give a sense of being "unprocessed" or "unfiltered" due to the degree of audio and visual "noise" that frequently permeates them. In addition, the videos feature numerous extreme close-up shots, making the objects feel literally "in your face" and adding to the images a sense of authenticity or aggressive honesty.[30] Further, although the videos vary in the extent to which they use explanatory text, many are notably stark with respect to linguistic explanation of their topics—and none seems to employ any sort of narrative voice-over to tie the images together. This general absence of vocal or textual media to tie the collage together suggests to the viewer a sort of minimal "interpretation" on the part of the authors, contributing to the feeling that the videos, rather than serving as a medium through which a processed, interpreted version of reality is transmitted, actually show the true, "basic essence" of a culture. And finally, beyond cinematic and packaging decisions, the content of the videos itself often might be considered raw. For example, an implication of vague illicitness (or explicit transgression) and hence a sort of rawness of "exposure" (as when the term "raw" refers to an open wound), pervades many of the scenes involving erotic components, as well as many of those moments that imply or symbolize violence toward people, animals, or cultures.[31]

Sublime Frequencies' *Isan: Folk and Pop Music of Northeast Thailand* is an exemplar of many of these techniques. The video juxtaposes clips of different types of Thai musical performances, both "traditional" (sacred ceremonies, *khaen* playing, *mawlum* singing) and "modern" (nightclub performances, pop singers, *molam* singing) with shots of the Isan region. Its soundscape and visuals come across as somewhat "unedited" or "unprocessed" because of their audiovisual noise: ambient sounds permeate the audio tracks; seemingly aimless panning is common; and shaking, grainy, and blurred images are pervasive throughout. This "noisiness" contributes to the sense that the material is coming to the viewer unfiltered or raw. For example, the opening twelve and a half minutes of the video feature a "festival demonstrating the rich cultural heritage of the four predominant tribes [of the area]: [Khmer, Suai, Lao, and Yo]. It [the festival] follows the birth of civilization in Isan, showcasing the local folklore in spectacular, processional magic."[32] In this scene, the ambient sounds of chattering, laughter, and other loud noises are as prominent as the ceremony's music, lending the sound an "unpolished" feeling due to the overlapping domains. In addition, the ceremony clearly has been shot with a hand-held camera, creating a "home video" style that is further emphasized by the abruptness of the cuts between scenes, challenging the viewer to create her own logic between them.

The ceremony is followed by one of Sublime Frequencies' characteristic "driving" transitions, during which the camera shoots from a moving vehicle: We journey down a dirt path lined with green trees and shrubbery, small buildings, and open-air structures. Throughout this excursion, we listen to the distant sounds of a Thai instrument, the *khaen,* and the more present sounds of a puttering motor presumably connected to whatever out-of-view vehicle the cameraman is riding. Again, it is clear that the images have been shot by a hand-held camera. The viewer is given a sense of visual ambience, brought into the atmospheric "background" of the location.

After about forty-five seconds of traveling down the dirt road, the scene shifts abruptly into what appears to be a musical demonstration of a *khaen,* which is played by a Thai musician identified only as "Mr. Ken" in the video's written materials. The camera focuses on Mr. Ken, who appears to be either sitting or standing in an outdoor structure that consists of a concrete floor covered by a roof, on a relatively sunny day. A traditional broom made of long, dry leaves lies on the ground, and some debris (cardboard, a trash can, tall wooden boards, a mattress tied with string) is stacked toward the back of the structure, next to a parked motorcycle. The camera zooms in closely on Mr. Ken and his instrument, at times moving so near that only the front of his face is visible, along with a few inches of the instrument he holds at his mouth. This use of extreme close-up shots (especially of body parts) is common in Sublime Frequencies' videos. Presumably it plays such a pivotal role in these works because it implies that the viewer is witnessing the subject's essence, raw and "up close"—that is, not hidden behind carefully constructed, sanitized ("cooked") images.

In addition, certain scenes in *Isan: Folk and Pop Music of Northeast Thailand* are imbued with a sense of the illicit. Toward the middle of the video, we see footage of singers and a band performing at a nightclub. This performance is described as "seductive" in the liner notes and is said to have taken place at the "infamous See-Saw Club," a "Gentleman's Club" from the "nocturnal and exclusive domains" of the urban centers of Isan.[33] The performers are not identified anywhere in the video's printed materials. Viewing a culture through the lens of the erotic is certainly a common strategy of exoticization, but it is not simply eroticism itself that lends this video a sense of illicitness.[34] The viewer does not, for example, know how old the girls are, the precise nature of their jobs, or anything about the Thai club other than that it is "exclusive." Rawness is invoked through a vague sense of transgression here; illicitness is predicated upon a sense of taboo by Western standards, something that involves the exposure of things that lie metaphorically "underneath" the surface—sex trafficking, for instance. The video, these images imply, has not been filtered or polished in the name of decency: What the viewer sees and hears is positioned implicitly as the raw, if uncomfortably ambiguous, truth.

A sense of the illicit is evoked in Sublime Frequencies' other videos in diverse ways. It is sometimes created through strategically constructed eroticism, as in the footage of sexy singers performing at nightclubs (prominent throughout the Southeast Asian videos); the play with phallus representations (in *Phi Ta Khon: Ghosts of Isan*); or the titillation of elaborately made up cross-dressers (in *Nat Pwe: Burma's Carnival of Spirit Soul*).[35] Illicitness is also created through implications of violence, as in the pervasive footage of bloodied animals or the guerrillas preparing for war in Banda Aceh, as well as the general sense of "danger" that Sublime Frequencies seems purposefully to instill into many of its videos, especially *Niger: Magic and Ecstasy in the Sahel* and *Musical Brotherhoods from the Trans-Saharan Highway*.[36] A sense of transgression also sometimes accompanies a sense of the uncanny in these videos, as seen, for example, in the bonus footage to *Sumatran Folk Cinema*, during which the camera pans slowly along a series of semirealistic statues of humans while solemn gongs resonate sporadically in the background.[37] While eroticism, violence, and eeriness do not universally connote illicitness in all films or film genres, here they are typically inflected with ambiguous, vaguely disturbing implications. In part, this is due to the combination of audiovisual juxtapositions that do not come together in the natural world. This is also due to the sense that, while we understand that what we are watching is real, it is often unclear exactly what the circumstances mean.

FROM AESTHETIC TO IDEOLOGY:
RAWNESS AND AUTHENTICITY

The concept of rawness, with its multilayered implications of natural, unprocessed coarseness and exposure, is thus a particularly useful lens through which to understand the aesthetic of Sublime Frequencies' videos. For the Sublime Frequencies team, however, rawness connotes not only the type of aesthetic and formal presentation discussed above, but also certain ethical, political, and economic values: honesty, lack of agenda on the part of the filmmaker, and the authenticity of noncommercial interests. When we view the Sublime Frequencies videos through the category of rawness, it becomes clear not only why the videos feature certain aesthetic choices, but also why the filmmakers maintain that their work resists the ethical and political problems of cultural representation implicated in other ethnographic films. In sum, Sublime Frequencies' aesthetic values are inseparable from its ideological commitments, and rawness is the link between them.

If rawness refers to that which is coarse and unprocessed, then its opposite, the "processed object," is that which is made safe or civilized. The processed object connotes compromise and artificiality—even deception. The Sublime Frequencies team argues that their work allows the viewer to process, or interpret, the material for herself. Therefore, they see as aesthetically compromised and ideologically based any work that explicitly promotes an agenda—any work that "cooks" or "digests" information for its audience, guiding and mediating the viewer's experience of the material.

Just as the text on its website conveys Sublime Frequencies' explicit commitment to rawness as an aesthetic category, the team's interviews avow their commitment to rawness as ideology. As noted above, Alan Bishop has declared that he finds narrators distracting because they force a political agenda by leading the viewer into one particular interpretation of visual events as they unfold. To take another example, Mayet has said that the label's works are essentially unfiltered, or "unadulterated," and therefore exempt from an overarching agenda.[38]

It is true that the performances being captured by the label were not created expressly for Sublime Frequencies' cameras, and that the company's videos "document" rather than "stage" a host of events that may not otherwise have ever been seen by most Western audiences. But of course, there *is* a technique to their filmmaking—even if it is a deliberately "messy" one, stylized to obscure the hand of the author. And if the documented performers do not "exist" for the camera, they are certainly aware of it in many shots, as is evidenced by the multitude of people in the videos who acknowledge that they are being filmed, whether by looking directly at the camera, speaking to it, or mugging.

Mayet's comments imply that the Sublime Frequencies team is able to approach these human subjects almost without their knowledge. His rhetoric bears some resemblance to the language of nature documentaries, along the lines of "we don't interfere when the polar bear is attacking and eating its prey." But despite the appearance that many of the people filmed do not notice the camera—especially when the camera zooms in on a random, far-away face in a large crowd—many, if not most, of the people being filmed are aware of it, a factor that necessarily affects their performance. Even without a narrator's voice to explain linguistically the filmmaker's objective, there is always an agenda of some kind; decisions have been made about what to film and how to film it. By trying so hard to avoid showing the role that their own editing decisions and aesthetic values have played in the final video, the Sublime Frequencies filmmakers end up obfuscating, in a potentially more insidious way, the camera operators and editors whose work necessarily lies behind the final cut. And thus we come to the heart of the difficulties that are posed by Sublime Frequencies' aesthetic-ideological allegiance to rawness.

For the Sublime Frequencies video team, aesthetic rawness seems to imply not only excitement and authenticity, but also a larger ideal centered on the idea of immediacy. In their interviews, advertisements, and DVD liner notes, the Sublime Frequencies filmmakers suggest that they offer their viewers a direct, unmediated experience of the recorded material.[39] The logic seems to be that because their material is raw—unfiltered, uncensored, and not always meticulously explicated—it offers the viewer immediate access.

Along these lines, Alan Bishop has remarked that, when he hears a song in another language, he generally prefers not to know the meaning of its lyrics:

> The lyrics are not an important thing to me. In fact, it [sic] can be a distraction. If I knew the language enough to know it was a horrible love song with stupid lyrics—like most of the popular songs are today in the English language that I hear—then it would be much more of a turnoff than if it would allow me to interpret it from the expressive capabilities of the vocalizing or of the sound itself, which allows me to create my own meaning for it, which elevates it into a higher piece of work for me.[40]

It seems that Bishop is claiming here that the very process of "understanding" can damage the experience of the sound and prevent the viewer or listener from having a transcendent moment. In this view, language, interpretation, explanation, and even *thought itself* on the part of the filmmaker mediate the viewer's encounter with another culture—and are therefore politically, ethically, and artistically unacceptable in the punk-rock, ethnographically aestheticizing, raw ethos of Sublime Frequencies. It is thus that the Sublime Frequencies team arrives at a position that disavows critical thought and traditional notions of instruction or interpretation.

CONCLUSION

An ideal of rawness is implied by the visual and aural features of the videos themselves as well as by Sublime Frequencies' marketing, from official publicity materials to the provocative public statements made by the label's team. Rawness is presented by the label as sensually "immediate," an ethnographically and artistically "authentic" ideal, and opposed implicitly by the company to the "inauthentic" works and practices of more mainstream and accepted enterprises. Ultimately, it is both through and because of a network of aesthetic-political associations related to the ideas of rawness and mediation that the Sublime Frequencies' works are unified with their ideas, leading the filmmakers to assert that first, their videos offer especially meaningful experiences of relatively unadulterated material; and second, because their videos operate within a system of values that purports not to follow the dicta of institutionalized Western rationality, it is misguided—even inappropriate—for a critic to subject the videos to any type of scrutiny founded upon Western notions about meaning. In other words, through the combination of their interviews, the packaging of their videos, and the aesthetics of the videos themselves, the Sublime Frequencies team implies that their video output is fundamentally resistant to the foundational systems underlying Western critical thought.

There is something commendable about the fact that Sublime Frequencies' filmmakers do not want to "impose" their perspective on the material they film. On a cultural-political level, many of us can understand a genuine desire not to take over someone else's story. On an aesthetic level, music as nonrepresentational sound travels well, and many have agreed that language can be a barrier to certain kinds of sensory experience. One need only think about discourses on the "sublime," absolute music, and "the drastic" to find corollaries with Sublime

Frequencies' ideas in more institutionalized settings. In this way, punk's DIY values and antiestablishment ideals meet Romanticism and discourses on transcendent art.[41] By rejecting post-Enlightenment scientific thought, emphasizing nonrational modes of experience, and encouraging "raw encounters" with music and cultures of the world, Sublime Frequencies appeals to mystical notions of meaning, keeping the cultural other mysterious and exciting.[42] The label thus has found a compelling method of re-enchanting a modern, industrialized, and increasingly disillusioned globalized world.[43]

But of course, the material *has* been interpreted, and *is* representational: Choices have been made about what material to film, how to film it, and how to package it. Each of these decisions has mediated the material in some way, and Sublime Frequencies' implicit denial of this, combined with the type of material they film and the way they film it, raises some extremely difficult and important dilemmas. The subject matter of these videos may indeed be "raw" and the performances "real"—but they are not, as has been claimed, "just pure sound and vision."[44] For when film is involved, you are always watching through someone's lens.

NOTES

1. Most famously, in recent academic conversations about supposedly "unmediated" ("live") performance as a category in opposition to performances that take place primarily through some kind of medium (television, film, etc.), Philip Auslander has thoroughly and compellingly critiqued the idea of such a thing as the unmediated, live performance existing. See Philip Auslander, *Liveness: Performance in a Mediatized Culture*, 2nd edition (London: Routledge, 2008).

2. Sublimefrequencies.com (accessed August 11, 2012). See CD SF048 and LP SF048, both entitled *Group Doueh: Treeg Salaam*.

3. This list reproduces excerpts selected from the *Oxford English Dictionary*, s.v. "raw": www.oed.com/view/Entry/158694?rskey=yuqYdW&result=2&isAdvanced=false#eid (accessed August 12, 2011).

4. The label has produced eleven videos to date, each of which features handheld footage of diverse kinds of musical performances from around the world, shot by one or more members of the Sublime Frequencies collaborators. The video output includes the following titles (in order of date of release, from earliest to most recent): *Nat Pwe: Burma's Carnival of Spirit Soul*; *Jemaa El Fna: Morocco's Rendezvous of the Dead*; *Folk Music of the Sahara: Among the Tuareg of Libya*; *Isan: Folk and Pop Music of Northeast Thailand*; *Niger: Magic and Ecstasy in the Sahel*; *Phi Ta Khon: Ghosts of Isan*; *Sumatran Folk Cinema*;

Musical Brotherhoods from the Trans-Saharan Highway; Palace of the Winds; My Friend Rain; Staring into the Sun.

5. See Karl G. Heider, *Ethnographic Film* (Austin: University of Texas Press, 1976). Heider's discussion of ethnographic film is fundamentally underpinned by the idea that "ethnographic films unite the art and skills of the filmmaker with the *trained intellect and insights of the ethnographer* [emphases mine]." Heider, ix. That is, "cinematographers must accept the scientific demands of ethnography." Heider, ix. And while these statements by Heider represent only the beginning of his more detailed ideas about the specific cinematic and textual features that ought to be present in ethnographic films, these ideas lie at the heart of the book, and do not seem to apply entirely to the type of ethnographic videos produced by Sublime Frequencies. For further discussion of ethnographic film, see also Emilie De Brigard, "The History of Ethnographic Film," in *Principles of Visual Anthropology,* 3rd edition, ed. Paul Hockings, 13–43 (Berlin: Mouton de Gruyter, 2003); Richard Breen and Judith Ennew, et al., eds., *Cambridge Anthropology, Special Issue: Ethnographic Film* (Cambridge: Cambridge University, 1977); Metje Postma and Peter Ian Crawford, eds., *Reflecting Visual Ethnography: Using the Camera in Anthropological Research* (Leiden: CNWS Publications, 2006); and Fatimah Toby Rony, *Third Eye: Race, Cinema, and Ethnographic Spectacle* (Durham, N.C.: Duke University Press, 1996). Finally, it is worth noting that the definitions of fieldwork and ethnography have become fairly contested terrain in today's anthropological world. Although many scholars continue to expect an ethnographer to engage in deep "immersion" in a site and its local people for a period of at least a year ("anthropology of immersion," as opposed to so-called "anthropology by appointment" or "anthropology lite"), other anthropologists are branching out toward a more inclusive model of ethnography. See Ulf Hannerz, *Anthropology's World: Life in a Twenty-First-Century Discipline* (New York: Palgrave Macmillan, 2010). Hannerz addresses various understandings of fieldwork as they have been put forth by anthropologists throughout the twentieth century, noting in particular the changing senses of the field that came with decolonization as well as with digital forms of technology ("Anthropology's world [. . .] is now also a cyberworld," 6). Ultimately, Hannerz advocates a "polymorphous engagement" and a pluralistic sense of fieldwork that legitimates a variety of approaches rather than only allowing a rigidly defined method based on participant-observation. On this idea, see especially pages 74–79. See also George E. Marcus and Judith Okely, "How Short Can Fieldwork Be?" *Social Anthropology/Anthropologie Sociale* 15, no. 3 (2007): 353–57. In sum, the question of whether Sublime Frequencies' videos count as "fieldwork" in the academic sense raises complex and fraught issues.

6. On the "found art" of Duchamp, see, for example, Francis M. Naumann, *Marcel Duchamp: The Art of Making Art in the Age of Mechanical Reproduction* (Ghent and New York: Ludion Press and H. N. Abrams, 1999). On collage art and its theorization, see Donald B. Kuspit, "Collage: The Organizing Principle of Art in the Age of the Relativity of Art," in

Collage: Critical Views, ed. Katherine Hoffman (Ann Arbor, Mich.: UMI Research Press, 1989). On analogous movements in music, see, for example, Brandon Labelle, *Background Noise: Perspectives on Sound Art* (New York: Continuum International, 2006).

7. Catherine Russell, *Experimental Ethnography: The Work of Film in the Age of Video* (Durham, N.C.: Duke University Press, 1999). Russell analyzes the ways in which different modes of representation blur and overlap in what she terms "experimental ethnographic cinema"—examples of which, she argues, can be found within the domains of a variety of recognized film genres (early cinema, or the "cinema of attractions," surrealist cinema, various kinds of nonfiction and documentary cinema, trance films, "found footage" films, and so on). Russell's theorization of the potentially complementary relationship between ethnographic film and "established" experimental film practices is productive when viewing Sublime Frequencies' work, as the label's videos seem to defy conventional generic categorizations. Russell, xi; xvii.

8. Pop culture critic Erik Davis has noted that, "*Folk and Pop Sounds of Sumatra Vol. 1* [. . .] offers only vague credits and no compensation to the original artists." In a polemical response to this criticism, Alan Bishop reportedly vowed to Davis that, "When it [the Sublime Frequencies CD based on Sumatra] starts selling like fucking Outkast, I'll fly to Medan and start handing out Benjamins to anyone who looks like these guys." Erik Davis, "Cameo Demons: Hanging with the Sun City Girls," *The Wire*, February 2004, www.techgnosis.com/scg.html (accessed August 11, 2011). Bishop later disavowed this callous statement, claiming "[i]t was obviously a fucking crack [. . .] If he [Davis] had done any research in any of my diatribes on the Web, he would've been able to see that it's not as black and white as that and it's not—in any regard—that we don't want to pay anyone; we do. It's just set up where it's really difficult to pay. You have to make that decision. Are you going to take the risk to do it or are you just going to not let it be heard?" Less polemically, Bishop has defended himself with the following: "We do pay some royalties. We have contracts with some artists, the ones that we can find or the ones that we can film or that we're in direct contact with. But in terms of archival recordings, it's a lot trickier." See Andy Beta's chapter in this volume. In response to the same kinds of criticism, Hisham Mayet has suggested acerbically that "critics should fight a much larger and nobler battle. Their time would be much better spent focusing on issues that are affecting all of us in much more sinister ways." Quoted in Mike McGonigal, "Beyond the Fringe: The Boundless Musical Geographies of Hisham Mayet and Sublime Frequencies," *Baltimore City Paper* (December 12, 2007). Retrieved from http://www2.citypaper.com/eat/story.asp?id=14958 (accessed August 10, 2011). Ultimately, it is impossible to discern the degree of "sincerity" in any statements given by members of this countercultural and sensationalist group, particularly considering their cultivation of their image as outsiders who aim to shock; nothing they say can be taken at "face value." Nonetheless, we may analyze their public statements productively on these issues within the context of their

public personae, examining how they express their official views and what this says about their work as a whole. Through a careful analysis of their comments in interviews, one sees that, while the group clearly is invested in portraying themselves as philosophically opposed to everything that the "legitimate" institutions of academic ethnomusicology and anthropology would stand for (compensation, verbal explanation, and so on), they nonetheless seem to base their final decisions regarding how to treat their subjects at least in part on practical considerations.

9. Although the viewer sees "credits" at the ends of all of the DVDs, for example, some of those attributions are far more detailed than others in terms of showing the names of the musicians playing in the videos. In response to this type of criticism, Alan Bishop has stated that he is "*not* concerned with [so-called] appropriate documentation." Charlie Bertsch, "Subverting World Music: The Sublime Frequencies Label," *Tikkun Magazine* (July 1, 2009). Retrieved from http://www.tikkun.org/article.php/Bertsch-subverting-world-music/print (accessed August 11, 2011). Cultural theorist and literary scholar Marcus Boon has analyzed the group's seeming blatant disregard for crediting the work of other musicians, and contextualizes Bishop's stance in a compelling way. Boon writes that, with Sublime Frequencies, "punk rock's aggressive style of appropriation, suspicious of authorities and experts [. . .] meets the more subtle but ubiquitous appropriations of traditional folk culture, in which everyone steals techniques from everyone else." Boon, "Sublime Frequencies' Ethnopsychedelic Montages," *Electronic Book Review: Music/Sound/Noise,* December 12, 2006, www.electronicbookreview.com/thread/musicsoundnoise/ethnopsyche (accessed August 11, 2011).

10. The videos and audio recordings rely in part upon unfamiliar, "exotic" sounds and images for their effect, opening the company to accusations of "Orientalism" and its attendant implications of cultural exploitation. Marcus Boon succinctly summarizes this critical trope about the group: "the argument goes that by not labelling or explaining what it is that we're listening to or seeing, SF [Sublime Frequencies] reduces the specificity of a particular cultural form in Morocco or Niger or Myanmar to a universalist, exotic sludge." Boon, "Sublime Frequencies' Ethnopsychedelic Montages." On this phenomenon in general, and on the relationship between cultural fascination with others and imperialist ideology in particular, see Edward Said's classic and influential *Orientalism* (New York: Vintage Books, 1978).

11. For several examples of early twentieth-century ethnomusicologists' unambiguously exoticist language about their subjects, see Kay Kaufman Shelemay, ed., *Ethnomusicology: History, Definitions, Scope* (New York: Garland, 1990). For a discussion of the connections between ethnographic writing and travel writing (a form of discourse also implicitly exoticist), see Mary Louise Pratt, "Fieldwork in Common Places," in *Writing Culture: The Poetics and Politics of Ethnography,* ed. James Clifford and George Marcus (Berkeley: University of California Press, 1986), 27–50. For a history of the discipline of anthropol-

ogy, see Thomas Hylland Eriksen and Finn Sivert Nielsen, *A History of Anthropology* (London: Pluto Press, 2001).

On ethically responsible documentation, see, for example, Mark Slobin, "Ethical Issues," in *Ethnomusicology: An Introduction*, ed. Helen Myers (New York: W.W. Norton & Company, 1992), 329–336. See also James Clifford and George E. Marcus, eds. *Writing Culture: The Poetics and Politics of Ethnography* (Berkley: University of California Press, 1986), an anthology that problematizes the idea that ethnography functions as a "transparent" mode of discourse that can truly represent another culture. Some ethnomusicologists, in order explicitly to redress past appropriations of cultural expression (often in the form of recordings), work in the area of repatriation, striving to give something back to communities who once served as subjects to the academic ethnographers' gaze. One might look, for example, to Aaron Fox's work with the Hopi and Iñupiaq (http://hopimusic .wordpress.com/ [accessed August 11, 2011]). In general, today's ethnomusicologists and anthropologists are highly concerned with the ethical and ideological issues raised by the work they do. While this preoccupation does not in itself guarantee ethical infallibility, it does suggest that such researchers are deeply invested and highly self-conscious about the ways in which they interact with the people they study. Moreover, ethnographic film is seen by many as especially in need of careful treatment of its subjects. See Heider, *Ethnographic Film*, 118–129. Here, Heider gives a cautionary statement regarding the different ways in which the people filmed in non-Western ethnographic films were treated in comparison with Western subjects: "As long as the subjects of ethnographic films were ten thousand miles away from the audiences, there seemed to be little real problem. But now that ethnographers are making films in the United States, and people in New Guinea are using films themselves, the situation has changed." Heider, *Ethnographic Film*, 121. In addition, although he warns that "the overloading of information is especially common in ethnographic films made by anthropologists," Heider is nonetheless an advocate of printed explanatory materials as an ethically obligatory accompaniment to ethnographic films, warning that "it is crucial to the ethnographicness of a film that they [the filmmaker's decisions] be explained, justified, and evaluated," and, in general, that "an ethnographic film must be supplemented by written material." Heider, *Ethnographic Film*, 87, 103, 127.

12. Michael E. Veal, personal correspondence, 2011.

13. On Sublime Frequencies' official website (sublimefrequencies.com), the company states that its goal is to pursue forms of "expression not documented sufficiently through all channels of academic research, the modern recording industry, media, or corporate foundations." Alan Bishop has also been cited as stating that "[w]e are covering areas where most ethnomusicologists don't go—many of them are not interested in pop or folk hybrid music." McGonigal, "Beyond the Fringe."

14. Hisham Mayet, quoted in Chris Toenes, "Hisham Mayet Travels the World Seeking Ecstasy in Sound: Filmmaker and Sublime Frequencies Co-Founder Seeks Ecstatic Truth,"

Independent Weekly, December 5, 2007, www.indyweek.com/indyweek/hisham-mayet -travels-the-world-seeking-ecstasy-in-sound/Content?oid=1205522 (accessed August 12, 2011).

While it is unclear where this "sidestep" quotation originates, it is used on many websites and blogs advertising Sublime Frequncies' wares. See, for example, http://www .umbusiness.co.uk/?p=534 (accessed August 12, 2011); http://porest-report.blogspot.com/ (accessed August 12, 2011); http://www.charliegillett.com/bb/viewtopic.php?f=54&t=9308 (accessed August 12, 2011); http://www.cargorecords.co.uk/release/14664 (accessed August 12, 2011).

15. McGonigal, "Beyond the Fringe." Emphases mine. And yet, although Sublime Frequencies generally does not employ narrative voice-overs in its videos, it is worth noting that some of the label's DVDs include more explanatory text in the liner notes than others. For example, there is a great deal of detail in the description in the liner notes of *Nat Pwe: Burma's Carnival of Spirit Soul,* DVD Sublime Frequencies SF004, 2003.

16. The group, which was active under this name from 1981 to 2007, consisted (after the first year) of a trio made up of Alan and Richard Bishop and Charles Gocher. See http:// www.suncitygirls.com/ (accessed August 11, 2011). Through hundreds of live performances and audio recordings on LP, cassette, and CD, the Sun City Girls produced an enormous number of extremely diverse musical performance pieces during the twenty-five years of their existence. Their work featured musical influences from musics of the Middle East, Southeast Asia, and Africa, often filtered through guitars and drumset (although they also used other instruments). The tone of their performances tended not infrequently toward abrasive noise, aggressive and "politically incorrect" parody and impersonation, dark and eerie surrealism (aided by the use of masks), and cynical irony. For more information on the group, see http://www.suncitygirls.com/ (accessed August 11, 2011).

17. For further discussion of the relationship between authenticity, individualism, and antiestablishment ideologies in punk aesthetics, see, for example: Angela Rodel, "Extreme Noise Terror: Punk Rock and the Aesthetics of Badness," in *Bad Music: The Music We Love to Hate,* ed. Christopher Washburne and Maiken Derno (New York: Routledge, 2004), 235–56; Philip Lewin and J. Patrick Williams, "The Ideology and Practice of Authenticity in Punk Subculture," in *Authenticity in Culture, Self, and Society,* ed. Phillip Vannini and J. Patrick Williams (Burlington: Ashgate, 2009), 65–83; and Stuart Borthwick and Ron Moy, "Punk Rock: Artifice or Authenticity?" in *Popular Music Genres: An Introduction* (New York: Routledge, 2004), 77–97.

18. Once again, this is why we cannot necessarily take anything that representatives of Sublime Frequencies say in public interviews at face value. Shock value seems to have been such an important part of the Sun City Girls that the trio might be considered not only experimental musicians, but also "performance artists" along the lines of the 1970s and 1980s artists who attempted via alienating acts to shock the public into critical thought.

For discussion of two of the more infamous performance artists of the late twentieth century, see, for example, Mary Richards, *Marina Abramović* (New York: Routledge, 2010); and Anna Ayres and Paul Schimmel, eds., *Chris Burden: A Twenty-Year Survey* (Newport Beach: Newport Harbor Art Museum, 1988).

19. Russell, *Experimental Ethnography,* xvii.

20. *Musical Brotherhoods of the Trans-Saharan Highway*, dir. Hisham Mayet, Sublime Frequencies SF041, 2005.

21. One can find many examples of Sublime Frequencies manipulating the subjectivity of the spectator via the camera's shifting perspectives, making the viewer feel as if she were located above, below, or within the activity, inside or outside the events unfolding on the screen. See, for example, *Phi Ta Khon: Ghosts of Isan*, dir. Robert Millis, Sublime Frequencies SF026, DVD.

22. See, for example, the opening ten minutes of both *Isan: Folk & Pop Music of Northeast Thailand*, DVD shot by Hisham Mayet and ed. Richard Bishop, Sublime Frequencies SF015, 2004, as well as *Musical Brotherhoods of the Trans-Saharan Highway*, dir. Hisham Mayet, Sublime Frequencies SF041, 2005.

23. For an example of stunning shots of landscapes, see the opening fifteen minutes of *Niger: Magic and Ecstasy in the Sahel*, dir. Hisham Mayet, Sublime Frequencies SF022, DVD. For examples of mugging, see especially *Palace of the Winds*, dir. Hisham Mayet, Sublime Frequencies SF047, DVD. Animals eating bloody and raw flesh can be found, for example, on *Musical Brotherhoods of the Trans-Saharan Highway*, dir. Hisham Mayet, Sublime Frequencies SF041, 2005. Shots of women singing and dancing onstage in nightclubs can be found on many of Sublime Frequencies' DVDs. See, for example, both the main footage and bonus footage of *Sumatran Folk Cinema*, dir. Mark Gergis and Alan Bishop, Sublime Frequencies SF040, DVD, 2007, as well as *Isan: Folk and Pop Music of Northeast Thailand*, shot by Hisham Mayet and edited by Richard Bishop, Sublime Frequencies SF015, DVD, 2004. Imagery of militant rebels can be found, most notably, in Sublime Frequencies' *Sumatran Folk Cinema*. This video includes footage of participants in the Free Aceh movement (GAM) shot by journalist-activists Billy Nessen and David Martinez. *Sumatran Folk Cinema*, dir. Mark Gergis and Alan Bishop, Sublime Frequencies SF040, DVD, 2007.

24. One Sublime Frequencies video that displays text on-screen during select moments is *Phi Ta Khon: Ghosts of Isan*, dir. Robert Millis, Sublime Frequencies SF026, DVD.

25. *Niger: Magic and Ecstasy in the Sahel*, dir. Hisham Mayet, Sublime Frequencies SF022, DVD.

26. *Sumatran Folk Cinema*, dir. Mark Gergis and Alan Bishop, Sublime Frequencies SF040, DVD, 2007.

27. *Phi Ta Khon: Ghosts of Isan*, dir. Robert Millis, Sublime Frequencies SF026, DVD; *Sumatran Folk Cinema*, dir. Mark Gergis and Alan Bishop, Sublime Frequencies SF040, DVD, 2007.

28. *Nat Pwe: Burma's Carnival of Spirit Soul*, Sublime Frequencies SF004, DVD, 2003; *Musical Brotherhoods of the Trans-Saharan Highway*, dir. Hisham Mayet, Sublime Frequencies SF041, DVD, 2005; *Sumatran Folk Cinema*, dir. Mark Gergis and Alan Bishop, Sublime Frequencies SF040, DVD, 2007.

29. See, for example, the treatment of animals (and the discussion of it on the "behind-the-scenes" footage) from *Planet Earth: The Complete BBC Series*, narr. David Attenborough, BBC Warner, DVD, 2007. Of course, one notable difference between animal documentary and Sublime Frequencies video is that animal documentaries typically do employ a great deal of narration (as their aim tends to be educational on the whole).

30. As Sublime Frequencies advertises on its website, their DVD entitled *Folk Music of the Sahara: Among the Tuareg of Libya* offers a "mind-blowing IN YOUR FACE document." See http://www.sublimefrequencies.com/item.asp?Item_id=12&cd=Folk-Music-of-the-Sahara:-Among-the-Tuareg-of-Libya (accessed August 29, 2011).

31. As advertised on the video's liner notes: "Take a forbidden look into the sultry Go-Go scenes of Gentlemen's Clubs [. . .]." Hisham Mayet and Alan Bishop, liner notes to *Isan: Folk and Pop Music of Northeast Thailand*, shot by Hisham Mayet and ed. Richard Bishop, Sublime Frequencies SF015, DVD, 2004.

32. Ibid. The language used to describe the ceremony is informative to a certain extent, but is not characterized by the degree of depth one would expect to find in more mainstream documentary or ethnographic films.

33. Hisham Mayet and Alan Bishop, liner notes to *Isan: Folk and Pop Music of Northeast Thailand*.

34. See, for example, Irvin C. Schick, *The Erotic Margin: Sexuality and Spatiality in Alteritist Discourse* (London: Verso, 1999).

35. *Phi Ta Khon: Ghosts of Isan*, dir. Robert Millis, Sublime Frequencies SF026, DVD; *Nat Pwe: Burma's Carnival of Spirit Soul*, Sublime Frequencies SF004, DVD, 2003.

36. *Niger: Magic and Ecstasy in the Sahel*, dir. Hisham Mayet, Sublime Frequencies SF022, DVD; *Musical Brotherhoods of the Trans-Saharan Highway*, dir. Hisham Mayet, Sublime Frequencies SF041, DVD, 2005.

37. *Sumatran Folk Cinema*. Sublime Frequencies SF040, DVD, 2007.

38. McGonigal, "Beyond the Fringe."

39. For example, Sublime Frequencies' official website includes the following advertisement for Hisham Mayet's video, *Musical Brotherhoods of the Trans-Saharan Highway*: "This film showcases an assortment of spectacular musical dramas presented live and *unfiltered* on the home turf of the world's most dynamic string/drum specialists performing and manifesting the ecstatic truth!" (emphasis mine). Retrieved from sublimefrequencies.com (accessed August 15, 2011). In addition, the liner notes to *Nat Pwe: Burma's Carnival of Spirit Soul* offer the following: "This film, without narrative spin, or agenda of judgment, captures the moods, intrigue, and exclusivity of this amazing

Burmese phenomenon." *Nat Pwe: Burma's Carnival of Spirit Soul*, Sublime Frequencies SF004, DVD, 2003.

40. Interview with Alan Bishop: see Andy Beta's chapter in this volume.

41. See for example, Carolyn Abbate, "Music—Drastic or Gnostic?" *Critical Inquiry* 30 (2004): 505–536. The label's implicit mysticist, antiscientific tropes could be considered in part to be an attempt to "immunize" their work "against refutation" (something many communities of modern thinkers would find problematic, for example, scientists in recent centuries, whose tests must rest on the assumption that others will correct their work if and when it becomes appropriate to do so). In a relevant discussion of music historian Carl Dahlhaus's intellectual precedents, musicologist James Hepokoski addresses the issue of cutting off critical discourse through immunization against refutation. See James Hepokoski, "The Dahlhaus Project and its Extra-Musicological Sources," *19th-Century Music* 19, no. 3 (1991): 221–46, 232.

42. It is also important to note here that the Sublime Frequencies team does not simply sustain an image of the other as mysterious and exciting through longstanding stereotypes and traditional clichés. More interestingly, it shows a contemporary image of the other, displaying emphatically hybridized (or "Western"-influenced) cultural forms in both music and fashion—and exoticizes that. In other words, Sublime Frequencies' videos do not present a simply nostalgic view of non-Western cultures, but rather, show many of the "natives" in jeans and tee-shirts, performing contemporary pop music. It is notable that, in so doing, the label does not attempt to "freeze" their subjects in a state of "primitiveness."

43. Indeed, a recent statement by Mark Gergis confirms that at least some members of the Sublime Frequencies team self-consciously affirm that their use of exotic sounds and images is in service of reenchanting a globalized world: "Western cautiousness with exotica is understandable, given centuries of colonial occupation and guilt, but really, in an age where we have practically seen and heard it all [. . .] [i]t's not wrong to look at another culture as exotic. In a world that is becoming increasingly homogenised and sterilised, I think we need to be very thankful that there is still this Other to be found." Gergis, quoted in Anna Ramos, "Conversation with Mark Gergis on his Sound Collection," in *Memorabilia. Collecting Sounds With . . .* Ràdio Web MACBA, March 2011.

44. Richard Bishop, quoted in Mike McGonigal, "Beyond the Fringe."

BIBLIOGRAPHY

Abbate, Carolyn. "Music—Drastic or Gnostic?" *Critical Inquiry* 30 (2004): 505–536.

Appadurai, Arjun. "Disjuncture and Difference in the Global Cultural Economy." In *Modernity at Large: Cultural Dimensions of Globalization*, 27–47. Minneapolis: University of Minnesota Press, 1996.

Auslander, Philip. *Liveness: Performance in a Mediatized Culture*. 2nd edition. London: Routledge, 2008.

Ayres, Anna, and Paul Schimmel, eds. *Chris Burden: A Twenty-Year Survey*. Newport Beach, Calif.: Newport Harbor Art Museum, 1988.

Bertsch, Charlie. "Subverting World Music: The Sublime Frequencies Label." *Tikkun*. July 1, 2009. www.tikkun.org/article.php/Bertsch-subverting-world-music/print.

Boon, Marcus. "Sublime Frequencies' Ethnopsychedelic Montages." *Electronic Book Review: Music/Sound/Noise*, December 12, 2006. www.electronicbookreview.com/thread /musicsoundnoise/ethnopsyche.

Born, Georgina, and David Hesmondhalgh, eds. *Western Music and Its Others: Difference, Representation, and Appropriation in Music*. Berkeley: University of California Press, 2000.

Borthwick, Stuart, and Ron Moy. "Punk Rock: Artifice or Authenticity?" In *Popular Music Genres: An Introduction*, 77–97. New York: Routledge, 2004.

Breen, Richard, Judith Ennew, et al., eds. *Cambridge Anthropology, Special Issue: Ethnographic Film*. Cambridge: Cambridge University, 1977.

Brooker, Peter. "Key Words in Brecht's Theory and Practice of Theatre." In *The Cambridge Companion to Brecht*, edited by Peter Thompson and Glendyr Sacks, 216–19. Cambridge: Cambridge University Press, 2006.

Clifford, James, and George E. Marcus, eds. *Writing Culture: The Poetics and Politics of Ethnography*. Berkeley: University of California Press, 1986.

Davis, Erik. "Cameo Demons: Hanging with the Sun City Girls." February 2004. www. techgnosis.com/scg.html.

De Brigard, Emilie. "The History of Ethnographic Film." In *Principles of Visual Anthropology*, edited by Paul Hockings, 13–43. 3rd edition. Berlin: Mouton de Gruyter, 2003.

Dolman, Larry. "Hisham Mayet of Sublime Frequencies" [interview]. *Blastitude* no. 19 (January 2006). blastitude.com/19/MAYET.htm.

Eriksen, Thomas Hylland, and Finn Sivert Nielsen. *A History of Anthropology*. London: Pluto Press, 2001.

Erlmann, Veit. "The Aesthetics of the Global Imagination: Reflections on World Music in the 1990s." *Public Culture* 8 (1996): 467–87.

Feld, Steven. "Notes on World Beat." *Public Culture Bulletin* 1, no. 1 (1998): 31–37.

Garofalo, Reebee. "Whose World, What Beat?" *The World of Music* 35, no. 2 (1993): 16–32.

Hallam, Elizabeth. "Texts, Objects and 'Otherness': Problems of Historical Process in Writing and Displaying Cultures." In *Cultural Encounters: Representing "Otherness,"* edited by Elizabeth Hallam and Brian V. Street. London: Routledge, 2000.

Hannerz, Ulf. *Anthropology's World: Life in a Twenty-First-Century Discipline*. New York: Palgrave Macmillan, 2010.

Heider, Karl G. *Ethnographic Film*. Austin: University of Texas Press, 1976.

Hepokoski, James. "The Dahlhaus Project and its Extra-Musicological Sources." *19th-Century Music* 19, no. 3 (1991): 221–46.

Kuspit, Donald B. "Collage: The Organizing Principle of Art in the Age of the Relativity of Art." In *Collage: Critical Views*, edited by Katherine Hoffman, 39–58. Ann Arbor, Mich.: UMI Research Press, 1989.

Labelle, Brandon. *Background Noise: Perspectives on Sound Art*. New York: Continuum International, 2006.

Lewin, Philip, and J. Patrick Williams. "The Ideology and Practice of Authenticity in Punk Subculture." In *Authenticity in Culture, Self, and Society*, edited by Phillip Vannini and J. Patrick Williams, 65–83. Burlington, Vt.: Ashgate, 2009.

Marcus, George E., and Judith Okely. "How Short Can Fieldwork Be?" *Social Anthropology/Anthropologie Sociale* 15, no. 3 (2007): 353–57.

McGonigal, Mike. "Beyond the Fringe: The Boundless Musical Geographies of Hisham Mayet and Sublime Frequencies." *Baltimore City Paper*. December 12, 2007. www2.citypaper.com/eat/story.asp?id=14958.

Myers, Helen, ed. *Ethnomusicology: An Introduction*. London: Macmillan, 1992.

Naumann, Francis M. *Marcel Duchamp: The Art of Making Art in the Age of Mechanical Reproduction*. Ghent and New York: Ludion Press and H. N. Abrams, 1999.

Postma, Metje, and Peter Ian Crawford, eds. *Reflecting Visual Ethnography: Using the Camera in Anthropological Research*. Leiden: CNWS Publications, 2006.

Pratt, Mary Louise. "Fieldwork in Common Places." In *Writing Culture: The Poetics and Politics of Ethnography*, edited by James Clifford and George Marcus, 27–50. Berkeley: University of California Press, 1986.

Ramos, Anna. "Conversation with Mark Gergis on His Sound Collection." *Memorabilia. Collecting Sounds With . . . "* Ràdio Web MACBA. March 2011.

Richards, Mary. *Marina Abramović*. New York: Routledge, 2010.

Rodel, Angela. "Extreme Noise Terror: Punk Rock and the Aesthetics of Badness." In *Bad Music: The Music We Love to Hate*, edited by Christopher Washburne and Maiken Derno, 235–56. New York: Routledge, 2004.

Rony, Fatimah Toby. *Third Eye: Race, Cinema, and Ethnographic Spectacle*. Durham, N.C.: Duke University Press, 1996.

Russell, Catherine. *Experimental Ethnography: The Work of Film in the Age of Video*. Durham, N.C.: Duke University Press, 1999.

Said, Edward. *Orientalism*. New York: Vintage Books, 1978.

Schick, Irvin C. *The Erotic Margin: Sexuality and Spatiality in Alteritist Discourse*, London: Verso, 1999.

Shelemay, Kay Kaufman, ed. *Ethnomusicology: History, Definitions, Scope*. New York: Garland, 1990.

Slobin, Mark. "Ethical Issues." In *Ethnomusicology: An Introduction*, edited by Helen Myers, 329–36. New York: W.W. Norton & Company, 1992.

Taylor, Timothy. "'Popular Musics and Globalization." In *Global Pop: World Music, World Markets*, 1–38. London: Routledge, 1996.

Toenes, Chris. "Hisham Mayet Travels the World Seeking Ecstasy in Sound: Filmmaker and Sublime Frequencies Co-Founder Seeks Ecstatic Truth." *Independent Weekly*, December 5, 2007. www.indyweek.com/indyweek/hisham-mayet-travels-the-world -seeking-ecstasy-in-sound/Content?oid=1205522.

Interview with Olivia Wyatt
Filmmaker and Photographer

Olivia Wyatt's documentary *Staring into the Sun*—funded with a shoestring budget using grants from Sublime Frequencies and money from Kickstarter—is a kaleidoscopic exploration of various tribal cultures in rural Ethiopia. Shot and edited by Wyatt, *Staring into the Sun*'s cacophony of music and images makes it more of a visual essay than a traditional documentary. By keeping commentary and ethnographic contextualizing to a minimum, the sights and sounds of the countryside speak for themselves without the benefit (or hindrance) of description. Moving between humor and seriousness, ritual and daily life, *Staring into the Sun* gives us an outsider's perspective on a variety of East African cultures, yet remains refreshingly unconcerned with their interpretation or valuing.

A Brooklyn-based filmmaker and artist, Wyatt had studied photojournalism at the University of Missouri before moving to New York several years ago to work for Magnum Photos and later Magnum in Motion. It was then that she first began making documentary films, including a number of films documenting voodoo rituals among New York's Haitian community. I spoke with the filmmaker about *Staring into the Sun*'s upcoming screening next week (along with a number of other incredible films) as part of [Brooklyn Academy of Music's] Saharan Frequencies series [2012].

JONATHAN ANDREWS: What prompted your interest in Ethiopia in the first place? How did the idea for the film first come about, and how did you manage to fund the project?

OLIVIA WYATT: Ethiopia fascinates me because there are around eighty diverse ethnic groups, and since the landscape is so harsh, many have maintained their traditions and are living as they have for thousands of years. So I decided to apply for a Fulbright to work on a project with the Dassanech tribe in Ethiopia. While I was applying, my boyfriend at the time sent me a link to the Festival of a Thousand Stars, which showcases the music of each of the 80 ethnic groups in Ethiopia. I said, "If I get the grant, we gotta go to the festival together."

Unfortunately, I did not get the grant, but the time of the festival was coming up and I still wanted to go. So I started writing to companies and magazines to see if anyone was interested in some photos or footage. Sublime Frequencies got back to me and said it was up their alley and they would be interested in distributing, but of course they would need to see what I brought back. So I started emailing friends of friends who had been there, found a translator, raised money on Kickstarter, and off I went by myself to Ethiopia.

JA: When you first departed, was there a particular place or event you wanted to visit or attend? How did the finished film ultimately conform or change from the idea you started out with?

OW: Initially I went to document the Festival of a Thousand Stars; however, when I arrived, the festival was canceled. I, of course, was slightly disappointed that I had trekked all the way over there for something that was canceled, but I couldn't let it stop me from making something and so I decided to just travel to as many of the tribes as I could in the areas they call home. I did this by hitchhiking my way across the country on the backs of Isuzu trucks, buses, camels, etc.

JA: How long did you stay with each tribe, and how did your relationships with them develop or change over time? Did the duration of your stay affect the aspects of daily life and the various events you were allowed to participate in?

OW: I packed visiting thirteen tribes into two and a half months and stayed with each tribe as long as I possibly could—but of course there were some that due to location I could only spend one or two days with, and one tribe I was only able to stay with for a few hours. When I would first arrive in most of the communities, the women would touch my skin, my breast, my hair. They would often adorn my body in some of their fashionable jewelry or clothing and braid my hair the way they braided theirs. It's strange, but I felt with most of the communities that my bond with the women was almost instantaneous.

Also, there was one time I arrived to document a Zar [a spiritual mystic or holy man], whose practices are not exactly legal. I traveled all through the night and up a hyena-infested mountain with someone from his tribe who had never even met him, and I was just fingers-crossed that he would even speak to me. When I arrived, his wife was screaming and holding tightly to their children (she thought

I was there to take them away), but he looked at me and through my translator said, "the spirits told me you were coming last night in my dreams, I know you are here to see a Zar ceremony, there will be one tomorrow evening, return with a bag of *khat*, some tobacco, and soda." I only spent a total of five hours with him, and truly feel that without the help of supernatural and/or spiritual forces, I never would have been invited to witness and document such a ceremony. I spent the most time with the Hamar tribe, and by the time I left a baby was named after me, so I would say that I immediately felt connections wherever I went, but obviously over the course of time these connections deepened.

JA: I'm curious to know—how was it traveling as a single woman in rural Africa? What kind of considerations did that pose?

OW: For the most part, people were just very curious and gentle with me, and I felt as though the men had a respect for me as a foreign woman traveling solo, that I did not see them have with women from their own communities.

However, there were some scary moments. I was hitchhiking on the backs of Isuzu trucks at night; because the roads are so hot they melt the tires during the day. They call the trucks "Al-Qaedas" because there are so many accidents and so many people die traveling on them. Also, it is illegal for me as a foreigner to ride in them. I eventually started pretending I was married to my translator so that this wasn't an issue, but initially they would hide me under chickens and whatnot in the backs of these trucks, and one time I was sitting next to a man who was missing an arm. When I asked what happened, he informed me that he used to drive one of these trucks and he lost it in a wreck.

I was the most frightened as a woman on one of these trucks when I was riding in the front of the truck and Yibltal (my translator/fake husband) was in the back. We couldn't communicate, and I was wedged in between two drunk men and a driver who was pretty high on *khat*. One of the men kept touching me. I would say *yellum* (no), but he would keep on doing it, and then the guy on the other side—the owner of the truck—would occasionally try to put his arm around me. These thoughts kept flashing through my head that they were going to lock the doors and have their way with me, so I made a scene and got the driver to stop the car, so I could communicate with Yibltal about what was happening and have him move into the front and the man with roaming hands moved to the back. This man was fired for his behavior as soon as we arrived in the next town.

There were other moments, too: going to jail, having AK-47s all around in some tribal areas, my translator getting punched and in a full blown fight with a man carrying an AK-47, traveling at night on roads that are known for hijacking, having cholera and dropping 20 pounds in one day. So many crazy incidents, but I don't think my gender pertains to many of these, only the one I mentioned of the men getting grabby in the truck.

JA: The role of music and ritual was central in your documentary—what can you say about the importance of music in these various cultures and these people's lives?

OW: Among the communities I visited in Ethiopia, music is a central part of their lives. I found that music was a way to connect with everyone, and everyone was involved in making it. They do it when they work, when they play, when they walk, when there is a celebration . . . always. Women even wear jewelry that doubles as percussive instruments. I really appreciate how much music and dance is incorporated into the lives of Ethiopians, as though it is one of the main threads keeping communities alive.

For me, music is the most basic and first form of communication, and I tend to agree that it predates verbal communication. For this reason, I am drawn to capturing music in other communities, because I feel it's a powerful way for foreign audiences to connect to the subjects of the film.

JA: The shots of the various dances and rituals in the film were fantastic. Did you just happen upon events that were already occurring or were some of them performed for your benefit?

OW: For the most part, I got lucky and ended up in places where things were naturally happening. Beyond the Zar spirit possession ceremony, some of the other things I lucked upon included weddings, and I was perhaps the luckiest to arrive at the Borena community the day after it rained so they were in the water wells working, which they only do on days after a rain. There were of course situations where I wasn't so lucky and I asked to see a performance—I would say about 30 percent of the film is like this.

JA: In *Staring into the Sun*, scenes of the various tribes are often interspersed with clips from Ethiopian television shows. What was your intention in juxtaposing these shots of village life with images as diverse as (what appear to be) music videos and newsreels? Also, where did you get those clips?

OW: I got most of these clips from the Ethiopian TV station. There is only one government-run TV station in Ethiopia, unless of course you are lucky enough to have a satellite, and on this station each tribe in Ethiopia is showcased for one hour each week. In this way, I feel that the government is honoring and helping to preserve the elements of each tribe that make them unique. I loved traveling to a part of the country in the northern part and hearing someone randomly singing a song from the south that they happened to catch on the TV.

There are certain tribal songs that are extremely popular across the country, for example the Hamar song that you see at the beginning of their section on the TV that then continues on with the women singing it live as they dance in a circle. This song is very famous all over Ethiopia, and I would hear communities everywhere singing their own version of that Hamar song. My motivation in incorporating and blending the TV footage with the documentary footage was simply to show the influence the tribal communities have on pop culture in Ethiopia.

JA: I know you've done a lot of work with the Haitian community and voodoo rituals here in New York, and there seems to be a real focus in your work on spiritual practices. Is there any connection between those previous projects and this film?

OW: I would say that everything I am naturally drawn to documenting is connected. I am extremely interested in anything tribal, religious, and ritualistic. I have found that within tribal communities there is extensive knowledge of and a symbiotic relationship between the people and their surroundings. Whether plants, animals, or the sea, there's knowledge so vast and so rich, yet that's something that I, personally—as a Westerner—feel so disconnected from. Often the elements of their surroundings also lend to the development of religious rituals where these aspects of nature are incorporated and worshiped in an animistic way. The Haitian community differs here because their worship is more ancestral rather than animistic, but to me both are magical and very closely linked.

JA: *Staring into the Sun* utilizes a nonlinear narrative with little use of dialogue or subtitles; the images work impressionistically, and the film remains relatively unconcerned with providing context. Can you talk about these stylistic/aesthetic decisions and why you made them?

OW: I am not an ethnographic filmmaker in the traditional sense, since my work is way more experiential and experimental. I do not seek to inundate a viewer with my personal opinion about what they are witnessing nor do I provide much information beyond what they would see and hear if they themselves were wandering aimlessly within the countries where I document. Essentially, I am allowing the viewer to take his or her own voyage. I want it to be a visceral, poetic, and mysterious experience; I want to force the audience to connect with the people in the film on the most basic level which, for me, is musical no matter where I go.

Between you and me, I will sometimes watch ethnographic films without the intended audio and have my own soundtrack playing of music from the country featured. For me this creates more mystery and enhances my experience as a viewer. Also, this work is done very much in the style of Sublime Frequencies' other films, which I have always been a huge fan of and inspired by, and it is a true honor and dream come true to have them releasing my work.

JA: It looked as if the whole film was shot in analog, rather than digitally. Was there a reason for that?

OW: Well, I lost a lot of work once while doing a project in Nepal during the Maoist Revolution. The project was all digital and I had a hard drive fail me. After that I went as analog as I could get, recording everything to tape, the audio to a Sony TCD5M cassette recorder with VU meters and the video to a Sony that captures onto an HD tape, so technically, the visual part is digital, but it is as analog as I can afford.

I just lost most of my equipment in Sandy so for my next project I am going to shoot digitally and on Super 8 millimeter film. I think I gotta go all digital with the audio though 'cause I am going to be using hydrophones, and the company that makes the ones I am going to use does so specifically for the Zoom, a digital audio recorder.

JA: This was your first film with Sublime Frequencies. How did your collaboration with them shape the project?

OW: I love the Sublime Frequencies style, always have, and was blown away when I first watched a film on their label, which was *Jemaa El Fna* by Hisham Mayet. When they showed an interest in the project, I shaped it to mimic their style, but looking back on it this has more to do with my respect for the way they were creating already, than the fact that they showed interest in the project.

JA: What are you currently working on?

OW: *Sea Gypsies*, which is a film exploring the culture of one of the smallest ethnic minority groups in Asia. Their lives revolve entirely around water. They can swim deeper than any other human being, their eye lenses change shape, and they can see farther underwater than any other human being, and they predicted the tsunami before modern scientists.

Unfortunately, a variety of sociopolitical groups are stripping them of their indigenous beliefs, and my goal is to capture and preserve as many aspects of their culture as possible, before it is completely altered. This will vary in so many ways from my previous work. I am going to shoot on Super 8 millimeter and digital format as I mentioned above. I will also have a narration of sorts, since my goal is to highlight the mythology, language, and other traditional beliefs. However, the film will lack a traditional documentary arc, therefore you could start and stop the film at any point in time or even just loop it, and the audio itself is going to flow more like an epic poem than anything else. I cannot say for certain as I have yet to shoot it, but I also envision half of the film taking place underwater.

This is also the first time I have a full team of people involved, which for me is really exciting. I will travel alone to work on the project, but there are some really incredible people involved in helping to make this happen. Women Make Movies is the fiscal sponsor, Kim Sherman (*Sun Don't Shine* and *A Teacher*) is one of *Sea Gypsies'* producers, Elisabeth Holm (Kickstarter film program director and *Welcome to Pine Hill*) is the other producer, and Will Oldham, aka Bonnie "Prince" Billy, is the executive producer.

NOTE

Sublime Frequencies recordist Olivia Wyatt has two visual projects on the label: *The Pierced Heart and The Machete* and *Staring into the Sun*. This interview was commissioned by and originally published March 6, 2013, on BOMBlog. © *Bomb Magazine*, New Art Publications, and its Contributors. All rights reserved. The BOMB can be read at www.bombsite.com.

DAVID FONT-NAVARRETE

Ambient Sound in Sublime Frequencies as Art (and/or) Ethnography

I. VARIOUS SOUNDS

The third Sublime Frequencies release, *Night Recordings from Bali*, begins with a collage of ambient sounds and musical performances: dogs barking, the recordist's footsteps, and a gamelan ensemble.[1] An edit between two tracks ("Gamelan Rehearsal" and "Monkey Forest Night") fades from a gamelan orchestra rehearsal to the nocturnal sound of insects and frogs. Do we also hear the unlikely sounds of birds in the night? On "Gamelan Gabor #1," a larger gamelan ensemble plays through a composition that ends with sustained, attenuating tones. Suddenly, the next track ("Rubber Television") cuts to a very similar sound of gamelan music: the tuning and timbres of the instruments are now familiar, but the music wobbles like an old, worn-out cassette tape. Is the new track an older, lower-fidelity recording of the same ensemble?

Voices modulated by theatrical drama take the sonic foreground, retroactively suggesting another dimension in the recording: We have been hearing background music from a soap opera, the sound doubly compressed via distorted broadcast airwaves and overloaded speakers. We quickly realize the recording has moved from a field recording of a musical performance to a recording of mass media on radio or television. The shaky, distorted timbres of "Rubber Television" signal a radical shift in media from a secondhand to a thirdhand recording. How and why do we listen to this recording of a recording of a recording? How do we situate the "source" of the recording, or ourselves? Further along, *Night Recordings from Bali* fades quickly from sounds at a funeral ceremony ("Cremation Procession [Rotating Coffin]") to frog and insect sounds ("Night Lotus Pool").

Then the album cuts abruptly to the middle of another gamelan performance ("Gamelan Gabor #2"), which then fades out.

On its webpage, Sublime Frequencies cites several "pioneering recording labels of the past" as inspiration.[2] The list includes Smithsonian Folkways, a label that is not only active (rather than "of the past"), but part of the national museum of the United States. While the Sublime Frequencies catalog is unified by an explicitly exotic, cross-cultural dimension (the products of "explorers"), it also represents a unique synthesis of avant-garde and documentary sensibilities. The label's concept-driven aesthetic connects its work directly to the artistic innovations of *musique concrète*, ambient music, and sound art. Moreover, many Sublime Frequencies releases also imply connections to theoretical concepts such as soundscapes, schizophonia, and acoustic ecology.[3]

This essay offers brief comparative notes on the Sublime Frequencies, Folkways, and Smithsonian Folkways labels. I explore the three labels' engagement with "ambient" sounds—meaning sounds "of the surrounding area or environment"—including field recordings (a broad, ambiguous term associated equally with experimental music, sound art, documentary projects, and ethnography) and other, more conspicuously altered recordings (i.e., processed, edited, or repurposed sounds).[4] Although ambient sound is most often considered incidental or extra-musical, it performs very different roles depending on its context: In musical, documentary, or ethnographic settings, it is most often used to convey a sense of authenticity and a direct relationship to place and time; however, in avant-garde settings, it is most often used to subvert and reorient conventional, mundane relationships between listeners and sounds.[5]

A brief, admittedly selective comparison of ambient sound in the Sublime Frequencies, Folkways, and Smithsonian Folkways catalogs sheds light on affinities and differences among the labels' respective approaches. More broadly, the comparison illustrates complex and often implicit relationships among artistic, documentary, and ethnographic modes of production. The distinctions among these three modes are by no means clear-cut; they overlap and blend into each other. I argue that the messy, ambiguous overlaps among artistic, documentary, and ethnographic modes constitute a dynamic tradition that is often more engaging and forward-thinking than that of any single mode. An experimental, avant-garde impulse runs through many labels specializing in exotic recordings, including Sublime Frequencies, Folkways, and—to a much lesser extent—Smithsonian Folkways. In this respect, Sublime Frequencies lies firmly along a historical continuum that oscillates between documentary and artistic approaches to sonic ethnography. While this essay strives to demonstrate and emphasize continuity, it also addresses some important differences among the three labels' approaches.

II. CUTTING UP SOUNDS
OF EXOTIC TIMES AND PLACES

Numerous releases on Sublime Frequencies incorporate ambient sounds: recordings of empty streets, crowded markets, footsteps through brush, animals, insects, and (often cacophonous) amplified music in public spaces. Radio transmissions—floating, invisible, public, and airborne—are also prominent. In Sublime Frequencies releases, ambient sound is most often employed as source material for audio collages: tracks on any given album function as distinct elements in a composite whole; sometimes single tracks include several distinct sources of sound mixed or spliced together; and the cuts between sources can be sudden and radical or remarkably smooth. (To my ears, the cuts invariably sound clever and purposeful.)

The label's *Radio* releases—*Radio Myanmar, Radio Algeria, Radio Thailand: Transmission from the Tropical Kingdom*, etc.—make explicit, sudden shifts between sources of sounds. On the other hand, *Streets of Lhasa* features several long, discrete tracks of ambient sounds: two tracks called "Streets of Lhasa" offer exactly what their titles promise; "Bian Jing" consists of twelve minutes of intense verbal exchanges among a group of Tibetan men; "Train" is a concise document of sound in movement; and "Peace on Top of the World" includes prominent—and, indeed, sublime—sounds of prayers and birds. *Street of Lhasa* is a relatively early Sublime Frequencies release, and it includes some of the most explicitly "ambient" recordings in their catalog. In general, the label's earlier releases include much more ambient sound than recent releases, which tend to adhere to relatively conventional notions of exotic music.[6]

Like other Sublime Frequencies releases featuring ambient sounds, Tucker Martine's *Broken Hearted Dragonflies: Insect Electronica from Southeast Asia* consists of "straight" field recordings that forgo conspicuous audio effects. But in this instance, the sounds of insects and their environment are recorded and arranged so that their entirely organic sound is convincingly rendered as ersatz electronic music; they would fit perfectly on an album of cutting-edge generative computer music. Given his expertise as an audio engineer and producer, Martine uses uncommonly sophisticated and deliberate recording and production techniques. But *Broken Hearted Dragonflies* is not really an audio collage. Instead, it takes a severe approach to ambient sound: Rather than serving as "background" for conventional documentary projects, the album insists on a listener's attention. When the dense frequencies of "Particle Swarm Intelligence" build up to a sustained, swirling crescendo, they become as difficult to "tune out" as a recording of a ringing fire alarm or a pounding jackhammer, demonstrating that ambient sound is emphatically *not* necessarily mellow. The sounds of a natural environment can be as extreme as feedback from electric guitars.

Describing his own exploration of insect and environmental sounds, composer David Dunn addresses concerns equally relevant to Sublime Frequencies. Dunn writes:

> There are many parallels in the collecting of sounds to other means by which we document and "bind time" in order to study, intensify experience, or cherish the past [. . .] Several recordists market their recordings as purist audio documentation of pristine natural environments with particular appeal to the armchair environmental movement. Personally I find something perverse about many of these recordings, as if the encoding of a semiotic referent in the form of an audio description of place could ever be something other than a human invention. Sometimes the sounds are intrinsically beautiful but are too often marketed as if their mere existence were somehow doing the environment a big favor. I can certainly understand arguments for the preservation of actual biohabitats but not as recorded sonic objects. The premise appears to be that these recordings will somehow sensitize the listener to a greater appreciation of the natural world when in fact they are more often perpetuating a nineteenth-century vision of nature and at best merely documenting a state of affairs that will soon disappear.[7]

If we extend Dunn's rationale from environmental to cultural dimensions of sound recording, several interpretations of Sublime Frequencies' work emerge. In one sense, the label appeals to "armchair" cultural tourists and voyeurs, marketing recordings across geographic, cultural, and socioeconomic divides as an act of "preservation." In another sense, Sublime Frequencies draws listeners' attention to some of the "perverse" dynamic and structural dimensions of recording, ostensibly sharing Dunn's intention "to invoke patterns of relationship intrinsic to the materials themselves."[8]

In general, though, ambient sounds in the Sublime Frequencies catalog are employed as raw materials for audio collages that reveal varying degrees of human presence, editing, and mediation. In a 2008 interview, Sublime Frequencies' Alan Bishop said: "Sound collage has always been one of my favorite mediums to work in, and with a shortwave radio, it's the perfect tool to create audio collage endlessly, spontaneously, on the spot, anytime and anywhere. The source material just happens to be better and more inspiring to me in the areas I've roamed—North Africa, the Mideast, South Asia, etc." (quoted in Andy Beta's chapter in this volume).

Rather than invoking "musical" or "natural" phenomena, Sublime Frequencies' ambient and thirdhand recordings often tune listeners in to mundane, pedestrian sounds. For example, we understand a recording of an Indonesian television program as "ambient" sound—a small, momentary portion of a cohesive, all-encompassing soundscape. It can also be understood as part of a more general artistic approach: We listen to a collage of radio broadcasts by Holger Czukay as art, just as we look at visual collages by Kurt Schwitters. But the exotic content and framing of Sublime Frequencies' albums are unmistakable and essential: An LP of edited "indigenous" radio programs from the United States would present a different set of abstractions, aesthetics, and ethical dimensions.

More recently, Bishop acknowledged the influence of the seminal "cut-up" techniques developed and popularized by William S. Burroughs and Brion Gysin: "I was familiar with the Burroughs/Gyson [sic] techniques and music collage in general but I was also employing these ideas with my own music at the time. Selective and geographical location Radio collage is a very practical idea that should have been widely utilized long before I did it but unfortunately that's not the case."[9]

"Cut-up" techniques can be traced directly to the avant-garde Dada movement of the early twentieth century, but they were named and popularized by Burroughs and Gysin in the 1950s. The basic technique involves the cutting of a text or image into pieces that are then rearranged to create an alternative, nonlinear version of the original. The process amounts to a type of abstraction through controlled randomization. According to Burroughs and Gysin, cut-ups are more usefully understood as a subconscious and spiritual process, closer to dreaming or divination than mechanics. Nonetheless, the procedures of a cut-up—including selection of source material—determine the results. Cut-up techniques are applicable to a variety of text- and image-based media but seem especially well suited to sound. Burroughs himself acknowledged, "John Cage and Earle Brown have carried the cut-up method much further in music than I have in writing."[10] Cut-up, as applied to audio recordings, gestures toward a paradoxical and fruitful relationship between the linear, temporal properties of sound and the nonlinear, fixed properties of audio recording media. Sounds are experienced *in time*, but recording technologies let us *rearrange, recombine,* and *reproduce* them.

Ambient sounds serve to index musical cultures, histories, and places. They can also lend a sense of authenticity and presence to a recording: We need only imagine the sound of a rooster in the background of a recording of "rural" music or the roar of a crowd in a "live" concert recording to appreciate the sense of place evoked by nonmusical ambient sound. Commenting on the Sublime Frequencies catalog, interviewer Joe Wensley says to Bishop:

> jw: To me they appear to be almost as abstract representations of the culture,
> like if you were to make one image from many photographs.
> ab: Yes—collage is collage any way you wanna slice it.[11]

To Wensley, the albums evoke very specific places through their geographical themes and titles, even though these places are (for most North American listeners) physically distant and quintessentially foreign. (Nearly every title for the first forty Sublime Frequencies releases includes proper place names.) Moreover, the recordings offer many distinctive sonic landmarks: spoken Arabic in Syria, Balinese gamelan ensembles, the plucking of *kora* strings in Mali. However, the arrangements of recordings and the catalog as a whole make oblique associations between places and sounds. As Wensley observes, the label's "representations" of cultures amount to abstract, artistic analogs of ethnography via sound. Many of the Sublime Frequencies releases employ ambient sounds to aesthetic and conceptual ends, simultaneously disorienting and grounding listeners.

Observing this paradox in the label's recordings, Michael Vazquez refers to the Bishop brothers' approach in Sublime Frequencies and their Sun City Girls band as "disorientalism." Vazquez notes that their recordings acquire "an extra poignancy precisely by dint of their obscurity."[12] Along similar lines, Charlie Bertsch juxtaposes the label's catalog with some of the thornier political dimensions of representations of non-Western people, places, and cultures in Western media:

> There are moments, listening to Sublime Frequencies compilations [. . .] when listeners lose their place. Instead of feeling transported to the faraway lands of their dreams, they hear this music as the mental wallpaper that it is: colorful, flat, and prone to misalignment. The sensation of being there gives way to the

confusion of "Where am I?" And that's precisely the effect label founder Alan Bishop and his collaborators are seeking to achieve [. . .] What listeners really need, in other words, is not orientation but disorientation.[13]

Here again, it is worth emphasizing that Sublime Frequencies' recordings reflect approaches that are both documentary and artistic—specifically, "artistic" in the sense of an avant-garde concept and aesthetic. Numerous tracks are dedicated entirely to sounds usually considered incidental or residual elements of an "ethnographic aesthetic"—sounds usually only heard in the background or at the beginning and end of more conventional recordings. These ambient sounds mark a "real" field recording, even if we only hear them before or after the "real" subject—that is, music or speech.

How does Sublime Frequencies' catalog of "neglected" sounds and people relate to more conventional "ethnographic" recordings of distinct (usually distant) cultures, times, and places? The label's prominent exoticism is certainly part of the equation, but its underground, artistic, and avant-garde sensibility is just as important. Sublime Frequencies' recordings are *made* exotic and abstract, and ambient sounds draw our attention to these disorienting qualities.[14] In this context, Sublime Frequencies' output can be understood as a set of complex interventions: (1) taking the notion of authenticity as a given; (2) discarding the notion of authenticity entirely; and/or (3) turning conventional notions of authenticity inside out.[15] Taken as a whole, Sublime Frequencies' output can be experienced as an organic, collaborative, and abstract collage of sounds from exotic locations. Paradoxically, the sounds are presented as being intimately associated with specific times and places, yet they often create a surreal set of juxtapositions that ensure listeners' awareness of an editor's hand at work.

All of this indicates an approach to ambient and nonmusical sound that is intimately related to avant-garde art movements of the mid-twentieth century. Pierre Schaeffer, the French polymath most closely associated with *musique concrète* (concrete or "real" music), describes his notion of "sonorous objects" in terms relevant to Sublime Frequencies: "When listened to by a dog, a child, or a Martian, or the citizen of another musical civilization, this signal takes on another meaning or sense."[16] As documents of exotic times and places devoid of substantial literal context, Sublime Frequencies' albums are *intended* to be interpreted in abstract ways; listeners are expected and disposed to perceive them as abstract forms whose meanings (if any) are open to subjective interpretations. The cumulative effect of the recordings draws listeners into a rich, novel world that is both "real" and imagined. Although the sources of ambient sounds on Sublime Frequencies CDs and LPs are sometimes referenced by track titles, it is difficult to know where or when the mediation of a given recording begins or ends. Are we hearing a live performance of music, a radio transmission, or background music in a television program?

Schaeffer designates sounds whose origins remain unseen, unclear, or unknown as acousmatic. "We have at our disposal the generality of sounds—at least in principle—without having to produce them; all we have to do is push the button on a tape recorder. Deliberately forgetting every reference to instrumental causes or preexisting musical significations, we then seek to devote ourselves entirely and exclusively to *listening* . . . Such is the suggestion of acousmatics: to deny the instrument and cultural conditioning. "[17]

Exploring this phenomenon from a rather different, but equally modern perspective, the Canadian theorist and composer R. Murray Schafer coined the term "schizophonia":

> The Greek prefix *schizo* means split, separated. Schizophonia refers to the split between an original sound and its electroacoustical transmission or reproduction. It is another twentieth-century development . . . Since the invention of electroacoustical equipment for the transmission and storage of sound, any sound, no matter how tiny, can be blown up and shot around the world, or packaged on tape or record for the generations of the future. We have split the sound from the maker of the sound. Sounds have been torn from their natural sockets and given an amplified and independent existence . . . The twentieth century has given us the ability to dislocate sounds in time as well as space. A record collection may contain items from widely diverse cultures and historical periods in what would seem, to a person from any century but our own, an unnatural and surrealistic juxtaposition.[18]

What do listeners gain from the acousmatic or schizophonic ways of hearing exotic sounds on Sublime Frequencies albums? Do the recordings create a different sense of engagement between people and places than more conventional—and arguably narrower—efforts to contextualize sounds, people, and places? Do the albums offer an engagement in the spirit of acousmatic sound, denying "cultural conditioning"?[19] Or an engagement that, according to more judgmental notions of schizophonia, is "unnatural and surrealistic"?[20] In my view, the acute tension and feedback between archival preservation and abstraction—including acousmatic re- and decontextualization of sound—is one of the label's distinguishing and most exquisite traits. Sublime Frequencies goes out of its way to hint at specific contexts for its sounds, not radical abstraction. Why else would albums offer such prosaic titles as *Bush Taxi Mali: Field Recordings from Mali, Radio Phnom Penh*, or (formulaically) *X (poetic name): Y (genre or instrument) from Z (place)*?

A related aesthetic and conceptual thread runs through the Sublime Frequencies catalog: The albums' producers conspicuously avoid being too precious with cultural and aural material. The recordings are edited and arranged meticulously, but their audio signal is often distorted into fuzzy, overdriven saturation. The overall effect of this recurring "low-fi" element in the catalog points to a rough sensibility, an aesthetic and ideological counterweight to the delicacy associated with avant-garde "fine" art.[21] This aesthetic also offers a parallel between sonic and social environments: "Exotic" sounds, locales, and cultures are intrinsically more gritty and down-to-earth, thereby resonating with the conventions of Euro-American counterculture. Compared to other labels' more "refined" approaches (recordings of pristine environments free of human noise or studio-produced music free of environmental noise), Sublime Frequencies cuts environmental sounds into its albums with the same roughness that characterizes its presentation of (conventionally) musical material. While the aesthetic element might sometimes derive from unavoidable, practical circumstances such as distorted or noisy "lo-fi" original tapes and static-tinged radio transmissions, they also demonstrate a conceptual relationship to acousmatic and schizophonic sounds.

The rough edges of these recordings are the sonic analogs of fingerprints, brushstrokes, signatures, and frames. The "real thing" is conveyed by foregrounding the medium and its manipulation. In other words, the recordings make it clear that *someone* recorded and edited the sounds, thereby pulling back a curtain between the sounds' sources and listeners and making the mediation of sound explicit. But they replace it with another curtain that obscures the sources and contexts of sounds. Ultimately, listeners' attention is drawn to various veils between the origins of sounds, their recording and editing, and the act of listening. The low fidelity of many of the recordings evokes the "real" people making and recording the sounds, reminding us that magic has the potential to dwell in any stage of the process: in the moment of performance, in edits, in collage, and in listening. This type of mediation acknowledges and encourages a certain type of reflexivity, vaguely analogous to anthropologists writing in the first person, to acknowledge their complex, messy relationships to other people: their subjects.

III. TRACING THE CONTOURS OF AN AMERICAN TRADITION IN FOLKWAYS, SMITHSONIAN FOLKWAYS, AND SUBLIME FREQUENCIES

While the history of Sublime Frequencies is described elsewhere in this volume, the following brief, fragmentary histories of Folkways and Smithsonian Folkways present affinities, parallels, and differences between and among these projects.[22] All three labels represent a U.S.-based approach to relatively "noncommercial" recordings: specialized, unique releases intended for small audiences.[23] They also incorporate elements of both traditional, exotic recordings and avant-garde approaches to sound, including numerous recordings of nonmusical and ambient sounds. However, the focus of the Smithsonian Folkways catalog has shifted gradually away from avant-garde and nonmusical sounds to focus on the production of high-fidelity recordings of traditional music genres. Finally, all three labels are nourished by a sense of mission that extends well beyond financial or purely aesthetic concerns.

Folkways Records is often associated primarily with American folk music, but it is also a seminal predecessor of multi- and cross-cultural "world music." Like the Sublime Frequencies catalog that it helped inspire, Folkways' releases include musical, documentary, and ambient sounds. The label's radical eclecticism weaves together art, documentary, science, and the experimental avant-garde. Aside from the traditional musical genres with which Folkways is most closely associated, lesser-known albums span an extraordinary collection of avant-garde, experimental, and documentary recordings. These include Bell Telephone Laboratories' *Science of Sound*, which explains aural phenomena such as "Frequency" and "The Doppler Effect"; Jew's harp recordings from Papua New Guinea, Ireland, Italy, the Philippines, the United States, Laos, and Kazakhstan; an astronaut's transmission from outer space; experimental magnetic tape compositions by the iconic Turkish composer İlhan Mimaroğlu; a chorus of frogs in Florida; and on and on.

Like Sublime Frequencies, Folkways began as a U.S.-based label that embraced eclectic music and sounds enthusiastically and unabashedly. Founded by Moses Asch in 1948, Folkways set out to fill gaps in the recording industry and marketplace. During much of its history, Asch and his assistant Marian Distler constituted the entire full-time staff. But despite its modest scale, Folkways released an extraordinarily large and diverse catalog over nearly four decades of business.[24] In this sense, Folkways can be understood as a predigital example of the Long

Tail, an economic and cultural phenomenon in which small quantities of diverse "niche" products amount to a larger portion of a market than popular "hits."[25]

In political and creative terms, Asch described himself as a "goddamn anarchist" and cultivated a powerful ideal—a mission—at Folkways:

> From [Asch's] set of vantage points at the margins of national, cultural, and political identity, Asch was able to grasp the importance of information that would enable others to understand those unlike themselves. He was in this sense a cultural "broker," who although neither attached to nor invested in a single cultural position, dedicated himself to the process by which others mediated understanding across cultural boundaries. His interests were not aligned with those whose music he made available nor with the audience for his records, but with the process of making sounds of other people comprehensible and significant.[26]

Making "other" peoples' sounds significant to listeners is clearly a goal shared by Folkways and Sublime Frequencies. The question of making sounds comprehensible is a very different matter. Alan Bishop has made a compelling argument for *lack* of comprehension as an open, multifaceted approach to musical sounds and—by extension—the people who make them: "The lyrics are not an important thing to me. In fact, it can be a distraction. If I knew the language enough to know it was a horrible love song with stupid lyrics—like most of the popular songs are today in the English language that I hear—then it would be much more of a turnoff than if it would allow me to interpret it from the expressive capabilities of the vocalizing or of the sound itself, which allows me to create my own meaning for it, which elevates it into a higher piece of work for me" (quoted in Beta's chapter in this volume).

The sense of abstraction that Bishop describes in terms of song lyrics—locating recordings as a point of departure for idiosyncratic, aesthetic experience—applies just as well to environmental sounds in the Sublime Frequencies catalog. In fact, this is the essence of acousmatic sound, by which even human language becomes dislocated from source or meaning.

While the Folkways catalog includes numerous environmental sounds, the albums have always been packaged with liner notes, most of which provide explicit context—a conspicuous contrast to Sublime Frequencies' early habit of providing precious little text with their albums. On the 1956 Folkways album *Sounds of a South African Homestead*, for example, Raymond B. Cowles's liner notes begin:

Throughout most of the lands assigned to Zulu and other aboriginal occupation [*sic*] very few of the bird songs recorded here will be heard again. It is only on some of the large white-owned farms, forest preserves and game refuges these birds can survive. The overcrowded lands of the Negro reservations have either been cleared of all bush or soon will be bare except for the scrub thorns and weeds that recapture abandoned land. Even the birds of the open grassland are scarcely managing to eke out a precarious existence in the "native areas," where overgrazing and spreading cultivation leave progressively less undisturbed habitats for their occupation.

The sounds of nature, primarily birds, are presented on Side A of the LP, while Zulu music is presented on Side B. In both instances, the objective is clearly to document beauty that seemed to be disappearing rapidly from existence.

Martine's *Broken Hearted Dragonflies* on Sublime Frequencies has a clear predecessor in the Folkways LP *Sounds of Insects* (1960), which was recorded and annotated by entomologist A. T. Gaul. While Martine's album is presented as an impressionistic and modern listening experience ("insect electronica"), Gaul's is presented as an enduring scholarly and scientific document. In his notes, Gaul includes an abundance of technical detail: "Wing beat tones [*sic*], and other of the audible insect sounds were picked up directly by an Astatic 77 dynamic cardioid microphone. The internal sounds of the activity of insect flight muscles were picked up through a special probe affixed to RCA 5734 electro-mechanical transducer tube feeding into specially built preamp." Likewise, Folkways' *Sounds of North American Frogs: The Biological Significance of Voice in Frogs* (1958) offers an entire album of frog sounds. Less scientific in tone but just as literal, Folkways' *Sounds of Yoga-Vedanta* (1962) is "a documentary of life in an Indian ashram."

Portable and affordable recording technologies—phonographs, magnetic tape, and digital devices—have played a crucial role in the development of both Folkways and Sublime Frequencies. Not incidentally, these same innovations have enabled new types of environmental, ambient sound recording and avant-garde musical experiments. For Folkways, the medium and the message coalesced beautifully: Accessible recording technology made exotic sounds much easier to record and publish, and a low-cost (albeit rigorous) workflow fit neatly within the label's eclectic, populist sensibilities. In this setting, field recordings by ethnographers became a vital source of material for the Folkways catalog.

The Ethnic Folkways series in particular offers recordings from a wide variety of sources: A 1947 issue of *Downbeat* magazine described it as "an educational rather than a musical set . . . of interest to anthropologists, folklorists and perhaps dance students."[27] The series was curated by Harold Courlander, among "a dying breed of self-trained ethnographers whose enthusiasm for and sensitivity to world ethnic music resulted in some of the most important collecting of the midcentury."[28] Initially, the Ethnic series offered recordings from Haiti, Cuba, and Ethiopia made by Courlander himself. A half-century later, an oblique line connects the work of Folkways and Sublime Frequencies: Both epitomize a radically eclectic, semi-outsider ("self-trained"), American approach to exotic music. These labels simultaneously embrace and stand apart from the conventions of "-ologies" and "-ographies" that characterize more formal, university-based scholarship.

Composer, pianist, and scholar Henry Cowell—whose work exemplifies the fertile relationship between avant-garde art and ethnography—also became closely involved with Folkways' Ethnic series. Cowell often employed non-Western traditional forms as a point of departure for his artistic experiments, and his liner notes provided detailed, rigorously researched information about exotic music on its own terms. In the notes to his five-volume *Music of the World's People*, he wrote: "All of this music contains richly rewarding values. That which may seem raucous at first may come to sound beautiful on further hearing, and at the very least, it will be found to be full of meaning and feeling. There is no better way to know a people than to enter with them into their musical life."[29] While tracks were paired meticulously with descriptive information, Cowell declined to organize the collection according to ethnicity, style, history, or geography. He instead offered an expansive "sampling of widely contrasted music from many levels of culture and many parts of the world."[30]

Harry Smith, best known as the force behind Folkways' legendary *Anthology of American Folk Music* (1952) and numerous influential, avant-garde films, represents another direct, crucial link between cultural flows traversing traditional music and a radical avant-garde. As explained by Cowell:

> Smith's imagination led him eventually to approach song neither narrowly as literature nor entirely as a window to the understanding of other cultures. Smith could conclude that his "projects are only attempts to build up a series of objects that allow some sort of generalizations to be made—regarding the popularity of visual or auditory themes." Yet he did not undertake the fieldwork or the writing that would have allowed him to make generalizations of this order about his collections. Rather, like the Beats with whom he would eventually join forces, the exploration of alien cultural forms in the end was a

self-referential project . . . In the arrangement of the music and notes within *Anthology* we see the operation of a lively avant-garde imagination for which folk music has become, above all, a mental plaything.[31]

This description of Smith's work could certainly be applied to the Sublime Frequencies catalog: Both approach the publication of lesser-known sounds for Western audiences as a dissident artistic endeavor, and the intuitive bases of their working methods serve as alternatives to more conventional scholarly or commercial approaches to similar material and themes.

The work of Tony Schwartz—another seminal figure in the history of Folkways—brings us back to the concept of ambient and environmental sound. A visionary sound engineer, collector, archivist, and theorist, Schwartz produced thirteen albums for Folkways.[32] According to Peter Goldsmith, "Schwartz's work was deliberately noncommercial, which must have appealed to Asch instantly. Asch immediately understood the purpose of Schwartz's work, and its spontaneity fit perfectly into Asch's idea of the authentic. At the same time, the idea that in 1952 one might find authentic folklore on the streets of New York was relatively novel. Schwartz provided Asch with the first concrete evidence that folklore was not an exclusively rural phenomenon, nor was it necessarily tainted or corrupted when transplanted to urban settings."[33]

Schwartz's now-classic recordings include *New York 19, Nueva York: A Tape Documentary of Puerto Rican New Yorkers*, and *Sound Effects, Vol. 1: City Sounds*. In *The World in My Mail Box* (1958), Schwartz applied a remarkable pre-Internet crowdsourcing approach to audio recording, which he introduced by declaring: "The widespread possession of the inexpensive magnetic recorder makes it possible for people all over the world to exchange recordings. This record will give you a few of the more than 10,000 folk recordings I have exchanged with people in more than forty countries. Although the exchange I established was mainly musical, you can see the possibilities for any type of audible material."[34] Schwartz's productions often employ narrative voice-overs offering the type of literal context typical of radio programs and documentary films, but his use of field recordings also includes abstract, collage-based conventions of avant-garde art.

Near the end of his life, Folkways founder Asch searched for a way to ensure that the label would carry on. After several unsuccessful attempts to sell the label outright, Asch began discussions with Ralph Rinzler, the artistic director of the Smithsonian Institution's Folklife Festival, who recognized the cultural and historical significance of the catalog. Shortly after Asch's death in 1986, his family formalized the donation of Folkways to the Smithsonian Institution with one crucial and unusual condition: Every recording would be made available to the general public, regardless of sales. The Folkways catalog became the basis for Smithsonian Recordings, a nonprofit record label of the United States' national museum. Ethnomusicologist and archivist Anthony Seeger was appointed the first director of Smithsonian Folkways, guided by a broad mission: "supporting cultural diversity and increased understanding among peoples through the documentation, preservation, and dissemination of sound."[35]

Since its inception, Smithsonian Folkways has acquired a number of important defunct labels, including Cook, Paredon, Monitor, and Dyer-Bennet. Like Folkways, the Cook Records catalog includes landmark non-Western music, as well as nonmusical and experimental recordings. A 1961 album titled *Radio Moscow and the Western Hemisphere*, now published and distributed by Smithsonian Folkways, resonates particularly well with much of the Sublime Frequencies catalog. A promotional text describes the recording as "an ambitious project to compile 'a digest of current Russian comment[ary]'":

> [T]his recording draws together excerpts of propaganda purportedly broadcast on Radio Moscow (we're promised an "all authentic shortwave recorded direct from Moscow"). These excerpts, out of context in their brevity and interpolation, cover a broad spectrum of topics including religion, segregation, the police state and US imperialism; all fall under the general heading of the Cold War. One radio voice assures us, "Yes, my friends, there are crackpots and malcontents in every society." All commentary is in English.

The goals of Smithsonian Folkways include an embrace of cultural and musical difference, amounting to an earnest effort to represent an exotic "other" to Western audiences with ethical integrity. In a 2007 interview, Smithsonian Folkways' associate director Atesh Sonneborn explained the label's basic approach:

> In the old, colonialist period . . . we've got collectors going out. The Smithsonian was founded on this principle. It comes out of the British model. You go to a far away place, you find things that are novel, exotic, strange, unique. You bring them back. We can bring them back without taking them. We can bring them back and give back to those who are willing to share. We can give back to the cultures. We can give back to the artists, or their heirs if they're no longer with us. This is not the old model. This is a new model of collecting . . .

Because much of what is in the collection is stuff that the audience that might encounter it by searching online would identify as . . . Strange. And when you identify Strange, you can respond to it with curiosity or fear. To enhance the curiosity, we have the original liner notes, which are a key element. We have stronger indexing than you find on any commercial website. And more and more, we have video and photographic content to provide far more than any liner notes—even great liner notes—could ever do . . . People have a gateway where they can really encounter the cultural "other" on their own terms, and on its own terms.[36]

Clearly, representing cultures "on their own terms" is not a simple matter: the very idea of collecting represents a complex, problematic interaction. For example, the liner notes to Smithsonian Folkways releases are very seldom composed by the musicians themselves. Likewise, listeners cannot encounter exotic music "on its own terms" through recordings that are produced, presented, packaged, and distributed in extremely standardized, specialized ways. The "old" model described by Sonneborn could be said to echo Sublime Frequencies' approach, but it is worth emphasizing that Sublime Frequencies does not presume to provide the same type of content or context as Smithsonian Folkways. Rather, Sublime Frequencies' approach can be understood as an attempt to bypass issues of representation and context by dealing with the recordings in a more intuitive, abstract way.

IV. CULTIVATING ART, ETHNOGRAPHY, MUSIC, AND SOUND

The Sublime Frequencies, Folkways, and Smithsonian Folkways labels represent distinct, yet closely related approaches to the dissemination of exotic music. Despite their profound influence, all three labels have a *very* small market. Their limited circulations allow extraordinary levels of independence and eclecticism; inversely, their eclectic and obscure offerings also place severe limits on their circulation.[37] For better and/or worse, the sounds come from far and wide, but their audiences are concentrated overwhelmingly in centers of political power and economic prosperity.

The sounds published by these labels performs two key functions: (1) contextualizing lesser-known traditions and artistic innovations, thus expanding our sense of collective diversity; and (2) conveying aesthetic and emotional content through distant and unfamiliar contexts, thus offering aesthetic and cultural escapism. In this abstract second function, musical and ambient sounds become vehicles for emotion and imagination—raw materials for various kinds of collage. However, Sublime Frequencies and Smithsonian Folkways have both moved away from ambient and experimental sounds, focusing instead on more conventional music recordings. In one sense, this is an unfortunate shift to a more conservative approach. Yet this change in focus also represents an admirable, conspicuous move from anonymity (nameless or "various" artists) to giving rightful authorship and credit to individuals and ensembles. The move away from ambient sound can also be understood as reflecting an innate difference between (a) musical recordings as commercially viable products and (b) ambient and nonmusical recordings as esoteric archival documents.

Many of the founders and innovators in the discipline of ethnomusicology have been intimately involved in recording, archiving, and publishing exotic sounds: Carl Stumpf, Erich von Hornbostel, and Curt Sachs developed the Berlin Phonogramm-Archiv at the beginning of the twentieth century, establishing a close relationship between recording and scholarship that has now endured more than a century. In a recent survey of approaches to sound within anthropology, Samuels et al. infer that "the invention of sound machines was part of a collection of epistemological practices of purification of sound, which sought to abstract sound from its immediate surroundings while noting its connectivity to place."[38]

Ironically, interviews with the cofounders of Sublime Frequencies have expressed contempt for ethnomusicologists and anthropologists:

(INTERVIEWER) LARRY DOLMAN: Have you gotten many criticisms, or should I say "critical readings," that accuse you of imperialist or colonialist tendencies? How do you respond?

HISHAM MAYET: If those criticisms have been made, then my response would be that it's really a kind of reverse imperialist/colonialist agenda. I think our presence out there encourages these people to appreciate their culture as it is, and by recording and distributing their art and aesthetic I think we are immortalizing their message to the world. You know anyone that makes that argument is guilty of an imperialist/colonialist agenda. I don't separate myself from "those people." I am one of them, so it's not as if one should treat them as if they belong in a fish tank or an anthropological museum, no! I sleep in their homes, eat their food and drink their tea. I think [Sublime Frequencies] is presenting this material as a living breathing form of human expression. It's not the academic, objective accountability of the material, it's about a raw, impressionistic and wholly subjective ecstatic experience. I hope that the material translates that passion.[39]

In this instance, an imagined "critical reading" places Mayet in a defensive posture, instigating a circular argument against a straw man. How does Mayet address "these people" and "their" culture while asserting that he is "one of them"? This "inside/outside" dilemma has been a central concern for anthropology and ethnomusicology since the 1980s, and both disciplines continue to depend on participant observation—that is, conducting "fieldwork" while living *with* people during extended periods of research into their ways of life. The goal of sharing a "raw, impressionistic and wholly subjective ecstatic" experience is not at odds with ethnography; on the contrary, a considerable and growing body of scholarship emphasizes precisely these goals.[40] The more important and interesting questions explore various ways that media—recordings, images, and texts like those published by Sublime Frequencies—simultaneously enable *and* limit transmissions of experience.

The work of Sublime Frequencies deftly avoids many of the pitfalls of disseminating art across cultural boundaries and grey areas, allowing listeners to encounter new and foreign sounds without presuming to explain or pigeonhole the sounds' sources or listeners. If we take the goal of ethnography to be the documentation and understanding of human culture, then the work of Sublime Frequencies occupies an intimate space and agenda within ethnomusicology and anthropology, particularly some of the powerful streams within these disciplines that emphasize artistic and subjective approaches to knowledge, experience, and truth.

Sublime Frequencies' primary audience seems to consist of Euro-American denizens of college radio, independent rock venues, and online arbiters of musical taste such as *Pitchfork* and *Vice*. That said, I suspect ethnomusicologists are more likely than members of any other profession to buy Sublime Frequencies releases, based—if nothing else—on an attraction to foreign, lesser-known cultures and their sounds. In this light, the scornful posture toward academics adopted by Mayet and Bishop is misplaced and unfortunate:

(INTERVIEWER) ANDY BETA: Ethnomusicology just left the field, climbed up inside the ivory tower, and has been firmly ensconced there ever since.
ALAN BISHOP: And they have their exclusivity and how they have their papers

written and recordings filed away and there's no access to them unless you're a member of their club. You have to kiss their ass to get in to it and pay them money to get in. That's the only way you can get it. Which is worse. I look at what we're doing as practical work in things like that, weighing our options and trying to do the best we can as we move along, learning as we go and we're making it up as we go along and sidestepping the whole thing and just getting our work done in the only way we have the means to do so without the funding and power machine that the institutions have. It still can make an impact.[41]

Mayet's and Bishop's disdain is difficult for me to understand. At its worst, it seems like the kind of reactionary, anti-intellectual stance more typical of the xenophobic right wing in the United States than Sublime Frequencies' populist, cosmopolitan xenophilia. Or perhaps it is simply part of a wholesale, defensive mistrust. Who are the models for Mayet's and Bishop's sinister, profit-driven vision? Not Jean Rouch, the artist-anthropologist who—like Mayet—made so many wonderful, heartfelt films in Niger.[42] Or Rouch's scion Paul Stoller, who also lived and conducted research in Niger. Or even Marcel Griaule, Rouch and Stoller's colonial-era predecessor in Niger.[43]

In my work as an artist and ethnomusicologist, I have found that artists and publishers are usually more concerned with money, prestige, and exclusivity than are academics. Likewise, I have met many ethnomusicologists whose primary interest lies in the warm-blooded, mysterious aspects of art and life. In fact, Sublime Frequencies' labors share a great deal with serious ethnomusicologists: most notably, a genuine commitment to the value of music, sounds, people, and places outside mainstream narratives.

Despite dubious claims to the contrary ("we're making it up as we go along"), the work of Sublime Frequencies has worthy predecessors. Some are mentioned in this essay, while many others are not; some, but not all, are based in powerful institutions; and only some are ethnomusicologists. The promotional mission statement for Sublime Frequencies quoted in the introduction to this volume mentions numerous "pioneering" labels of the past.

In this light, the history of Sublime Frequencies is not being written on a blank slate. To the contrary, this essay is meant to emphasize continuity and affinity be-tween the work of Sublime Frequencies and other labels more closely associated with anthropology and ethnomusicology. My view is that Sublime Frequencies is intimately related to labels like Folkways and Smithsonian Folkways. Viewed collectively and in historical context, they constitute a vibrant publishing tradition that blurs distinctions among art, documentary, and ethnography, conjuring a no man's land in which strategies for the sonic representation of culture collapse into one another or expand. However, a comparative view also emphasizes the exceptional, enduring, and radical nature of Asch's work at Folkways. Ambient and nonmusical sounds play an intrinsically important—and sadly, often neglected—role in documenting and understanding our world and its people; they are also a useful indicator of a recording label's orientation within the larger fields of art and culture. As these venerable labels' histories continue to unfold, ambient sounds may reflect the extent to which they confine themselves to a narrow musical marketplace or expand the scope of their contributions to create a more diverse, artful, and eclectic record of our world.

NOTES

1. Alan Bishop, *Night Recordings from Bali,* Sublime Frequencies, SF003, CD, 2003.

2. Sublime Frequencies' website, sublimefrequencies.com.

3. R. Murray Schafer, *The Soundscape* (Rochester, Vt.: Destiny Books, 1993). For a recent review of these issues from an anthropological perspective, see David W. Samuels, Louise Meintjes, Ana Maria Ochoa, and Thomas Porcello, "Soundscapes: Toward a Sounded Anthropology," *Annual Review of Anthropology* 39 (2010): 329–45.

4. This use of the term "ambient sound" should not be confused with "ambient music," coined by Brian Eno in 1978 (*Ambient 1: Music for Airports*, EG Editions, LP, 1978), and subsequently used to designate a subgenre of electronic and electroacoustic music. See Mark Prendergast, *The Ambient Century: From Mahler to Trance—The Evolution of Sound in the Electronic Age* (New York: Bloomsbury, 2000), for a thought-provoking, ambient-themed (and mostly Euro-American) history of music in the twentieth century. See Simon Reynolds, "Brian Eno: Taking Manhattan (By Strategy)," *Red Bull Music Academy,* April 25, 2013, www.redbullmusicacademy.com/magazine/brian-eno-in-nyc-feature, for an account of the approach to "ethnomusicological" and "exotic ethnic" sounds adopted by Eno and his collaborators, including David Byrne, who recalled, "We would hole up and make fake ethnographic records, with the sleeve notes and everything . . . We'd invent a whole culture to go with it."

5. An analogous relationship between ethnography and visual art is explored in Alex Coles, ed., *Site-Specific: The Ethnographic Turn* (London: Black Dog Publishing, 2000). Along similar lines, Kristine Stiles recently used sonic metaphor to describe Robert Rauschenberg's collage-based, multimedia interventions in visual art as "a cacophony of cultures." Stiles, ed., *Rauschenberg: Collecting and Connecting* (Durham, N.C.: Nasher,

2014). It is worth noting that a robust literature on this relationship exists in Latin America. See Juan Carlos Olivares Toledo, *El umbral roto: escritos en antropología poética* (Santiago de Chile: Fondo Matta/Museo Chileno de Arte Precolombino, 1995), and the larger body of work published in Chile by Fondo Matta.

6. I use the term "exotic" in a mostly literal and commonsense way, as a synonym for "unfamiliar," "foreign," or "outside." But it is intended as a necessary provocation. First, referring to "exotic" recordings and cultures invokes some of the messy and inherently problematic dimensions of this essay's subject: U.S.-based labels that specialize in marketing and selling recordings of non-Western music and sound to Western audiences. Inevitably, questions of authenticity and ownership quickly arise. However, my use of "exotic" is not necessarily pejorative; it should not be confused with Euro-American traditions of exoticism that tend to aestheticize or objectify "Other" people and cultures as *essentially* obscure, primitive, or dissimilar.

7. David Dunn, "Nature, Sound Art, and the Sacred," in *The Book of Music and Nature*, ed. David Rothenberg and Marta Ulvaeus (Middletown, Conn.: Wesleyan University Press, 2001).

8. Ibid., 9.

9. Joe Wensley, "Interview: Founder of Sublime Frequencies Alan Bishop," *Sweet and Sound* (February 2010), www.sweetandsound.co.uk/2010/02/interview-founder -of-sublime-frequencies-alan-bishop/. On Burroughs and Gysin, see Olivares Toledo, *El umbral roto*; Daniel Odier, *The Job: Interviews with William S. Burroughs* (New York: Grove Press, 1974); William S. Burroughs, *The Soft Machine* (New York: Grove Press, 1966 [1961]); Burroughs, *The Ticket That Exploded* (New York: Grove Press, 1967 [1962]); Burroughs, *Nova Express* (New York: Grove Press, 1964), as well as briongysin.com (accessed August 11, 2011).

10. Quoted in Odier, *The Job*, 33.

11. Quoted in Wensley, "Interview: Founder of Sublime Frequencies Alan Bishop."

12. See Michael C. Vazquez, "Disorientalism," *Bidoun*, 2010, www.bidoun.org /magazine/10-technology/disorientalism-by-michael-c-vazquez/.

13. See Charlie Bertsch, "Subverting World Music," *Tikkun*, www.tikkun.org/article. php/Bertsch-subverting-world-music.

14. Sublime Frequencies' use of ambient sounds raises intriguing practical questions regarding the label's workflow (planning, selection, editing, design, reproduction, distribution, sales, etc.), criteria for publication (both implicit and explicit), and network of audiences and distribution. Unfortunately, these questions remain beyond the scope of this essay.

15. Some notable examples of ethnomusicologists' engagement with these issues include Steven Feld, "From Schizophonia to Schismogenesis: On the Discourses and Commodification Practices of 'World Music' and 'World Beat,'" in *Music Grooves: Essays and*

Dialogues, ed. Charles Keil and Steven Feld (Chicago: University of Chicago Press, 1994); Feld, "A Sweet Lullaby for World Music," *Public Culture* 12, no. 1 (2000): 145–71; Jocelyne Guilbault, "Interpreting World Music: A Challenge in Theory and Practice," *Popular Music* 16 (1977):31–44; Guilbault, "On Redefining the 'Local' through World Music," in *Ethnomusicology: A Contemporary Reader*, ed. Jennifer C. Post (New York: Routledge, 2006); Louise Meintjes, "Paul Simon's Graceland, South Africa, and the Mediation of Musical Meaning," *Ethnomusicology* 34, no. 1 (1990): 37–73; Timothy D. Taylor, *Global Pop: World Music, World Markets* (New York: Routledge, 1997); Taylor, *Strange Sounds: Music, Technology & Culture* (New York: Routledge, 2001); Taylor, *Beyond Exoticism: Western Music and the World* (Durham, N.C., 2007); Paul Théberge, "Ethnic Sounds": The Economy and Discourse of World Music Sampling," in *Music and Technoculture*, ed. René T. A. Lysloff and Leslie C. Gay, Jr. (Middletown, Conn.: Wesleyan University Press, 2003); and Hugo Zemp, "The/An Ethnomusicologist and the Music Business," *Yearbook for Traditional Music* 28 (1996): 36–56. For a review, see Martin Stokes, "Music and the Global Order," *Annual Review of Anthropology* 33 (2004): 47–72. See also Huib Schippers, "Tradition, Authenticity, and Context: The Case for a Dynamic Approach," *British Journal of Music Education* 23, no. 3 (2006): 333–49; and David Font-Navarrete, "'File Under Import': Musical Distortion, Exoticism, and *Authenticité* in Congotronics," *Ethnomusicology Review* 16 (2011), ethnomusicologyreview.ucla.edu/journal/volume/16/piece/460.

16. Pierre Schaeffer, "Acousmatics," in *Audio Culture: Readings in Modern Music*, ed. Cristoph Cox and Daniel Warner (New York: Continuum, 2004 [1966]), 79.

17. Ibid., 81.

18. R. Murray Schafer, *The Tuning of the World* (New York: Alfred A. Knopf, 1977), 90. See also Schafer's *The Soundscape*. For a recent and provocative contribution that suggests listening "against" and "beyond" soundscapes, see Stefan Helmreich, "Listening Against Soundscapes," *Anthropology News* 51, no. 9 (2010): 10.

19. Schaeffer, "Acousmatics," 81.

20. Schafer, *The Tuning of the World*, 90; and Feld, "From Schizophonia to Schismogenesis."

21. See also David Novak, "The Sublime Frequencies of New Old Media," *Public Culture* 23, no. 3 (Durham: Duke University Press, 2011): 603–34.

22. For detailed histories of Moses Asch's Folkways Records, see Peter D. Goldsmith, *Making People's Music: Moe Asch and Folkways Records* (Washington, D.C.: Smithsonian Institution Press, 1998); Tony Olmsted, *Folkways Records: Moses Asch and His Encyclopedia of Sound* (New York: Routledge, 2003); Richard Carlin, *Worlds of Sound: The Story of Smithsonian Folkways* (New York: HarperCollins, 2008).

23. Of the three labels, Smithsonian Folkways is the only one that employs a not-for-profit structure.

24. See Goldsmith, *Making People's Music;* Olmsted, *Folkways Records;* and Carlin, *Worlds of Sound.*

25. Chris Anderson, *The Long Tail: Why the Future of Business Is Selling Less of More* (New York: Hyperion, 2006).

26. Goldsmith, *Making People's Music,* 4–5.

27. Ibid., 200.

28. Ibid., 198.

29. From Henry Cowell's liner notes to *Music of the World's People: Vol. 1* (1951). Available at www.folkways.si.edu/albumdetails.aspx?itemid=902.

30. Goldsmith, *Making People's Music,* 235.

31. Cowell, liner notes to *Music of the World's People,* 239–41. Smith's original booklet for the *Anthology of American Folk Music* is available at www.folkways.si.edu/albumdetails .aspx?itemid=2426.

32. See www.tonyschwartz.org and David Suisman, "Listening to the City," *Smithsonian Folkways Magazine,* 2012, www.folkways.si.edu/magazine/2012_fall_winter/cover_story .aspx.

33. Goldsmith, *Making People's Music,* 247.

34. Ibid.

35. See www.folkways.si.edu/about_us/mission_history.aspx (accessed August 11, 2011).

36. Personal communication.

37. In the case of Smithsonian Folkways, a commitment to accessibility is expressed as a mandate to keep their entire catalog "in print." See www.folkways.si.edu/about_us /mission_history.aspx.

38. Samuels et al., "Soundscapes," 330.

39. Larry Dolman, "Hisham Mayet of Sublime Frequencies," *Blastitude,* 2006, http:// blastitude.com/19/MAYET.htm.

40. For one scholar's example, see Paul Stoller and Cheryl Olkes, *In Sorcery's Shadow: A Memoir of Apprenticeship among the Songhay of Niger* (Chicago: University of Chicago Press, 1987); Stoller, *Fusion of the Worlds: An Ethnography of Possession among the Songhay of Niger* (Chicago: University of Chicago Press, 1989); Stoller, *The Cinematic Griot: The Ethnography of Jean Rouch* (Chicago: University of Chicago Press, 1992); Stoller, *Embodying Colonial Memories: Spirit Possession, Power, and the Hauka in West Africa* (New York: Routledge, 1995); Stoller, *Sensuous Scholarship* (Philadelphia: University of Pennsylvania Press, 1997).

41. See Andy Beta's chapter in this volume.

42. See *Jean Rouch: Screening Room with Robert Gardner,* dir. by Robert Gardner (1980; Watertown, Mass.: Documentary Educational Resources, 2004), DVD; Jean Rouch, *Ciné-Ethnography,* ed. Steven Feld (Minneapolis: University of Minnesota Press, 2003); Stoller, *The Cinematic Griot.*

43. See James Clifford, "Power and Dialog in Ethnography: Marcel Griaule's Initiation," in *Observers Observed: Essays on Ethnographic Fieldwork* (Madison: University of Wisconsin Press, 1983).

BIBLIOGRAPHY

Anderson, Chris. *The Long Tail: Why the Future of Business Is Selling Less of More*. New York: Hyperion, 2006.

Bertsch, Charlie. "Subverting World Music." *Tikkun*. www.tikkun.org/article.php/Bertsch -subverting-world-music.

Burroughs, William S. *Nova Express*. New York: Grove Press. 1964.

——. *The Soft Machine*. New York: Grove Press, 1966 [1961].

——. *The Ticket That Exploded*. New York: Grove Press, 1967 [1962].

Carlin, Richard. *Worlds of Sound: The Story of Smithsonian Folkways*. New York: HarperCollins, 2008.

Coles, Alex, ed. *Site-Specific: The Ethnographic Turn*. London: Black Dog Publishing, 2000.

Cowell, Henry. Liner notes to *Music of the World's People: Vol. 1* (1951). Available at www .folkways.si.edu/albumdetails.aspx?itemid=902.

Dolman, Larry. "Hisham Mayet of Sublime Frequencies." *Blastitude*. 2006. blastitude. com/19/MAYET.htm.

Dunn, David. "Nature, Sound Art, and the Sacred." In *The Book of Music and Nature*, edited by David Rothenberg and Marta Ulvaeus, 95–107. Middletown, Conn.: Wesleyan University Press, 2001.

Eno, Brian. *Ambient 1: Music for Airports*. EG Editions, LP, 1978.

Feld, Steven. "From Schizophonia to Schismogenesis: On the Discourses and Commodification Practices of 'World Music' and 'World Beat.'" In *Music Grooves: Essays and Dialogues*, edited by Charles Keil and Steven Feld, 257–89. Chicago: University of Chicago Press, 1994.

——. "A Sweet Lullaby for World Music." *Public Culture* 12, no. 1 (2000): 145–171.

Font-Navarrete, David. "'File Under Import': Musical Distortion, Exoticism, and *Authenticité* in Congotronics." *Ethnomusicology Review* 16 (2011). ethnomusicologyreview. ucla.edu/journal/volume/16/piece/460.

Goldsmith, Peter D. *Making People's Music: Moe Asch and Folkways Records*. Washington, D.C.: Smithsonian Institution Press, 1998.

Guilbault, Jocelyne. "Interpreting World Music: A Challenge in Theory and Practice." *Popular Music* 16 (1997): 31–44.

——. "On Redefining the 'Local' through World Music." In *Ethnomusicology: A Contemporary Reader*, edited by Jennifer C. Post. New York: Routledge. 2006.

Helmreich, Stefan. "Listening Against Soundscapes." *Anthropology News* 51, no. 9 (2010): 10.

Jean Rouch: Screening Room with Robert Gardner, dir. by Robert Gardner (1980; Watertown, Mass.: Documentary Educational Resources, 2004), DVD.

Meintjes, Louise. "Paul Simon's Graceland, South Africa, and the Mediation of Musical Meaning." *Ethnomusicology* 34, no. 1 (1990): 37–73.

Mellow, James R. "The Stein Salon Was the First Museum of Modern Art." *New York Times*. December 1, 1968. www.nytimes.com/books/98/05/03/specials/stein-salon.html.

Odier, Daniel. *The Job: Interviews with William S. Burroughs*. New York: Grove Press, 1974.

Olivares Toledo, Juan Carlos. *El umbral roto: escritos en antropología poetica*. Santiago de Chile: Fondo Matta/Museo Chileno de Arte Precolombino, 1995.

Olmsted, Tony. *Folkways Records: Moses Asch and His Encyclopedia of Sound*. New York: Routledge, 2003.

Prendergast, Mark. *The Ambient Century: From Mahler to Trance—The Evolution of Sound in the Electronic Age*. New York: Bloomsbury, 2000.

Reynolds, Simon. "Brian Eno: Taking Manhattan (By Strategy)." Red Bull Music Academy. April 25, 2013. www.redbullmusicacademy.com/magazine/brian-eno-in-nyc-feature.

Rouch, Jean. *Ciné-Ethnography*. Edited and translated by Steven Feld. Minneapolis: University of Minnesota Press, 2003.

Samuels, David W., Louise Meintjes, Ana Maria Ochoa, and Thomas Porcello. "Soundscapes: Toward a Sounded Anthropology." *Annual Review of Anthropology* 39 (2010): 329–45.

Schafer, R. Murray. *The Soundscape*. Rochester, Vt.: Destiny Books, 1993.

——— . *The Tuning of the World*. New York: Alfred A. Knopf, 1977.

Schaeffer, Pierre. "Acousmatics." In *Audio Culture: Readings in Modern Music*, edited by Cristoph Cox and Daniel Warner, 76–81. New York: Continuum. 2004 [1966].

Schippers, Huib. "Tradition, Authenticity, and Context: the Case for a Dynamic Approach." *British Journal of Music Education* 23, no. 3 (2006): 333–49.

Small, Christopher. *Music, Society, Education*. Middletown, Conn.: Wesleyan University Press, 1996.

Stiles, Kristine, ed. *Rauschenberg: Collecting and Connecting*. Durham, N.C.: Nasher Museum of Art at Duke University, 2014.

Stokes, Martin. "Music and the Global Order." *Annual Review of Anthropology* 33 (2004): 47–72.

Stoller, Paul. *The Cinematic Griot: The Ethnography of Jean Rouch*. Chicago: University of Chicago Press, 1992.

——— . *Embodying Colonial Memories: Spirit Possession, Power, and the Hauka in West Africa*. New York: Routledge, 1995.

——— . *Fusion of the Worlds: An Ethnography of Possession among the Songhay of Niger*. Chicago: University of Chicago Press, 1989.

——— . *Sensuous Scholarship*. Philadelphia: University of Pennsylvania Press, 1997.

Stoller, Paul, and Cheryl Olkes. *In Sorcery's Shadow: A Memoir of Apprenticeship among the Songhay of Niger.* Chicago: University of Chicago Press, 1987.

Sublime Frequencies. Website. www.sublimefrequencies.com.

Suisman, David. "Listening to the City." *Smithsonian Folkways Magazine.* 2012. www.folkways.si.edu/magazine/2012_fall_winter/cover_story.aspx.

Taylor, Timothy D. *Beyond Exoticism: Western Music and the World.* Durham, N.C.: Duke University Press, 2007.

———. *Global Pop: World Music, World Markets.* New York: Routledge, 1997.

———. *Strange Sounds: Music, Technology and Culture.* New York: Routledge, 2001.

Théberge, Paul. 'Ethnic Sounds': The Economy and Discourse of World Music Sampling." In *Music and Technoculture,* edited by René T. A. Lysloff and Leslie C. Gay, Jr., 93–108. Middletown, Conn.: Wesleyan University Press, 2003.

Vazquez, Michael C. "Disorientalism." *Bidoun.* 2010. www.bidoun.org/magazine/10-technology/disorientalism-by-michael-c-vazquez.

Wensley, Joe. "Interview: Founder of Sublime Frequencies Alan Bishop." *Sweet and Sound.* February 2010. www.sweetandsound.co.uk/2010/02/interview-founder-of-sublime-frequencies-alan-bishop/.

Zemp, Hugo. "The/An Ethnomusicologist and the Music Business." *Yearbook for Traditional Music* 28 (1996): 36–56.

Zorn, John. Liner notes to *The Big Gundown: John Zorn Plays the Music of Ennio Morricone.* Elektra Nonesuch 9 71939–2, CD, 1986.

INTERLUDE

Sublime Frequencies
Listener Interviews

MICHAEL E. VEAL

Interview with Chris Becker

Composer

JANUARY 24, 2015

MICHAEL E. VEAL: How did you encounter the Sublime Frequencies recordings, and how do they factor into your own creative process?

CHRIS BECKER: Back when I was a student in Ohio—I remember walking the halls, and there was one faculty member in particular, a guy named Vaughn Wiester, who's a trombone player and big-band director. And he would just stop us and give us records . . . It was outside-the-classroom learning, right? You never knew when Vaughn was gonna pop up, kind of like Santa Claus, and say, "Hey, have you checked this out?" And we were freshman, sophomores—we hadn't heard of this stuff. And a lot of this stuff he was giving us was music from around the world. For example, there was a great recording on Nonesuch of the [Balinese] *Ketjak*, the "Monkey Chant," where the chant took up one whole side of the record.[1] So, music from around the world, or outside of America started coming to me that way.

I'm kind of speaking about "world music" in very broad terms. It's almost like you were digesting the music and you didn't really look at the long history behind it. It's kind of like, "I like Brazilian music"—well, what does that mean? Well, that's something that maybe comes later. Or, "I like the Monkey Chant"—well, what is it? "Well, I don't know, but it sounds cool." At that point, it's just sound. The critical thinking part of it comes later.

So, all this kind of leads me to the spirit of how I came across Sublime Frequencies. Other composers might speak very specifically about musical influences—you know, "This impacted the way I started playing guitar," for instance, or, "I wrote some songs after hearing this particular artist." I can speak to the Sublime Frequencies recordings as a composer and an engineer, as somebody mixing music.

The first recording on that label that came across my radar was the *Bush Taxi Mali* album.[2] I liked the idea of going out "in the street," as it were, and capturing things as they happen in real time. What struck me was hearing a recording where "the sounds of the field" are just as important as "the music." It wasn't just recordings of musicians. I like the fact that street sounds themselves—the ambience of the city—are also a part of the recording and, for me, the composition. It's not, "We've got four musicians on the stage, we fan them out, we make sure the mix is beautiful, etc., and you cut when they're done making music." It's that what you hear on the radio, what you hear outside the window, the sound of animals around you, the sound of conversation—I think all of that makes recordings so alive. And that's something that is a big part of the music that I make—this idea that everything can go into the pot. As a composer, I'm saying, "I can shape this—I can take all of this field stuff and I can turn it into something else, and take people on an imaginary journey into wherever I want to take them."

The Bishop brothers, they've introduced things like just turning the radio on and recording, like, "What's playing in Egypt?" or "What's playing in Syria?" I like that as an attitude, but I also like it compositionally and artistically. You know, a transistor kind of aesthetic.

There's also a quote, I don't remember if it was Richard or Alan Bishop. But they talked about the recordings they started making around the world during their travels, and one of them said something to the effect of, "You don't need a grant, you don't need thousands of dollars to do this, you don't need to go to school to study, you don't need to do tons of research, you've just gotta go do it." Even as the Sun City Girls, they were putting out one recording after another. Regardless of how you might feel about the music, there's this whole culture of folks out there who are just passionate about making sound, making a statement, being creative. They're not necessarily trained musicians—but they make one cassette after another—beautifully designed, with draftsmanship and artwork. I think that's something really important. That sense of industry—you keep making stuff. Keep putting it out there . . . There's a spirit there that's important, and kind of keeps me going: Do It Yourself. After all, the industry has changed drastically since the *Bush Taxi Mali* recording [2004], and the issues that musicians have to deal with are still shaking themselves out.

I came up at a time when there was no Internet; you learned by just trading fanzines or notebooks or getting together and playing records—that whole punk world with bands like Black Flag, Hüsker Dü—and I think a lot of that I carried into the conservatory, where maybe it didn't really belong [laughs]. But it's wonderful to blend everything. It's that kind of punk rock aesthetic, but applied to an area that, at least in our society, the academics have traditionally been in charge of. So, if I'm interested in something, if I want to do it, I find a way to do it, because I have a passion for it.

NOTES

1. *Golden Rain*, originally released on the Nonesuch Explorer series in 1969 as Nonesuch H-72028.

2. *Bush Taxi Mali,* Sublime Frequencies SF012, 2004.

Interview with Ethan Holtzman

Keyboardist and Co-Founder

of Dengue Fever

JANUARY 17, 2015

E. TAMMY KIM: Tell me what you know about the label Sublime Frequencies?

ETHAN HOLTZMAN: Several years ago, we did a show with a band called Neung Phak, and I think Mark [Gergis] was in it. I've just always loved Sublime Frequencies. They put out music from wherever they want, and it really hits home for a lot of people. For example, our singer Chhom Nimol, she had to leave Phnom Penh during the Pol Pot regime during the 1970s, so she was living in a Thai refugee camp, and while she was there, she was listening to music and absorbing a different culture. She's hearing this music there, so when we started the Thai Isan, *molam* styles of music, it was fun for Nimol. We played those records from Sublime Frequencies—she could dance, she understands the music, too.

ETK: When did you first hear about Sublime Frequencies?

EH: I think we probably played a show at Amoeba [record store in San Francisco], and then they gave us a [store] credit for playing there that day. So I'm looking around then and that's when I first saw—there's all these albums, they all look interesting. I don't have all of them by any means; I just have a few of them. Some of the albums, there are two or three songs that are great and some not as great. It's worth it, though, because you get a whole story about an area.

ETK: How do you think Sublime Frequencies is different from old "world music"?

EH: There were a few different labels that were starting up and doing different things [in the early to mid-2000s]. I was terrified early on when someone was like, "You do world music?" I was like, "No, no!" World music is the cool music now; it's just music from other places. When you're in a band, though, it's a different thing. "We're gonna book you for world music festivals." "We're gonna put in you in the world music section." But I've come to realize, I do like music from all across the globe. I'm thinking of old records I saw that weren't Sublime Frequencies but looked like they could be. A Turkish psychedelic rock album, another from Peru. Sublime Frequencies branded themselves in a way where they have kind of a hipness to them. "This is cool, these guys are cool. They're going out to these countries and grabbing weird recordings and just putting it out." Just-check-it-out kind o' vibe. A lot of DJs collect it all. . . .

I like all the artwork. It's interesting to me. It doesn't seem like a Smithsonian world album. It feels like you're finding something that's like, "Ah, yeah! That's exactly what I was looking for"—something that's different, something that has spirit in it.

ETK: What are your thoughts on Sublime Frequencies' *Cambodian Cassette Archives* release?

EH: I liked it. I put out my own *Electric Cambodia* [album]—songs from decades ago that were hard to find. The stuff I originally got, it was stuff somebody had already released. *Cambodia Rocks* is a real good compilation, [too,] and that was on [the label] Parallel World. That was one that my brother had gotten. I had gotten some cassettes on my first trip, and my brother was like, "I got [the same thing] from Aquarius Records in San Francisco." [That was] the real good Cambodian psychedelic rock from the late 1960s—that's what we started playing as a band.

ETK: What was Nimol singing when you first "discovered" her?

EH: When we first saw Chhom Nimol sing in Long Beach, it was at a nightclub called Dragon House, a Chinese-Cambodian buffet supper hall. There was a huge stage and eight girls dancing slowly, dressed up. They would sing slow, romantic Cambodian songs. They played the "Electric Slide."

ETK: Are there political aspects to your music?

EH: With Cambodia, for our singer's best interest, we try not to get too involved or vocal about it. She doesn't want to have people hate her or try to hurt her when she's there. We just try to do the right thing and help out. We work with a lot of good charities. We have political opinions, but you can't just say, "Hun Sen is a backstabbing crook"—and I don't even know if he is, but you could get iced over there. It was always, "Let's get this music heard. Let's let people see it." Because it's such a beautiful body of music. I guess that's politics in a sense.

ETK: What do you think about Sublime Frequencies' practice of rereleasing old music?

EH: I don't know what they're doing; I just know what we did. On *Electric Cambodia*, we didn't write any of those songs. Some of the artists on the album have passed away. We just said the profits will go to [the charity] Cambodia Living Arts unless somebody comes out and says, "That's my song." We're not talking a lot of money, but we did send a check to them recently. We've worked with some surviving relatives of the artists, so they've gotten some money.

ETK: Who is Dengue Fever's audience?

EH: I wish I could answer that in a couple months, after I tour and see, because it's been four years. But our audience is like, there's a lot of people from America who come to our shows, then there's a lot of Cambodians, younger or older, too. We've played in Cambodia three tours, and when we play over there it's all mixed. I would think [our audience] would just be music fans. Like, what kind of music fans are KCRW (Los Angeles-area public radio) fans? Those are the people who listen to us—and a handful of Cambodians.

PART THREE

Local Forays

Trekking Africa

JULIE STRAND

Bush Taxi Mali
Taking the Long Way Home

Any traveler to sub-Saharan Africa knows that the experience is a veritable assault on the senses: A swirling chaos of new sights, odors, flavors, and sounds overwhelm the visitor. The physical sensations of the densely populated, urban tropical climate infiltrate the body. It's quite a lot to get used to, and the true test of a Western traveler's mettle is how easily he or she adapts to such a wholly foreign environment, as most newbies will have very little frame of reference from which to interpret the dense sensory output of these surroundings. Once the new environment becomes navigable, however, it quickly becomes apparent that sound holds more importance in West Africa than it does in the Western world: It is used to interpret space, time, events, people, and history.

The primacy of sound in West Africa, including speech and music, has roots in the social and cultural needs of African societies in the precolonial period. Early African civilizations were primary oral cultures that first encountered written systems via Muslim migrations beginning in the seventh century, then more forcefully through European colonization in the eighteenth century.[1] The preliterate African soundscape developed around heavy reliance upon speech and sound to communicate meaning, create literary art, and preserve history. Vast bodies of oral literature were generated during this period, and musical practices were integrated with oral traditions to fuse the two forms of sonic expression and codify the performance of history, culture, and identity. For example, the Mande ethnic groups of West Africa, a dominant cultural presence in Mali, have a special artisan class they call *jeli* (or *griot* in French) whose social responsibility is to preserve oral histories, genealogies, and folktales, with the aid of music.[2] This is one of the many ways in which sound, and music in particular,

Bush Taxi Mali: Field Recordings from Mali (SF012) takes
the form of an imagined, sonic travelogue.

function simultaneously as public record, vital communication, social contract, and poetic art form.

The Republic of Mali, a landlocked country in the middle of West Africa that straddles the edge of the Sahara Desert and spans the Sahel grasslands into the tropical savanna, is as intensely rich an aural environment as a visual one. Like all people, Malians rely heavily on these two senses to negotiate their environments, but sound in particular is a primary organizing principle in daily life. The Malian soundscape is characterized by a rich variety of archetypal sounds that have evolved over the centuries.[3] Walking through the neighborhoods of Bamako on a Sunday afternoon, one can hear drummers, singers, and spectators in the streets, celebrating a wedding, child-naming ceremony, or other local gatherings for reasons both sacred and secular. The sounds of transport are defined by the whine of motorbikes, clattering bicycles, sputtering diesel engines, and drivers happily beeping their horns to greet others and accentuate the music emanating from their car stereos. Local markets are dominated by the deafening sounds of recorded music, popular and traditional, pouring out from cassette and CD stalls. The tinny sounds of televisions escape from local eateries and watering holes, where locals gather to enjoy football games, local programming, and foreign sitcoms and soap operas (dubbed in French). The persistent cacophony of local fauna—roosters, chickens, goats, dogs, sheep, birds, and donkeys—provides a counterpoint to the audio collage of music, children, engines, spirited conversation, and the sounds of manual labor.

In the West, it's not difficult to come across images from Mali or neighboring West African countries: women dressed in brightly colored prints, stunning landscapes of red earth vibrating against sparse, green foliage, and intricately designed artwork, masks, and other accoutrements of traditional life. Visitors to the region may have a mental picture of what they will see in Mali, but it is much harder to imagine what one will hear. Travelers who come to Mali specifically interested in sound often find that aural experiences create their most compelling memories—but it is precisely these experiences that are so ephemeral and difficult to recount later. One way of preserving these sounds is to create a snapshot: While photographs can tell one story about a region and the people who live there, recorded sound gives a different, more interactive sense of place. Especially in a country like Mali, where music is but one element of a broad local soundscape, an audio postcard can provide a unique reenactment in time of one's travels.

Sublime Frequencies' *Bush Taxi Mali* provides one such sonic missive, tracing the travels of Tucker Martine, a music producer who spent one month in rural and urban Mali in the fall of 1998 in search of interesting sounds to capture and share with his friends back home. His field recordings were then sculpted into a pastiche of edited sounds that include musical performances intermingled with environmental sounds, supplemented with insightful liner notes that provide a sense of personal experience and context. In many ways, Martine's Sublime Frequencies recordings subvert the grand tradition of ethnographic field recordings that came to prominence in the twentieth century.[4] Rather than giving a survey of dominant musical traditions of the region, paired with ethnographic photos and background notes intended to educate the listener, *Bush Taxi Mali* bears some of the neo-psychedelic hallmarks of much of the Sublime Frequencies catalog: CD artwork that features a layered mashup of lo-fi images representing people and places in the recording and an editing aesthetic that juxtaposes a heterogeneous array of sounds taken from different sources.

The result on *Bush Taxi Mali* is a virtual and vicarious reenactment of Martine's aural journey through one of the most sonically rich environments on the planet. However, unlike the early ethnographic recordings of the Library of Congress, the French Ocora label, or the iconic UNESCO recordings of the 1960s and 1970s,

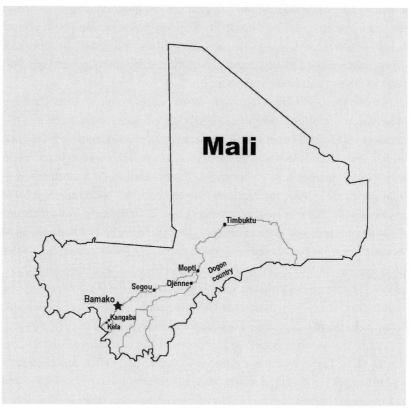

The Republic of Mali, highlighting Martine's ports of call: the capital city of Bamako,
Kela, Kangaba, Segou, Djenne, Mopti, and Dogon Country. The distance by road
between Kela and Mopti is roughly 400 miles/650km. Most of Martine's itinerary
followed the Niger River, branching off in Mopti to the Bani River, which runs
through Djenne. Timbuktu is included for reference only. Although only seasonally
navigable today, the Niger River is an historically vital local waterway that has
provided transportation through West Africa for millennia, from its tropical sources
in the Guinea basin, up through the Sahel regions of Mali, reaching its summit at
the edge of the Sahara around Timbuktu, and continuing its way back down into the
oil-rich Niger Delta region of Nigeria. Planning a journey that follows such a path,
which really could be done only by bush taxi today, follows ancient trade
and migration routes imbued with centuries of local history.

Bush Taxi Mali is decidedly self-reflexive and nonpedantic. Martine's notes only provide scant information about the musicians and performance contexts, without the depth of background information that the more pedagogic series are known for. However, just as most Sublime Frequencies releases presumably are engineered to both disorient their listeners and open their minds to new types of sounds, *Bush Taxi Mali* falls somewhere in the middle, between surreal streams of unreferenced radio transmissions and ethnographic primary-source recordings that seek to educate audiences about foreign cultures through their music.[5]

This raises the question: What does one learn from listening to this collection of sounds from the field? Perhaps even more importantly: What would one expect, or even want, to learn from it? The answer, of course, depends upon the listener. Some listeners come to the recording as world music enthusiasts, seeking to expand their repertoire of musical knowledge to a new, obscure part of the world, as yet unexplored. Some are simply looking for a vicarious, exotic travel experience, while others want to find new sounds to inspire their own musical works. And those who are fortunate enough to have visited the region hold the recording as an audio keepsake from their own epic travels in Africa.

I fall into the last category, having traveled a very similar route to Martine's only a year and a half before he did. The sounds in this collection evoke in me an intense nostalgia, only subsequently colored by academic analysis. Having spent over two years living in this and other regions of West Africa, I can't help but feel a sense of home when I listen to these recordings, however long ago and far away that home may be to me now.

But I am not alone in this emotional response. Part of the appeal of this collection is that Martine manages to create a sense of familiarity nestled within the sonic exotica that initially hits the listener's ear. The recording invokes feelings that are universal: passion, longing, jubilation, fatigue, childhood exuberance, the bustle of urban life, the solitude of rural landscapes, the comfort of daily routine, a sense of home. We all articulate our sense of home in different ways, both within a single culture and among different ones, but the connection to our most basic needs as humans is unmistakable. Somehow, in the soul of this collection of musical and nonmusical sounds undoubtedly foreign to most non-African ears, the exotic makes way for the ordinary, disorientation yields to a curious sense of familiarity, and the seemingly disjointed, collage-like structure paves a path to the comfortable sounds of everyday human life.

In the following analysis, one of my goals is to demystify the unfamiliar sounds in *Bush Taxi Mali* by giving context, background, and cultural history not already provided by the liner notes and track titles. Timbre, repertoire, function, and the settings of these sounds may not be immediately familiar to most listeners, but human voices, plucked strings, flutes, the beating of drums, and ambient sounds of both urban and rural landscapes resonate with nearly everyone, particularly among the cosmopolitan, arguably eccentric, adventurous audience that the Sublime Frequencies label tends to attract.

TRAVELING MALI BY BUSH TAXI

Because this recording represents a journey, it's important to understand the basics of transportation in the West African Sahel. For shorter trips, many locals opt for a bicycle or *mobylette* (moped), especially given oppressive African fuel prices.[6] For longer trips, wealthier Malian nationals and expats move across the country in private, air-conditioned cars designed to shield them from the outside environment. For most others, including foreign travelers on a budget, there remains the most proletarian mode of West African public transport: the bush taxi.

Though decidedly lacking in comfort—I have spent many an arduous journey across the West African savanna wedged hip bone–to–hip bone—bush taxis are a basic, affordable form of public transportation relied upon by locals. For foreign travelers, bush taxis are not only the cheapest way to get from point A to point B, they also offer a singular, raw experience of backcountry travel in rural West Africa and are the best way to see Mali and meet Malians. There are three types: (1) your standard, rattletrap West African taxi devoted to rural routes between smaller cities and villages; (2) variations on the Peugeot 504, a seven-seat minibus often crammed with ten to twelve people and a few goats and sheep strapped up top for good measure; and (3) the *bâché*, a pickup truck with a tarp stretched across a metal frame, sheltering makeshift wooden benches installed in the bed, quite possibly the most humble form of motorized travel on the continent.

In any of these vehicles, a traveler might share hours of amicable conversation over the course of an inevitably long journey. Despite the potential language barrier (very few Malians speak English and French becomes scarce in rural areas), the bush taxi is one of many places where foreign tourists experience the overflowing hospitality that characterizes social encounters throughout West Africa. Across cultural, social, economic, or other differences, travel partners will readily share food, offer to let you hold their babies, and express avid curiosity about where you're from, while opening up about their own lives and daily life in Mali. One hears endless streams of local gossip; family tales, both tragic and uplifting; hopeful plans for the future; and questions, so many questions, about the strange and wonderful world that you, as an outsider, a *tubabu*, have come from.[7] These lively exchanges, during endless hours of pounding rides through oppressive heat and the choking, reddish dust that blankets everything inside and outside the vehicle, are among my fondest and most miserable memories of Mali.

Stepping off a bush taxi, one feels beaten, exhausted, sore, and filthy, but also exhilarated, liberated, and ready to take on the next adventure, which might be as prosaic as wandering into the closest watering hole for food and a lukewarm beverage. Anyone who has traveled the African countryside in this way knows that it is not easy to communicate these memories to others, and that recounting such stories to friends back home always fails to capture their exquisite rawness. The tracks on *Bush Taxi Mali* go a long way in this regard: They capture the moments between punishing treks in these unpretentious vehicles—when your senses are heightened to their extreme and you've never felt more alive.

THE AUDIO-CULTURAL LANDSCAPE OF MALI

One of the most surprising realizations that Western tourists have when visiting Africa is the broad ethnic diversity that exists within even a small geographic region. The cultural landscape presented in *Bush Taxi Mali* draws from three of the larger and more well-known ethnic groups in the country: the Mande, the Dogon, and the Fula, each completely distinct in language and cultural history but tied together by political-geographic boundaries. The majority of the music on the CD represents the Mande, possibly the most celebrated musical culture of the region, and in particular, the *ngoni* lute, an instrument central to the *jeli* tradition explained below. Layered over some of the Mande's most iconic musical practices, such as the *ngoni* and *balafon* music of the *jeli*, is an experience of everyday life, similar to what one encounters riding a bush taxi. Martine's field recordings allow the listener to eavesdrop (via his mediated presentation) on sounds of daily life in this immensely diverse corner of the world.

As is evident on this disc, Sublime Frequencies is one of the few labels that privileges ambient sound as an essential component of the recording. There are many examples of more conventional ethnographic recordings that include the occasional crowing rooster or chirping crickets to suggest a natural performance setting, authenticating the featured subject matter and partly concealing the otherwise contrived nature of the production. Listeners of ethnographic recordings like to imagine themselves as flies on the wall of a purely organic music-making setting, as though they've stumbled across a performance. The sprinkling of certain natural sounds throughout the recording, therefore, helps encourage this suspension of disbelief while supplying familiar contextual details.

The integration of daily sounds and musical recordings in *Bush Taxi Mali* takes this process a step further, drawing upon deep and varied stores of ambient sound that represent an acoustemology of the region, a broad sonic palette that represents one's way of knowing and being in the world.[8] In *Bush Taxi Mali*, these sounds are nothing more than what Martine regularly encountered during his travels, and he recorded them in public, just as he did the musical performances presented to him. Some of the ambient noises provide a constant backdrop and are barely noticeable (street sounds, natural sounds), while others happen only occasionally and signal events (calls to prayer, honking horns, the sound of a popular TV show playing next door). These sounds are just as important as musical interludes in representing an ethnographic reality of Mali—perhaps even more so.

Beyond the unique situational nature of the local soundscape, environmental sounds complement musical ones in creating an overall aesthetic of disorientation. This sonic exotica delights listeners with a new, strange palette drawn from vastly different cultural contexts, without being explicitly pedagogical about them. This is another way that *Bush Taxi Mali* and the Sublime Frequencies label diverge from the established ethnographic recording tradition. Rather than setting out to educate and inform the audience about the people who made the music, the sonic product itself is the focus. Disorientation occurs when the raw, hyper-real, and minimally contextualized recordings take the listener from a sense of being there to the confusion of, "Where am I?"[9] The answer depends on the perspective of the ethnographer-recordist, in this case Martine, and the environmental sounds included in the collection are the key to understanding his experiences in Mali, as they situate the music within reality, not some imagined, romanticized ideal of a "pure" Malian culture.

The editing of the source recordings on this disc is therefore crucial to understanding Martine's singular journey from late 1998. In order to communicate as wide a range of places, impressions, and experiences as possible in a 55-minute recording, Martine often combines recordings from different sources on the same track, "like documentary filmmakers who piece together found footage."[10] At times jarring, the sonic edits quickly take the listener from a musical performance in a village to a walk past market stalls in another city many miles away. For example, in Track 8, "Kah Mohno (Dogon)," following a recording from

Dogon country, Martine appends an unidentified snippet of Mande music, presumably from either Kela or Kangaba, and then sounds of the local market in Mopti.[11] This is not a survey of Malian musical practices, highlighting a carefully balanced selection of local music traditions; this is Martine's tour of a handful of towns and regions in the country, the specific places he visited, the people he encountered, and the period of time he was there.

But the track order does not follow the chronology of Martine's itinerary: Other considerations guided his decisions of editing and sequence. Martine's aesthetic sensibility came into play to create a texture that alternates among timbres of ambient sounds, string instruments, voices, flutes, and drums. We're brought into Martine's world and aesthetic logic. While *Bush Taxi Mali* does not include some of the iconic instruments associated with Mali—the *jembe* drum, the *kora* harp—it does present a thoughtful, compelling sample of the most interesting sounds that Martine heard.

The result is a varied progression of music and sounds that rest comfortably on foreign ears, never too much of one thing at a time. The ambient soundscape sprinkled throughout the compilation is quite varied in itself, as discussed above, and signals both the general, permanent fixtures of West African life as well as particular details: the musical selections on the radio, the specific languages spoken, or the unique whine of the most common brand of motorbike in the area.

Periodic returns to these ambient episodes, between beautifully performed tracks of music, remind the listener of the journey, of movement through space and time. A sense of motion is best communicated through these excerpts, usually appended to the end of a track or, at other times, taking up a track in its entirety. Martine's rapid editing style gives the listener a sense of physically passing through vignettes of daily life: Snippets of overheard conversations blend into sounds of a television, then bits of loud market sounds, layered over traffic sounds from the nearby street. Again, nothing is dwelled upon for very long, only a few seconds of each sound fragment.[12] The goal is not to indulge too much in any single episode, not to learn too much of the individual stories unfolding in each scene, but to create sonic wallpaper, a backdrop infused with unique elements of the Malian soundscape, accompanying each passage to the next destination. Adding to the sense of movement are deliberate placements of transportation sounds: footsteps, cars, bicycles, and motorbikes.[13] These transitional passages act like mortar between the bricks of the main source recordings, holding the collection together while maintaining the theme of movement and travel.

BREAKDOWN OF LOCATIONS, SOURCE MATERIALS, AND ETHNIC GROUPS REPRESENTED MUSICALLY ON THE CD *BUSH TAXI MALI*

Track	Name	Location	Ethnic group	Instruments/Sounds
1	Morning in Djenne: Les Cheveux de Sunjata	Djenne, Kela, or Kangaba	Mande	• Ambient village sounds, walking → • Two *ngoni*, voice →
2	Radio Bamako	Bamako	N/A	• Radio transmission collage: traditional music, popular music, news broadcasts, static
3	Rihlah	Kela	Mande	• Solo *ngoni*
4	Fouta Djallon	Mopti	Fula	• Solo flute, soft drums
5	Autorail	Kela	Mande	• Solo voice
6	Mopti Niger Walking	Mopti	N/A	• Ambient village market sounds: conversations, music from the radio, people eating, traffic, children playing, sounds of feet walking on a dirt road →
7	Segou[a]	Kela or Kangaba	Mande	• Two *ngoni*
8	Kah Mohno (Dogon)	Dogon, [Kela?], Mopti	Dogon, Mande, or N/A	• Children's chorus, clapping → drum ensemble → • Male and female *griot* voices, *balafon* → • Ambient street sounds from Mopti; motorbike, walking
9	Kaita [sic][b]	Kela or Kangaba	Mande	• *Balafon, ngoni,* and voice → • Ambient street sounds: bicycles, cars, walking, popular and traditional music from radios, babies crying
10	Deni Meba	Segou	Mande	• Solo *ngoni,* goat bleating in the background

Track	Name	Location	Ethnic group	Instruments/Sounds
11	Bambaran Wedding Celebration	Segou	Mande	• Ambient sounds during an outdoor wedding cel-ebration: voices speak-ing/singing through a distorted PA, drums heard in background; fades to echo sounds of wedding in distance, birds singing? → • Ambient street/market sounds, faint music heard behind voices
12	Sanan Kouya	Kela or Kangaba	Mande	• Two *ngoni* → • Ambient street sounds: voices, music from radio/TV, cars/motor-bikes →
13	O Mansa Mousa	Kela or Kangaba	Mande	• Solo guitar, female voice
14	Dogon Country at Night	Dogon country	N/A	• Ambient, nighttime rural village sounds: roosters, crickets, goats, sheep, faint human voices, then a loud donkey braying in the distance, echoing off the cliffs

Bulleted items indicate more than one source recording in a track; arrows indicate an edited crossfade to the next track or source recording within a track.

a. While the musicians identified this as their "song of Segou" to Martine, it is actually a version of the Mande *jeli* standard, "Kulanjan," which is also the name of a type of bird indigenous to the region.

b. The correct title of this song is "Kaira."

SELF-REFLEXIVITY AND THE PERSONAL
JOURNEY THROUGH MALI

A crucial element to understanding the contexts of these recordings is its track-by-track liner notes. Such notes have long been used to establish the authenticity of world music recordings—small nuggets of information provided to give meaning and a frame of reference to foreign sounds. Liner notes and their accompanying artwork, therefore, can hold great power over how the listener perceives and understands the music. One of the benefits of representing people and places with a collection of audio recordings, as opposed to a static set of photographs, is that audio is dynamic and multifaceted, moving forward in time while presenting layers of aural information that may fuel mental pictures. Without adequate mediation in the form of liner notes, it's possible that listeners will rely only on their own, potentially misguided and essentialized preconceptions about the culture.

Martine's approach to this task was to use his personal experiences, emotional responses, and interpretations of events to usher the listener through his arrangement of the collection. Almost all *Bush Taxi Mali*'s liner notes are written by hand, presumably Martine's, which both personalizes them and lends a casual feel to the production. The track list on the back of the CD is printed on what looks like yellow notebook paper, giving a sense of immediate authenticity, as if this were a page from the actual notebook Martine carried and jotted his notes in throughout his travels. The track titles are printed over faded remnants of an old list called "Mali Mixes," a *scriptio inferior* that looks like some of his technical notes on the raw field recordings. Some similar notes were included in the margins of the top-layer track list, with Martine's personal impressions of some of the tracks. Notes like "hypnotic—banjo like," "good 'til :56," and "roll off some low rumble" convey his perspective on these sounds, his feelings about them, and his associations.

The palimpsest-style of the track list on the CD's exterior is an outward indication that this collection emerged through a layered, multistep process, and that our experiences of the sounds included in the final product are mediated by Martine's editing hand. We get a sense of the raw materials that went into the final product, which have been carefully considered, worked, and reworked until they became truly personalized. The "Mali Mixes" notes also appear inside the CD booklet, layered over a photo of three musicians who play most of the *ngoni* and other Mande tracks that constitute the majority of music on the disc.

Their photos blend into a collage of Malian stamps and images from Martine's passport, still more visual signs of travel and movement, and further indication of the highly personal nature of the CD package.

The heavily worked album art mirrors Martine's editing style in the studio. According to him, *Bush Taxi Mali* was an exercise in learning about recording and manipulating audio. These skills fed into the development of his successful career as a producer and recording engineer, as he later earned a Grammy nomination for engineering in 2007.[14] Martine claims to be largely self-taught. His interest in learning about recording equipment, paired with wanderlust and curiosity about sound around the world, led to a practice of making mixtapes of his global sonic travels for his circle of friends in Seattle. His then-nascent yet highly adept recording and editing rigor were already evident on *Bush Taxi Mali*, which has a much more polished sound than many Sublime Frequencies recordings, despite the admitted rawness of the source recordings.[15]

Martine's decision to forego general background notes for individual track notes enriches each track as a singular vignette and omits a greater cultural context for the work as a whole. The tracks are therefore linked not by a common ethnic or geographic theme laid out by the producer but by an inner logic that allows the listener to create his or her own personal web of meaning and intertextuality. Furthermore, his use of esoteric place names, instruments, and other local nomenclature provides exotic appeal for world music dilettantes, minus the didactic cultural arcana typically valued by area specialists. The result is that the listener feels just informed enough to have a sense of what the recordings represent, without really knowing exactly what the recording is supposed to represent. The impression is more emotional and sensual than factual.

For example, the first track of the recording, "Morning in Djenne, Les Cheveux de Sunjata," is explained thus: "An early morning walk around Djenne followed by the griots I met in Kela playing a lovely tale of Sunjata under the stars. 2 ngoni, balafon, and voice." First, Martine has set up a framework of time. By beginning the recording with morning sounds, he creates an expectation that the collection of tracks is meant to represent the passing of a day. This expectation is confirmed by the reference to nighttime in the title of the last track, "Dogon Country at Night." Certainly, the geographic spread represented across the recordings would be impossible to cover in a single day, but reality is suspended in service of the idea that a typical day in Mali may simply include a similar variety of sounds. The ethnic diversity of the country is therefore alluded to within the diurnal framework, and the foreignness of the ethnic landscape is softened by the universality of the passage of a single day.

The note for the opening track also introduces a number of foreign names and terms. The *ngoni* instrument, the most prevalent sound in the collection, is explained elsewhere in the liner notes, but this brief description leaves many questions in the mind of the listener: What are *griots*? Who or what is Sunjata? What is a *balafon*? Where is Djenne, and why did he go there? How do I even pronounce "Djenne"?[16] The esoteric nature of the information included may provoke more questions in the listener than it does elucidate the setting, but that is part of the thrill of many Sublime Frequencies' recordings: encountering something that is so far from one's realm of acquaintance that the specific details about the sounds matter less than the experience of the encounter.

Nevertheless, this confusion is quickly abated by the familiar sound of footsteps on gravel at the beginning of the recording. And while walking can be considered universal, the sound is set against an archetypal backdrop that situates one aurally within a specific cultural and acoustemological setting only recognized by those familiar with the locale. In this case, Martine fades in typical domestic sounds associated with morning in the West African Sahel: roosters and birds calling back and forth, the plaintive bleats of sheep and goats, tinny morning news broadcasts from radios and television, the final, pre-sunrise chatter of crickets, and the gentle voices of women preparing breakfast and commencing domestic duties. Certainly, most listeners have no idea what morning sounds like in Mali or anywhere else they have not been, but this track communicates an unmistakable sense of beginning that appropriately ushers the listener into the "day" of the CD.

These sounds dissolve into two iconic instruments of the Mande: the *bala* or *balafon*, a wooden, gourd-resonated xylophone; and a pair of *ngoni,* three- to five-stringed lutes that have been determined to be among the prototypes for the modern-day banjo.[17] The Mande are one of the largest ethnic groupings in Mali, comprising the Bamana, Maninka, and other satellite ethnolinguistic groups. The Bamana language (also called "Bambara"), is the *lingua franca* in southern Mali, and despite the rich ethnic diversity found throughout this enormous country, Mande culture dominates much of Mali's ethnic landscape.[18] The intrepid traveler in Mali wishing to pick up a few local phrases will likely be taught some standard greetings and numbers in Bamana, and both live and recorded music heard in the southern, nondesert portion of the country is dominated by Mande traditions. This music also holds a significant presence in academic studies of the region and commercially available recordings. The prevalence of this culture in Mali and surrounding regions, both physically and in the foreign consciousness, is echoed in *Bush Taxi Mali*.

Among the Mande, certain types of music-making are restricted to an inherited class of musicians known locally as *jeli*, though Martine cites them in his notes with the pan-ethnic, French-derived term *griot*.[19] The *jeli* in Mande culture, similar to *griots* in other cultures, hold the social and cultural responsibility of preserving history in a traditionally oral culture. Local histories, folklore, and genealogies comprise much of what *jelis* spend their lives learning, and this precious information is preserved with the aid of music. In addition to vocal arts, *jelis* may also specialize in one of three instruments, the *bala*, the *ngoni*, or the *kora*, a 21-stringed harp. The songs accompanied by these instruments literally embody the history, culture, and social norms of the Mande peoples and their common roots in the thirteenth-century Mali Empire ruled by Sunjata Keita. This ruler is referenced in the opening track, titled "Les Chevaux de Sunjata" (Sunjata's Horses), part of the Mande repertoire that has preserved cultural history for centuries.

The instruments and repertoire of Mande culture appear in ten of the fourteen tracks in this collection. The *ngoni* is featured in six. Why this focus on a single instrument when Mali offers such a rich variety of instruments and musical traditions? We again see the impact of Martine's personal preferences in these selections. Perhaps the fact that the *ngoni* is a lute, similar to the guitar and many other Western string instruments, makes it more familiar to him and his intended audience. A photo of the *ngoni* players who appear on this recording is included in the CD booklet, with a caption that describes the instrument, its design and playing technique, and refers to its link to the American banjo. Adjacent to this photo is that of another musician playing guitar, a direct connection between the two instruments.

This brief photographic reference highlights an important, familiar association for the Western audience: the *ngoni*'s relationship to the guitar and banjo. Here is another way in which a sense of "home"—of Martine's own North American culture—is brought into this collection. The photo and accompanying notes are not simply information intended to arm the listener with an image and basic understanding of the instrument featured in the recording. The associations drawn here between African and American instruments help communicate the sense of homey familiarity that Martine undoubtedly felt when he heard the *ngoni* during his travels. The performance style of the instrument differs from that of most American string instruments, but the acoustic timbre of a plucked lute taps deeply into the American musical psyche. This is the sound of folk music, bluegrass, Appalachia, and the American South. Martine is the son of a songwriter and grew up in the capital of the country music industry, Nashville, Tennessee. The *ngoni,* therefore, not only hearkens back to the music of Martine's personal history, but also represents the roots of American music. Martine has exploited these associations in Western consciousness and extended American roots music back to Africa with these field recordings. The transatlantic musical connection is not unique in itself, but Martine's method of doing so by drawing upon emotional responses to instrumental timbre, the plucked strings of the *ngoni*, and other sounds on *Bush Taxi Mali*, reflects his personal reactions to and associations with the music.

We learn even more about Martine's extramusical experiences in Mali by how he contextualizes the tracks in this collection, helping the listener share in his travels rather than ethnographically informing us about the music in each track. We imagine ourselves in his shoes, seeing, hearing, and smelling the surroundings he did. His notes for "Kah Mono (Dogon)" demonstrate this:

> After a couple of days hiking into the Dogon country, I was told there would be a big celebration that night. The Hogan (spiritual chief of the village) wished to honor me, their guest[,] with a feast and some music. Here you can hear the Dogon children singing a song—noticing the microphone—and then competing amongst themselves for the microphones [*sic*] attention. Keep in mind this is at least a 2 day hike from any cars, roads, electricity, etc. Many of these kids had never seen a microphone and were simultaneously excited and scared by it. They completely lit up when I played it back for them! Then the adults took charge by kicking in the drums . . . and I have added another snippet of Mopti street sounds at the end.

While we discover the name of the spiritual leader and learn basic local protocols for honoring guests, the vivid imagery included here reflects Martine's experiences of the situation, including the children's reactions and the remoteness of the location, rather than information about the Dogon themselves. In fact, the Dogon are known internationally for their valuable artwork, including intricately carved doors that were unfortunately pilfered from the region throughout the twentieth century by enthusiastic collectors. Tourists also flock to Dogon country to see the stunning Bandiagara Escarpment, a 500-meter sandstone cliff that stretches 150 km across the region and overlooks the Dogon villages built beneath. On the face of the escarpment are ancient structures built by the Tellem, a race of smaller people, not unlike the BaAka or other small-bodied forest people in Central Africa, who inhabited the region before the Dogon arrived in the fourteenth century.[20]

It is a long, onerous journey to Dogon country from the nearest source of basic amenities like electricity and running water. Climbing up the escarpment to explore the ancient Tellem houses, paths of smooth, shiny rocks are evident on the otherwise craggy surface, eroded by centuries of bare Dogon feet, visiting the granaries and sacred burial grounds that some of these dwellings are used for today. The overwhelming feeling of remoteness in Dogon country is unlike anything I've felt anywhere else in Africa—or the world, for that matter. One night, lying atop a small hut to sleep, I witnessed a spectacular meteor shower that accentuated the immensity and isolation of this strange and beautiful place.[21] I wrote in my notebook:

It was a perfectly clear night, I almost felt like the dry heat of the day might have burned all the clouds away. We were many miles away from any electricity or major sources of light, so there was nothing obstructing our magnificent view of the heavens. A telescope would have been ideal at that moment (yeah, and who's going to haul a telescope all the way out to Dogon country?) because it seemed like I could see every single star in the sky. I just lay there, gazing at the immensity of it all, when I noticed the stars were moving everywhere in the sky, leaving tiny little trails behind them—it was a meteor shower! The entire sky was filled with tiny shooting stars, and in the distance, a huge crescent moon, rising above the minaret of the village mosque. The sky went on forever in all directions, and I was thinking that I have never seen anything like this before, and may likely never again.[22]

Back in the late 1990s, it seemed that life had changed very little over the centuries in remote, rural Dogon country. Plastic flip-flops and modern tee-shirts worn by kids were the only signs that I hadn't stepped back 300 years in time. The children's fascination with Martine's microphone is understandable, given that their isolation did not allow for frequent interaction with modern technology. At the same time, they are like children everywhere—curious, eager to show off what they know, and vying for adult attention. The children who appear in the track "Kah Mono" express this exuberance in their earnest singing, each verse increasingly ardent. There is an urgency to their song as they compete to sing into the microphone and impress the foreign traveler.

Then the adults take over with drums and a whistle, the children's voices fading into the background but still audible. There is something so foreign yet so familiar about this setting—children and adults participating in ordinary evening activities while entertaining guests, exchanging curiosities, each displaying their exotic memorabilia to the other. The feeling of community and family is unmistakable, and the foreignness of the sights, tastes, smells, and sounds dissolve into a feeling of warmth and domestic familiarity.

The addition of street sounds from Mopti to the end of this track may seem like a non sequitur, an editing decision motivated purely by a need for aesthetic variety. A previous note tells us only that Mopti is a "largely Fulani" town in Mali where the flute track "Fouta Djallon" was recorded, and seems to have nothing to do with the Dogon. However, the city of Mopti, located in the "waist" section of Mali, is the last city with any reliable amenities before Dogon country, and the place one goes to organize tours there.[23] Any trip to Dogon country, therefore, begins and ends in Mopti. This bit of editing, then, recreates the realities of traveling to this region. Dogon country and Mopti, which have no real ethnic or cultural connection, are forever associated with one another in the mind of anyone who has made the long, hot, and spectacular trek through Dogon country.

The musical tour, spanning seven distinct rural and urban locations, more than a half-dozen different types of instruments, and three major ethnic traditions, ends not where it began, but back in Dogon country, with the nocturnal soundscape of rural Mali. The sounds heard in Track 14, "Dogon Country at Night," could be heard nearly anywhere in rural Africa at night, but the striking geography of the Bandiagara Escarpment in Dogon country creates a natural echo effect, reminiscent of some of the filters and other studio techniques Martine employed during his editing process. The metaphor of the day inscribed within *Bush Taxi Mali* closes, and the audience is treated to a setting and sound that may be unusual to the foreign listener, but is very common in rural Africa. Martine sets the scene: "After the celebration mentioned with track 8, the folks kindly showed me to the rooftop upon which I was to sleep. As I lay there, gazing out at the clearest sky I will ever see—I heard the comotion [sic] of the village settling down. The way these sounds reflect off of the cliffs is amazing and pretty apparent here when the donkeys get going."

This is an excellent example of how sound represents physical space in Mali— as it can everywhere. In this case, the specific nature of the donkey bray echoing off the escarpment creates an aural manifestation of the physical attributes of the environment: tall, rocky cliffs overlooking villages on a flat surface below and stretching sideways as far as the eye can see, the enormity of the space that amplifies the echoes, and the occupants of this space, of which humans seem to be the minority. This is soundscape at its best, where sound interacts directly with the physical environment, responding and being shaped by it. It is not humans or human-made music clashing with the environment; it is nature (animal) meets nature (stone cliffs), rendering human cultures as bystanders to a much greater drama.

This drama is heightened by the choice of sounds in this track as well as their persistence everywhere in Mali and the West African Sahel. The terrifying racket of a donkey's bray shattering the peaceful night air is something one simply has to get used to in West Africa, just like the other discomforts of heat, dust, bad smells, the perennial sound of babies crying, and waking at 5:00 a.m. to the distorted, piercing sounds of the morning call to prayer from the neighborhood mosque. Travel helps one grow: stepping out of one's comfort zone, stretching personal limits, and building tolerance for things once thought intolerable. I learned to put up with quite a bit over the two-plus years I spent in West Africa, but the sound of a donkey never fails to stop me cold in my tracks and rattle my nerves.

Animal sounds, like all other sounds mentioned here, are a natural part of the Malian soundscape, and the donkey solo in Track 14 is a fitting and humorous way to close the collection. In addition to bringing nightfall to the "daytime" of the CD, it is a final reminder of how much of African life is integrated with nature. The ambient sounds in *Bush Taxi Mali* express this best: crickets audible behind many of the musical performances, the sounds of feet against unpaved earth, and even the unexpected accompaniment of a bleating goat to the solo *ngoni* performance in Track 10, "Deni Meba." Martine, like most Western tourists in Africa, was likely struck by how much human life interacts with the natural world in Mali, even in urban settings. Animals are slaughtered for meals right in the home courtyard, bits of earth (dust) and insects insinuate themselves into every part of your belongings and person, chickens constantly scurry about underfoot, and sheep and other domestic livestock are sometimes brought right into the house overnight to protect them from theft. Life, death, and nature are everywhere in Mali—and throughout the African continent. Music is but one part of this, just as it comprises only a portion of the Malian acoustemological soundscape.

FINDING HOME IN A MALIAN BUSH TAXI

Martine collected nineteen hours of audio during his month-long journey through Mali, and the 55 minutes included in *Bush Taxi Mali* were carefully selected and edited to tell a story of these travels, his impressions, and his experiences there. Which sounds were excluded—undoubtedly encountered and possibly even recorded, but not included? Many iconic sounds in the Malian soundscape are missing from the disc: the perennial calls to prayer from innumerable local mosques; the Mande *jembe*, easily the most well-known African drum across the globe; and the Mande *kora*, a 21-string harp and the third member of the *jeli* instrumental triumvirate, most notably played by Malian *jeli* and international recording star, Toumani Diabate.[24] Their omission can again be chalked up to the editing process that Martine used to personalize the collection, for *Bush Taxi Mali* is not supposed to be a generic survey of common styles.

I want to make one final point about timing. Contemporary sound studies are rooted in the idea that endemic, archetypal sounds define the soundscape of a location, and that observing the ways they change can reveal greater social and technological processes. Over time, new sounds have made their way into the daily soundscapes of West Africa since Martine's visit: The introduction of the cell phone is likely the most profound technological and acoustic change, but there are also newly imported, quieter, Japanese-built motorbikes and an increase in electronic games heard both indoors and out. Sometimes, changes in a soundscape can reflect more insidious processes. The current soundscape of Mali in particular reveals some of the dramatic changes that have taken place there in recent years. The 2012 *coup d'état* and resulting Islamist takeover of Mali's major northern cities had devastating effects on the region, as the introduction of Sharia law precipitated the brutal enforcement of extremist social rule and a ban against all forms of music in the North.[25] In the south, including the capital city of Bamako, fearful Malians cancelled events and closed down performance venues, while rebels from the north systematically confiscated musical instruments and equipment and menacingly threatened local artists, sending some to seek asylum in neighboring countries.[26]

By early February 2013, the Malian military had regained control of the north with the aid of a French-led international coalition. Sharia rule was then lifted, and Malian musicians in particular rejoiced. Still, local residents fear the return of rebel forces, and life has not yet returned to normal. Many venues remain closed, and Malians are not out socializing or enjoying traditional festivities as much as they had in the past. The current soundscape is tempered by this fear, as the memories of a particularly violent form of religious rule, one that does not reflect the distinctively tolerant, peaceful Muslim culture of Mali, are still fresh in communal memory. If Martine had made this voyage fourteen years later than he did, his recordings would have reflected a quite different soundscape. Timing is therefore crucial to understanding the acoustemology of a place, and the gradual return to normal life in Mali will be measured in part by how much of the preconflict soundscape returns. The return of prolific and public music-making in particular is a sign of a healthier, resilient community, as music in Mali is so closely intertwined with history, communication, celebration, emotion, and identity.

Bush Taxi Mali is Martine's personal, virtual tour of Mali by a form of transport that allows close, constant contact with the surrounding environment. His ride does not require the passenger to endure hours of physical discomfort as the countryside whizzes by; instead, the world passes by at a pace just slow enough to catch fleeting glimpses of Malian life. The sensation is a familiar one, not unlike passing by houses on a residential street or scanning a tableau of windows on the side of an apartment building. Each scene has its own story, but the larger narrative is not concerned with the details of these individual stories. It instead communicates a sense of home, where close interactions take place, meals are shared, confidences are exchanged—and where one goes in search of the comfort and security that all humans crave.

Infused with these personal experiences, *Bush Taxi Mali* communicates important aspects of a tourist's sonic experience in the country: how sound represents physical space, structures the passage of time, represents history and ethnic identity, and offers the perceptive listener an intimate glimpse into the daily lives of Malians. It is the details that make the sounds Malian, but the framework in which they are presented convey a universality that any listener can identify with. Daily life initially may look and sound different in different corners of the world, but it is quickly recognizable in its varied minutiae. The specific sounds, timbres, and contexts constructed for this album draw the listener into Martine's impressions of this human journey. *Bush Taxi Mali* takes its listeners by the hand, shows them something foreign and exciting, and then demonstrates how these exotic sounds are mundane in their own environments, allowing us to find a sense of ourselves and our own ideas of home within this exotic sonic landscape.

NOTES

1. Defined as "cultures with no knowledge at all of writing" in Walter J. Ong, *Orality and Literacy: The Technologizing of the Word* (New York: Routledge, 1982), 1.

2. Many other African ethnic groups have similar social and historical roles for specialists in music, a performing art that provides a structured backdrop for epic histories, folk tales, and genealogy-rich praise songs.

3. By "archetypal sounds," I refer to Murray Schafer's classification of soundscape elements, including keynote, signals, and soundmarks, but I also use the term "archetypal" in its more general sense of being typical of an area, and not Schafer's specific definition of "those mysterious ancient sounds, often possessing felicitous symbolism, which we have inherited from remote antiquity or prehistory." *The Tuning of the World* (New York: Random House, 1977), 9.

4. Martine also recorded and edited two other Sublime Frequencies releases: *Broken Hearted Dragonflies: Insect Electronica from Southeast Asia* and *Eat the Dream: Gnawa Music from Essaouira.*

5. Ryan Brown, interview with Alan Bishop, 2006, www.indieworkshop.com/archive /interviews.php?id=114; Charlie Bertsch, "Subverting World Music: The Sublime Frequencies Label," *Tikkun*, July 1, 2009, www.tikkun.org/article.php/Bertsch-subverting -world-music/print.

6. Gasoline prices in West Africa can range anywhere from two to four times the cost in the United States.

7. *"Tubabu"* is a pan-linguistic term common in the Sahel, generally understood as "white person," but used to refer to any non-African.

8. Steven Feld, "Waterfalls of Song: An Acoustemology of Place Resounding in Bosavi, Papua New Guinea," in *Senses of Place*, ed. Steven Feld and Keith Basso, 91–135. Santa Fe: School of American Research Press, 1996.

9. Bertsch, "Subverting World Music," 77.

10. Ibid.

11. See map of Mali for relative distances of these locations.

12. This sense of quickly passing by a landscape is also reflected in the image printed on the CD itself and the background of the CD tray. Both feature a blurry photograph of a tree, presumably taken through the window of a moving bush taxi.

13. The theme of movement and travel that persists throughout the CD is also evoked by the selection of the fifth track, "Autorail," a local, French-derived term for the train. The installation of railways by colonial powers in the nineteenth and early twentieth centuries marked a revolution in transportation technology across West Africa. While they were constructed mainly by locally conscripted laborers and often symbolize the brutality of colonial oppression in Africa, they also represent modernization, links among remote

regions of the continent, and a means to access goods, services, and a broader range of employment opportunities for migrant workers living in rural areas.

14. The nomination was for the CD *Floratone* by guitarist Bill Frisell and drummer Matt Chamberlain (Blue Note Records, 2007). Martine described the album as an improvisation that he and his colleague Lee Townsend recorded, then compositionally structured in the editing room. Personal communication, 2013.

15. Ibid.

16. Most nomenclature in former French colonies follows French phonetic spelling. In order to produce a hard "j" sound, as in "jelly," the "j" is preceded by a silent "d," so "Djenne" is pronounced, "jen-nay."

17. See Cecilia Conway, *African Banjo Echoes in Appalachia: A Study of Folk Traditions* (Knoxville: University of Tennessee Press, 1995).

18. Mali is the 24th largest country in the world with an area of 1,240,192 square kilometers, slightly less than twice the size of the state of Texas. The Mande ethnic group comprises roughly 50 percent of the nation's population, estimated at 15.5 million. Central Intelligence Agency, *CIA World Factbook,* "Country Demographics and Area Comparisons," www.cia.gov/library/publications/the-world-factbook/geos/ml.html. The encyclopedic linguistic reference, *Ethnologue,* lists 56 living languages spoken in Mali, though 80 percent of its population speaks dialects of the Mande language Bamana (Bamanankan) to varying degrees, as either a first language or a *lingua franca* "Mali," *Ethnologue,* www .ethnologue.com/show_country.asp?name=ML.

19. The term *griot* was developed by the French from a number of local names for a professional musician of inherited status who preserves local histories through performances of music and speech as part of his cultural duty and profession. See Eric Charry, *Mande Music: Traditional and Modern Music of the Maninka and Mandinka of Western Africa* (Chicago: University of Chicago Press, 2000); and Patricia Tang, *Masters of the Sabar: Wolof Griot Percussionists from Senegal* (Philadelphia: Temple University Press, 2007), for more on roots and definitions of these terms.

20. Many visitors to Dogon country have noted that the remaining Tellem villages closely resemble Anasazi cliff dwellings in the Four Corners region of the United States.

21. The intense, 115-plus-degree April sun in Dogon country bakes the rocky ground all day, and the heat radiating from it at night is so intense that most people sleep on rooftops to escape it.

22. Field notes, April 17, 1997.

23. Despite its remote location, enough tourists come through Mopti looking for tours to Dogon country, Djenne, or Timbuktu, that the local police station requires all tourists to register with them and get a large purple stamp in their passport as evidence, helping local officials keep track of foreign traffic in this small town.

24. Mali is 90 percent Muslim, 1 percent Christian, and 9 percent purely indigenous religions. "Mali," *CIA World Factbook*.

25. The *adhan*, or Muslim call to prayer, may sound like musical singing to an outsider, but is considered sacred chant by practitioners, and therefore outside the realm of secular music-making.

26. For more about the ramifications of recent bans on music by Islamist extremists, see Andy Morgan, "Mali: No Rhythm or Reason as Militants Declare War on Music," *The Guardian*, October 23, 2012, www.guardian.co.uk/world/2012/oct/23/mali-militants -declare-war-music; Robin Deneslow, "Mali Music Ban by Islamists 'Crushing Culture to Impose Rule,'" *The Guardian*, January 15, 2013, www.guardian.co.uk/music/2013/jan/15 /mali-music-ban-islamists-crushing; and CBC News, "Mali's Musicians Defiant in Face of Music Ban," January 22, 2013, www.cbc.ca/news/arts/story/2013/01/21/mali-music.html.

BIBLIOGRAPHY

Bertsch, Charlie. "Subverting World Music: The Sublime Frequencies Label." *Tikkun*. July 1, 2009. www.tikkun.org/article.php/Bertsch-subverting-world-music/print.

Brown, Ryan. Interview with Alan Bishop. 2006. www.indieworkshop.com/archive /interviews.php?id=114.

CBC News. "Mali's Musicians Defiant in Face of Music Ban." January 22, 2013. www.cbc .ca/news/arts/story/2013/01/21/mali-music.html.

Central Intelligence Agency. "Country Demographics and Area Comparisons." *CIA World Factbook*. www.cia.gov/library/publications/the-world-factbook/geos/ml.html.

Charry, Eric. *Mande Music: Traditional and Modern Music of the Maninka and Mandinka of Western Africa*. Chicago: University of Chicago Press, 2000.

Connell, John, and Chris Gibson. "Vicarious Journeys: Travels in Music." *Tourism Geographies: An International Journal of Tourism Space, Place, and Environment* 6, no. 1 (2004): 2–25.

Conway, Cecilia. *African Banjo Echoes in Appalachia: A Study of Folk Traditions*. Knoxville: University of Tennessee Press, 1995.

Deneslow, Robin. "Mali Music Ban by Islamists 'Crushing Culture to Impose Rule.'" *The Guardian*. January 15, 2013. www.guardian.co.uk/music/2013/jan/15/mali-music-ban -islamists-crushing.

Feld, Steven. "Waterfalls of Song: An Acoustemology of Place Resounding in Bosavi, Papua New Guinea." In *Senses of Place*, edited by Steven Feld and Keith Basso, 91–135. Santa Fe: School of American Research Press, 1996.

Feld, Steven, and Donald Brenneis. "Doing Anthropology in Sound." *American Ethnologist* 31, no. 4 (2004): 461–74.

"Mali." *Ethnologue*. www.ethnologue.com/show_country.asp?name=ML.

Martine, Tucker. Personal communication. March 18, 2013. Portland, Ore.

Morgan, Andy. "Mali: No Rhythm or Reason as Militants Declare War on Music." *The Guardian*. October 23, 2012. www.guardian.co.uk/world/2012/oct/23/mali-militants -declare-war-music.

Ong, Walter J. *Orality and Literacy: The Technologizing of the Word*. New York: Routledge, 1982.

Schafer, R. Murray. *The Tuning of the World*. New York: Random House, 1977.

Skinner, Ryan Thomas. "Bush Taxi Mali: Field Recordings from Mali" (Review). *Journal of American Folklore* 124, no. 493 (2011): 214–15.

Sublime Frequencies website, www.sublimefrequencies.com.

Tang, Patricia. *Masters of the Sabar: Wolof Griot Percussionists from Senegal*. Philadelphia: Temple University Press. 2007.

Interview
with Tucker Martine

Tucker Martine has recorded three titles for Sublime Frequencies: *Bush Taxi Mali: Field Recordings from Mali*, *Broken Hearted Dragonflies: Insect Electronica from Southeast Asia*, and *Eat the Dream: Gnawa Music from Essaouira*. We met on the rainy evening of March 18, 2013, at Branch Whiskey Bar in Portland, Oregon, to talk about his experiences with the label.

JULIE STRAND: How did you become involved with Sublime Frequencies?

TUCKER MARTINE: Well, I lived in Seattle for ages, so I've known [label co-founder] Alan Bishop for a long time through the Seattle music scene. His background is from the band Sun City Girls, which is kind of a wild, art-rock band, so I knew him through being a person in Seattle involved with music, ending up at some of the same places, and having a lot of the same friends. He knew that I was doing a lot of traveling and field recording, so he told me that he'd started a label and said to let him know if I had anything that he should check out.

JS: So when you made these recordings, did you already have these trips planned, or did you go to any of these places specifically to record for Sublime Frequencies?

TM: No, I never went with Sublime Frequencies in mind. In fact, I think all those trips were completed before the label even existed. The Moroccan recordings had already been released by Tinder Records, in the Bay Area, but then went out of print because the label folded, so when Alan expressed excitement about releasing those, too, I went for it.

JS: Which recording did you submit first?

TM: I gave him the Mali one first, because the Moroccan ones at the time were still tied up with the other label. It's all confusing anyway because the Moroccan recordings were made in 1994, before the Mali recordings (1998), but Sublime released them later. So, the Mali one was released first, and then the insect recordings were released.

JS: Yes, *Broken Hearted Dragonflies*, tell me about that one.

TM: I gave that one to Alan mostly just thinking, "Oh you'll get a kick out of this, I know you like esoteric stuff." His wife was from Burma, which is where a lot of those recordings are from, so I just kind of passed it along, more just knowing he was one of the few people in the world I knew who would actually go home and spend time listening to it. And he immediately called and said he wanted to put it out. [laughs]

JS: So that one was done in Burma mostly?

TM: Burma, Thailand, and Laos, but mostly in Burma. There are just a few little, odd things that I wove in from other places because they were part of the same trip.

JS: Tell me about your editing aesthetics in these recordings—were they all purely your own inspiration?

TM: Yes, exactly. The Moroccan one was the first such thing that I had done, and they were just recordings I had made. It's like, somebody who likes to take pictures when they travel, I just like to make recordings. So I just did it for myself, and I made up some cassettes from Morocco to give to friends, which eventually ended up in the hands of some people who wanted to put them out because they were starting a world music label. That really gave me the bug. It was so great to get the music and sounds, and then to figure out how to try to weave it all together so that it feels like a coherent story.

JS: I heard that you collected over 19 hours of audio for the *Bush Taxi Mali* recording. How did you choose what to include in the collection?

TM: I really just went for the sounds that spoke to me. I had a list that I narrowed down to my favorites, and then I tried to figure out how to weave them together. Sometimes something wouldn't fit in so I would axe it, or sometimes I would realize I need more environment sounds to put between these two tracks, so I'd go digging through [the recordings]. It was a lot like a puzzle, you get a couple of pieces that give you a clue to what's next, but you won't know until you get the next piece.

JS: There's a lot of *ngoni* (three-stringed traditional lute) throughout the recording, why does that instrument play so prominently in this collection?

TM: Well, I had sought after the *ngoni* stuff. It was just a sound that captivated me, and I kept hearing it on recordings from Mali, and it drew me in. I couldn't quite place it, and I couldn't quite picture it. This was before the Internet was readily available, so I was really driven by that intrigue of not knowing where the sound came from or how it was made. Then when I was in Mali, whenever I was in a situation where I might do some recording, I expressed enthusiasm about the *ngoni*.

JS: One of the things people have noticed about *Bush Taxi Mali* is its higher production value and more polished sound compared to a lot of the other Sublime Frequencies releases. Is that just a result of it being your style?

TM: Yeah, and it's where I was at the time. I know [Sublime Frequencies] likes it really raw, which is great because there have been a lot of labels that have covered more polished-sounding stuff. But mine were still just done with a stereo mic and me out there in the fields and in the dirt.

JS: What else were you doing in this time period in your own career?

TM: Nineteen ninety-four was my second year in Seattle, and I was trying to save up money to buy recording equipment. I was very taken with people like Brian Eno and John Cage, who were using the recording studio as a compositional tool. I was really driven toward exploring that and ended up recording other people as I went along, just as a way to learn the gear and understand recording better.

JS: What do you spend most of your time doing now? I know that you have the studio and you're a producer.

TM: Pretty much doing that, yeah. I'm making records all the time, and most of them are a fairly long process, so I end up with only a handful a year. That's the thing about record-making, it takes three months to make something 40 minutes long that hopefully sounds effortless. I hope I have the patience for it as I grow older.

JS: How do you see these three projects that you did for Sublime Frequencies fitting into your overall body of work and your creative aspirations?

TM: Sometimes I really think it's a shame that I haven't continued to do more of those types of recordings, but I also think it's dangerous to think that you can just go do something like that at any time. I think part of what was so special is that I went on those trips fully prepared for none of that to happen. If I went on a trip that was all about that type of project, there would be all this pressure. It would be so fraught with disappointment, especially if stuff wasn't coming together at every turn.

So, the Sublime Frequencies projects feel to me really, really related to what

I'm doing now. I'm always looking for the spontaneous, unconscious moments that happen in a recording, even if it's a collection of three-minute songs that's very composed. The field recordings have helped teach me that a lot of the most special moments are the accidental ones and the ones that no one is looking for or looking to make, but if you have the ear to notice when they happen, they really can be some of the most special moments.

MICHAEL E. VEAL

Dry Spell Blues
Sublime Frequencies across
the West African Sahel

I. DRY SPELL BLUES: THE DELTA

It have been so dry,
you can make a powderhouse out of the world
Well, it have been so dry
you can make a powderhouse out of the world
Then all the moneymen [are] like a rattlesnake in his coil

Son House, from "Dry Spell Blues," 1930[1]

In June 1964, blues enthusiasts Dick Waterman and Nick Perls climbed the front steps of an apartment building in Rochester, New York, where they had finally tracked down the singer and guitarist Son House, a legend of the Delta blues and a strong influence on iconic blues masters such as Robert Johnson and Muddy Waters.[2] With a style shaped by his riff-based bottleneck-guitar playing and impassioned, churchified vocals, House melded the rhythmic drive of the country blues with the impassioned delivery of the country preacher. Although he had not played in years at the time of Waterman and Perl's visit, rapturous press was soon proclaiming House's "rediscovery," and the singer's reemergence is considered a defining moment of the 1960s' blues boom, which revived the careers of older, rural bluesmen for the folk festival circuit and the new recording market in American folklore.[3] House and other, older blues performers were soon given recording contracts and tours of America, Europe, and beyond, and

The raw, droning sound on *Group Inerane: Guitars from Agadez
(Music of Niger)* (SF034) and other Sublime Frequencies African
guitar albums resonates with the Mississippi blues tradition.

the release of House's 1964 collection *Father of the Delta Blues* was probably *the*
seminal of event of the folk-blues revival.[4]

House's example is significant in that it demonstrates the role of sound recordings in the preservation and revitalization of musical traditions. He might well
have remained in relative obscurity had his earlier recordings (for Paramount in
1930 and the Library of Congress in 1941–1942) not caught the ears of Waterman,
Perl, and their colleagues.[5] In today's lingo, these men would be known as "crate
diggers," music enthusiasts who spend hours thumbing through stacks of records
in the hope of discovering novel sounds and the performers behind them. Sound
recordings were the medium that allowed the music of the Mississippi Delta to
transcend space and time, and to bridge formidable social, racial, and national
barriers. Suddenly, middle-class white Americans and Europeans were clamoring
for the sound (and in some cases, *to sound like*) elderly, rural African-American
men who, in their primes, might as well have lived, to refract James Baldwin, in
"another country." The comparison is relevant, since the recorded documenta-

tion of America's rural musical traditions—whether made for commercial or academic purposes—primed a generation of musicians and record collectors for their embrace of ethnographic recordings of the wider world's traditional music that were made by ethnomusicologists and cultural anthropologists. These two modes, the local and the global, would later fuse in the sonic imaginings of some listeners, and the forms of collecting, connoisseurship, and crate-digging these recordings inspired would be a strong shaper of America's post–World War II music culture. In this sense, House's theme of "Dry Spell Blues" could also refer to the American "world music" impulse and its continual search for exotic sounds, a search the Sublime Frequencies label would undertake in its turn-of-the-twenty-first-century forays into Africa's music.

Historically, the style of guitar playing that evolved in the Mississippi Delta and other parts of the American South was strongly traceable to West African traditions of string playing that had traveled to the United States via the transatlantic slave trade.[6] For African Americans of House's generation, however, "Africa" might as well have been Neptune; it was a symbol feared, despised, and misunderstood in the African-American imaginary due to the cultural disruptions of slavery and its distortions of black history. And though the symbol of Africa began to be regenerated in the post–World War II contexts of African and Caribbean nationalism, and African-American civil rights and Black Power, most young African Americans of the 1960s dismissed the country blues as an anachronistic music redolent of the old South, racial oppression, docility, and servitude.[7]

By the time of the 1960s' blues revival, then, the type of acoustic, rural blues associated with House, Robert Johnson, and others appealed mainly to white Americans whose interest in the music was either folkloric or had been stoked by British blues rockers such as The Yardbirds, The Bluesbreakers, or The Rolling Stones, who publicly proclaimed their admiration for the old blues masters.[8] In this way, the existential state of the solitary, wandering bluesman—a state of being consolidated in the relatively individualized labor of American slavery and intensified as a byproduct of the increasing opportunities for itinerant labor that followed Emancipation—became a state accessible to Americans of all backgrounds.[9]

Musically, of course, the blues language of pentatonic riffs, "blue note" inflections, and swing rhythms had been a central dialect of American popular music since the Jazz Age. What changed in the 1960s was the specific embrace of the *guitar* blues—in its origins, a rural music of low social status, whose structural code had been electrified in the 1950s by Delta musicians such as Muddy Waters and Elmore James who migrated to northern industrial cities such as Chicago. It was later radically rewritten by musicians whose aesthetics had been transformed by the mind-altering substances associated with the 1960s' counterculture, by the trickle-down technologies of the Cold War with their sci-fi implications for musical sound, and by a youth culture in full visionary mode. Thus, between the 1930s and the 1970s, the guitar blues traveled a trajectory across categories of rural folk music to national folklore, until its core innovations were soaked up into the common practice of American vernacular and popular traditions.

While the structural qualities of the blues were being subsumed into the mainstream of American popular music, they were gradually acquiring a different shade in African-American culture during the 1960s, as scholars and historians began to invest the music with greater significance. Social scientists began to valorize the form as an important folk root of African-American culture. Literary figures distilled an idea of the blues as a philosophical essence of African-American culture and began to mine blues lyrics for the foundations of a distinctly African-American existential outlook.[10] Most significantly, it was the confluent interests of folklorists, ethnomusicologists, cultural anthropologists, and cultural nationalist currents associated with civil rights and Black Power that coalesced in an examination of the blues as musical evidence of African survivals in the Americas and that led to a gradual resignification of the music in trans-African terms.[11] At the same time that guitarists such as Jimi Hendrix, Jeff Beck, Jimmy Page, and Eric Clapton were recalibrating the guitar blues for the aesthetics of the Space Age, the word "blues" began to circulate around the Black Atlantic, providing a new cultural inflection for a broad range of African string-based musics. These were typically played by itinerant musicians, featuring droning string instruments supporting semispoken or declamatory vocals, and were generally plaintive, melancholy, or reflective in tone. With such a constellation of cultural and economic pressures on the blues symbol—coming simultaneously from rock, African-American music, world music, the global discourse on blackness, and the ongoing American search for ever more exotic sounds, it was only a matter of time before the emergence of the idea of African "guitar heroes," borne of a moment of pan-Africanist idealism and rationalized on the terms of British/American guitar rock.

II. ANOTHER COUNTRY

Hendrix does have one big trip in mind. "I'm gonna go to Memphis, Egypt,"
he said, in a curious tone. "I had a vision and it told me to go there.
I'm always having visions of things and I know that it's
building up to something really major."
Steven Roby, Hendrix on Hendrix [12]

In Africa itself, the concept of a "guitar hero" was actually nothing new, although its particular form of heroism had as much to do with currents of nationalism and postcoloniality as it did with technological and stylistic innovation. Though the instrument historically had been looked down upon in Africa as one of low social status since its introduction in the late nineteenth century (it was cheap to acquire, relatively easy to learn, unconnected with more deeply rooted indigenous musical traditions, and generally associated with the urban poor), sub-Saharan Africa has in fact been one of the world's richest spheres of guitar playing since World War II, and the instrument was central to most of the continent's popular styles from the 1950s through the beginning of the digital age in the 1980s. Viewed one-dimensionally, its introduction might seem a marker of Western musical imperialism, but the guitar's true history in Africa has been a prismatic, syncretic dialogue between Western popular music and indigenous musical traditions. In its electrified form, the guitar would acquire as many subtle shadings during the early decades of African popular music as it had during the birth of rock and roll: postwar Africa was a constellation of guitar dialects carved out of the raw fusion of melody, rhythm, tone, and electricity. The distinctive six-string personalities that emerged across the continent were comparable to those at the foundation of electric blues, rock and roll, and soul, such as Elmore James, Scotty Moore, Bo Diddley, Chuck Berry, Steve Cropper, Jimmy Nolen, Duane Eddy, and Roebuck "Pops" Staples.

It is generally accepted that the guitar was introduced to Africa by the Portuguese in the fourteenth century, while its regional spread throughout the continent is largely attributed to the movement of merchant sailors (of Kru ethnicity from present-day Liberia, Sierra Leone, and Côte d'Ivoire) around the African coasts in the early decades of the twentieth century. Historians of highlife such as John Collins have credited the Kru as disseminators of a style of guitar-playing (dubbed "palmwine" and which Collins refers to as "African guitarism"), in which contrapuntal figures are created by a characteristic alternation between a bass line played with the thumb and arpeggiation by the other fingers.[13] Spreading the European guitar as part of their wares, historical accounts suggests that the Kru transplanted this style of guitar-playing at various African points of commerce (and future capitals) along the West African coast and up the Congo River Basin: Dakar, Conakry, Accra, Cape Coast, Lagos, Port Harcourt, Leopoldville (Kinshasa), and others. By the 1950s, the electric guitar had become widely available and, at each point, new genres germinated at the intersection of the new instrument and local musical traditions.

Best known among these African traditions are two highly influential corridors of guitar playing. First is the Mande cultural sphere in parts of The Republic of Guinea, The Gambia, Mali, Burkina Faso, and Senegal in which techniques of indigenous string and keyed percussion instruments (such as the *kora* harp, the *ngoni* lute, and the keyed *balafon*) were transferred onto the guitar. A similarly influential evolution took place along the Congo River, where musicians in the new capitals of Kinshasa and Brazzaville mapped patterns from indigenous string, keyed percussion, and lamellophone instruments (such as the *likembe* thumb piano) onto this new instrument.[14]

The guitar's significance extended beyond its sonic qualities. As the second half of the twentieth century unfolded, the guitar could be found at the heart of the popular traditions that provided the soundtrack for various nations' post–World War II march to national independence. Its lustrous melodies, often laid over the adapted Cuban *montunos* that were central to the formation of so many popular African styles, transmuted the euphoria of nationalism and independence into musical sound.[15] With its optimistic feel, shimmering melodicism, and the organic, expansive sound of the reverb units of the era, the guitar music of independence-era Africa vaguely recalls psychedelic music of the 1960s. In reality, chemical interventions were rarely necessary; these heady sonic constructions, Baroque in their structural complexity, were driven mainly by the utopian visions of nation-building. It was the guitar's initial disconnection from traditional repertoires and contexts that provided it an innocuous and stealthy profile, enabling popular styles to become agents of social change. The subsequent rapprochement with traditional musics would be catalyzed by the cultural imperatives resulting from national independence: essentially, the need to concoct a music that was modern but that was simultaneously clearly rooted in tradition.

It was within these contexts of sonic and political potency that bona fide electric guitar virtuosi began to emerge in the late 1960s, including Barthélémy

Attisso with Senegal's Orchestra Baobab, Boubacar Traoré with Mali's Rail Band, Sekou Diabate with Guinea's Bembeya Jazz National, and Nicholas Kasanda ("Dr. Nico") with various bands in former Zaire (now Democratic Republic of the Congo). Playing with the most popular dance bands in these nations, they were "heroes" in the sense that their melodies, cast in the electric hues of African modernity, were dramatic embodiments of the hopes and dreams of new nationhood. In the final analysis, as much as it was connected to social change, the electric guitar in West Africa, unlike in the American South, was not typically an instrument of rebels or outsiders. These artists did fully embrace rock's institution of the guitar solo, an art form distilled from the solitary existential state of the country bluesman. But they repositioned it within the polyrhythmic net of interlocking parts characteristic of West African's tropical forest belt, in a way that re-redefined the individualism of the rock-guitar solo in terms of a sonic, structural encoding of community and reciprocity.

What is interesting and telling, from the point of view of the ongoing pan-African musical "conversation," is that a similar fusion was being architected simultaneously on the other side of the Atlantic. Guitarists of color like Jimi Hendrix and Carlos Santana, having been knighted as guitar heroes within the exploding soundscape of the 1960s' counterculture, found themselves answerable to the pressing political issues of the day and were consequently working to reposition the individualism of the lead guitar solo within a more inclusive, communalist, and ultimately Africanist aesthetic. At the Woodstock Festival in 1969, for example, Hendrix debuted his Gypsy Suns, Moons and Rainbows band, which expanded his power-trio format to include a second guitarist, a West Africa–inspired percussionist, and a Latin-Caribbean percussionist. The full-blown psychedelic freak-out of his previous power trio was replaced in the new band with an emphasis on repeating and interlocking riffs and rhythm patterns.[16] Santana also appeared at the Woodstock Festival with a sound that grafted his blues-rock guitar style over a rhythmic foundation adapted from Afro-Cuban music.[17] The closest Hendrix ever came to West Africa was in 1968, with his two-part evocation of the Benin-Haiti-New Orleans *Vodoun* corridor in "Voodoo Chile"/"Voodoo Child (Slight Return)," and with a brief 1969 vacation in Morocco. But Santana actually appeared in Ghana in 1971 as part of the legendary "Soul to Soul" festival held in Kwame Nkrumah's Black Star Square, where his performance was rapturously received and praised as the most "African-sounding" of all the visiting performers.[18] Santana was essentially playing an edgier, more aggressive version of the kind of fusion that musicians in places such as Guinea, Senegal, and the Congo had been working at since the 1950s.

Even in areas of the continent that Western performers were less likely to visit in those years, the same cultural process was powered by sound recordings. Manthia Diawara's *In Search of Africa* chronicles a "mini-Woodstock" held in Bamako in the early 1970s, a listening party organized with his friend "Sly"—in which the electric guitar retained all of its political potency across cultural borders:

> The imagination of the youth in Africa at the time was captured by the defiant images of George Jackson, Angela Davis, Muhammad Ali, Eldridge Cleaver, Malcolm X and James Brown . . . We dressed to resemble our black American heroes . . . We decided to organize our own Woodstock-in-Bamako, to educate people. Sly and I knew the names of all the musicians who had played at Woodstock, and we wanted to make sure that our Woodstock-in-Bamako would present the real thing . . . When we arrived, the speakers were blaring "With A Little Help From My Friends" by Joe Cocker. There were many people who had copied our style—that is, they were dressed like Jimi Hendrix, George Harrison, Richie Havens, Buddy Miles, Sly Stone, Frank Zappa, Alice Cooper and James Brown. But there were some who had donned traditional hunter suits; tight-fitting trousers and mud-cloth blouses oversewn with cowrie shells and mirrors. Some of them wore hunters' elongated hats, which covered their ears and cheeks all the way to their chins. They had bows and arrows, and they looked like Simbon initiates . . . There was smoke in the air, and Sly and I felt really good about ourselves. Soon Jimi Hendrix's "Voodoo Child" filled the air, and by then we were on top of the world.[19]

This moment of cultural frisson in Mali, during which youth cultures emerged as a result of the growth of leisure time and money in the post–World War II era, was repeated all over sub-Saharan Africa and was in the Malian case artfully immortalized in Malick Sidibé's photographs of Bamako's nightlife in the 1960s and 1970s.[20] In almost every image, a record player sits somewhere in the background, while partygoers pose, grasping vinyl records as if they were ritually charged objects. In fact, they *were* objects in a political and historical ritual, one that used a remarkably urbane form of music connoisseurship to assert Africa into a modernity that had previously been denied it, while giving that modernity an African inflection. As chronicled by Sidibé, these ritual objects included recordings by soul singers James Brown and Ray Charles, *Charanga* singer Johnny Pacheco, French chanteuse Françoise Hardy, jazz organist Jimmy Smith, releases from Guinea's state-run Syliphone label, The Beatles, and Hendrix. The electric guitar was gradually taking its place among them.

Diawara and his friends embraced musicians like Hendrix in the early 1970s in part because the efflorescent fusion of indigenous music and rock guitar was still consolidating. By the 1970s, local guitarists had worked out this fusion. In fact, the ebullient guitar solos heard on Guinea's state-run Syliphone label suddenly soared an octave higher in the 1970s, thanks to the intervention of Roger Mayer's Octavia—a combined octave-splitting-and-distortion device originally custom-made for Hendrix and not commercially produced at the time, but which inexplicably had found its way to the Voix de la Révolution studios of post-independence Guinea.[21] In addition to the handful of Hendrix songs on which it features (including "Purple Haze, "One Rainy Wish," and "Who Knows"), its sound endures on the other side of the Atlantic as a signature of the short-lived, halcyon days of Guinean independence on songs such as "Moussogbe" (Bembeya Jazz National, 1973) and "Kogno Koura" (Balla et ses Balladins, 1972).[22]

These younger musicians were proud citizens of African modernity, but simultaneously conceived of their art as in stylistic dialogue with Western rock-guitar practices, in political solidarity with the 1960s' counterculture and Black Power sentiments as articulated in the United States and, by the 1970s, increasingly drawing its spiritual power from the wellsprings of traditional African culture. The cover of the first volume of the 1976 compilation *Assalam Aleikoum Africa*, for example, features a striking photo of an unnamed guitarist clad in an ensemble of giant leaves and the traditional garb of a medicine man, standing in front of a traditional raffia hut. He holds a Gibson ES-335, a guitar strongly associated with the blues in general and B. B. King in particular. But the instrument is not plugged into an amplifier; the cord stretches from the instrument to a forbidding ritual mask strung up on the side of the hut.[23] The image says much about the symbolic sources powering the music. This African generation's embrace of the rock aesthetic enabled it to differentiate itself from the foreign music that had dominated at the time of independence, and which gradually was being stigmatized as "colonial" in the literal or symbolic sense: "copyright" cover versions of Western pop music (in the Anglophone areas) and/or Cuban models (in the Francophone areas). And as the album image suggests, in many places this remaking was accomplished by cloaking the new instrument in the aura of indigenous, traditional models of music-making.

Extending outward from the music, however, the "Afro-rock" aesthetic contained a generational and countercultural implication that the time was drawing

near for the hard questions to be asked of African independence and postcoloniality. These questions had much to do with the issues of nation, religion, ethnicity,
class, and the global distribution of Africa's natural resources.

III. DRY SPELL BLUES: THE DESERT

Most of these African guitar traditions pull toward a center of gravity that aligns
with the Atlantic coast, the area of historical encounter with Westerners. However, another trajectory of African guitarism orients northward and northeast-
ward toward the West African Sahel and further, into the Sahara Desert, North
Africa, and the music cultures of the Middle East. Encompassing portions of
Cameroon, Nigeria, Niger, Chad, Burkina Faso, Senegal, and Mauritania, the
music cultures of the West African Sahel/Western Sudan resonate with a different aspect of the blues. The idea of "two centers" of cultural gravity is, of course,
a reflection of the broader historical reality of the Sahel as a crossroads between
the global "East and West," understood largely in religious terms. Nations with
a north-south orientation such as Nigeria or Cameroon tend to be split between
a remote, Muslim north and a coastal, cosmopolitan and Christian south while
(overwhelmingly Muslim) nations with an east-west orientation such as Senegal
and Mali tend to be split between a remote east and a more cosmopolitan west.

The Republic of Niger occupies a peculiar place within this regional scheme.
An area of former "French West Africa" that gained its independence in 1960, it
is geographically the largest country in West Africa but also a landlocked country
of which roughly 80 percent is composed of the Sahara Desert. With limited
natural resources, the country has not been as woven into the global economy
as other African countries, and it regularly ranks toward the very bottom of
the United Nations Human Development Index.[24] It goes without saying that,
unlike bordering nations such as Nigeria, Ghana, and Mali, the musical culture
of Niger remains remote to the West, and even to most connoisseurs of African
music. Although the traditional music of its various ethnicities have been well
documented by (mainly French) ethnographic labels such as Nonesuch, Ocora,
and Playasound, it has not had a vibrant tradition of popular music and its best-
known art form is not music, but the annual Guerewol festival, an androgynous
spectacle in which young, male Fula cattle herders dress up and preen outra-
geously to attract the attention of young women.[25] In general, however, Niger's
art culture is not well known in the wider world and the good-natured clowning
of the Guerewol does not mirror Niger's relatively tough postindependence his-

tory, which has encompassed periods of protracted drought, military coups and countercoups, and widespread poverty and illiteracy.

At first glance, few Westerners would ever imagine this remote, sparsely populated, and semiarid part of Africa as a source of any kind of rock music. And in general, the musical sound of this area is more austere than the tropical-belt musics, due mainly to the narrower range of materials historically available in the desert environment to be fashioned into musical instruments. But it was here that the Sublime Frequencies label planted its proverbial flag, documenting a unique form of Saharan electric-guitar music that it and other labels eventually sold to the world as a form of "blues." This is not as surprising as it may initially seem, given that, culturally speaking, the West African Sudan and Western Sahel regions are connected closely to the Middle Eastern context in which the Western guitar historically evolved. Expanding beyond the "great bend" of the Niger River (roughly between Bamako, Mali, and Niamey, Niger) into Northern Africa and the Sahara Desert, the region contains a plethora of bowed and plucked string instruments that have proliferated across the huge geographic expanse of the Muslim world, from West Africa to Southeast Asia, and which, in their westward flow across the Atlantic, have influenced the blues culture of the United States.[26] The musical connection is reinforced by the nomadic and seminomadic cultures that populate this area, whose lifestyles resonate to varying degrees with the American country blues as a musical, social, and philosophical practice.

At length the day arrived when I was to set out on my long wished for excursion . . . For what can be more interesting than a considerable town, said to have once been as large as Tunis, situated in the midst of lawless tribes, on the border of the desert . . . and protected as a place of rendezvous and commerce between nations of the most different character, and having the most various wants? It is by mere accident that this town has not attracted as much interest in Europe as her sister town, Timbuktu.

German explorer Heinrich Barth, 1850[27]

The town that so captured Heinrich Barth's imagination in the late nineteenth century was Agadez, a desert outpost of the Tuareg and other nomadic groups. Sometimes referred to as the "blue men of the desert" because their skin is often stained by their characteristic indigo-dyed clothing, the Tuareg are a cluster of nomadic, desert-dwelling Berber tribes numbering approximately one million people split among the nation-states of Algeria, Niger, Mali, and Libya (with smaller communities in northern Nigeria and Burkina Faso). Historically, they controlled the trans-Saharan trade routes linking the sub-Saharan interior with the major cities of the Mediterranean, and Agadez enjoyed its apex in the fourteenth and fifteenth centuries as a stop on the caravan routes from Kano and Timbuktu (in present-day Nigeria and Mali, respectively) to North Africa. Its gradual decline began after it was sacked by the Moroccans in the fifteenth century, but as late as the late nineteenth century was still considered a far-flung outpost of the Ottoman Empire.

Somewhat similarly to the Kurds of southwest Asia, the Tuareg have maintained a contentious relationship with the governments of the various nation-states among which their region of the Sahara has been apportioned. This has particularly been the case in Mali, which borders Niger in the southwest. The Tuareg's claims of political marginalization and physical dispossession have erupted in several uprisings: 1962 to 1964, 1990 to 1995, 2007 to 2009, and the most recent, in 2012. The 2012 rebellion, in fact, was more far-reaching in its consequences than the previous uprisings. Reports indicate that this resurgence of Tuareg nationalism, resulting from the contentious efforts of several groups, was intensified by the return to Mali of armed Tuareg soldiers who had long been disaffected with the central government's bias toward the Bamana-speaking majority in the south.[28] These soldiers previously had received military training from General Muammar al-Qadaffi in Libya, and later had been conscripted to fight alongside Qadaffi as his regime was under siege in 2011. By the time of the 2012 rebellion, the rebels were fighting instead for the creation of a secessionist, Tuareg-controlled state to be called Azawad that would comprise most of northern Mali. Ultimately, however, the more broad-based and Islamist Ansar Dine faction usurped the leadership of the rebellion, imposing Sharia law in the occupied territory and banning a number of activities, including, ironically, music. In northern Malian cities such as Gao, Mopti, and Timbuktu, musicians began to be harassed and jailed, and sometimes even had their limbs amputated by militants who considered music, in accordance with a radically strict interpretation of Islamic law, able to inflame the passions.[29]

This conflict between the settled, historical empire-builders of the south and the nomadic, desert-dwelling tribes of the north is reflected in the very different sounds of their respective musical forms. But as strongly secular Muslims with interests that diverged from both the Bambara in southern Mali and the fundamentalists to the north, the Tuareg were ultimately pawns in a broader wave of Islamist sentiment sweeping across the western Sahel. Northern Mali eventually was subdued by the Malian government with support from a transnational military force led by France, but, at the time of writing, the musical life of the north has yet to return to its former level of activity. Western commentaries often noted the irony of the fact that music, one of Mali's strongest imports, was being banned. But they ignored the fact that northern Mali had always been, in effect, a different country from southern Mali. The North was essentially a lawless region dominated by the Tuareg and other nomadic peoples who had controlled the area for centuries, and within which colonial geographic boundaries were relatively meaningless. Understanding this area as fragmented into "northeastern Mali" and "southwestern Niger" is less meaningful than understanding it as a transnational desert region defined by the Tuareg and other nomadic and seminomadic peoples. Mali's global profile as a powerhouse of African music was based largely on the music of the *jelis* and *griots* of the south. At least, until Sublime Frequencies came along . . .

Until fairly recently, the best known of the so-called "Tuareg blues" bands was Tinariwen, who grew out of the uprisings of the 1960s and 1970s and were the first to elaborate the Tuareg's concerns in a rock medium, to an international audience. The group's leader/guitarist Ibrahim Ag Alhabib was inspired by the music of Hendrix and other Western pop musicians, but has a touch and sound on the instrument more reminiscent of guitarists like John Lee Hooker and James "Blood" Ulmer, and Tinariwen albums such as *Aman Iman* are compelling collections of Tuareg blues crafted for the ears of the global world music audience.[30] But while Tinariwen's recordings are shaped by high production values, tuneful pop songcraft, funky, dance-oriented bass lines, and a vaguely clubby aesthetic, a cluster of younger groups gradually emerged with a much rawer sound and delivery. Group Bombino (led by guitarist Omara "Bombino" Mochtar) and Group Inerane (led by guitarist Bibi Ahmed) emerged from Agadez, while Group Doueh (led by Salmou "Doueh" Baamar) hail from Dakhla, in the disputed territory of Western Sahara. These bands formed the nucleus of Sublime Frequencies' campaign of documenting and selling the electric guitar music of the region. Sonically, their music finds its closest kinship with the "desert blues" of the late Malian guitarists Ali Farka Touré (who hailed from Niafunké, near Timbuktu) and Lobi Traor Traoré, and the little-known guitar music of nearby Mauritania (which has also sometimes been described as "blues").[31] Unlike the complex figuration of Congolese styles, the intricate filigree of the Mande styles, or the dense polyrhythms of the coastal areas, the Agadez groups' Sahelian string aesthetic has the rawness of a garage band, offering a form of "African rock" that is most true to the term. Traded around the region's thriving cassette culture, it seems inevitable that this particular sound would attract the attention of Sublime Frequencies, twenty-first-century crate-diggers whose sensibility is fundamentally shaped by punk rock. With previous guitar-related releases (in whole or in part) from India, Thailand, Jordan, Indonesia, Myanmar, and Iraq, one of the label's most important contributions has been highlighting electric guitar repertoires of the non-Western (and particularly Muslim) world. In rapid succession, the label issued a series of albums in its "Guitars from Agadez" series.[32]

If Syrian *dabke* singer Omar Souleyman was Sublime Frequencies' ace in the hole because his hyped-up, electronic rhythms resonated with the Western techno/electronica crowd, the Tuareg blues was another ace because of its resonance with Western punk-, indie-, and blues-rock sensibilities, and also because it could be marketed as an exotic form of guitar rock. Presented to the global audience as guitar heroes and rhetorically written into the transnationalized blues currents flowing across the Atlantic, groups like Bombino, Doueh, and Inerane help extend a form of blues-rooted, guitar heroicism that, in the context of the digital age, has fallen largely out of fashion in the West. It helps that this is also a form of rock that literally comes from "as far away as Timbuktu." The sound of distorted guitars is a familiar element to Western ears, but the unusual tunings and microtonal inflections of the Agadez groups fuel fantasies of remoteness for the dwellers of information-dense hipster locales in the United States such as Berkeley, Williamsburg, and Portland.

As with the recent Western popularity of Konono No 1's recordings of distorted Congolese thumb pianos, an aesthetic of dereliction provides an aura of authenticity to the crudely electric tones here.[33] Sublime Frequencies' 2005 video *Niger: Magic and Ecstasy in the Sahel*, for example is, by turns, a helpful and confounding companion to the Niger recordings, presenting the viewer with panoramic vignettes of Nigerien music, including two segments of electric guitar music. Filmed in rustic settings with musicians playing on cracked cymbals, jerry-rigged sound systems, cheaply produced electric guitars, and with vampire bats hanging from the ceiling, the film largely depicts circumstances that a typical Westerner would interpret as impoverished. While aerial shots of Agadez show a city plan of highly regularized, geometric organization, the Niger video tends to present either "broken" geometries (decrepit buildings, outskirts of towns, mud huts) or arid, organic settings such as stretches of desert. To some extent, this may be a reasonably accurate depiction of parts of Niger, but it tends to reinforce an impression of physical dereliction and cultural isolation. There are no clear scenes of Niamey, the nation's capital (a city of modern office buildings, paved roads, and hotels), or of any standard of living remotely comparable with that familiar to most of Sublime Frequencies' audience. After all, the Sahel Sounds label recently has released two volumes of *Music from Saharan Cellphones*, full of Sahelian beats given a FruityLooped, Auto-Tuned hip-hop inflection that tie the musical life of some of the remotest regions of the Sahara directly to what is being produced in New York City and Los Angeles.[34] But Sublime Frequencies' only semi-nod to the outside world on this DVD is oblique and incidental, a brief market scene in Agadez where French hip-hop can be heard playing in the background.

Truth be told, there is something about the coarse, droning music of the group Ouragan Del Air ("Air of the Desert") and Group Inerane (which closes out the DVD) that is strongly reminiscent of Mississippi blues musicians like John Lee Hooker or Junior Kimbrough. And when it is amplified to the high volume that the Niger bands play on the American and European club circuit, with the melodies of indigenous Tuareg lutes such as the *imzhad* or *tinidit* mapped onto distorted guitars and articulated from within a continuous electric drone, the results come across as a coarse, exotic, and Middle East–inflected sound reminiscent of the early Velvet Underground, the alternate tuning universes of Glenn Branca and Sonic Youth, or a more organic angle on the currently fashionable term "Afropunk."[35]

This is a very different sound than what is typically heard and seen in the coastal and tropical-belt nightclubs of African capitals such as Lagos, Accra, Dakar, Abidjan, or Kinshasa, and it also contrasts strongly with the classicist tropes through which the blues and African music have often been linked. In contrast to much of the guitar music of the immediate postindependence era, this is not a music that celebrates the nation-state. The widely known modern music of artisans such as the Mande *jelis,* for example, derives from the artistic traditions of the empire of Mali, which reached its political apogee between the thirteenth and fifteenth centuries. As noted by Diawara, while these styles have commanded respect and admiration throughout the world, they have also factored into their respective societies in a fairly conservative manner that differs from the outsider impulse often considered to be at the root of the blues.[36] Having evolved within the imperial African context of the Mali empire, theirs is an artistic practice implicated in ancient and colonial-era power dynamics that often have worked to the disadvantage of the Tuareg and other nomadic peoples of the Sahara. In the hands of musicians such as Bombino and Doueh, then, the guitar is returned to its "blue" history with a postutopian sound that reinvests blues-inflected guitar rock with an embattled sensibility and an aura of rebel discontent and lawlessness while indexing secession, ethnic tension, desertification, and the contested African nation-state. Like Johnson, House, and other roaming bards of the Mississippi Delta, the raw simplicity of Saharan rock comes up against narratives of classicism, nation, and religion—reinhabiting the historical status of the blues as an outsider music, providing an intoxicating and hard-rocking juxtaposition of familiarity, remoteness, and frontier intrigue for the Western audience. The ground-level political realities are harsh but at the same time allow those behind Sublime Frequencies to position themselves as the intrepid, bad boys of musical ethnography. Consider the label's press for the release of its fifth volume of Tuareg rock, a compilation featuring the music of the Nigerien group Koudede:

> The circumstances surrounding these recordings are the stuff of which legends are made: In January 2012, a major insurgency brewing in the far north of Mali turned Timbutku's Festival au Désert into a heavily fortified spectacle. Just one day after the festival, rogue Tuareg rebels launched a full takeover of northern Mali, armed to the teeth with weapons from the Libyan war that ended in the murder of Col. Gaddafi, the spiritual father of the Tuareg in their struggle with the surrounding governments. By the time Koudede's group made it back to the capital city of Bamako—with Sublime Frequencies' Hisham Mayet in tow—discord had flared between the mostly Bambara ethnic south and the Tuareg community in the capital region. With a Tuareg exile already in progress, Koudede decided after much hesitation to follow through with a live concert at Toumast—the Tuareg compound in Bamako—in defiance of advice that all Tuareg should leave the city immediately. Recorded on location at Toumast by Hisham Mayet in January 2012, these two tracks are a scorching distillation of the urgency and fire in Koudede's music: the pure sound of his people and their constant struggles. Limited edition of 700 copies.[37]

Viewed in the context of its overall oeuvre, Sublime Frequencies' Nigerien sojourn makes perfect sense; the philosophy and aesthetics of the electric guitar clearly lie at the heart of their mission, reflected in their rendering of a wide range of the world's musics through a prism of punk-inflected distortion.[38] But in this period of tense, complicated relationships between the United States and the Muslim world, what can the music of Saharan nomads signify for the Western rock audience? Does that audience even make distinctions between various African nations, ethnicities, localities, or varieties of Islam? The musicians promoted by the label play music with a good beat and an undeniably compelling approach to the electric guitar. But, as Leah Caldwell chronicles in a recent article on Omar Souleyman, the political context is sometimes lost in translation.[39] Generally and generationally speaking, Sublime Frequencies' audience tends to engage with world music as one of the endless sounds made accessible by globalization, a very different perspective than that of the baby boomers, who tended to engage it via narratives of nationalism and decolonization.

Nonetheless, the texture of the music emanating from Agadez may ultimately have a political utility in and of itself. Even though most of Sublime Frequencies' audience probably would be surprised to learn that the Agadez bands (similarly to Omar Souleyman) are what we would refer to as "wedding bands" singing various local genres of romantic poetry, the distortion of their sound is given a different kind of context in America by the explosion of interest in Islam and Middle Eastern culture following the World Trade Center attack in September 2001. If one result of this has been the large-scale demonization of Muslims, the other is the proliferation of Middle Eastern and Arabic Studies programs in American colleges and universities. To an extent, Sublime Frequencies' chronicling of the music of the Muslim world is situated within this ambivalence. But the Saharan bands' aggressive, distorted sound may also have a more personal utility for the label's founders. Not only do they share various Middle Eastern backgrounds, but the label's home base is Seattle, the culturally monochrome context of grunge rock. Sublime Frequencies has pursued local guitar repertoires in other areas of the world, such as Thailand, Turkey, and India.[40] But the Agadez recordings clearly hold a special appeal in their hearts, given their attraction to outsiderness and distortion. What could be more dramatically suited to their own sensibilities and their cultural outlook than the music of nomadic, guitar-wielding desert rock rebels? As Mark Gergis told Chris Rolls:

[G]rowing up half Arab in America is different than not growing up half Arab. I'll never really know what it would be like to peacefully eat bologna sandwiches in grade school without being called Khomeini-face or Gaddafi or something. I vowed artistic revenge on my classmates at an early age . . . Growing up around a lot of Middle Eastern hospitality, food, music and values has definitely made me see things differently than a non-Arab American. The U.S. has waged war on my Dad's country for over half my life, so I have always had a unique perspective on that as well. Especially when people in the trash suburb I grew up in would come into our market with "Fuck Iraq" T-shirts on and ask us "Where you from"?[41]

How relevant is this to the on-the-ground realities in the Sahara? How, despite the producers' intentions, does Sublime Frequencies factor into the West's Orientalist tendency to project its own fears, fantasies, and desires onto the Muslim world, instead of engaging with its actual cultural and political realities? Agadez today lies near the midpoint of the recently completed Trans-Saharan highway, known mainly as a trading market for various goods: camels, silver, leather, and . . . uranium. Niger's music culture may not be widely known, but the country supplies almost 10 percent of the world's uranium—most of it under the control of the French nuclear energy commission Areva NC, which mines it for French use while selling off the surplus.[42] Substantial uranium (and petroleum) deposits have also been discovered in other parts of the region such as northern Mali and Chad. Perhaps unsurprisingly, most international coverage of the Tuareg rebellion has failed to mention the fact that the proposed Azawad secession (and the French intervention), like most attempted secessions of the postcolonial era, was likely powered by the world's ongoing scramble for Africa's natural resources.[43] Opinions vary on France's motivations to control a larger share of the region's deposits of "yellowcake" uranium, or about the substance as a pretext for the American "counterterrorist" presence (via unmanned drones) in the area.[44] Either way, the Tuareg, other Saharan peoples, and their region of the Sahara—whether within the borders of Mali, Niger, Mauritania, or other regional nation-states—are now implicated in global affairs in a more direct way. In fact, a close view reveals that Niger is directly implicated in several of Africa's political hotspots; the northern part is tied into Algeria and Libya, while the southern part is tied not only into northern Mali, but also into northern Nigeria, where a wave of Islamic fundamentalism has flourished as an articulation of local petro-politics. Similarly to secessionist tensions in Democratic Republic of the Congo and Nigeria, the global scramble for Africa's natural resources continues to wreak havoc across the region. However circumspect Sublime Frequencies has been in its liner notes, and however much its founders deign to share with their audience, interviews with the label's founders reveal them to be acutely sensitive observers of these events. As Hisham Mayet commented in 2011 when asked about the events of the so-called "Arab Spring":

[W]e have friends in all of these countries. Libya is going through an intense revolution. I was born there and have a lot of close relatives that are in the middle of it. My dad is exiled now to Egypt now because of it. Syria is just completely falling apart . . . Egypt was insane. We've got friends there as well. It's definitely created a more extreme environment for us to be around. We're into it and we're not. We're happy when it's an organic process, like Egypt. We're kind of unhappy when we realize that a lot of these revolutions, be it in Syria or Libya . . . are really being orchestrated by the West. That's a situation where we know there are malevolent forces creating chaos for their own greed and thirst for destruction.[45]

CONCLUSION: "WHY I SING THE BLUES"[46]

A passage of melodious string and choral music provides the soundtrack for a chapter of the *Niger* DVD, titled "Agadez," which takes the viewer on a surreal tour of the town, filmed at variable speeds. The vaguely wistful feel of the passage is reminiscent of the final scene of the *Woodstock* film, which portrays the festival's garbage-strewn aftermath, and under which the melancholic strains of Hendrix's "Villanova Junction Blues" play.[47] With its passages of vaguely Aeolian and Phrygian harmony, Hendrix's ballad evokes the bluesy, the mythical, and the exotic at the same time that it hazily reinforces the visual narrative of a trip being over. But whether the trip is taken to the outer regions of consciousness, through an improvisation, or across cultural borders, we can be sure that it has been chronicled somewhere within a blues song. This shouldn't be surprising, since the country blues historically was felt as a music of everywhere and of nowhere. It was a music of everywhere because it was played by itinerant musicians always on the move. And it was a music of nowhere because the musicians were socially liminal and often despised, playing their music on the outskirts of town, the edge of society, and out of the reach of faith.

What do the tropes of "nowhere," "somewhere," or "everywhere" mean today, in our digitally disembodied yet endlessly connected age, when you can, more or less, communicate with anyone, anywhere with the push of a few buttons? We are simultaneously everywhere because of the conveniences of digital culture and nowhere because of the social alienation created by our increasing dependence on these very devices. The bands promoted by Sublime Frequencies are increasingly visible on the global stage but, like country blues singers in their day, it is likely that their cultural reality will remain remote to global audiences whose energy demands have arguably (and ironically) fueled the evolution of their music. Perhaps this is why the Saharan bands are singing the blues. The term "Tuareg" is actually an Arabic word that, based on their remote desert existence

and pre-Islamic animist beliefs, translates into English as "abandoned by God."
At the end of the day, however, we are all linked by the very real, physical issue
of resources and their central role in human affairs. Son House wrote "Dry Spell
Blues" to chronicle the drought that devastated the Mississippi Delta in 1930,
but the title could just as easily refer to the desolation and despoliation of the
desert, as Bombino sang in 2013:

> The desert
> I am in the desert
> Full of nostalgia
> In the desert
> Without water I was sitting, meditating
> On the problems facing the desert . . . [48]

NOTES

1. Son House's "Dry Spell Blues" is contained on *Masters of the Delta Blues: The Friends
of Charlie Patton* (Yazoo 2002, 1991).

2. For an account of Son House's life and music, see Daniel Beaumont, *Preachin' the
Blues: The Life & Times of Son House* (Oxford: Oxford University Press, 2011).

3. For background on these events, see Betsy Bues, "Hunt for Blues Singer Ends in
City," *Rochester (NY) Times Union*, July 6, 1964.

4. See Son House, *Father of the Delta Blues: The Complete 1965 Sessions*, Sony/Legacy
CD 48867, 1992.

5. House's Paramount recordings are widely available: "Dry Spell Blues" (parts 1 and
2), "Preaching the Blues" (parts 1 and 2), "My Black Mama" (parts 1 and 2), and "Walking
Blues" are available on *Masters of the Delta Blues*, and "Mississippi County Farm Blues" and
"Clarksdale Moan" are available on *The Stuff That Dreams Are Made Of* (Yazoo 2202, 2006).

6. The banjo, for example (understood to be an American adaptation of West African
spiked-lute instruments such as the *ngoni* of Mali and Guinea or the Senegambian *xalam*), is
only the most obvious adaptation of this string instrument type and way of playing. See Cecilia Conway, *African Banjo Echoes in Appalachia* (Knoxville: University of Tennessee, 1995),
and Gerhard Kubik, *Africa and the Blues* (Jackson: University of Mississippi Press, 1999).

7. Of course, this stereotype was largely based in a misguided understanding of the
blues. In their primes, bluesmen such as House and Johnson were by no means docile
and servile. They were itinerant, womanizing, brash, and sometimes violent men, plying
their trade in juke joints where the humiliations of daily life could be drowned out mo-
mentarily in hard liquor, hard rocking blues, and spontaneous eruptions of violence. Son
House claimed that every juke party he played ended with the attendants scattering from

a fight that broke out (see Beaumont, *Preachin' the Blues*). Legend has it that Johnson died as a result of his womanizing, poisoned by the jealous husband of a love interest while playing at one of these juke joints (see Tom Graves, *Crossroads: The Life and Afterlife of Blues Legend Robert Johnson* [Memphis, Tenn.: Devault-Graves, 2012]). House himself did time in prison for murder, an experience immortalized in his 1938 recording "Mississippi County Farm Blues." The urban-based assertions of black manhood associated with Black Power in the 1960s may have seemed new, but they had been built upon earlier strategies of masculine survival that had accumulated over the centuries in the hard life of the Deep South. Those survival mechanisms are encoded into the language of blues masculinity.

8. For sources on the British blues boom, see Christopher Hjort, *Strange Brew: Eric Clapton and the British Blues Boom, 1965–1970* (London: Jawbone Press, 2007), or Bob Brunning, *Blues: The British Connection* (London: Helter Skelter Press, 2003).

9. For an interesting perspective on the existential qualities of the blues and their roots in the labor structure of slavery, see the chapter "The Rise of a Sung Literary Genre," in Kubik, *Africa and the Blues.*

10. For example, see James H. Cone, *The Spirituals and the Blues: An Interpretation* (Maryknoll, N.Y.: Orbis Books, 1972).

11. Two examples of this, separated by several decades are Samuel Charters, *The Roots of the Blues: An African Search* (New York: Da Capo, 1981), and Kubik, *Africa and the Blues.*

12. Jimi Hendrix interviewed by Nancy Carter in 1969, as quoted in Steven Roby, *Hendrix on Hendrix: Interviews and Encounters* (Chicago: Chicago Review Press, 2012), 195.

13. See Section One ("Roots") of John Collins, *West African Pop Roots* (Temple University Press, 1992).

14. Lamellophones are instruments constructed with metal "tongues" tuned to varying lengths. For a history of the guitar in the Mande tradition, see Eric Charry, *Mande Music: Traditional and Modern Music of the Maninka and Mandinka of Western Africa* (Chicago: University of Chicago Press, 2000). For the Congolese tradition, see Gary Stewart, *Rumba on the River: A History of the Popular Music of the Two Congos* (London: Verso, 2000).

15. See Richard M. Shain, "Roots in Reverse: *Cubanismo* in Twentieth-Century Senegalese Music, *International Journal of African Historical Studies* 35, no. 1 (2002).

16. See Hendrix's *Live at Woodstock* (MCA MCA3–11987, 1999).

17. See Santana's *The Woodstock Experience* (Columbia 88697 48242 2).

18. Santana's performance is contained on the DVD *Soul to Soul* (Rhino R2 970327, 1971).

19. Manthia Diawara, *In Search of Africa.* (Cambridge: Harvard University Press, 1998), 100–102. *Simbon*, a term found frequently throughout the *Sundiata* epic, refers to an association of Mande hunters.

20. See André Magnin, *Malick Sidibé* (Zurich: Scalo, 1998).

21. For background on Roger Mayer and the Octavia, see Tom Hughes, *Analog Man's Guide to Vintage Effects* (n.p.: For Musicians Only, 2004).

22. Bembeya Jazz National's "Moussogbe" can be found on Bembeya Jazz National, *The Syliphone Years* (Sterns, 2004); and Balla et ses Balladins' "Kogno Koura" can be found on Balla et ses Balladins, *The Syliphone Years* (Sterns, 2008). Hendrix's "Purple Haze" can be found on *Are You Experienced* (Reprise Records, 1967); "One Rainy Wish" can be found on *Axis: Bold as Love* (Track Records, 1967); and "Who Knows" can be found on *Band of Gypsys* (Capitol, 1970).

23. Various Artists, *Assalam Aleikoum Africa,* Volume One (Antilles 7032, 1976).

24. See the 2013 version of this report at: http://hdr.undp.org/en/statistics/.

25. These recordings include: *Africa: Drum, Chant and Instrumental Music* (Nonesuch Explorer 9–72073–2, 1976); *Hunters of the Dallol Mawri* (Ocora C560170, 2005); *Nomades du Désert* (Playasound PS 65009, 1987); *Les Nomades du Niger: Peuls, Bororos et Tuaregs* (Fremeaux & Associates FA 5290, 2010); *Nomades du Niger: Musique des Touareg, Musique des Bororo* (Ocora OCR 29, 1989); *Niger: La Musique des Griots* (Ocora OCR 20, 1964), and *Tuareg Music of the Southern Sahara* (Folkways FE 4470, 1960).

Fascinating to Westerners due to its visually striking and seemingly androgynous character, the *Guerewol* has been famously documented by *National Geographic*. An image of the ceremony adorns the cover of free jazz saxophonist Ornette Coleman's 1988 album *Virgin Beauty* (Legacy Recordings), and the Guerewol iconography is also represented on the cover of Miles Davis's 1969 album *Bitches Brew* (Columbia G2K-40577).

26. The close kinship of these instrument types is reflected in etymological similarities between their names despite their wide geographic dispersal: the bowed *rebab/rabab* found in numerous varieties from North Africa to Indonesia, the Moroccan *sintir* lute and the Central Asian *santoor* zither, the North Indian *sitar*, the Persian *tar* or *setar* lutes, and the Western guitar—itself historically of Persian origin.

27. "Journey to Agades" (sic) from Heinrich Barth, *Travels and Discovery in North and Central Africa London* (London: Ward, Lock & Co., 1890), 162–63.

28. These organizations include Ansar Dine, the National Movement for the Liberation of Azawad, and the Movement for Oneness and Jihad in West Africa.

29. See Sujatha Fernandes, "The Day the Music Died in Mali," *New York Times*, May 19, 2013.

30. Tinariwen, *Aman Iman: Water is Life* (Independiente ISOM 65CD, 2007).

31. For representative recordings of these artists and traditions, see Ali Farka Touré, *Radio Mali* (World Circuit, 2006), Lobi Traor *Traoré, Bamako Nights* (Glitterbeat, 2013), and Moudou Ould Mattalla, *Mauritania—Guitar of the Sands* (Buda Musique, 2006).

32. Group Doueh: *Guitar Music from the Western Sahara* (SF030, 2007), *Treeg Salaam* (SF048, 2009), *Beatte Harab* (SF063, 2010), *Zayna Jumma* (SF066, 2011); Group Inerane: *Guitars from Agadez*, Volume 1 (SF034, 2007), *Guitars from Agadez*, Volume 3 (SF061, 2010); Group Bombino: *Guitars from Agadez*, Volume 2 (SF046, 2009).

33. For example, the label press for Konono No 1 reads: "Some instruments used by these bands already sound 'distorted' when played acoustically, like the buzzing Kasaian drum featured in many songs; most of them are original creations or re-creations, made by the musicians themselves. We already know the electric *likembe*, or thumb piano, pioneered by Konono No 1, with its pickups made of copper telephone wire wound around crushed car alternator magnets . . . Some other bands use, for example, electric guitars reassembled from parts with origins as diverse as Bulgaria, China and Mexico, hi-hats made from hubcaps and film cans on top of a front axle and wheel held upside down, rattles made of a steel spring and sardine cans, jugs made of a drain pipe glued onto a calabash with gaffer tape, etc." From the Crammed Discs website: http://www.crammed .be/index.php?id=34&art_id=41&bio=full (accessed December 24, 2013).

34. *FruityLoops* and *Auto-Tune* are two types of digital music production software commonly used in the production of hip-hop, for the purposes of editing and pitch correction, respectively.

35. Devon Maloney, "What Is Afropunk?" *Village Voice*, August 21–27, 2013.

36. See Diawara, "Return Narratives," in *In Search of Africa*, 86–119.

37. From www.sublimefrequencies.com/item.asp?Item_id=88&cd=Koudede---Guitars -from-Agadez-Vol.5 (accessed June 27, 2013).

38. The trend of engaging with the music of the non-West through the aesthetics of distortion is nothing new. For example, experimental composer Karlheinz Stockhausen did it with his 1967 work *Telemusik*, a collage of world music fragments treated to various processes of filtering. The Beatles recorded Indophile songs such as "Blue Jay Way," which treated the drones of Hindustani music with pitch-shifting effects such as flanging and phase shifting. John McLaughlin's jazz-rock fusion supergroup Mahavishnu Orchestra overlaid the odd-time *tala* structures of Indian classical music with distorted lead guitar playing. More recently, the recent *Congotronics* project has filtered the traditional *likembe* thumb pianos of the Congo-Kinshasa area through a prism of distortion. The sound of Congotronics groups like Konono No 1 initially may have distorted due to faulty amplification, but the altered sound was seized upon by its Belgian producers and sold to Westerners as a sort of exotic, Afro-punk sensibility.

39. See Leah Caldwell, "Syria: On the Cusp of Hipness, Then Fading," 2013, http:// lareviewofbooks.org/essay/syria-on-the-cusp-of-hipness-then-fading/.

40. See *Bollywood Steel Guitar* (SF043), *Omar Khourshid: Guitar El Chark* (SF052), *Shadow Music of Thailand* (SF042), among several other guitar-oriented releases.

41. See Gergis's interview with Chris Rolls at: http://www.fecalface.com/SF/blogs-main menu-63/116-music/1346-interview-mark-gergis-aka-porest (accessed December 21, 2013).

42. For a profile of uranium mining in Niger, consult http://world-nuclear.org/info /Country-Profiles/Countries-G-N/Niger/#.UhZPVRb5JYI.

43. See Lydia Polgreen, "Battle in a Poor Land for Riches beneath the Soil," from *New*

York Times, December 14, 2008, http://www.nytimes.com/2008/12/15/world/africa/15niger.html?pagewanted=all (accessed December 11, 2013).

44. For an example asserting France's motivation in this regard, see R. Teichmann, "The War in Mali. What You Should Know: An Eldorado of Uranium, Gold, Petroleum, Strategic Materials," *Global Research,* Centre for Research on Globalization, January 15, 2013, www.globalresearch.ca/the-war-on-mali-what-you-should-know/5319093 (accessed June 16, 2013). For the counterposition, see Ron Adams, "France Does Not Need Mali's Uranium Despite All Conspiracies to the Contrary," *Atomic Insights,* http://atomicinsights.com/france-does-not-need-malis-uranium-despite-all-conspiracy-sites-to-the-contrary/ (accessed June 16, 2013). For one perspective on U.S. motivations, see Wayne Masde, "Obama's Military Presence in Niger: U.S. Control over Uranium under the Disguise of Counter-terrorism," *Global Research,* Centre for Research on Globalization, March 3, 2013, www.globalresearch.ca/obamas-military-presence-in-niger-uranium-control-under-the-disguise-of-counter-terrorism/5325002 (accessed August 25, 2013).

45. From Andrew Tonry's interview with Hisham Mayet, *Portland Mercury,* June 30, 2011, www.portlandmercury.com/endhits/archives/2011/06/30/interview-sublime-frequencies-co-founder-hisham-mayet (accessed December 24, 2013).

46. "Why I Sing the Blues" is a song made famous by B. B. King. The best-known version was recorded for the Bluesway label in 1969 and can be found on *B. B. King: King of the Blues* (MCA MCAD4–10677).

47. See *Woodstock* (Warner Home Video, 2009).

48. Group Bombino, "Her Tenere" from *Nomad* (Nonesuch 534291, 2013).

BIBLIOGRAPHY

Adams, Ron. "France Does Not Need Mali's Uranium Despite All Conspiracies to the Contrary." *Atomic Insights.* January 24, 2013. http://atomicinsights.com/france-does-not-need-malis-uranium-despite-all-conspiracy-sites-to-the-contrary/ (accessed June 16, 2013).

Barth, Heinrich. *Travels and Discovery in North and Central Africa London.* Ward, Lock & Co., 1890.

Beaumont, Daniel. *Preachin' the Blues: The Life and Times of Son House.* Oxford: Oxford University Press, 2011.

Brunning, Bob. *Blues: The British Connection.* London: Helter Skelter Press, 2003.

Bues, Betsy. "Hunt for Blues Singer Ends in City." *Rochester (NY) Times Union,* July 6, 1964.

Caldwell, Leah. "Syria: On the Cusp of Hipness, Then Fading." 2013. http://lareviewofbooks.org/essay/syria-on-the-cusp-of-hipness-then-fading/.

Charry, Eric. *Mande Music: Traditional and Modern Music of the Maninka and Mandinka of Western Africa.* Chicago: University of Chicago Press, 2000.

Charters, Samuel. *The Roots of the Blues: An African Search.* New York: Da Capo, 1981.

Collins, John. *West African Pop Roots.* Temple University Press, 1992.

Cone, James H. *The Spirituals and the Blues: An Interpretation.* Maryknoll, N.Y.: Orbis Books, 1972.

Conway, Cecilia. *African Banjo Echoes in Appalachia.* Knoxville: University of Tennessee, 1995.

Diawara, Manthia. *In Search of Africa.* Cambridge: Harvard University Press, 1998.

Fernandes, Sujatha. "The Day the Music Died in Mali." *New York Times,* May 19, 2013.

Graves, Tom. *Crossroads: The Life and Afterlife of Blues Legend Robert Johnson.* Memphis, Tenn.: Devault-Graves, 2012.

Hjort, Christopher. *Strange Brew: Eric Clapton and the British Blues Boom, 1965–1970.* London: Jawbone Press, 2007.

Hughes, Tom. *Analog Man's Guide to Vintage Effects.* n.p.: For Musicians Only, 2004.

Kubik, Gerhard. *Africa and the Blues.* Jackson: University of Mississippi Press, 1999.

Magnin, André. *Malick Sidibé.* Zurich: Scalo, 1998.

Maloney, Devon. "What Is Afropunk?" *Village Voice,* August 21–27, 2013.

Masde, Wayne. "Obama's Military Presence in Niger: U.S. Control over Uranium under the Disguise of Counter-terrorism." *Global Research,* Centre for Research on Globalization. March 3, 2013. www.globalresearch.ca/obamas-military-presence-in-niger-uranium -control-under-the-disguise-of-counter-terrorism/5325002 (accessed August 25, 2013).

Polgreen, Lydia. "Battle in a Poor Land for Riches Beneath the Soil." *New York Times,* December 14, 2008. http://www.nytimes.com/2008/12/15/world/africa/15niger. html?pagewanted=all (accessed December 11, 2013).

Roby, Steven. *Hendrix on Hendrix: Interviews and Encounters.* Chicago: Chicago Review Press, 2012.

Shain, Richard M. "Roots in Reverse: *Cubanismo* in Twentieth-Century Senegalese Music." *International Journal of African Historical Studies* 35, no. 1 (2002).

Stewart, Gary. *Rumba on the River: A History of the Popular Music of the Two Congos.* London: Verso, 2000.

Teichmann, R. "The War in Mali. What You Should Know: An Eldorado of Uranium, Gold, Petroleum, Strategic Materials." *Global Research,* Centre for Research on Globalization. January 15, 2013. www.globalresearch.ca/the-war-on-mali-what-you-should -know/5319093 (accessed June 16, 2013).

Tonry, Andrew. Interview with Hisham Mayet. *Portland Mercury,* June 30, 2011. www. portlandmercury.com/endhits/archives/2011/06/30/interview-sublime-frequencies -co-founder-hisham-mayet (accessed December 24, 2013).

Middle East Steps

JOSEPH SALEM

Engineering Social Space
The "Silent" Structures of Alan Bishop's
Radio Palestine

Indeed, to collage elements from impersonal, external sources—
the newspaper, magazines, television, billboards—is to understand,
as it were, that, in a technological age, consciousness itself becomes
a process of graft or citation, a process by means of which
we make the public world our own.

Marjorie Perloff, The Futurist Moment

Radio Palestine, eighth in the Sublime Frequencies catalog, is advertised as a "super-sonic collage" featuring "Cairo Orchestral/Greek Sartaki/Palestinian Folk/ Jewish and Euro-hybrid music styles/Jordanian reverb guitar . . . all placed deep within the mirage of an 18-year-old time capsule of news, commercials, radio plays, UFO signals, Secret agent messages and chainsaw shortwave."[1] In truth, *Radio Palestine* juxtaposes over 200 distinct samples in a mimetic portrayal of the discursive noise surrounding the eastern Mediterranean, placing particular emphasis on this region as a hotbed of sociopolitical conflict. Throughout the disc, various forms of signal processing create an aural landscape that is both a hypostatized reflection of, and a dynamic commentary on, the shifting cultural boundaries that divide the Mashriq region.

My description of *Radio Palestine* comes from hearing it as a postmodern collage that reveals meaningful relationships between the editorial voice of its producer, Alan Bishop, and the evocative representations provided by its radio-phonic samples. More specifically, a directed study of radio and collage formats

Radio Palestine: Sounds of the Eastern Mediterranean (SF008)
juxtaposes over 200 distinct samples of music and sound.

and their relationship to specific postmodern discourses can provide guidance for analyzing the production of *Radio Palestine* as carefully crafted social commentary. Following this model, I use two well-known commentaries on the aesthetics of radio and collage to develop a hermeneutics for engaging the material format, the aural content, and the suggestive, extramusical commentary of *Radio Palestine* as a sublime constellation of overdetermined signifiers.

The liner notes of the disc—which, like many Sublime Frequencies recordings, are decorated with hyperstylized images of cultural tokens—contain only one paragraph of text and a separate track listing, while a brief aside cites editing and artwork contributions. Based on this information, one assumes that the disc represents the singular vision of Bishop, as it was first recorded, edited, and produced by him in 1985, before its final editing with Scott Colburn in 2003.[2] The liner notes also showcase a panoramic photograph of a small girl with a bandage over her right eye, overlaid by Bishop's journal-like reminiscence. The text, written in the past tense (one presumes in November 2003 about an event in 1985), describes Bishop's initial rendezvous and subsequent stay with an influential man in Haifa. Bishop outwardly emphasizes the social importance and eccentric hospitality of his friend "Mohammed"; this leads to a subliminal, but no less postured, emphasis on the powerful, *musical* foundation of their friendship. The text also states that Bishop had been traveling for at least a month prior, that he kept in touch with Mohammed for two years after he returned to the States, and that he dedicates the disc, with noteworthy affection, to the "*one and only* Mohammed from Haifa" (my emphasis—the irony should not be lost).

In light of these materials, it is likely that the track listings of *Radio Palestine* reconstruct a journey through the eastern Mediterranean. Indeed, while it remains unclear if or when the contents of *Radio Palestine* come from purchased recordings, radio broadcasts, or live performances, various key words, phrases, and broadcast centers referenced throughout the disc allow us to situate some of its contents geographically onto a map of the region.[3] As this exercise demonstrates, the disc may reflect Bishop's own extended stay in the region, his independence as a traveler, and his passion for associating the boundless, geographic ambiance of radio with his on-the-ground experience of a number of locations.

Putting aside an exploration of Bishop's more personal experiences, the following three sections develop a case-specific approach to reading the format and content of *Radio Palestine* as a commentary that is more concerned with producing an abstract representation of a physical region than a private travelogue. Starting with the implications of the title of the disc, I argue that radio and recordings have unique powers to mediate particular sociocultural contexts, and that *Radio Palestine* presents a multifaceted reflection of the eastern Mediterranean that combines the multiplied aspects of cubist painting with the complex referential planes of collage. These various layers of signification prepare a review of Jean-François Lyotard's aesthetics of the sublime in order to articulate the signifying potential of associative relationships in *Radio Palestine*. Once the relationship between the formal characteristics of collage and radio is made more explicit, I use a structural analysis of *Radio Palestine* to propose a rich constellation of genres, styles, and associative relationships across the aural surface of the disc, all shaped by Bishop's tacit authorial voice.

RECORDINGS AND RADIO

At heart, Sublime Frequencies represents a project of ethnographic preservation. The record label's promotional website self-describes "a collective of explorers dedicated to acquiring and exposing obscure sights and sounds" that are "not documented sufficiently through all channels of academic research, the modern recording industry, media, or corporate foundations."[4] In addition, an extended list of "inspirations" mentions canonic ethnographic labels.[5] The emphasis on exploration, documenting and sharing, and exposing "rare or obscure" forms of expression all point toward a singular—some might say myopic—vision of ethnomusicological research. This is because, unlike Sublime Frequencies, the goals of ethnomusicologists have continually developed away from the simplistic adoption of these practices by problematizing the use of external sources and emphasizing the disruptive force of our own preconceptions and agendas on our ability to observe, record, and/or report our observations of others. Thus, it is without condoning the stated agenda of Sublime Frequencies that I emphasize the nuanced complexity of *Radio Palestine* as a particular manifestation of the label's agenda, even when my goal is to bias us toward appreciating the inherent strengths of the disc over its shortcomings.

Of course, the use and misuse of recording technology are as old as the gramophone itself. In the earliest stages of cylinder recording, critics and advocates alike were fascinated with the effects of disembodied sound: the phantom resonance of distant voices or the playback of African instruments in London. While contemporary listeners are less impressed by such technological feats, the paradox of "the recording" as an authentic source of documentation—where records simultaneously ensure an accurate representation of a performance and separate sound from source, event, and time—continues to rely on the disembodied mediation of sounds. Any project assuming to capture, document, or present "sights and sounds" from "obscure" sources must deal with the inability of these mediated materials to "speak for themselves" with the same immediacy as live observations. This is a direct challenge to the aesthetics of Sublime Frequencies.

This judgment is not meant to be ethical. To make a conceptual leap from the specific to the general, Michael Chanan writes, "The integrity of the musical work of the past, its intimate unity with the time and place of performance, what Walter Benjamin called its aura, has been destroyed. Music has become literally disembodied, and the whole of musical experience has been thrown into a chronic state of flux. . . . And this is both a symptom and one of the causes of the condition of postmodernism."[6] This is also a symptom of, and justification for, Sublime Frequencies' promoted aesthetics, as the label continually asserts that its products capture something like the aura of various events, people, and soundscapes, even while its products flaunt the authorial anonymity inherent in mechanical reproduction. Perhaps Chanan's postmodernism is less a reference to some hypothetical or ideal listening practice than an attempt to capture the seemingly endless network of signifiers attached to any recorded performance.[7] The same is true for Sublime Frequencies: It is an end-oriented label, concerned more with the consumption and reception of its products than in an idealized representation of some single, reified cultural image. Like it or not, it is a celebration of the signifying potential of art, albeit an amoral one.

In fact, unlike some multimedia formats (such as the DVD, which Sublime Frequencies also embraces), the choice to create *Radio* discs aims to *compound* the disembodied nature of mechanical reproduction by further obfuscating the mediation between a performer, his or her recording, and the spectator. As Alan Weiss describes, radio uses the anonymity of its source to utilize an impersonal, public signal for a two-part function: first, the controlled consumption of a "private" experience in the home; and second, the creation of a shared cultural identity. He writes: "Thus the paradox of radio: a universally public transmission is heard in the most private of circumstances; the thematic specificity of each individual broadcast, its imaginary scenario, is heard within an infinitely diverse set of nonspecific situations, different for each listener; the radio's putative shared solidarity of auditors in fact achieves their atomization as well as a reification of the imagination."[8]

By challenging the "*putative* shared solidarity of auditors," Weiss argues that the individualized perspective of private auditors of radio may assist the formation of an idealized cultural imagination that does not exist in any real sense; in other words, Weiss's radio allows listeners to wrongly assume that their opinion of a broadcast is equally shared by all other listeners. Similarly, different FM bands can segregate the public into divisive factions based on listener demographics, just as a single radio station may create a voluntary cultural space for a divided population to comingle. Finally, radio waves can penetrate the liminal spaces between the inhibitory boundaries of place, region, race, and space, turning the negative space of such semantic distinctions into imaginary amphitheaters for audiences of all types. Thus the social mechanics of radio reproduction: How better to manufacture a new cultural identity, to promote an unforeseen cultural solidarity, than to make admission anonymous, effortless, and available within the comfort of your own home?

CONFLICTS AND COLLAGE

Really, the composition of this war was not the composition of all
previous wars, the composition was not a composition in which there
was one man at the center surrounded by a lot of other men but a
composition that had neither a beginning or an end, a composition in
which one corner was as important as another corner,
in fact the composition of cubism.[9]

Gertrude Stein, Picasso, 1938

Cubism involves the synthesis of multiple adumbrations or aspects of an object
as a more or less coherent whole, even while the angles and disjunctions that
separate the individual adumbrations of these objects are maintained against the
backdrop of the work.[10] In contrast, the temporal unfolding of *Radio Palestine*
never offers the wholeness or synthesis of a static image, but Bishop's commitment to simultaneously portraying a number of contrasting views of a perpetu-
ally troubled region can still be elucidated by the epigraph above. The overlap
between Stein's cubism and Bishop's editing is similar to the relationship between
cubism and collage more generally, where the former focuses on a singular title
and subject, while the latter embraces a cacophony of postmodern signification. Through its dynamic embrace of the postmodern, collage can provide the
conceptual framework needed to relate the various fragments of *Radio Palestine*
to the genres and categories scattered throughout the disc.

In "The Invention of Collage," Marjorie Perloff plainly addresses the most
basic characteristics of collage before challenging the ontological stability of the
genre as a governing structure for works of art.[11] First, Perloff establishes that
collage "always involves the transfer of materials from one context to another,
even as the original context cannot be erased."[12] Second, "each element in . . . collage has a dual function: it refers to an external reality even as its compositional
thrust is to undercut the very referentiality it seems to assert."[13] Third, "when
the object is called upon 'to play an increasingly important role,' its difference
is foregrounded."[14] And finally, edging increasingly toward the postmodern,
"collage thus challenges us to read the signs and decode the symbols, to take
the scrambled clues and put them into a more orderly sequence"—but certain
examples are so dense, "so dizzying a spiral of inciting fragments, sounds, and
colors, so shrill a torrent of spectacle and noise, that we can never perceive
[them] as a coherent image."[15] Thus, the relationships within a collage continue

to spiral outward, stressing the boundaries of the modernist work concept by creating increasingly layered networks of signification.[16] It is easy to extrapolate further: A modernist discourse, where the stability of forms and systems creates a foundation for self-reference and reflection within the work of art, becomes a postmodern condition, where the distinction between part and whole, figure and ground, becomes so relative as to challenge any single, coherent interpretation of the work. In effect, the aesthetics of collage stress the boundaries of the modern work through a magnification, rather than denial, of traditional signifiers: An overdetermined network of relationships capsizes into Lyotard's postmodern aesthetics of the sublime.

COLLAGE À LA PERLOFF

Collage *transfers material* from one context to another without erasing the original context. For this reason . . .

Objects in a collage have a "dual function": they refer both *inside and outside* of an artistic frame *simultaneously* as well as *independently.*

Emphasis on a particular object as an isolated signifier produces greater difference between it and other juxtaposed objects.

Collage asks us to create an ordered sequence from a multitude of objects, thus creating "so dizzying a spiral . . . so shrill a torrent of spectacle and noise, that we can never perceive [them] as a coherent image."

For these reasons, Jean-François Lyotard's postmodern aesthetic is particularly apt for integrating the various forms of representation in collage. This is not because Lyotard clarifies the aesthetics of Kant and Burke, but rather because his theory of the sublime locates the source of our response to awe-inspiring artistic abundance in the distinction between the "presentable" (clearly representational) and the "unpresentable" (abstractly conceptual).[17] It is worth recalling Lyotard's discussion of the sublime directly:

Here, then, lies the difference: modern aesthetics is an aesthetic of the sublime, though a nostalgic one. It allows the unpresentable [i.e., abstractly conceptual] to be put forward as the *missing* contents; but the form, because of its recognizable consistency, continues to offer the reader or viewer matter for solace and pleasure. . . . The postmodern would be that which, *in the modern*, puts forward the unpresentable *in presentation itself;* that which denies . . . the consensus of a taste which would make it possible to share collectively the nostalgia for the unattainable; that which searches for new presentations, not in order to enjoy them but in order to impart a stronger sense of the unpresentable.[18]

In short, Lyotard's "presentable" includes forms and concepts that relate to our shared tastes and values, the basis of any "classical" style of art, while his "unpresentable" captures the conceptual power in art to convey concepts that go beyond the limits of conventional signifiers. This means that three layers of signification are actually encapsulated within Lyotard's modern and postmodern aesthetics: the classical, where the relationship between signs and signifiers remains fixed (although tainted and tempered by nostalgia for modern spectators); the modern, where the "spaces between" classical signifiers create a layer of conceptual commentary on the process of signification itself; and the postmodern, where the conceptual play of both of these modes of representation is captured in the formal structure of the work. Lyotard conflates these three layers of signification by first reducing them into two aesthetic categories—the modern and the postmodern—before insisting that all three forms of representation can coexist within the same artistic material. For Lyotard, then, the real distinction between modern and postmodern aesthetics is not absolute—a modern *or* postmodern work—but is rather a difference in how various layers of signification *simultaneously* communicate nonrepresentational concepts or ideas within a given form.

This is precisely why Lyotard's theory relates so well to *Radio Palestine*. Combining Perloff and Lyotard, a postmodern collage uses conventional, "classical" forms to signify meaning, challenges these representations with jarring juxtapositions, and then frames this process as a sublime play of overdetermined signifiers. Put more figuratively, these three layers of representation correspond to the "Palestine" of *Radio Palestine*: It is at once a nostalgic time capsule of genres and traditions; a boundless broadcast space of coexisting, but sharply contrasting, factions; and finally, a spiraling dialectic of utopia as "ideal place" and "no place" at once—a true presentation of the "unpresentable."

DECONSTRUCTING THE COLLAGE

The table that follows is a breakdown of *Radio Palestine* by track. Bold timings represent single samples that exceed ten seconds in length; *italic* timings represent *collections* of fragments that, due to the style of the disc, I treat as conglomerate, if internally divided, groups. A brief glance shows that the vast majority of *Radio*

Palestine's samples are less than ten seconds in duration, as a limited number of the table entries are bold, and most of the italic entries represent combinations of samples that are less than one to two seconds each.[19]

The following table is helpful because it deconstructs (literally, as in deconstructing a tent) the rough and raw aural landscape of *Radio Palestine* into its component parts. In order to isolate Bishop's editing technique, I sorted the samples according to broad, generic categories: *News Broadcasts, Western Music, Regional Music* (based on references to scales, harmonies, and instruments of the Middle and Near East), *Sound Art/Electronic Music, Ceremonial Music,* and finally, format-defined content such as DJ shout-outs and *Advertising.* These categories are not meant to capture or classify the inherent meaning of any specific example (such as interpreting the musical content of a prayer broadcast). Instead, to deconstruct the editing in this way is to critique the role of its producer.

My analytical process continued beyond segregating the streams of continuous samples on *Radio Palestine.* I went as far as re-editing select audio samples to create new tracks that grouped similar categories of samples together; for example, I extracted all of the *News* samples from the disc and compiled them as a single track. The point of all of this de- and re-constructing is simple: I wanted to test the formal qualities of the collage by flexing and relieving the tension between Bishop's aggressive juxtapositions. This content was then presented to a number of colleagues who provided feedback on how my samples were perceived by other listeners.

One immediate effect of my edits was the clarification of the "classical," or first layer, of semantic content of *Radio Palestine*; that is, reorganizing the samples into complementary groups to emphasize the meaning of individual samples over and above the strong, contrastive juxtapositions that characterize the disc. Meanwhile, my generic categories provide a context of similar musical styles that allow the samples to speak beyond individual snippets of radio broadcasts to something closer to a panoramic image of the radio dial: By emphasizing the inherent meaning of any particular example relative to a broader network of similar signifiers, a constellation of genres, types, and normative forms emerges as a second layer of semantic content. One could equate this stage to the stations on a radio dial (Top 40, soft rock, R&B, punk), where the expectation is that each song is to be appreciated relative to similar, rather than radically different, titles. Finally, the distance between these classifications and the harsh, but carefully organized, reality of Bishop's original tracks is precisely where I locate the sublime representation of "unpresentable" politics of *Radio Palestine.* Importantly,

TRACK BREAKDOWNS FOR *RADIO PALESTINE* ACCORDING TO CUTS BETWEEN WELL-DEFINED SAMPLES

Key: Bold = music or news 10 seconds or longer; *italics* = scans or groups of scanned "fragments" that combine to form homogenous groups; * = samples used in my re-edits.

Track 1/ *Madame Foyer*

TIME	DESCRIPTION	CATEGORY
0:00–0:47	Voiceover with Repetitive Instrumental Refrain	Narration + Music
0:48–0:58*	News [English]: "Finger in Eye"	News
0:59–1:03*	News [English]: "Further upheaval"	News
1:03–1:05	Homophonic Orchestral	Regional Orchestral
1:06–1:15*	News [English]: "Role of RFA"	News
1:16–1:53	Airwave/Dial Scans/Cuts	Sound Art
1:53–2:00	Homophonic Orchestral	Regional Orchestral
2:00–2:06	Airwave/Dial Scans/Cuts	Various
2:07–2:56	Oud Solo w/Ensemble [FADE OUT]	Regional Ensemble

Track 2/ *Falafel Eastern*

TIME	DESCRIPTION	CATEGORY
0:00–0:03*	Test Signal Beeps	Sound Art
0:03–0:09	Homophonic Orchestral	Regional Orchestral
0:10–0:25	Piano and Voices	Regional Folk
0:26–0:31	Narration [Foreign] w/Music	Narrations + Music
0:32–0:34	Scans/Cuts	Various
0:35–0:48*	Classical Organ (End on HC ↠)	Western Classical
0:49–2:20*	Instrumental Pop (Starts with ↠ PAC!)	Western Pop
2:21–2:26	Airwave/Dial Scans/Cuts	Various
2:26–2:59*	"Spoken" Easy Listening [English]	Western Pop
3:00–3:12	Airwave/Dial Scans/Cuts	Various
3:13–3:23	Male Vocals [Foreign] w/Ensemble	Regional Vocal
3:23–3:43	Female w/Ensemble (elec.)	Regional Club
3:43–3:49	Male Vocals [Foreign] w/Ensemble	Regional Vocal
3:59–4:16	Airwave/Dial Scans/Cuts (Long Fragments)	Various
4:16–4:47	String Solo w/Drone [FADE OUT]	Regional Ensemble

Track 3/ Bedouin Sparklers

TIME	DESCRIPTION	CATEGORY
0:00–0:52	Oud w/Drone	Regional Ensemble
0:52–1:00	Homoophonic Orchestral	Regional Orchestral
1:00–1:04	Airwave/Dial Scans/Cuts	Various
1:04–1:41	Vocals [Foreign] w/Orchestra	Regional Vocal
1:41–1:53	Oud w/Ensemble	Regional Ensemble
1:53–1:59	Test Signal Beep	Sound Art
1:59–2:04	Airwave/Dial Scans/Cuts	Various
2:04–2:13	Static/Art	Sound Art
2:13–2:15*	. . . "Broadcasting" . . .	DJ
2:15–2:20	Male Oratory	Ceremonial
2:20–2:28	Electronica Pop	Regional Club
2:29–2:45	Airwave/Dial Scans/Cuts	Various
2:46–3:41	Male [Foreign], Oud w/Orchestra	Regional Vocal
3:42–4:05	Public Oratory	Atmospheric
4:05–4:57	Male [Foreign], Oud w/Ensemble [FADE OUT]	Regional Vocal

Track 4/ Tangental Psychedelico

TIME	DESCRIPTION	CATEGORY
0:00–0:21	Western Instrumental Folk	Western Folk
0:22–0:35	Ariwave/Dial Scans/Cuts	Various
0:35–1:02*	Male [Foreign] w/Guitar	Serenade
1:02–1:10*	News: [English] "Geneva Arms Talks"	News
1:10–1:18*	Classical Guitar	Western Classical
1:18–1:20	Fragment	Fragment
1:20–1:35	Voices [Foreign] w/Piano	Regional Folk
1:35–1:40	Airwave/Dial Scans/Cuts	Various
1:40–1:53	Voice [Foreign] w/Ensemble	Western Pop
1:54–2:00*	Baroque Chorus w/Orchestra	Western Classical
2:00–2:03	Children's Voices [Foreign Dialogue]	Regional Vocal
2:04–2:50	Oud w/Ensemble	Regional Vocal
2:51–3:00*	Drone w/Solo	Ceremonial
3:00–4:51	Vocals [Ahhh] w/piano and electronics	Western Pop
4:51–6:33	Airwave/Dial Scans/Cuts (Longer Fragments)	Sound Art
[5:11–5:20]*	DJ [English]: "Sorry!"	DJ
6:33–7:04*	Voices [Foreign] w/ Ensemble [FADE OUT]	Western Pop

Track 5/ Solitaire Oriental

TIME	DESCRIPTION	CATEGORY
0:00–1:04	Very Distorted "Funk" (electronica)	Regional Club
1:04–1:15	Game-Show Filler (!)	Western Pop
1:15–1:20	Distortion	Sound Art
1:20–3:22*	Jordanian Reverb Guitar	Regional Pop
3:22–4:46	Drum Instrumental	Regional Folk
4:47–4:58	Airwave/Dial Scans/Cuts	Various
4:59–5:34*	News [English]: "Small Matter of Humans" [ABRUPT ENDING]	News

Track 6/ Beirut Cocktail/Khartoum Entrée

TIME	DESCRIPTION	CATEGORY
0:00–0:21	Voice [French] w/Ensemble	Regional Cocktail
0:22–0:31	Advertisement [Foreign]	Narration + Music
0:31–0:40	Narration [Foreign]	Narration
0:40–0:48	Scans/Cuts [Traditional]	Regional Ensemble
0:48–1:32	Voice [Foreign] w/Ensemble	Traditional/Folk
1:33–1:35	Voice Fragment [Foreign]	Fragment
1:35–1:47	Voice [French] w/Ensemble	Regional Cocktail
1:47–1:52	Fragment	Regional Orchestral
1:52–2:11	Street Noise	Sound Art
2:12–2:29	Narration w/Music	Narration+ Music
2:30–2:34	Fragment	Regional Ensemble
2:34–3:08	Voice [Foreign] w/Ensemble	Regional Ensemble
3:08–3:37	Distortion (over music)	Sound Art
3:37–4:13	Voice [Foreign] w/Ensemble	Regional Ensemble
4:13–4:16	Airwave/Dial Scans/Cuts	Various
4:16–4:21	Test Signal Beeps	Sound Art
4:22–4:28	Airwave/Dial Scans/Cuts	Various
4:28–4:44	Scans—Prayers/Poetry?—Scans	Ceremonial
4:44–5:05	Airwave/Dial Scans/Cuts (Longer)	Various
5:05–5:51	Drum, Cymbals, Dance [FADE OUT]	Regional Folk

Track 7/ *Voice of Peace?*

TIME	DESCRIPTION	CATEGORY
0:00–0:16	Narration [Foreign], Scans/Cuts	Narration + Music
0:17–0:23	DJ [English]: "Voice of Peace"	DJ
0:23–3:03	Vocal (Foreign) w/Orchestra	Regional Ensemble
3:04–3:05	Fragment	Regional Vocal
3:05–3:32	DJ [Foreign AND English]: "Voice of Peace" [FADE OUT]	DJ

Track 8/ *The Aswan Slip*

TIME	DESCRIPTION	CATEGORY
0:00–0:09	Airwave/Dial Scans/Cuts	Various
0:10–1:17	Vocal [Foreign] w/Ensemble [FADE OUT]	Regional Folk

Track 9/ *Ramadan with Crowbar*

TIME	DESCRIPTION	CATEGORY
0:00–0:54	Text [Foreign] + Music "Ramadan"	Sound Art
0:54–0:56	Voice [Foreign] Fragment	Fragment
0:56–1:05	Female Oration	Oratory
1:05–1:10	Narration [Foreign]	Narration
1:10–2:02*	Prayer/Recitation w/Drum	Ceremonial
2:02–2:16*	Airwave/Dial Scans/Cuts "Ramadan"	Ceremonial
2:16–3:08	Distortions (over narration and music)	Sound Art
3:09–3:34*	News [English]: "Killed a Soviet Advisor"	News
3:35–3:36	Airwave/Dial Scans/Cuts	Various
3:37–4:32*	News [English]: "Boeing from Beirut" [FADE OUT]	News

Track 10/ Night in Ancient Egypt

TIME	DESCRIPTION	CATEGORY
0:00–0:11	Ambient Sounds	Sound Art
0:12–0:47	Voice [Foreign] w/ Orchestra	Regional Ensemble
0:47–0:57	Airwave/Dial Scans/Cuts	Various
0:57–1:07	Solo Instrumental	Folk
1:07–1:09	Voice [Foreign]	Fragment
1:09–1:19	Guitar, Strings	Western Pop
1:19–1:21	Fragment	Fragment
1:22–1:34	Voices [Foreign] w/Ensemble	Regional Dance
1:34–1:52	Male, Orchestra (soft rock)	Regional Ensemble
1:52–2:09	News [German]	News
2:10–2:20*	Prayer	Ceremonial
2:20–3:00	Electronica "Ancient Egyptian Mythology" [FADE OUT]	Regional Club/Pop

Track 11/ Exploding Briefcases of Cairo

TIME	DESCRIPTION	CATEGORY
0:00–0:01	Narration [English]	Fragment
0:01–0:13	Guitar/Oud	Regional Ensemble
0:13–0:22*	"Exploding Distortion"	Sound Art
0:22–0:34*	"El Falis Noche" + Ambient Sounds	Narration + Sound
0:34–1:14*	Orchestral/Sentimental	Western Ensemble
1:14–1:17	Distortions	Sound Art
1:17–1:24*	Prayer/Recitation [Foreign]	Ceremonial
1:25–1:32	Airwave/Dial Narration/Cuts [Foreign]	Fragments
1:33–1:58	Homophonic Orchestral Music	Regional Orchestral
1:58–2:07	Male Voices [Foreign]	[News]
2:08–2:13	British Narration [English]	Narration
2:14–2:41	Airwave/Dial Scans/Cuts	Various
2:42–3:25	Oud w/Ensemble (Drone and Drums)	Regional Folk
3:25–3:30	Voice [Foreign]	Fragment
3:30–4:08*	Ambient/Prayer/Recitation	Ceremonial
4:08–4:11	Fragments	Fragment
4:11–4:16	Conversation	Fragment
4:16–4:24*	Distortion	Sound Art
4:25–4:31*	Fragments, Wobbles	Sound Art
4:32–4:40	Voice [Foreign] w/Orchestra	Regional Ensemble
4:41–4:49	Airwave/Dial Scans/Cuts	Various
4:49–5:04*	Distortions/Airwave/Dial Scans/Cuts	Sound Art
5:04–5:09*	Narration and Music	Narration + Sound
5:10–5:13	Airwave/Dial Scans/Cuts	Various
5:13–6:37	Orchestra w/Instrumentals [FADE OUT]	Regional Orchestral

Track 12/ Trenchcoat Heatwave, Buffet-Style

TIME	DESCRIPTION	CATEGORY
0:00–0:05	Instrument Fragment	Regional Folk
0:05–0:13	Narration [Foreign]	Narration
0:14–0:19	Fragment	Fragment
0:19–0:25	Female Narration	Narration
0:25–0:29	Narration [Foreign] (distorted)	Narration
0:29–0:35	Native Flute Solo	Regional Folk
0:35–0:59	Voice [Foreign] w/Oud	Regional Ensemble
0:59–1:02	Distortion	Sound Art
1:02–1:37*	News [English]: "Meeting President Reagan"	News
1:37–1:52	Voice [Foreign] with Oud and distortion	Regional Folk
1:52–2:08	Airwave/Dial Scans/Cuts (Distorted)	Sound Art
2:08–2:32*	Dramatic Orchestral	Regional Orchestral
2:32–2:37	Narration [Foreign]	Narration
2:37–2:44	Airwave/Dial Scans/Cuts	Various
2:44–2:56	Voice [Foreign] w/Ensemble	Regional Ensemble
2:57–3:05	Airwave/Dial Scans/Cuts	Various
3:05–3:48	Instrumental Groove with Narration [Foreign] [FADE OUT]	Regional Pop

Track 13/ ElectriCAIRO

TIME	DESCRIPTION	CATEGORY
0:00–1:24	Distortions (over multiple signals/narration) [ELIDED]	Sound Art

Track 14/ How Are You, Mr. Criminal?

TIME	DESCRIPTION	CATEGORY
0:00–0:09*	DJ [English]: Mocking "Voice of America"	DJ
0:09–2:05	Voice [Foreign] w/Ensemble [FADE OUT]	Regional Folk

Track 15/ Psychic Iman INC.

TIME	DESCRIPTION	CATEGORY
0:00–0:27*	Distortions (Warble over Narration)	Sound Art
0:27–0:58*	Voices [Foreign] w/Oud	Regional Folk
0:59–1:17	Narration → Drama	Narration
1:17–1:23	Voice [Foreign] w/Ensemble	Regional Ensemble
1:24–2:20*	Very, very Distorted Electric Pop	Sound Art
2:20–2:21	Fragment	Fragment
2:21–2:24	Narration [Foreign]	Narration
2:25–2:38	Very Distorted Oud	Regional Folk
2:38–2:44	Fragment	Fragment
2:44–2:49*	Narration [Foreign] Jordianian Guitar	Narration + Music
2:49–3:00	Airwave/Dial Scans/Cuts	Fragments
3:00–3:20	Women/Children [Foreign] w/Ensemble	Regional Folk
3:21–3:29	Airwave/Dial Scans/Cuts	Various
3:29–3:39*	Narration [Foreign] + Chopin	Narration + Music
3:39–3:42	Airwave/Dial Scans/Cuts	Various
3:42–4:07	Distorted Soundtrack/Concerto	Regional Orchestral
4:07–4:08	Airwave/Dial Scans/Cuts (w/channel bleeding)	Various
4:08–4:27	Voice [Foreign] w/Ensemble	Regional Folk
4:27–4:57	Distortion [FADE OUT]	Sound Art

Track 16/ Freedom Fighters

TIME	DESCRIPTION	CATEGORY
0:00–0:01	Narration [English]:"I created Reptiles"	Narration
0:01–0:14	Street Noises [w/English Cussing]	Sound Art
0:15–0:18	News: "In the Evening"	News
0:18–0:19	Fragment [Foreign Voice]	Fragment
0:19–0:38	News [English]: "How far away are they?"	News
0:39–0:43	News: PLO oppressed	News
0:44–0:50	News: Expulsion of PLO starts	News
0:50–0:54	News: Creation of Bilateral	News
0:55–0:56	Gunfire	Fragment
0:56–1:06	"Terrorists" [ABRUPT ENDING]	News/Sound Art

Track 17/ Lo-Fi Nubia

TIME	DESCRIPTION	CATEGORY
0:00–2:36	Voices [Foreign] w/Ensemble [FADE OUT]	Regional Folk

this "distance" is a formal one, represented not by the samples themselves, but by their arrangement or the spaces between them.

While the aural content of my reconstructions cannot be reproduced here, I can still convey their primary effect: One immediately senses how grouping the samples by categorical sameness does not entirely resolve the formal dissonances of style, region, and format so essential to the aural effect of *Radio Palestine*. Some categories are based on musical themes, while the aural content of others varies widely. For example, I define the category *Western* not by the musical origin of the samples, but by their ability to be mistaken as center-dial European or American radio content. In contrast, the *News* broadcasts are internally structured around regional and international political events, almost entirely from an internal, British perspective, and are almost exclusively reported in English. Another one of my group categories, *Place Makers*, refers to samples that evoke specific settings, such as cocktail bars, broadcast stations, and cosmopolitan centers. Finally, the category *Sound Art* implies that various distortions on the disc are not the result of radio broadcasts, but are actually studio "compositions" created by Bishop to artfully shape the ambience of the disc. To put it simply, each of my alternate tracks required a different *type* of grouping—these were groupings made not by *musical* genre, but by *functional* category, not by musical tradition but by semiotic function. In this sense, the groups highlight all three layers of representation in *Radio Palestine* by making the analyst aware of how the materials "represent" as individual samples, as members of a genre, as radio broadcasts, and as elements in a collage.

In the following section, I invite the reader to listen to a number of samples from each category (these are the same tracks I used for my own edits). In addition to specific track listings, I provide a brief explanation as to why each category has analytic relevance for my analysis of the disc. As with the rest of my analysis, I focus more on interpreting the structural implications of the collage format as a hermeneutic method and less on isolating or providing concrete interpretations of Bishop's actions or the sounds of *Radio Palestine*.

NEWS BROADCASTS

Track 1/ Madame Foyer: 0:48–0:59, 0:59–1:03, 1:06–1:15
Track 4/ Tangental Psychedelico: 1:02–1:10
Track 5/ Solitaire Oriental: 4:59–5:34
Track 9/ Ramadan With Crowbar: 3:09–3:32, 3:37–4:32
Track 12/ Trenchcoat Heatwave, Buffet-Style: 1:02–1:37

In *Radio Palestine*, news broadcasts politicize the landscape with time-capsule references to then-contemporary events. It is worth noting that many of the news broadcasts in *Radio Palestine* are placed in close proximity to one another.[20] Hence, diverse updates combine to produce journalistic "news flashes." However, unlike typical radio updates, these reports are spliced, *cut up* (they do not start with clear beginnings and endings); they do not interrupt or *cut into* an ongoing station broadcast. The news flashes thus draw attention to themselves as recorded, edited, and reproduced out of context. This processing inserts an editorial chasm between the *content* of the broadcast and its significance *as* a broadcast. Formally, this has the effect of broadening the distance between the original function of the news and our perception of it as a historical document.

EXAMPLE 1: NEWS TRANSCRIPTIONS

Track 1/ Madame Foyer: 0:48–0:59, 0:59–1:03, 1:06–1:15

" 'That's no way to treat a friend,' said one White House Official. And the secretary of State, Mr. Schultz, has accused Congress of 'Sticking its Finger in King Hussein's eye.' " (British Accent)

" . . . seems to be vital if further upheavals are to be prevented" (British accent)

" . . . There's been a lot of speculation about the future role of the RFA . . ." (British accent)

Track 4/ Tangental Psychedelico: 1:02–1:10

"But they promised to support the United States' efforts at the Geneva Arms Talks, and called on the Soviet Union to take on a positive attitude." (British accent)

Track 5/ Solitaire Oriental: 4:59–5:34

" 'There's just the small matter of human beings involved, like the Jewish families who've been persuaded to live in nice little flats on the West Bank by an Israeli administration promising eternal protection and security. Or, the thousands of Palestinians still living in the hobbles of Shatila and Burj el-Barajneh [Palestinian refugee camps] in Beirut, while the macho men of Amal and whatever Palestinian faction is in charge there these days, slug it out with expensive arms and ammunition, or highjack airplanes at will. Is that facing up to reality?' he asked Jack Thomson recently in Amman." (British accents)

Track 9/ Ramadan With Crowbar: 3:09–3:32, 3:37–4:32

"... Fighters killed a Soviet advisor ... and Afghan commando leader and 11 more soldiers in the same area June 1st. The sources also said Soviet troops are returning to Kabul from the Konar valley in Eastern Afghanistan where they waged a three-week offensive against resistance fighters. The Soviet units broke through guerrilla positions, lifting a nine-month rebel siege of the government garrison at Barakok [?]." (British accent)

"... drama began shortly before the regular Jordanian airline flight to Amman was due to take off from Beirut airport. Some of the passengers were still on the tarmac identifying their baggage when a carload of gunmen, firing in the air, raced up to the Boeing 727. They stormed on board and ordered the pilot to fly to Tunis. The plane took off, but there wasn't enough fuel for a flight to Tunis, so the pilot landed at Larnaka airport in nearby Cyprus, for refueling, before taking off again and heading for Tunis. But the Tunisian authorities made it quite clear they did not want to the airliner to land there ..." (British accent)

Track 12/ Trenchcoat Heatwave, Buffet-Style: 1:02–1:37

"'... to meet President Reagan if that is the case.' 'I'm not all that sure that the decision has been made. I have read press reports, as have others I'm sure, that Gorbachev will not come, but I am not totally persuaded of that. But even so I think that what the Soviets are saying, is they do not want a meeting that just is a handshake and an hour's small talk—I think they're talking about a substantive summit. The Reagan Administration is wary of a substantive summit.'" (British broadcaster, American interviewee)

Example 1 is a transcript of some of the English news samples from *Radio Palestine*. Remembering that the content of these examples is overtly decontextualized, an examination of the transcripts reveals provocative consistencies. For example, it is clear that the producer of *Radio Palestine* is concerned with political events and regional conflicts, such as the Cold War and American and British politics.[21] In these few samples, the pro-Shi'a Amal Movement of the Lebanese Civil War, the highjacking of an airliner by Fawaz Younis, the war in Afghanistan, the Geneva Summit, and Israeli-Palestinian politics of the West Bank are all referenced. Yet, despite such consistencies of content, it is difficult to pinpoint any political bias in the media landscape. Instead, the excerpts bypass politically charged positions in order to convey a volatile climate of competing international interests in the region. Furthermore, the majority of these clips are critically distanced: They are not presented *in the moment of*, but rather *as commentary on*, iconic events. Together, temporal displacements and a lack of controversial issues keep the listener at a safe distance from the contexts of the original broadcasts.[22]

Finally, these clips remain in dialogue with the content of the disc at large: As studio broadcasts, they contrast the charged field journalism of "Freedom Fighters"; as English broadcasts, they stand out against many Arabic narrations; as spoken text, they provide a respite from the musical content; and as studio news, they stress the radio broadcast over and against musical culture. Likewise, the formal characteristics discussed above stress the role of these broadcasts as once-meaningful messages for an ossified political past, a distant, hermetically sealed reminder of a day in the life. As such, the news portions of the disc provide implicit rather than explicit evidence of political commentary by *Radio Palestine*'s producer. Not coincidentally, it is the oddly neutral tone of these broadcasts that shapes their impact as much as the selective content of their reports.

WESTERN/EUROPEAN MUSIC

Track 2/ Falafel Eastern: 0:35–0:48, 0:49–2:20, 2:26–2:59
Track 4/ Tangental Psychedelico: 1:10–1:18, 1:54–2:00, 6:33–7:04

While these clips could combine with other samples to produce different and unique categories, they are grouped here as signifiers of American or European domestic music. This categorization is appropriate because of the general paucity of these genres on *Radio Palestine*: Other categorizations would be too inclusive to articulate a clear, distinct purpose for these samples.

Each of these musical samples participates in at least two "classical" semantic planes simultaneously. First, musical traits mark each excerpt as a (once) foreign influence. Second, the fact that these samples were broadcast (some as recordings, others live) implies an assimilation of Western traditions within a given geographic region. The tension between these two semantic planes leads to broader questions of cultural assimilation: How do non-Western cultures assimilate Western music? How, once assimilated, does such music become "indigenous" to a culture? And finally, what role does such music have as part of an ethnographic document, particularly for Western listeners? As a result, this category, with its classical guitar and orchestra, its Leonard Cohen guitar fadeout, and its carefully fashioned organ-to-rock cadence, provokes listeners to reconsider what it means for music to be "native" to any area or culture, particularly in a region so permeated by disparate colonial and political influences.

Track 4/ Tangental Psychedelico: 2:51–3:00
Track 6/ Beirut Cocktail/Khartoum Entrée: 4:28–4:44
Track 9/ Ramadan With Crowbar: 1:10–2:02, 2:02–2:16
Track 10/ Night in Ancient Egypt: 2:10–2:20
Track 11/ Exploding Briefcases of Cairo: 1:17–1:24, 3:30–4:08

Without dividing *Radio Palestine* into compartmentalized categorizes based on speculations of their real-life use and function as original sound events, overt references to religious or public rituals are distinct enough to allow for generic categorization as ceremonial music. These samples are treated like most others: as fragmented representations of something more complete or as naive eavesdrops of an anonymous spectator. It is generally through subtle references, then, that *Radio Palestine* hints at the influence of sacred traditions in this old and fertile region. Nonetheless, these samples do draw special attention to themselves when juxtaposed against the ongoing flow of *Radio Palestine*: The melismatic recitation of texts, the thin or nonexistent instrumental textures, and the broadcasting of prayer over loudspeakers all have distinct aural signatures. This allows them to contrast with the acoustic streams of *Radio Palestine*'s tracks as unique contributions highlighted through a type of negative energy, as moments of pause, aural breaths, or brief meditations. The strength and autonomy of these signifiers, their ability to represent specific, identifiable functions, becomes all the more powerful when recognized by those familiar with the religious contexts of the broadcasts. At the same time, listeners who have not participated in these traditions may find them to be provocative of a rare and radical otherness—a feeling that is otherwise carefully controlled by Bishop's use of English disc jockeys and BBC news.

RADIO DISTORTION/SOUND ART

Track 2/ Falafel Eastern: 0:00–0:03
Track 6/ Beirut Cocktail with Khartoum Entrée: 4:16–4:21
Track 11/ Exploding Briefcases of Cairo: 0:13–0:22, 4:16–4:31, 4:49–5:04
Track 15/ Psychic Iman INC.: 0:00–0:28, 1:24–2:20
Track 16/ Freedom Fighters, 0:01–0:14, 0:56–1:06

Perhaps the most unexpected characteristic of *Radio Palestine* is its remarkable sound art. As these samples show, the producer of *Radio Palestine* uses noise in conjunction with music to create a new type of radiophonic sample, one that, importantly, did not exist in 1985 Palestine—at least not with such studio polish. One can interpret this transformation from noise to music using various strategies. For example, these fragments can be analyzed as sound art; as attempts at replicating actual radio distortion; as failed attempts at the natural effects of radio technology; as overt, self-referential reminders of the medium; as mechanized exaggerations of the ambient noise of the region; or, in combination, as postmodern markers of authenticity in a mechanically reproduced object. Any one of these interpretations could lead to interesting results. However, a particular example suggests that it is most fruitful to stress the overt and intentional shaping of electric distortion as an aesthetic object.

The track "ElectricAIRO" is one minute and twenty-four seconds of continuous distortion. There is little doubt that the electric manipulation of sounds is foregrounded, while the underlying (music) samples create a homogenous background. This becomes particularly clear when a separate music track enters around 0:53 to act as a counterpoint to the ongoing distortion track. Lest there be any confusion, "ElectricAIRO" closes with each sub-track ending separately, allowing the instrumental music to fade into the next track while the distortions fade out to silence. Thus, unlike the more subtle examples manipulated throughout *Radio Palestine*, the counterpoint between the separate music track and the continuous distortion leaves little doubt about the overt dialogue between distortion-as-music and traditional radio content in "ElectricAIRO."

For this reason, "ElecticAIRO" is a macrocosmic example of the microcosmic examples listed above, with the caveat that Bishop uses a variety of types of electronic manipulation throughout the disc. In contrast to reminders of the radio format itself—a category treated separately below—these distortions interact with other music examples as a violent aesthetic force, perhaps portraying forces of terror in the region at this time. No parallel in reality is necessary; instead, formal similarities secure the association: These distortions are a force in and of themselves, yet they lack any material substance, any governing code; they are defined by a common appetite for manipulating, distorting, and controlling other samples at piecing volumes; they attack arbitrarily, with no warning, assaulting the music and the listener alike; they terrorize the ear at piercing volume. A specific, mimetic representation of this trope, the first sample—near the beginning of "Exploding Briefcases of Cairo"—literally shocks the listener as high decibels of intense, broad-spectrum noise blast out a calm musical interlude. With samples as suggestive as this one, it is easy to consider this sound art as a separate category of music-making, one that contributes to the effect of *Radio Palestine* in unique and inimitable ways. Oddly, this is also the only type of sample that seems to exist autonomously from the region itself, indicating, perhaps, that these samples are the only *explicit* content—political or social—offered by Bishop.

PLACE MAKERS

Track 4/ Tangental Psychedelico: 0:35–1:02
Track 5/ Solitaire Oriental: 1:20–3:22
Track 6/ Beirut Cocktail/Khartoum Entrée: 0:00–0:21, 1:35–1:47
Track 11/ Exploding Briefcases of Cairo: 0:22–0:34, 0:34–1:14
Track 12/ Trenchcoat Heatwave, Buffet-Style: 2:08–2:32
Track 15/ Psychic Iman INC.: 2:44–2:49, 3:29–3:39

Place Makers offers a competing musical force to the *Western* category above. This is because, under their current categorization, these samples reference specific social atmospheres. There is a musical tension here, where the Beirut cabaret, the subtle elitism of Chopin, the electric guitar reverberations of Jordan, and even East Asian strings and gongs all suggest specific places or venues over and above a particular musical work.

Of course, for a listener more acquainted with the region, many more samples on *Radio Palestine* may hint at specific locations. It is their tacit emphasis on atmosphere rather than tune, on the naming or identifying of a place or region rather than a genre or tradition, that sets these samples apart. Recognizing how samples as brief as five or ten seconds so powerfully evoke specific atmospheres is important for considering how diverse and vivid the collage landscape of *Radio Palestine* is for travelers of the region: Even when shorter bursts of music participate in the formal juxtapositions, autonomous signifiers can present a variety of distinct places in rapid succession, bringing together unlikely cultures in a strongly segregated social landscape.

DJS AND ADVERTISEMENTS

Track 3/ Bedouin Sparklers: 2:13–2:15
Track 4/ Tangental Psychedelico: 5:11–5:20
Track 7/ Voice of Peace: 0:17–0:23, 3:05–3:32
Track 14/ How Are You, Mr. Criminal?: 0:00–0:09
Track 15/ Psychic Iman INC: 3:29–3:39

With the introduction of DJs, advertisements, and broadcast signatures in general, *Radio Palestine* explicitly references its source media. Station calls identify Voice of Peace, a radio station broadcast from the coastal waters of Tel Aviv from 1973 to 1993, and Voice of America, the official external broadcasting service of the U.S. government. Both stations broadcast primarily in English, although Voice of Peace also incorporated French, Arabic, and Hebrew segments. For an English-speaking listener, these examples offer unique points of orientation throughout *Radio Palestine*: They are the strongest reminders of the radio format and of Bishop's own travel throughout the region.

Indeed, while other samples clearly represent Arabic language channels with station calls, radio dramas, and advertising role-plays, the use of English radio journalists and disc jockeys is one feature that continually signals Bishop's use of recordings as a travelogue. While this is a rather mundane and conventional interpretation of Sublime Frequencies soundscapes, it remains a vital part of any interpretation of Bishop's intentions. For while any English-speaking listener is automatically sensitized to these references to station and region, one cannot always assume that Bishop intended this response so much as he reproduced his own experience, the samples that caught his own ears. This does not change the fact that Bishop uses these samples, or how they point the listener toward Western-oriented broadcasting that combine with English news broadcasts to continually stress a particular type of cultural infusion of Western practices into the region during Bishop's travels. But it does imply that the carefully crafted structure of *Radio Palestine* is a different object of study than Bishop's own experiences and intentions.

———

The occasional asterisks in the preceding table denote the specific tracks used in my re-edits of the disc; they also reveal an important characteristic of Bishop's editing. When cross-referenced against my "category" columns, one can see just how carefully he juxtaposes different types of content throughout the disc. Of course, my analysis of the disc can never be complete, and my categories remain subjectively defined. Still, I assert that any analysis of the *structure* of the disc — the variety of samples and the inherent musical differences between them — will result in a similar type of cubist collage, albeit viewed from another perspective. My examination shows that *Radio Palestine* is produced to distribute more than traditional music from a particular place or region; and even more so, that it was engineered with far more creative intention than a random collection or catchall time capsule requires. Indeed, the disc's cuts, splices, and juxtapositions carefully montage a number of variations on a theme, where the heterogeneous differences among samples become deemphasized precisely because of their artful dissociation from one another.

It is for this reason that merely rearranging the samples disrupts their signifying potential. Ultimately, my edits reinforce the power of the collage and its relation to cubism: Three layers of signification—from the immediate recognition of music, through its perceived cultural context by each individual listener, to its reception as one of many signifiers among a radiophonic collage—become increasingly dependent on their aural, rather than cultural, context. Bishop has created a landscape of airwaves, a utopian no place, a mass and collection of acousmatic bodies, spirits, and voices that matches the transient landscape of the Palestinian condition. It is an imaginary landscape, one in the hearts and minds of its perceivers, but also one that, like the subject of a cubist painting, seems to deny the recognition of the specific, identifiable edges, borders, and perimeters intuitively sensed and desired by its audience.

For while the rough-and-tumble editing, modal scales, and recognizable languages and rituals of *Radio Palestine* create a number of one-to-one correspondences to specific cultural spaces, the rapid juxtaposition of these samples constantly reorients the listener toward the broader context of the disc. Slowly, radio waves erode the concrete borders that divide the region, making space for the politics of form to shape the soundscape. The format is ideal: Radio has, in a region suffering from an excess of political, social, institutional, and territorial boundaries, a passport to trespass—to intermingle, to penetrate—all spaces equally. Combined with collage, radio reveals the "unpresentable" content of *Radio Palestine:* an exhausting, poignant, disorienting, and at times, extremely sentimental journey through a utopia too diverse to quantify. It is in this final layer of signification that, despite its English broadcasts, despite its false radio distortions and its free, disembodied sounds floating without names, faces, or dress, *Radio Palestine* succeeds.

The influence—and perspective—of Sublime Frequencies' Bishop is clear. His process of recording, documenting, and selectively editing is never free of bias, editorial scars, or overt political commentary. But he has found a way to expose "unpresentable" cultural processes, the struggle and conflict they entail, without focusing on any single perspective or concrete object. In short, he *has* captured the *inability to* capture the elusive Palestine of the eastern Mediterranean.

NOTES

1. *Radio Palestine: Sounds of the Eastern Mediterranean*, recorded, edited, and assembled by Alan Bishop, *Sublime Frequencies* SF008, 2003.

2. The liner notes state plainly that the disc was "Recorded, Edited, and Assembled by Alan Bishop in 1985" before adding the bit about final editing. *Radio Palestine*, liner notes.

3. Bishop's liner notes mention an interest in tracking down "old records by Farid El Atrache, Sabah, and Oum Khoultoum," as well as receiving many records from Mohammed and local retailers.

4. Sublime Frequencies website, www.sublimefrequencies.com/ (accessed 13 December 2008).

5. The list includes Ocora, Smithsonian Folkways, Ethnic Folkways, Lyrichord, Nonesuch Explorer, Musicaphon, Bärenreiter, Unesco, Playasound, Musical Atlas, Chant du Monde, B.A.M., Tangent, and Topic. www.sublimefrequencies.com/

6. Michael Chanan, *Repeated Takes: A Short History of Recording and Its Effects on Music* (London: Verso, 1995): 18.

7. Recent writings on absolute music in the Western tradition have problematized the idea of authentic modes of listening since the pre-modern—not postmodern—era. For this reason, it is more fruitful to consider "postmodern" modes of listening as bypassing "authentic" modes of listening altogether to focus on how new performance traditions—including digitized music and headphone listening—depend on and are shaped by new forms of mediation. Chanan himself makes such an observation on page 9 of his text. For standard examples of writings on performance practices of pre-modern music, see Daniel Chua, *Absolute Music and the Construction of Meaning* (Cambridge: Cambridge University, 1999), and Richard Taruskin, *Text and Act: Essays on Music Performance* (New York: Oxford University, 1995).

8. Alan Weiss, *Phantasmic Radio* (Durham: Duke University, 1995), 6.

9. As quoted in Marjorie Perloff, *The Futurist Moment* (Chicago: University of Chicago, 1986), 74. Stein is referring to World War I. Perhaps it is relevant that the history of the "modern" eastern Mediterranean began with the British Mandate for Palestine in 1915, during the heart of the cubist movement.

10. For example, "In cubist collage . . . the introjected fragment—say, the newspaper page or the violin *f* [of Picasso's *Still Life with Violin and Fruit*, 1913]—retains its alterity even as that alterity is subordinated to the compositional arrangement of the whole." Perloff, *The Futurist Moment*, 52.

11. Ibid., 44. It is worth noting that Perloff uses two standard modernist examples throughout this discussion: Pablo Picasso's *Still Life with Violin and Fruit*, 1913, and Carlo Carrà's *Demonstration for Intervention in the War*, 1914.

12. Ibid., 47. My ordering of the following ideas does not follow Perloff's original organization.

13. Ibid., 49.

14. Ibid., 52. The quotation is from Apollinaire, *Les Peintres cubistes*, 1913.

15. Ibid., 61–3. Here, Perloff is referring to Carlo Carrà's *Demonstration for Intervention in the War*, 1914, as a specific instance of a common structure.

16. A defense of this process, where inherent meaning is defended against the slippage of absolute relativism even while inherent meaning is itself understood as construction of relative social forces, can be found in Donald Kuspit, "Collage: The Organizing Principle of Art in the Age of the Relativity of Art," reprinted in *Collage: Critical Views*, ed. Katherine Hoffman (Ann Arbor: UMI Research, 1989), 39–57.

17. In fact, Lyotard seems to think most traditional readings of Kant and Burke are faulty, or "nostalgic," because these readings stress a coherent synthesis in the sublime as an idealized wholeness for "solace and pleasure." In this sense, Lyotard's understanding of the sublime contrasts strongly with many contemporary readings of Kant's aesthetics not because he stresses the pain, angst, or awesomeness of the sublime, but rather because he insists that the (postmodern) sublime cannot be based on a clear, coherent organization of semantically stable elements. For one representative example, compare Lyotard's position below with Andrew Bowie, *Aesthetics and Subjectivity: From Kant to Nietzsche*, 2nd edition (Manchester and New York: Manchester University Press, 1993), especially 8–13 and 43–47; for a more complete example of Lyotard's position, see Jean-François Lyotard, "Answering the Question: What Is Postmodernism?," in *The Postmodern Condition: A Report on Knowledge*, trans. Geoff Bennington and Brian Massumi (Minneapolis: University of Minnesota, 1984), 80–81.

18. Lyotard, "Answering the Question," 81. Emphasis added.

19. Throughout, it should be remembered that my breakdown of the disc is constructed loosely in at least three ways: (1) all timings are rounded to the second; (2) genre styles and types are not defined in relation to known or confirmed originals; (3) "category" designations are based on my repeated exposure to the tracks and my intuitions as a listener, not on strict rules of length, type, or style; thus, boundaries between categories are fluid.

20. Track 16/ Freedom Fighters is an extreme case: The entire track is a sequence of dramatized field reports.

21. Likewise, Track 16/ Freedom Fighters—not transcribed here—documents local and regional terrorist activity.

22. A major exception is the shock and violence of the self-contained track 16/ Freedom Fighters; however, as this track comprises "field" rather than "studio" broadcasts, it is worth questioning its inclusion in the category "news broadcasts" altogether.

BIBLIOGRAPHY

Bowie, Andrew. *Aesthetics and Subjectivity: From Kant to Nietzsche*, 2nd edition. Manchester and New York: Manchester University Press, 1993.

Chanan, Michael. *Repeated Takes: A Short History of Recording and Its Effects on Music.* London: Verso, 1995.

Chua, Daniel. *Absolute Music and the Construction of Meaning.* Cambridge: Cambridge University, 1999.

Kuspit, Donald. "Collage: The Organizing Principle of Art in the Age of the Relativity of Art" In *Collage: Critical Views*, edited by Katherine Hoffman (Ann Arbor: UMI Research, 1989), 39–57.

Lyotard, Jean-François. "Answering the Question: What is Postmodernism?" In *The Postmodern Condition: A Report on Knowledge*, trans. Geoff Bennington and Brian Massumi. Minneapolis: University of Minnesota, 1984.

Perloff, Marjorie. *The Futurist Moment.* Chicago: University of Chicago, 1986.

Taruskin, Richard. *Text and Act: Essays on Music Performance.* New York: Oxford University, 1995.

Weiss, Alan. *Phantasmic Radio.* Durham: Duke University, 1995.

SHAYNA SILVERSTEIN

The Punk Arab

Demystifying Omar Souleyman's
Techno-Dabke

In June 2011, on a hot afternoon in north Chicago, large crowds turned out for a local music-and-arts festival curated by The Empty Bottle, a bar and alternative-music club. Mark Gergis of Sublime Frequencies introduced the main act: "From northeastern Syria, from the Jazeera region and the Hassake governate, from the villages of Ras al-Ayin and Tal Amir, please welcome to the stage, Omar Souleyman!"

Souleyman entered the stage in his signature brown *thobe* (gown), red-and-white checkered *keffiyeh* (headwrap), and aviator sunglasses, and raised both arms to acknowledge his fans. He began the set with a *mawwal* (nonmetered, improvised, sung poetry) in colloquial Syrian Arabic, to which keyboardist Rizan Sa'id responded with Kurdish instrumental fills. After a few verses, Souleyman paused just long enough to grab the crowd's attention. Then, with an electrifying shout—"Eeeeeeya!"—he broke into 'ataba and dabke (popular Levantine Arab performance genres) and gestured for the crowd to start dancing to Sa'id's hammered beats. Some dancers synchronized their steps to the rhythms while others flailed their arms. A young woman wearing a *keffiyeh* started to *dabke* (the word is both verb and noun for the Arab line dance distinguished by a foot stomp), leading a chain of people in a small circle close to the stage.

"*Ya achti!*" (Hey sister!) Souleyman said, affectionately greeting me backstage at the 2011 Do-Division Festival. We had been introduced the previous year at a festival in northern Belgium by Raed Yassin, a Lebanese sound artist helping out as cultural liaison for Souleyman's tour. I asked Souleyman how the tour was

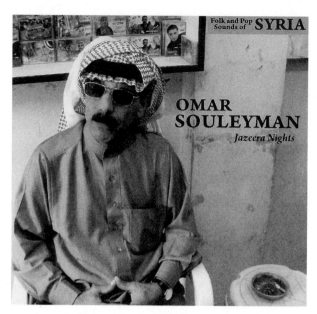

Omar Souleyman, the Syrian wedding singer featured on
Sublime Frequencies albums including *Jazeera Nights* (SF055),
now performs around the world.

going. "It is good," he said. "No accidents and good money." I wondered if he
was referring to the mishaps of earlier tours—the theft of summer earnings in
Belgium and a relative's mishandling of profits. He continued, "They are dancing.
It is good to be here. I like Chicago."[1]

Since his international debut on the Sublime Frequencies label, Souleyman
has gained broad appeal beyond Syria and the Arab world. The first Syrian
wedding singer to cross over to Western audiences, he is embraced as a world-
music phenomenon by consumers of punk, dancehall, house, techno, and world
beat who dance ecstatically at his live shows. From Chicago to the acclaimed
Glastonbury Music Festival in the UK, Souleyman is a global commodity sought
after by independent music lovers and global ravers.

He first came to the attention of Sublime Frequencies in the late 1990s, when
musician, producer, and collector Mark Gergis—in search of Syrian *sha'bi* (popular) music—encountered his cassettes in a working-class Damascus street stall.[2]
Several years later, Gergis contacted Souleyman for permission to distribute his
recordings on the Sublime Frequencies label. Their collaboration resulted in

the 2007 release of *Highway to Hassake*, a folk-and-pop compilation featuring 13 tracks of *'ataba*, *dabke*, and *choubi* recorded at live events.[3]

In 2009, Gergis released a YouTube video collage, *"Leh Jani"* ("When I Found Out"), in conjunction with the album.[4] *"Leh Jani"* did more for Souleyman's career than any other project. Supplementing a track of the same name on *Highway to Hassake*, the video depicts Souleyman and his band at various venues, from a local nightclub to outdoor and indoor weddings. The video insinuates the relaxed sexual mores and delirium of wedding dance parties in the borderlands of the Middle East. Souleyman appears as a detached yet controlled "boss" of the Arab street. Titillating and exotic, *"Leh Jani"* became a "gateway cut" for many Souleyman fans, including Qu Junktions, a UK-based organization for independent music, which contacted Sublime Frequencies in 2009 to propose a European tour. With a debut at the Sonár Festival in Barcelona, this tour launched Souleyman's career in the West. To the amazement of Sublime Frequencies and its followers, "one of the surprising hits at Sonár 2009 was none other than Syrian megastar-in-waiting Omar Souleyman."[5]

No longer a workingman's singer from an isolated region of Syria, Souleyman is today a sensation among alternative music fans in Europe and North America. His hipness hinges less on his "legacy status" in Syria (a misleading embellishment conceived by Sublime Frequencies) than on his surreal performance style. Journalist Andy Morgan writes: "to the hip, [Souleyman's] an adorable techno-*naif*, a strange apparition from another world . . . for them, the very fact of his improbable existence is already half the charm."[6] By casting Souleyman's music as "new old media" and promoting him as an iconoclast, Sublime Frequencies capitalized on the free flow of globalization and digital culture and targeted outsider audiences, from experimental-music connoisseurs to lovers of global pop and electronic dance music.[7]

This essay focuses on the reception of Souleyman's concerts during his period working with Sublime Frequencies (2006–2011).[8] Charting his rise from a local vocalist whose recordings were wedged between Damascus cassette stalls to an internationally recognized artist, his crossover to Western audiences is situated within the cultural context in which he began working in Hassake in the 1990s. Not quite the "legendary" Syrian singer that Sublime Frequencies has touted, Souleyman promoted his parties and adapted to changing conditions in ways typical of popular singers in his region. The trajectory of his career since he began working with Sublime Frequencies is, however, emblematic of how the label fosters cross-cultural understanding—striking the nerve of the exotic. In the context of post-9/11 politics in the West, the Souleyman project taps into an exotica hyperbolized by Islamophobia. By critiquing the popular music discourse surrounding live concerts and situating these concerts in local contexts, this essay suggests that Souleyman's popularity is driven by countercultural desires for authenticity, cultural tolerance, and political activism.[9] Motivated by antihegemonic resistance to homogeneity and insularity, fans problematically inscribe Souleyman's *"techno-dabke"* within discourses of race and class that historically have shaped the circulation of non-Western popular musics.

ANALOG SYRIA

In 1997, Mark Gergis headed to the Middle East, motivated by personal and political interests. He had lamented the erosion of Iraqi music under Saddam Hussein—and would later produce *Choubi Choubi!* (2005) to abate the loss of Iraqi popular dance music—but, unable to visit his paternal homeland of Iraq, Gergis looked toward Syria, and specifically Syria's border with Iraq, as a substitute destination for his musical pilgrimage.[10] He was also interested in bringing Syrian music to a larger audience, in light of a cultural isolation borne of its quasi-socialist economy and Baathist politics under the Assad regime.

Gergis's musical fascination with the Middle East was tied to both his Arab-American identity and his adolescence in Detroit. In a 2008 interview with the online art and skate magazine *Fecal Face*, Gergis recalled being mocked and feared by his neighbors in suburban Detroit during the first Gulf War: "People in the trash suburb I grew up in would come into our market with 'Fuck Iraq' T-shirts on and ask us 'Where you from?' . . . I vowed artistic revenge on my classmates at an early age."[11]

This experience connected Gergis to Sublime Frequencies founder Alan Bishop, who also grew up outside of Detroit. Bishop's first encounter with Arab music was through a recording of Farid al-Atrash on *oud* (Arabic lute), introduced by his grandfather, a Lebanese-American musician who frequently invited friends over to play Arab music in his basement.[12] The two met in the late 1990s through northern California's alternative music scene, where they connected over their mutual sense of alienation, punk affinity, and Middle Eastern heritage. Through Sublime Frequencies, Bishop and Gergis would aim to counter gross misperceptions of Arab culture in America by redistributing popular musics from the region and producing "obscure sights and sounds" through collage and cut-up techniques (e.g., *I Remember Syria*, 2004).

This penchant for analog culture drew Gergis to Omar Souleyman. Gergis took an interest in the lowbrow cassettes that circulated pop and dance tracks through Syria's informal music economy. The low fidelity of these tapes appealed to his taste for distorted and experimental sounds, and also happened to deemphasize the foreignness of the Arabic language. As a punk musician and indie music producer, he saw the potential for the "incredibly fast and gritty *dabke* music blaring in the street stalls of every city."[13] Of Souleyman's music, Gergis said:

> [A]fter collecting and listening to hundreds of (*dabke* singers), I deduced that while there are similar acts in the country, none really matches the distinct character of the Souleyman sound. His longtime collaboration with Rizan Sa'id, the Kurdish keyboard player, has yielded some of the rawest and most urgent-sounding examples of "new wave *dabke*" I've heard, and it definitely stands apart from others, to me. Souleyman's voice is unique as well, whether he's singing or MC-ing, there's a rugged beauty to it that is genuine and very likeable.[14]

Yet Gergis did not immediately market Souleyman's music. In fact, after sitting on his cassette collection for many years, it was only when a friend asked him for a compilation of Souleyman's tracks that Gergis experienced a breakthrough. He listened again to how "the fidelity varied wildly and some tapes were unmarked and pitched or edited poorly."[15] Not himself an Arabic speaker, Gergis enlisted the help of Raed Yassin, a multimedia artist based in Beirut, to help approach Souleyman in 2006 for permission to distribute his recordings with Sublime Frequencies. Souleyman considered this an opportunity to reach audiences beyond the Middle East and trusted Gergis.[16] What resulted, with help from Yassin and Alan Bishop's support, was the Sublime Frequencies release *Highway to Hassake*.

THE HASSAKE HOMELAND

Before signing with Sublime Frequencies, Souleyman was a *mutrib*, or wedding singer, who had spent over a decade building a thriving career in eastern Syria and beyond—but he had not always been oriented musically. Not until 1994, encouraged by friends to sing for local *ḥaflāt* (party events) in Ras al-Ain, did he leave behind years of manual labor to pursue this line of work. But once he decided to perform professionally in 1994, he said, he "literally had a party every day. There would be a waiting list for me to sing at weddings."[17]

As a *mutrib*, Souleyman developed strategies that made him very popular. His sets would begin with a *mawwal,* or nonmetered vocal improvisation, that set the tone for the festivities and established his artistic authority and individual touch. The rest of the set would alternate between *mawwal* (pl. *mawawīl*), *'ataba, dal'una,* and other upbeat dance forms typical of *sha'bi* music, each differentiated by their prosaic construction, poetic meter, rhyming patterns, and rhythms. The band played polymetric arrangements of *leff, baladi,* and *waḥda* rhythmic patterns typical of *sha'bi* and other popular musics broadcast on Arab radio and television in the 1970s and 1980s. His audiences would participate collectively in the *dabke,* a regional line dance distinguished by a signature foot stomp and improvisational movements.[18] In traditional fashion for a wedding singer, he also served as master of ceremonies, making toasts to the bridal party with wit and grace, and picking up village dialects to cater to local tastes and preferences. Depending on the occasion, he, like other wedding singers, would offer tributes to popular political and religious figures, regardless of his personal views or affiliations.[19] Flexible and agile, able to adapt and improvise anywhere, he was transformed from an average wedding singer into a *fanān,* or artist. Souleyman has said that he was recognized as a *fanān* not only in his local village but throughout Hassake.

To a Syrian ear, what distinguishes Souleyman from other Syrian wedding singers is the syncretic blend of Turkish, Iraqi, and Kurdish sounds typical of the Hassake region. Souleyman is from Ras al-Ain, a village on the Turkish border that reflects the diverse heritage of Armenian, Assyrian, Kurdish, Turkish, and Syrian Arab communities in the region. Performance genres are quite fluid in Hassake, as in other border zones, and Souleyman was known for customizing his sets for audiences as familiar with Kurdish *govend* and Iraqi *choubi* as Syrian *dabke.*[20] Souleyman worked closely with several musicians, including Ali Shaker on *baǧlama saz* (long-necked lute) and keyboardist Rizan Sa'id, to arrange these sets.[21] His partnership with Sa'id, who would become a fixture of Souleyman's band, goes back to 1996. Sa'id is recognized regionally for his Kurdish style of playing and he brought with him a distinctly Kurdish intonation, rhythmic complexity, and song repertoire. Sa'id also adapted the *choubi* style of Iraqi dance music to the keyboard by sampling a *khishba* or *zanbour* drum and intermittently disrupting the metric groove with repetitive strikes that sound like gunshots.

Souleyman's sounds evoke a complex set of ethnic and regional distinctions that reinforce sociocultural differences within Syria. Whereas Damascus is often valorized as a cosmopolitan urban center and the seat of political and economic power in Syria, in contrast, nonelite populations from northeastern Syria are marginalized as rural, popular, and underclass.[22] Since before the Syrian war, Hassake was isolated economically and politically by the state and suffered from limited access to education, health care, and other social services. Political antagonism between Kurdish nationalists and the Baathist regime led to intense government surveillance of residents throughout the area, and, like that of the neighboring governorates of Deir el-Zour and Raqqa, Hassake's agricultural economy suffered from major droughts since 2006 that impoverished many. In search of opportunities for seasonal work, thousands left eastern Syria for greater Damascus between 2005 and 2011.[23] These various "push" factors—drought, labor migration, and political isolation—arguably led to the Syrian uprising that broke out in March 2011.[24] The Syrian war and the emergence of the Islamic State in 2014 inflamed the region's extreme isolation to the point of crisis. At the time of this writing, Souleyman has sought refuge in Turkey, where he lives with his family when not touring Europe or North America.

In the context of a declining regional economy in the 2000s, Souleyman began to work in the Gulf region, drawing on his knowledge of the Gulf dialect and culture to appeal to these new audiences. The video that brought Souleyman to the West's attention, "Leh Jani," portrays Souleyman as a lower-class wedding singer who performs primarily at Khaliji ḥaflāt (Gulf- and Iraqi-based parties) rather than in Syrian venues. As such, the video indexes Gulf-based cultural referents rather than Syrian or Kurdish signifiers. For instance, Souleyman acts as MC and sings at weddings where the bride and groom wear formal Bedouin attire rather than the Western ensembles that many Syrian couples rent or purchase. The video captures him in a besht, or formal robe popular in the Gulf. Relatedly, the video enhances the sha'bi (popular) and more vulgar aspects of Khaliji culture: "Why are the pretty girls from Mosul?" scrolls across the screen in Khaliji dialect.

In keeping with most sha'bi videos, "Leh Jani" reflects the lo-fi aesthetics of the late 1990s, when a "new wave" of technology altered traditional performance dynamics in Syrian sha'bi culture and widened access to music production equipment.[25] The video evokes dated television shows; the camerawork and audio are discontinuous and choppy. The audio imperfectly aligns with Souleyman's rhyming and verse structure, and the camera tends to focus on the upper bodies of dancers rather than on their footwork in the dabke line. It also focuses more on promotion and entertainment than on the display of artistic talent. The production studio's name and contact information scroll across the screen at regular intervals, often cutting off the content of the recording.

Souleyman worked within a system that cheapened musical labor, including his own.[26] He was subject to Syrian "cassette culture": informal networks that produce and distribute recordings of live shows for low-cost, local consumption through local street vendors.[27] This circulation occurs outside the nationalistic state output heavily promoted by the Ministry of Culture and centered in Damascus, and serves as the primary conduit for working-class entertainers such as Souleyman.[28] Cheap recordings allow individual wedding singers to market themselves and book their calendars: Souleyman released some 500 such cassettes and CDs over 20 years. Despite this proliferation of recorded material, he remained on the social and political periphery of Syrian *sha'bi* music, performing sounds from the Hassake border, pursuing Khaliji consumers, and constantly adapting to local performance conditions.

THE FEVER PITCH OF *TECHNO-DABKE*

As a wedding singer, Souleyman's priority is to make people dance. And on tour in Europe and the United States, it is the danceability of his music that has won him so many fans. "[T]he Syrian musician turned the energy dial to maximum," *The Telegraph* wrote, of his performance at the 2011 Glastonbury Music Festival. Souleyman "had the whole crowd at the West Holts Stage dancing their socks off."[29] Jon Garelick of *The Phoenix* described a similar scene at a Boston show in 2012:

> Dancing was general—line dances, circle dances, break dances. At one point, a kid who had been at the heart of the melee—in full white *thawb* gown and *keffiyeh*—broke from the crowd, ran to the back of the room, and puked. A woman danced by, her face completely veiled by a *keffiyeh*, but wearing a black tank-top and cheetah patterned short shorts, mid-riff exposed. By the end of the show, she was on stage with another woman, her headdress now wrapped around her hips, shimmying wildly.[30]

Souleyman's fever-pitch popularity in the West is largely due to the perceived translatability of *dabke* rhythms to Euro-American tastes and dance styles.[31] *Dabke* as a musical form and beat traditionally accompanies the prescribed line dance that goes by the same name. Yet its regular, fast-paced, duple meter and high-energy sound invite all kinds of global dance expressions. At the 2010 Summerdance Festival in downtown Chicago, for example, audiences danced to Souleyman with salsa, polka, African dance, belly dancing, and EDM movements.

His music is said to conjure a "familiar yet foreign feel in its Syrian manifestation" of Western popular forms.[32] Souleyman remarked in an interview, "you know, I came here to Europe and found out that the people not only can handle my *dabke* sound but they like it very much and were dancing to it."[33]

As with Khaliji parties in the Gulf, Souleyman developed new strategies to accommodate his new audiences. Increased schedule demands and a lack of familiarity with communities in the Gulf had affected his ability to engage effectively with the local dynamics of a given party, the quality that had distinguished him from other wedding singers. Looking to maintain his competitive edge and provide his clients with a "unique show," he began collaborating with local poets, such as Mahmoud Harbi, who provided him with rhyming lines of *mawawīl* and bridal party toasts, rather than improvise these himself. When Souleyman began touring Europe, he did so with Harbi, and the poet exoticized the show. At a 2010 concert in Brussels, a young woman said, "the poet whispering in his ear was so cool . . . Like a mystery, inexplicable. I asked myself, what is he saying?"[34] The following year, however, Souleyman returned to Brussels without Harbi. He explained that shows abroad had fixed programs—in contrast to live weddings that require customized songs and speeches—eliminating the need for improvised poetry. In place of the poet, virtuosic keyboardist Rizan Sa'id assumed a more prominent role. By reducing the role of vocals, poetry, and improvisation in his touring arrangements, Souleyman again adapted his performance to a new audience. What he lost in exotic allure he gained in Sa'id's musical contribution.

For most fans, Souleyman's appeal has less to do with the multicultural tropes of world music and more with the repetitive groove of electronic dance music. Around the same time that Souleyman came to Björk's attention (discussed later in this essay), the 2009 Sonár Festival launched him into the Western concert market. While festival organizers slotted him into their expansion of "geographical frontiers" to Africa and the Middle East (though, nominally, Souleyman was the only Middle Eastern artist), journalists related his "high octane" *dabke* mostly to punk and electronic dance music.[35]

For instance, reviewers likened the rhythmic drive of *techno-dabke* to techno and house grooves. One blogger noted that "one of the most striking similarities to have hit me is that of the omnipresent Arabic wedding ululation to the pea whistle of hardcore rave.[36] Whether hardcore or a "thumping house beat," in "La Sidounak Sayyada" ("I'll Prevent the Hunters from Hunting You"), these impressions are driven by rhythmic groove.[37] As well, reviewers often comment on how the intensity of his music contrasts with his aloof, affectless stage presence. He appears "straight as a board" and "stationary" to the extent that he "barely moves onstage."[38] His "expressionless" performance seems to contradict the "hyped-up" nature of *dabke*.[39] In the context of dance festivals and nightclubs, this emotional flatness can be seen as coextensive with electronic dance music's synthetic, hypnotic timbres, beat patterns, and aesthetics.

Punk has also been a persistent touchstone in Euro-American accounts of Souleyman's music. In 2010, *The Wire* cast Souleyman's *Jazeera Nights* album as pure punk, or "the most joyful, jouissant and probably unintentionally punk celebration of pure sound since the earliest days of Hardcore Techno."[40] Allusions to punk became contagious. Journalists stressed the punk-like aesthetics of Souleyman's fast, aggressive, and hard-edged beats and stripped-down instrumentation. One reviewer commented that Souleyman is "too abrasive to be party music" because his "anthemic energy" is "raw and bloody."[41] The same reviewer compared *dabke* to spazzcore, a "spastic" punk-derived music that despite being "ostensibly chaotic, is very demanding in terms of precision and physical endurance."[42] Aaron Leitko of the *Washington Post* suggested that "the volume and intensity of [Souleyman's] music recalled the '70s proto-punk band Suicide, which made similar, if less technically capable, use of keyboards and drum machines to generate minimalist pounding. But that's still a bit of a stretch."[43]

These accounts cater to the punk sensibility of the Sublime Frequencies' consumer—the kind of listener Andy Morgan has called the "gentleman with a punk attitude." By recontextualizing Souleyman in relation to punk aesthetics, his music becomes a signifier of punk culture. Moreover, punk consumers express their antiestablishment, subversive, and DIY attitudes by listening to *techno-dabke* with a "simultaneous aesthetic and activist disposition."[44]

Not unrelatedly, *techno-dabke* has also been connected to Jamaican dancehall. Analogies to dancehall hyperbolize Souleyman's beats in order to stress the similarly hard, percussive beats of *techno-dabke* and dancehall. Dave Segal noted in a review of *Jazeera Nights* that he "sounds like a Middle Eastern analogue to dancehall, with its hyper-adrenalized aura and stridently emotional vocals."[45] Bill Meyer of the *Chicago Reader* speculated in 2010 that "manic tommy-gun drum bursts over rhythm loops could pass for samples from impossibly sped-up dancehall reggae records."[46] One blogger compared beats in Souleyman's "La Sidounak Sayyada" to the "applause riddim" in dancehall artist Sean Paul's "Temperature."[47] *The Wire* related Souleyman's role onstage to that of a Jamaican toaster or MC.[48] Ben Yaster of *Dusted Magazine* also asserted that "Souleyman is as much a toaster as he is a troubadour—his refrains are chanted rather than sung."[49]

Such comparisons underscore the politics of otherness in punk and electronic dance music cultures. Like *dabke*, dancehall is a street-based sound system that encompasses dancing to minimalist beats and vocals improvised by an MC. Dancehall emerged in inner-city Kingston in the late 1970s at a moment of sociopolitical and often violent conflict between Jamaica's two major political parties. Snubbed by the Jamaican elite for its subversion of middle-class values and ideologically opposed to roots reggae and Rastafari philosophy, dancehall flaunts sexuality and violence in its lyrics.[50] From reggae to dancehall, Jamaican dance musics historically have been co-opted by electronic dance music producers and punk musicians who "cross genre frontiers and seek out examples of 'otherness' to match their sense of alienation."[51] Just as sociopolitical affinities are projected onto lower-class urban black imaginaries through the embrace of dancehall outside of Jamaica, Western fans of *techno-dabke* embrace Arab otherness in a post-9/11 world of xenophobia.

These sentiments were reflected among audiences throughout Souleyman's 2010 European tour. At a club event at Recyclart, an alternative arts hotspot in Brussels, Souleyman shared a roster with Gergis (billed as "world music DJ"), a *rai* band from Algeria, and several other DJs from Brazil and Australia.[52] The crowd raved enthusiastically on the dance floor during Souleyman's set—shimmying, jiving, breaking. One young woman championed the broader cultural significance of Souleyman's appearance at Recyclart: "This is so Brussels! It is a mixed crowd and there are some here of Arab descent. It's a space to dance and share good vibes among those who follow music circuits and festivals, and among those who desire a place to mingle among those 'in the know.' This is what Recyclart hopes to be on a good night."[53] At Recyclart, Souleyman's presence assured audiences of a globalized network of cultural resistance and solidarity that appeals to aesthetic and activist visions for a more inclusive Brussels.

Similar hopes played out at Souleyman's appearance at an annual arts festival in Kortrijk, a modest city in the Flemish-speaking area of Flanders. The main stage of the Kortrijk Congé festival was located on Buda-Eiland, an area located on the periphery of the historic city center (now a major shopping district and one of the largest pedestrian zones in Belgium). Kortrijk Congé invited Souleyman to participate in a festival that aims to bring awareness to local community issues through the arts.[54] He appealed to their visions of pluralist public space and active cultural citizenship, which resonate more broadly within the history of linguistic politics that has long divided the northern and southern provinces of Belgium. Language is a site of contestation between opposing groups of French and Flemish speakers in Belgium, who maintain separate political parties, newspapers, television channels, and libraries as well as public administration—differences have undermined politics to the extent that there is a movement for a Flemish homeland.[55] Socially aware and politically motivated, the Flemish festival organizers were keen to promote Souleyman as part of their vision. In Flemish Kortrijk, Souleyman's "folk-psychedelic" spoke to the politics of the vernacular and values of social justice, accompanied by a trace of the ecstatic. Orientalized yet modern, traditional yet reimagined, Souleyman stood for the Flemish ideals of intercultural dialogue, social welfare, and civil society.

Souleyman, Sa'id, and Ali Shaker say that this festival was one of their favorites. At 1:30 a.m., they performed their "boombox-street-party-feel" to a crowd of several hundred ecstatic ravers. Party favors were tossed to the crowd, large plastic balls bounced over their heads, and they waved glowsticks high in the air. As they packed up their equipment after the show and prepared to drive on to the next day's stop, they told me backstage that the *jaw* (atmosphere) was *mutarab* (enchanting); the audience was *zarif* (cool). "It should be like this," they affirmed.

BJÖRK CROSSINGS

In June 2009, indie star Björk endorsed "Syrian techno" in a broadcast on National Public Radio's *You Must Hear This* program.[56] Her endorsement not only introduced Souleyman to NPR listeners, but also marked *dabke*'s crossover from Arab and Arab-American cultures to mainstream American culture. Björk related his work to her aspirations for populism and experimentalism through the unity of acoustic and electronic sounds in dance music (Dibben 2009). Her endorsement facilitated Souleyman's crossover into the alternative music industry, increased his visibility, and introduced him to her fan base.

In 2011, Björk invited Souleyman to collaborate in her *Biophilia* project. An album and a series of interactive visual apps built for iPad by David Attenborough, *Biophilia* is a foray into voice and computer-generated images. At once gaming, art, science, and music, *Biophilia* represents Björk's experiments at the intersections of nature and technology.[57] The project has been interpreted as a way of "naturalizing technology" by offering an intimate and emotionally powerful alternative to technological determinism in popular dance music.[58] The multimedia project resists the predictability of standardized dance tracks and pop music through the affective power of Björk's voice and its user-centered interactive software design.

Like her earlier projects, *Biophilia* was produced through a collaborative ethos that is central to Björk's creative process.[59] She explains, "I can make all the skeleton and song writing, but then when I am almost finished I am curious to get the real virtuosos in the field to add like some sort of acrobatic things."[60] Björk was intrigued by Souleyman's collaborations with the poet Mahmoud Harbi: "I always heard interesting stories that he has one man called Mahmoud Harbi who is a longtime collaborator—he writes poems for Souleyman. When they are really warmed up and going for it at a good-times party, Harbi stands next to him on stage and chain-smokes. Then he will whisper poetry in his ear that he's writing at the moment. Omar will sing it immediately in the microphone and run around the room, exciting people there. I thought it was quite exciting for a poet and an MC to work together."[61]

She contacted Souleyman, who agreed to remix "Crystalline Series."[62] Working from their studio in Hassake, Souleyman and Sa'id dubbed over Björk's tracks to produce "Crystalline," "Tesla," and "Mawwal."[63] The One Little Indian label released the remix as a 12-inch LP in July 2011 in conjunction with two other remixes—by Matthew Herbert and Serban Ghenea, respectively.

The A-side "Crystalline" is reconceived as a traditional *dabke* track that opens with an instrumental introduction of alternating melodic phrases on keyboard and *buzuq* supported by a downtempo groove. Synthesized *tabl* drum enters as Souleyman breaks into an *'ataba* style of vocalization: "Ehhhh!" These serve to introduce a sample of Björk's vocals from her "Crystalline" track, backed softly by instrumental embellishments and a steady percussive beat. The track shifts between their two voices in alternating sections until they start to sing over each other in ascending and wailing vocal breaks that shatter the soundscape. The remix supplants the frenetic dubstep, bell sounds, and synthesized sonic bursts in the original with *choubi* percussion on the Iraqi *khishba* drum. The juxtaposition of these percussive sounds with Arabic vocal ululations and a *tabl* breakbeat reinforces Souleyman's aesthetic traditions.

On the B-side, "Tesla" and "Mawwal" tend even more to the traditional *dabke* sound in terms of timbre, texture, instrumental arrangement, and melismatic vocals. Both tracks open with instrumental solos—Rizan Sa'id on keys and Ali Shaker on *buzuq*—supported by a drone and heavy in reverb and echo. Creative adaptations play out in the manipulation of voice, rhythm, and studio effects. The remix "Tesla," named after the tesla coil synth that provides a bassline for the original "Thunderbolt," imitates the original's lush texture and samples Björk's voice extensively. While the correlations of "Mawwal" to Björk's compositions are less explicit, the placement of "Mawwal" at the end of the LP is a clever reversal of its conventional function as an introductory nonmetered vocal section that introduces a dance set.

Acclaimed by media and fans, "Crystalline Series" is an "ecstatic" remix that blurs cultural boundaries of Western and non-Western artists and aesthetic boundaries of improvised vocals and synthesized beats. The broader social significance of this collaboration lies in the subversion of cultural logics associated with non-Western music, indie punk, and EDM.

CONCLUSION

More so than other releases by Sublime Frequencies, the Souleyman project is laced with intimate undertones and political overtones. Gergis and Bishop have said that their personal experiences with xenophobia in Detroit and alienation from mainstream American society since the Gulf War, respectively, motivated them to take on this project. They have challenged public perceptions of Syria and Iraq through tours and albums of Souleyman, *Choubi Choubi!*, and *I Remember Syria*. Yet they also resist overtly politicizing those sounds they promote as antihegemonic. Both Gergis and Bishop have declined press interviews (as of this writing) since the Syrian crisis began. They severely restricted media access to Souleyman, who, when available, has spoken about music but refrained from discussing politically sensitive topics, such as his status as a Syrian refugee in Turkey. The Sublime Frequencies team has eschewed metanarratives—academic, political, or otherwise—in favor of reiterating how Souleyman enchants audiences worldwide through sound and sight. Though their resistance to hegemonic institutions stems from and inspires productive affective alliances, the lack of a metanarrative has enabled the commodification of *techno-dabke* in ways that seem contrary to Sublime Frequencies' position.

Rather than taking to *dabke* as a distinct genre with its own aesthetic categories, Euro-American consumers depend on musical metaphors that liken Souleyman's sounds to punk, techno, and dancehall, as well as to world music. Audiences perform global dance styles from open-ended interpretive movements to salsa, bellydance, and rave; journalists fetishize him (and occasionally critique such fetishization) as an anomaly within contemporary popular culture. In order to make *dabke* digestible for non-Arabs, consumers draw on the discursive frameworks that shape alternative and electronic dance musics;

quite literally, they consume *techno-dabke*. These efforts generally resist contextualizing Souleyman and his music within Arab society; nor do they attempt to situate his experiences within the shifting dynamics of popular culture in the Middle East. Such mediations not only perpetuate the mystique surrounding Souleyman's presence in the West, but ironically reproduce the very logics of the global media commons that Sublime Frequencies originally set out to resist in its experimentalist approach to new old media.

Techno-dabke reinforces the divide between globalized cultural consumption and the ethnomusicological tradition at the same time that it mediates sonic and embodied encounters with alterity. These mediations are situated in the post-9/11 rise of Islamophobia and racialization of Arab bodies, which, as this essay points out, have framed the consumption of Souleyman's live concerts.[64] While newly shared spaces of pleasure and leisure have been produced by these encounters, they are predicated on the performance of antihegemonic stances among youth, from Brussels and Glastonbury to Chicago and LA. As discussed above, these concert-going youth position themselves as advocates of racial tolerance, religious pluralism, and multiculturalism through the production of Arab musical difference. Yet even as their consumption of Omar Souleyman's *techno-dabke* resists insularity and homogeneity, these culturally and artistically elite audiences arguably fail to achieve the decolonizing gesture that they aspire toward. Rather, the commodification of *techno-dabke* reproduces existing relations of race and social class in popular music.

Today, Souleyman is an A-list entertainer who performs for global events, such as the 2013 Nobel Peace Prize Ceremony (alongside Morrissey and Mary J. Blige, among others). His music has been arranged by Kronos Quartet and produced by Kieran Hebden of Four Tet. In his journey from local wedding gigs to the global music industry, his music has represented the syncretic sounds of Hassake and exoticized difference from the Arab world, countercultural resistance, and, in the backdrop of the Syrian war, the iconic refugee displaced by unfathomable violence. His music speaks for the complexities of these moments, in their various scales and contexts, and for the uncanniness of encounter. Though he parted ways with Sublime Frequencies in 2011, Souleyman's popularity reflects the label's keen ear for what sounds cross over and enchant countercultural listeners in the West. Ironically, Souleyman is now an iconic figure in the very industry that Sublime Frequencies, and its fans, seek to resist.

NOTES

1. Personal correspondence with Mark Gergis. July 2010. Belgium.

2. *Sha'bi* literally translates as "of the people." *Sha'bi* practices, which range from popular music to food-based customs, are typically associated with street culture and traditional ways of life in ways that refer to the popular aesthetics of the working class.

3. Omar Souleyman, *Highway to Hassake (Folk and Pop Sounds of Syria)*. SF031, CD, 2007, www.sublimefrequencies.com/item.asp?Item_id=34&cd=Omar-Souleyman:-Highway -to-Hassake-(Folk-and-Pop-Sounds-of-Syria).

4. Mark Gergis, "*Leh Jani*" ("When I Found Out"), 2009. www.youtube.com /watch?v=pgRUHIeaKOk.

5. Field Day Festivals, 11 June 2011, www.fielddayfestivals.com/features_and_audio /omar-souleyman-live/.

6. Andy Morgan, "The Dabke Demon," *fRoots,* October 2010.

7. David Novak, "The Sublime Frequencies of New Old Media," *Public Culture* 23, no. 3 65 (September 21, 2011): 603–34.

8. At the end of 2011, Souleyman departed Sublime Frequencies to work with Mina Tosti. Under her management, he has collaborated with British electronic musician Four Tet, performed at the 2013 SXSW alternative music festival, and contracted "La Sidounak Sayyada" (I'll Prevent the Hunters from Hunting You) for string quartet arrangement by world-music pioneers Kronos Quartet. I wish to thank Tamara Turner for sharing materials from her personal correspondence with Tosti.

9. Ethnographic research for this study was conducted through interviews, participation-observation at electronic dance music festivals in the United States and Europe, and analysis of popular media discourse. I also draw extensively on fieldwork carried out in Syria (2004–2008) in which I focused on popular *dabke* practices and the production of ethnic and national identity (Shayna Silverstein, "Mobilizing Bodies in Syria: Dabke, Popular Culture, and the Politics of Belonging," PhD diss., University of Chicago, 2012).

10. Personal correspondence with the author, June 2009, Chicago, Ill. See also Morgan, "The Dabke Demon"; Chris Rolls, "Interview: Mark Gergis aka Porest," *Fecal Face,* November 18, 2008; Alex Behr, "This Is Your Brain on Souleyman: Interview with Mark Gergis," *Evil Monito,* May 1, 2010.

11. Rolls, "Interview."

12. Brandon Stosuy, "No Sleep Til Beirut: A Conversation with Alan Bishop," *Arthur Magazine.* September 2005.

13. Rolls. "Interview."

14. Quoted in Behr, "This Is Your Brain on Souleyman."

15. Ibid.

16. According to Yassin, he and Gergis became acquainted through experimental

music networks in Lebanon and the States. Gergis contacted him to ask for assistance as a cultural liaison and translator. Yassin helped to place the initial phone call to Souleyman and offered translations for *Highway to Hassake* liner notes. He also joined Souleyman's tours in 2009 and 2010 to translate and facilitate everyday arrangements. Personal correspondence with Raed Yassin, May 2006, Beirut, Lebanon. I also wish to thank Wills Glasspiegel for sharing materials taken from a personal interview with Souleyman, conducted over Skype with a translator.

17. Andy Beta, "Omar Souleyman: The Wedding Singer," *Spin,* October 22, 2013. This claim is contestable as village locals have noted that local restaurants would not offer him performance opportunities. Personal correspondence with Salah Ammo, October 2014.

18. Silverstein, "Mobilizing Bodies in Syria."

19. Consider, for instance, the song "Bashar Ya Habibi Shaab" (Oh Bashar, Beloved of the People), which is popularly hailed as a pro-Assad tribute among regime supporters. Just as Souleyman disavows political affiliations, he chooses to position himself as nonoppositional in order to maintain his artistic legitimacy in an authoritarian state that censors cultural production and demands compromises from artists and intellectuals. Shayna Silverstein, "New Wave Dabke: The Stars of Musiqa Sha'biyya in the Levant," in *Out of the Absurdity of Life*, ed. Theresa Beyer and Thomas Burkhalter (Solothurn, Switzerland: Traversion Press, 2012).

20. These popular dance musics embody distinctions based on language, ethnicity, and place. Whereas *choubi* and *dabke* have been staged as nationalist cultural traditions since the mid-twentieth century, the more limited circulation of Kurdish *govend* reflects Kurds' status as a stateless ethnicity residing in places characterized by strong nationalist sentiments.

21. Syrian wedding bands typically consist of electronic keyboard, several percussionists on *riqq* (tambourine), *darbukka* (goblet-shaped drum) and *tabl* (double-headed barrel drum), and local instruments *bağlama saz* (long-necked lute) and *mijwiz* (reed instrument) that articulate Turkish and Arab musical aesthetics, respectively. Additional instruments may include electric bass, electric or acoustic *oud* (short-necked lute), and violin.

22. These attitudes are likely related to the marginalization of Hassake within Syrian constructions of nationhood. Much of what is considered Syrian is centered on Damascene customs and traditions that boast of Damascus as the "cradle of civilization." Christa Salamandra, *A New Old Damascus: Authenticity and Distinction in Urban Syria* (Bloomington: Indiana University Press, 2004). According to this worldview, Bedouin identities serve as nostalgic tropes of a pre-modern history that is set apart from modern worldviews and experiences. Relatedly, local dialects signify distinctions between social groups in ways that sustain class and ethnic divisions within Syria. Amanda Terc, "Syria's New Neoliberal Elite: English Usage, Linguistic Practices and Group Boundaries" (Ann Arbor: University of Michigan, 2011). The use of a Bedouin dialect and other stylistic tropes in Souleyman's music therefore may lead to opinions that his singing style is "rough," "harsh," and essen-

tially untranslatable for Damascene speakers. As well, the Kurdish and Turkish elements in his style are considered non-national from the perspective of most Syrians. Cultural and linguistic practices help parse the ways in which Hassake identity is culturally alien from dominant constructions of Syrian identity. In Syria's domestic music industry, Souleyman's profile is fairly obscure in comparison to nationally recognized singers such as Ali El Dik, Wael Khoury, and Samara El Samara. His relatively peripheral position in the Syrian music industry may explain why he is more open to pursuing tours for non-Arab audiences outside of the Middle East.

23. Myriam Ababsa, *Raqqa: Territoires et Pratiques Sociales D'une Ville Syrienne* (Beirut: IFPO, 2009).

24. See James L. Gelvin, *The Arab Uprisings: What Everyone Needs to Know*, (Oxford: Oxford University Press, 2012); International Crisis Group, *Popular Protest in North Africa and the Middle East (VI): The Syrian People's Slow Motion Revolution*, July 6, 2011.

25. Silverstein, "New Wave Dabke."

26. Salah Ammo, personal correspondence with author, October 2014.

27. Manuel, *Cassette Culture*. See Ted Swedenburg, "Egypt's Music of Protest," *Middle East Report* 265 (2012), for the recent emergence of a YouTube culture of popular distribution, specifically *mahrajan* popular music in Cairo since 2007.

28. Cécile Boëx, "The End of the State Monopoly over Culture: Toward the Commodification of Cultural and Artistic Production," *Middle East Critique* 20, no. 2 (2011): 139–55. As discussed earlier, tribute songs to political and religious figures such as Bashar al-Assad, Nasrallah, or Imam Ali are common among popular singers. These tribute songs gain popularity through small media and social media rather than through national television or radio broadcasts controlled by state institutions.

29. Lucy Jones, "Glastonbury 2011 Top Ten Highlights," *The Telegraph*, June 28, 2011.

30. Jon Garelick, "Dengue Fever and Omar Souleyman at the Paradise: International Sounds of Love," *The Phoenix*, June 5, 2012.

31. Such translatability is contestable and likely related to the particular contexts in which Souleyman's *dabke* is performed. For instance, Algerian-French *rai* producers intentionally standardized rhythms for the club scene in France by adapting complex triplet patterns into a duple groove that was easier for French clubgoers. Marc Schade-Poulsen, *Men and Popular Music in Algeria: The Social Significance of Raï* (Austin: University of Texas Press, 1999).

32. Luminous Insect, "Dabke—Sounds of The Syrian Houran," *Enochian Tapestries*, July 15, 2012.

33. Moritz Gayard, "Interview: Omar Souleyman," electronicbeats.net, February 16, 2012.

34. Personal interview with author, Brussels, Belgium, July 2010.

35. The roster of African musicians included Konono No 1 (Congo), Mulatu Astatké

(Ethiopia), Mujava (South Africa), Buraka Som Sistema (Portugal/Angola), and Culoe de Song (South Africa), playing genres from "Afro-house" to *kuduro*.

36. Luminous Insect, "Dabke—Sounds of the Syrian Houran."

37. Chizzly St. Claw, "Review of Omar Souleyman, *Dabke 2020*," *Tiny Mix Tapes*, 2009.

38. Damon Krukowski, "Souleyman: Dabke 2.0 Sound of Syria comes to Hub," *Boston Globe*, October 31, 2010, boston.com.

39. Rebecca Aranda, "Omar Souleyman at The Echo Last Night," *OC Weekly Blogs*, July 13, 2011; Aaron Leitko, "Omar Souleyman Takes His Brand of Syrian Folk-pop to the 9:30 Club," *Washington Post*, June 7, 2012.

40. Peter Shapiro, "Omar Souleyman | Soundcheck," *The Wire*, July 2010.

41. Emerson Dameron, "Omar Souleyman—'Atabat' (*Dabke 2020*)," *Dusted Magazine*, May 12, 2009.

42. According to urbandictionary.com: "Punk-derived music that generally incorporates lots of time and tempo changes (imparting the 'spastic' quality referred to in the name), spazzcore is often, while ostensibly chaotic, very demanding in terms of precision and physical endurance. The term was first applied to Frodus, and Shelby Cinca is generally credited as the inventor of the term" (last accessed January 3, 2013).

43. Leitko, "Omar Souleyman."

44. In his study of the aesthetic politics of Australian "post-punk" culture, Graham St. John identifies the "explosion of simultaneous aesthetic and activist dispositions [in which] post-punk actors intervene to express difference and/or make a difference in varied responses to conditions of inequality, injustice, and despoliation. A punk trajectory would be sustained through proximity to the 'streets' and commitment to a 'cause.' " St. John, "Making a Noise—Making a Difference: Techno-Punk and Terra-ism," *Dancecult: Journal of Electronic Dance Music Culture* 1, no. 2 (2010): 28.

45. Dave Segal, "Review of 'Jazeera Nights,' " *The Stranger*, June 14, 2010.

46. Bill Meyer, "The List: June 24–30, 2010," *Chicago Reader*, 24 June 2010.

47. David Drake, http://kingdrake.com/blog/omar-souleyman, 2009.

48. Shapiro, "Review of 'Jazeera Nights.' "

49. Ben Yaster, "Omar Souleyman—*Highway to Hassake (Folk and Pop Sounds of Syria)*," *Dusted Magazine*, November 1, 2007.

50. Jamaican dancehall has been characterized as "a fast-moving form of reggae with a hard percussive beat, a bass that echoes like a seismic tremor in your gut, a music with an irresistibly deep groove" by Jordan Levin in the *Miami Herald*. "A vocalist/DJ raps ('toasting' or 'chanting') over a track that usually consists of just a rhythmic bassline, drums, maybe guitar . . . A dancehall DJ is musician, producer, and showman all in one." See Levin, "Dancehall DJs in the House," *Miami Herald*, 26 April 1996.

51. Michael E. Veal, *Dub: Soundscapes and Shattered Songs in Jamaican Reggae* (Wesleyan, Conn.: Wesleyan University Press, 2007), 225.

52. Also playing that night were Mark Gergis as "World Music DJ"; Cheb Eb El Farah, a *rai* genre wedding band from Morocco; DJ Maga Bo from Brazil/America; and an Australian DJ then based in Barcelona who goes by Suckafish P. Jones. The series was part of a "Holidays" summer festival that included film series, workshops, and special events and was funded by municipal, national, and private sponsors.

53. Interview with author, July 9, 2010, Brussels, Belgium.

54. Kortrijk Congé was curated by local arts organizations including Buda (film and artspace), De Kreun (concert hall), Passerelle (Flemish contemporary dance), Unje Zorgelozen (theater), Kunstencentrum, and the city of Kortrijk. The organizations collaborated to generate awareness and funds for social issues including social welfare for disadvantaged children and social discrimination on the basis of race and ethnicity. The festival ran from sunset to sunrise and was presented at arts galleries, temporary street installations, and an outdoor stage serviced by a full bar and food vendors.

55. Generally, French-speaking communities in southern Belgium are lower-income with higher rates of unemployment and receive greater welfare benefits, conditions that build resentment in Flemish areas in northern Belgium.

56. Björk, "You Must Hear This: Omar Souleyman," *National Public Radio,* June 29, 2009, www.npr.org/2009/06/29/106047345/you-must-hear-this-omar-souleyman (accessed February 1, 2012).

57. The Biophilia app includes a score, an essay by musicologist Nicola Dibben, a game by which the user controls musical changes, and links to purchase songs through download. "Graphic rendering" of songs like "Crystalline" and "Cosmogony" collide with Björk's breakbeats. The project's art directors, known for their post-punk aesthetics, won "Best Recording Package" at the 2013 Grammy Awards. In addition to the app and album, the Biophilia project encompasses a tour of eight cities over three years, a website, a documentary, a music education program, and two remix collaborations solicitated by Björk at the time of the project's release in the summer of 2011.

58. Ian Biddle, "Vox Electronica: Nostalgia, Irony and Cyborgian Vocalities in Kraftwerk's Radioaktivität and Autobahn," *Twentieth Century Music* 1, no. 1 (2004): 81–100. Biddle relates issues of technology, modernity, and the electronic voice to argue for how synthetic timbres and beat patterns "empty out" subjectivity and convey emotional flatness. He is interested in how concepts of technology and technological progress become elided with the use and sound of electronic technology in music. Biddle proposes that these elisions align technology with modernity and modernity with industrialization such that the synthesized sounds and beat patterns of electronic music in Euro-American musical cultures have acquired industrial and mechanical associations.

59. Björk embraces the ethos of collaboration and mutualism among those whom she considers peers—recording engineers, instrumental improvisers, experimental vocal artists, film and art directors. She shared that "I have many months of working like that

but then I always arrive to point where it seems too indulgent and lonely . . . And I get overexcited about someone I find brilliant and I want to write with her/him" (posted in online forum, cf. Nicola Dibben, *Björk* [Bloomington: Indiana University Press, 2009], 135). Björk attributes her desire to build collaborative working relationships to her working-class childhood and the influence of her father's union job, her musical background in punk, and her response to the hierarchical working practices she experienced with film director Lars von Trier (*Dancer in the Dark*) (Dibben, *Björk*, 137).

60. Interview with Björk, quoted in Dibben, *Björk*, 134.

61. Björk, "You Must Hear This: Omar Souleyman."

62. Although sources remain unclear about Souleyman's professional or aesthetic interests in this project, Wills Glasspiegel has suggested that Souleyman attributes his success and distinction in the Middle East to his open ear and interest in rock, pop, and jazz rhythms. In collaboration with Sa'id, he modifies these styles for the popular traditions of *dabke, 'ataba,* and *mawwal* by mixing and programming beats on his keyboard. See Glasspiegel interview in this volume.

63. Sources are also unclear about the extent to which musical editing was carried out exclusively by Souleyman and Said or whether recording engineers affiliated with Sublime Frequencies also contributed to the remix project.

64. Nadine Naber, and Amaney A. Jamal, eds., *Race and Arab Americans Before and After 9/11: From Invisible Citizens to Visible Subjects* (Syracuse, N.Y.: Syracuse University Press, 2008).

BIBLIOGRAPHY

Ababsa, Myriam. *Raqqa: Territoires et Pratiques Sociales D'une Ville Syrienne.* Beirut: IFPO, 2009.

Aranda, Rebecca. "Omar Souleyman at The Echo Last Night." *OC Weekly Blogs,* July 13, 2011.

Behr, Alex. "This Is Your Brain on Souleyman: Interview with Mark Gergis." *Evil Monito,* May 1, 2010.

Beta, Andy. "Omar Souleyman: The Wedding Singer." *Spin,* October 22, 2013.

Biddle, Ian. "Vox Electronica: Nostalgia, Irony and Cyborgian Vocalities in Kraftwerk's Radioaktivität and Autobahn." *Twentieth Century Music* 1, no. 1 (2004): 81–100.

Björk. "You Must Hear This: Omar Souleyman." *National Public Radio,* June 29, 2009. www.npr.org/2009/06/29/106047345/you-must-hear-this-omar-souleyman (accessed February 1, 2012).

Boëx, Cécile. "The End of the State Monopoly over Culture: Toward the Commodification of Cultural and Artistic Production." *Middle East Critique* 20, no. 2 (2011): 139–55.

Damai, Puspa. "Babelian Cosmopolitanism: Or Tuning in to 'Sublime Frequencies.'" *CR: The New Centennial Review* 7, no. 1 (2007): 107–38.

Dameron, Emerson. "Omar Souleyman—'Atabat' (*Dabke 2020*)." *Dusted Magazine*, May 12, 2009.

D'Andrea, Anthony. *Global Nomads: Techno and New Age as Transnational Countercultures in Ibiza and Goa*. London: Routledge, 2007.

Dibben, Nicola. *Björk*. Bloomington: Indiana University Press, 2009.

El Hamamsy, Walid, and Mounira Soliman, eds. *Popular Culture in the Middle East and North Africa*. London: Routledge, 2013.

Garelick, Jon. "Dengue Fever and Omar Souleyman at the Paradise: International Sounds of Love." *The Phoenix*, June 5, 2012.

Gayard, Moritz. "Interview: Omar Souleyman." electronicbeats.net, February 16, 2012.

Gelvin, James L. *The Arab Uprisings: What Everyone Needs to Know*. Oxford: Oxford University Press, 2012.

Huq, Rupa. "Raving, Not Drowning: Authenticity, Pleasure and Politics in the Electronic Dance Music Scene." In *Popular Music Studies*, edited by David Hesmondhalgh and Keith Negus, 90–102. London: Arnold, 2002.

International Crisis Group. *Popular Protest in North Africa and the Middle East (VI): The Syrian People's Slow Motion Revolution*. July 6, 2011.

Jones, Lucy. "Glastonbury 2011 Top Ten Highlights." *The Telegraph*, June 28, 2011.

Krukowski, Damon. "Souleyman: Dabke 2.0 Sound of Syria comes to Hub." *Boston Globe*, October 31, 2010. boston.com.

Leitko, Aaron. "Omar Souleyman Takes His Brand of Syrian Folk-pop to the 9:30 Club." *Washington Post*, June 7, 2012.

Levin, Jordan. "Dancehall DJs in the House." *Miami Herald*, 26 April 1996.

Luminous Insect. "Dabke—Sounds of the Syrian Houran." *Enochian Tapestries*, July 15, 2012

Mamdani, Mahmood. *Good Muslim, Bad Muslim: America, the Cold War, and the Roots of Terror*. Random House Digital, Inc., 2005.

Manuel, Peter. *Cassette Culture: Popular Music and Technology in North India*. Chicago: University of Chicago Press, 1993.

Meyer, Bill. "The List: June 24–30, 2010." *Chicago Reader*, 24 June 2010.

Morgan, Andy. "The Dabke Demon." *fRoots*, October 2010.

Naber, Nadine, and Amaney A. Jamal, eds. *Race and Arab Americans Before and After 9/11: From Invisible Citizens to Visible Subjects*. Syracuse, N.Y.: Syracuse University Press, 2008.

Nance, Susan. *How the Arabian Nights Inspired the American Dream, 1790–1935*. Durham: University of North Carolina Press, 2009.

Novak, David. "The Sublime Frequencies of New Old Media." *Public Culture* 23, no. 3 65 (September 21, 2011): 603–34.

Rodgers, Tara. *Pink Noises: Women on Electronic Music and Sound.* Chapel Hill, N.C.: Duke University Press, 2010.

Rolls, Chris. "Interview: Mark Gergis aka Porest," *Fecal Face,* November 18, 2008.

St. Claw, Chizzly. "Review of Omar Souleyman, *Dabke 2020.*" *Tiny Mix Tapes,* 2009.

St. John, Graham. "Making a Noise—Making a Difference: Techno-Punk and Terra-ism." *Dancecult: Journal of Electronic Dance Music Culture* 1, no. 2 (2010): 1–28.

Salamandra, Christa. *A New Old Damascus: Authenticity and Distinction in Urban Syria.* Bloomington: Indiana University Press, 2004.

Schade-Poulsen, Marc. *Men and Popular Music in Algeria: The Social Significance of Raï.* Austin: University of Texas Press, 1999.

Segal, Dave. "Review of 'Jazeera Nights.'" *The Stranger,* June 14, 2010.

Shapiro, Peter. "Omar Souleyman | Soundcheck." *The Wire,* July 2010.

Silverstein, Shayna. "Mobilizing Bodies in Syria: Dabke, Popular Culture, and the Politics of Belonging." PhD diss., University of Chicago, 2012.

———. "New Wave Dabke: The Stars of Musiqa Sha'biyya in the Levant." In *Out of the Absurdity of Life*, edited by Theresa Beyer and Thomas Burkhalter. Solothurn, Switzerland: Traversion Press, 2012.

Stokes, Martin, ed. *Ethnicity, Identity, and Music: The Musical Construction of Place.* Oxford, UK: Berg, 1994.

Stosuy, Brandon. "No Sleep Til Beirut: A Conversation with Alan Bishop." *Arthur Magazine,* September 2005.

Swedenburg, Ted. "Egypt's Music of Protest." *Middle East Report* 265 (2012).

Terc, Amanda. "Syria's New Neoliberal Elite: English Usage, Linguistic Practices and Group Boundaries."Ann Arbor: University of Michigan, 2011.

Traber, Daniel S. "L.A.'s 'White Minority': Punk and the Contradictions of Self-Marginalization." *Cultural Critique* 48, no.1 (2001): 30–64.

Veal, Michael E. *Dub: Soundscapes and Shattered Songs in Jamaican Reggae.* Wesleyan, Conn.: Wesleyan University Press, 2007.

Yaster, Ben. "Omar Souleyman—*Highway to Hassake (Folk and Pop Sounds of Syria).*" *Dusted Magazine,* November 1, 2007.

WILLS GLASSPIEGEL

INTERPRETED BY RAED YASSIN

EDITED BY NADER ATASSI

Interview with Omar Souleyman
and Rizan Sa'id

The following interview with Syrian *dabke* singer Omar Souleyman and his keyboardist, Rizan Sa'id, took place in a backstage trailer at the Central Park Summer Stage in June of 2010. The performance marked Souleyman's New York City debut, and this interview was his first in-person interview in the United States.

As a journalist and fan of Souleyman's music, I was thrilled to interview him on behalf of the public radio program *Afropop Worldwide*. Media artist and Sublime Frequencies collaborator Raed Yassin interpreted my questions and answers in Arabic. The interview was filmed by Kalimah Abioto and is available online. Nader Atassi, researcher at the Arab Studies Institute and Syrian-American activist, later corrected and edited the interview transcript based on the original audio recording.

Before the interview began, I learned that Souleyman and his crew had encountered substantial difficulties in entering the United States—equipment was lost temporarily and a member of Souleyman's band (the poet who whispers inspiring lyrics in Souleyman's ear mid-performance) had not been able to procure a visa. Despite these difficulties, Souleyman and Sa'id gave a strong performance—the New York City crowd was riveted and they stayed dancing hard for over an hour on a balmy summer afternoon.

The fact that it was Souleyman's first performance in New York imparted gravitas to the event. Dedicated fans were eager to welcome Souleyman across what was, for many of us, a substantial linguistic and cultural gap. For other, casual listeners in the New York City crowd, however, Souleyman's performance provided the opportunity to hear something familiar outside the halls and cultural walls that usually frame *dabke* music and dance.

Souleyman was followed on the Central Park bill by Tinariwen, a Tuareg guitar group from the Sahel, whose lilting, minor-key drones provided a pentatonic counterpoint to Souleyman's hard and fast, keyboard-driven wedding music. Tinariwen's desert blues drifted into the backstage trailer where I interviewed Souleyman and Sa'id.

In the years since this inaugural New York City performance, Souleyman has returned to the United States almost a dozen times. His relationship to the United States and his American agents has also shifted: Souleyman left the Sublime Frequencies label in 2011 and in 2013 released a new record with the Domino records affiliate, Ribbon Music, produced by Kieran Hebden. As of this writing, amid the ongoing Syrian civil war, Souleyman has continued to tour in the United States and across the world. When he is not on the road, he lives with his wife and children as a refugee in Turkey.

WILLS GLASSPIEGEL: How would you describe *dabke* to someone who doesn't know much about it?

OMAR SOULEYMAN: First of all, this music is our music, an Arab dance music. Any person who hears this music will want to dance. Whenever I am on stage, my mission is to make those who don't dance *dabke*, dance *dabke*. In other words, I want to teach people to *dabke*, God willing.

WG: What is distinct about your style of *dabke*?

OS: What changes *dabke* is the rhythm. I use my country and *choubi* as inspiration. And I have my own style of singing and of *dabke* as a whole. *Dabke* is rhythm and that rhythm is different in different countries throughout the Middle East.

WG: What is the area you're from?

OS: It's called Hassake. It's in northeast Syria, and I come from a village called Tal Amir and from Ras al-Ain.[1]

WG: What is the inspiration for your lyrics?

OS: The subject of the lyrics is all romantic, words of love, words of flirtation, words about dancing.

WG: How did you feel when your music was brought to listeners outside your country?

OS: When I first started as an artist, I was hoping to become successful in Syria—and outside of Syria. I wanted to be a star. And everything I have hoped for has become reality, and I am very happy about this.

WG: How did you meet Sublime Frequencies?

OS: I met Mark Gergis in 2006. I said I would sign to release about two thousand tapes—Mark seemed like a nice guy. I'm thankful to them for promoting my music in a good manner, and they worked hard with me to make this happen and to bring me to Western countries.

WG: Maybe we could talk a little bit about the role of the keyboard, Rizan. How would you describe what you're playing and how do the drums or the melody fit in? How do you play both at the same time?

Rizan Sa'id: I work for different people, not just Omar. The keyboard is like my very own laptop. I work on programming it all the time, to explore it and make different programs for each singer that I work with. There are special programs for Omar, and I have other music for people who do different stuff.

WG: Would you ever be interested in making beats for a Western artist?[2]

RS: Arabic music, the style that I'm doing, is so far from Western music. I'd like to do it, but I don't think it would work. What's special about what I do, is that I incorporate pop beats, some from the Western world, and then modify them and apply them to Arabic music. We are mixing influences from the Arab world, from Turkey, from the West, so that when Westerners listen to it, they like it; when Arabs hear it, they like it; when Kurds hear it, they like it; when Turks hear it, they like it. The biggest indicator of this is that we do concerts for Kurdish people, for Arabs, for Christians.

WG: What American influences have inspired you?

RS: My experience comes from the recording studio. I always listened to rock, pop, and jazz, and when I'm listening, I think about how I can incorporate parts of this foreign music, or patterns or beats, into Arabic music. Sometimes I do songs where, at first, you think it's a Western song, like as an intro with a melody, but then it turns into a surprise and it will be an Arabic song.

WG: Omar, is your music at all controversial within the Muslim community in your region?

OS: No, no, not at all. Of course there are some who are extremist, but that's another issue. In every place, there are extremists and people who are not extremists.

WG: What is it like to be a star musician in your own community?

OS: The treatment I receive in Syria is respectful, from the state and the country, the people. My flavor is different from other people's flavor: the *dabke* was slow, I made it faster. Rizan and I have worked together for 13 to 14 years. We would sit at home and say, "The *dabke* needs to be faster. It needs to be slower," so that, little by little, people got used to the faster *dabke*. But people are now used to this faster *dabke*. There were many times I had a show and there were very few people, so I didn't perform. I am unable to sing if there isn't a crowd.

WG: Please describe your live performance style.

OS: An artist should be an artist in style, not just in terms of voice. In Syria, I don't walk on the street. If I go out three or four times a day, people will start knowing me. If there is a show but I'm not officially invited or getting paid to play, I won't go. If there's an event and you're inviting me just to go, I won't come. Because I am looking for fame and the respect of the people.

WG: I've heard that sometimes someone will whisper poetry in your ear while you're performing.

OS: This is very particular to my role as a wedding singer in my region. I want to make a special, unique wedding for everybody, so I have a poet friend who [improvises poetry about the people attending]. I sometimes have three weddings to do in one week, so I need him to help me change the lyrics. But being here (abroad), I don't need that poet because everything is fixed, and it's a different situation than being in a wedding. . . .

I only sing my own style of music . . . , and I don't like to cover songs. If somebody asks me to do someone else's song at a wedding, I won't sing it, no matter how nice it is.

NOTE

1. In February 2013, years after this interview took place, Souleyman's hometown of Ras al-Ain became a flashpoint in the ongoing Syrian conflict. Due to its status as a multicultural border town, it was thought that Ras al-Ain's capture by rebel forces would be "a prelude to the opposition controlling the region's remaining areas, and securing the northern oil fields." *Al Monitor*, February 21, 2013, http://www.al-monitor.com/pulse /politics/2013/02/ras-al-ain-agreement-syria.html#ixzz2YPPWyhZq.

2. A year after conducting this interview, Souleyman and Sa'id remixed Björk's "Crystalline."

Asian Emissions

STANLEY SCOTT

Radio India
Eternal Dream or Ephemeral Illusion?

SCREAM: "Yaaaaaaa-Hoooooooo!"
ORCHESTRAL STRINGS (jagged bow-strokes):
"Dadadada Dá, Dadadada Dá Dadada!"

Thus begins "Radio Delhi #1," the first selection on *Radio India: The Eternal Dream of Sound*, Sublime Frequencies' double-CD set of sound collages drawn from recordings that Sublime Frequencies co-founders Alan and Richard Bishop made in northern India in 1989 and 1996. Indian film buffs will recognize the song as "Chahe Koi Mujhe Junglee Kahe," from the 1961 Hindi movie *Junglee* (Beltangady, M.). In this *filmi geet,* the singer declares that people may call him a "junglee" savage, but they can say what they will, because he knows his love is true.[1] The original film recording featured the impeccable pronunciation and tuneful singing of superstar playback singer Mohammed Rafi, but "Radio Delhi #1" features a cover version, in which his voice is replaced by the more strident, metallic twang of a Hawaiian guitar.[2] Two minutes into this first collage, the drone of a *shehnai* (Indian oboe) ensemble overlaps with and then supplants the *filmi* orchestra, and the remaining three minutes of the track feature the opening section of a free-rhythm, meditative classical *alap,* a duet between masters of the double-reed *shehnai* and the *santur* (Indian hammered dulcimer).[3] At the 4:50 mark, with no break, a string orchestra cuts abruptly into the unfolding improvisation, providing manic, melodramatic background music to another Bombay film. "Radio Delhi #2" has begun, without segue or pause.

Intrigued by these unlikely juxtapositions, the listener reaches for the liner notes, hoping to find the names of the artists and an explanation of the logic

Radio India: The Eternal Dream of Sound (SF014), a two-CD set,
provides little context for a wide range of tracks, all but one a
patchwork of radio broadcasts.

behind the transitions. What one finds instead are images meant to evoke an iconic India: a cover photo of a man and boy minding cows in a semiarid pasture, a back panel showing the Taj Mahal tinted a garish pink against an electric turquoise sky, a color panel of two South Indian *Kathakali* dancers in full costume, another of an astonished and disheveled Bollywood actress, four black-and-white panels featuring a hand-drawn map of India showing the sites of communal disturbances, graffiti political slogans in English and Bengali, a list of nineteen recorded tracks, an image of the Goddess *Kali* floating over a *Shiva lingam*, and one paragraph of liner notes.[4] No musicians are named, and no organizing principles are provided. The liner notes confirm what the reader has already begun to suspect: In this sonic landscape, you, the listener, must find your own way.

READING THE TEXT

To unravel the puzzle presented by *Radio India*, I have chosen to read each of its elements—aural, written, and visual—as parts of a multifaceted text. I begin with a consideration of the approach presented in the liner notes, where the editor, Sublime Frequencies' co-founder, Alan Bishop, presents the reader with a set of intriguing paradoxes. Those notes, taken together with the recordings themselves, raise important questions. Whose music is this? What messages are being conveyed about Indian culture? What is the collagist's aesthetic approach? Is *Radio India* aural ethnography, in which case the focus would be on representing Indian radio culture, or is it experimental sonic art, in which case the aim would be to transform these radio excerpts into something new, thereby changing their function and meaning? If it attempts to be both at once, are the values guiding the experimental sonic artist compatible with those that inform musical ethnography?

The idea of musical collage is not new. Experimental sonic artists in the tradition of John Cage, who began creating radio collages in the early 1950s, often work outside the boundaries of traditions in which music is meant to convey predetermined meanings.[5] Like much abstract visual art, experimental music embraces an ambivalence that more traditional expressions avoid. If the composer treats all acoustic sources as equal, then excerpts of conventional genres (love songs, hymns, political anthems, etc.) ostensibly become pure sound sources—equal to traffic noise, running water, birdsong, and radio static—and all are fair game for the sonic collagist.

The actual effect of juxtaposing culturally charged musical materials with less "meaningful" sounds, however, belies the notion that "all sounds are created equal." In Cage's radio collages, original sources are often so fragmented, processed, and overlaid that their original identity and significance are lost, but in *Radio India,* most excerpts are long enough for the original sources and meanings to be apparent to knowledgeable listeners. This effect is heightened by the fact that, among the world's music cultures, India's is particularly affect-prescriptive. In Indian classical music, every *raga* is meant to evoke one or more of the nine *rasas* (aesthetic moods such as eros, pathos, valor, awe, and humor) outlined in the *Natyasastra*, India's oldest extant musical treatise.[6] Indian popular music, consisting primarily of film songs, is every bit as emotion-driven as the classical genres. Therefore, the sorts of excerpts that predominate in *Radio India*'s collages necessarily evoke some of the meaning and emotion inherent in the source recordings.

Ethnographic recordings, in contrast to experimental sonic collages, are designed to illuminate cultural meaning. Sonic excerpts, in this realm, usually are accompanied by explanatory texts, which provide contextualization, elucidate significance, and comment on musical form and aesthetics. Ethnomusicologists also tend to favor recordings of complete performances, because they present a truer, more complete picture of musical practice in its cultural context than short excerpts can provide. Musical meaning unfolds over time, and excerption can have the effect of interrupting a story partway through, leaving us wondering what the author intended.

Radio India's collages fall in between the pure-sound compositions of Cage and the culturally illuminating recordings of musical ethnographers; the excerpts are too evocative to lose their original meaning completely, but lack the contextualization and interpretation that characterize ethnomusicological presentations. Is *Radio India,* therefore, a hybrid? What is its intent? Are we to appraise its success by the standards of pure sonic art, or by those of musical ethnography?

I offer partial answers to these questions in the discussion that follows. After discussing the liner notes, I analyze the sound and form of the recordings, and the aesthetic approach of the collagist. I then proceed to a consideration of reception, drawing on published Western reviews as well as interviews with several South Asian listeners living in the United States. These responses reveal a new level of complexity, in which *Radio India*'s aesthetic approach elicits positive responses from some (but not all) members of its targeted Western audience, but collides head-on with some cultural values of India's musically educated, radio-listening public. Finally, I discuss *Radio India*'s ambivalent nature as both sonic art and aural ethnography, and the conflicts inherent in that seemingly polarized identity.

LINER NOTES: UN-KEY TO
AN INCREDIBLE SONIC MUSEUM

In the liner notes, producer Alan Bishop describes India as an "incredible Museum of Sound." He then declares the recording itself to be a "Radio collage with minimal contextual identification," "a map without a key," "an encyclopedia without an index," and "sound as eternal dream."

By defining this recording as a map, Bishop challenges the reader-listener to ask, "What is the use of a map without a key?" We use maps to provide orientation, to guide us to places where we want to go, to help us to understand landscapes. Minus a key, a map loses most of these orienting functions, which are supplanted by others: aesthetic, mnemonic, proprietary, and creative. We may enjoy the un-keyed map as an object of art, we may place it on a wall or in a scrapbook to remind us of where we have been, we may point to it to lay claim to ownership of our prior experiences on the ground it represents, and we may mine it for inspiration in creating our own imaginary landscapes.

By proclaiming the double CDs' lack of contextualization in a liner-notes broadside, Bishop announces that this is no ordinary map; regarding orientation, you, the consumer, are on your own, and the aesthetic, mnemonic, proprietary, and creative functions will predominate. The listener is given a few pages from Bishop's own sonic scrapbook, along with the information that the recordings were made by him and his brother Richard Bishop in 1989 and 1996. Each recorded track, all but one a patchwork of several radio broadcasts, is given minimal identification: "Radio Varanasi," "Radio Jaipur," "Radio Hill Station," and so on. None of these titles identify particular radio stations or broadcasts. As with the artists' names, no broadcast dates or call letters are provided.

In designating this set of sonic collages as an encyclopedia, Bishop invites a second question: "What is an encyclopedia without an index?" Encyclopedias, in which entries are ordered alphabetically, *are* indexes, so we may assume that "encyclopedia without an index" means an encyclopedia without order.

Encyclopedias are meant to provide quick access to general information about "everything." Their scope is vast (encyclopedic), but navigation through this universe of knowledge is possible because of alphabetization, without which the reader would be lost in an ocean of words. Without this order, an encyclopedia loses its function as a quick, easy way to get information. If it serves any purpose, then, it must be of a different nature. We may open it at random, and allow chance to decide what we will and will not learn. We may sample bits and pieces of its world, evoking a sort of intoxication in the overwhelming flow of information. We may abandon as hopeless the effort to make sense of it, which has a certain consciousness-altering virtue; since understanding is not possible, we are forced to go with the flow. Or we may allow ourselves to be entertained by the endless variety of the informational flood, all the while hoping that, in the fullness of time, serendipitous sampling will allow us to understand something of the whole span of knowledge.

One difficulty with presenting *Radio India* as an encyclopedia is its narrow scope; it is a selection of recordings chosen from two trips to India, more a patchwork of gleanings than a broad overview. Sublime Frequencies' rationale for inclusion and exclusion is unstated, and the scope of the entire sample is limited by the unknown agendas of the producers of the original broadcasts. Is this therefore aleatory music, in which chance procedure determined what would be included? Or is this a collage of found objects, in which the intentions of the original artists are redirected by the collage-maker? Since Bishop has selected and shaped these excerpts into their present form, it seems the latter: a collage of found objects. Like much contemporary art (and *unlike* most Indian music), *Radio India* leaves it to the viewer (listener) either to find meaning in it or simply to experience it without indulging in interpretation. In the few clues Bishop gives us, he seems to prefer the second response, decrying analysis and commentary. The intention is, perhaps, to encourage a Zen-like immersion in the sound itself, without the mediation of contextualizing language. Be this as it may, the collagist-recordist has chosen to present these particular sounds, in these particular groupings, and in this particular order. His very choices and ordering leave the imprint of his thinking on the recording, and thoughtful listeners may be forgiven for asking, "What is this meant to convey?"

In describing India as a "Museum of Sound," Bishop emphasizes the value of the sonic elements in *Radio India* as cultural artifacts. Most museums, however, contain carefully selected items, collected and presented with the idea of representing "good" or "representative" samples meant to reveal something about the culture from which they emerge. Although India, vast and complex as it is, *might* be viewed as a museum, a collection of artifacts, it is not the Louvre or the Metropolitan. It is, instead, a living, changing culture, producing an uncountable number of *objets d'art* from which a percentage of a percentage might be selected for display in a museum. In this sense, India is not the museum or collection; the museum is that which Sublime Frequencies has chosen to display, limited to broadcasts from a handful of north Indian cities, representing only three of India's dozens of languages, and only a fraction of its hundreds of musical genres. On what basis, then, has Sublime Frequencies selected and grouped these particular sonic creations? I consider this question below, when I come to the question of musical sound and form.

The album's subtitle, *The Eternal Dream of Sound,* echoes both ancient Hindu conceptions about music and the eighteenth- to twentieth-century trope of India's "golden age." This golden age, proposed by British Orientalists and embraced by Indian nationalists under British rule, was a two-edged concept. For the British colonialist, it placed Indian economic independence, and the will to wield political power, safely in a mythical past. For the Indian nationalist, the golden age provided not only the emblem of former glory, but also the desire for its return and the motivation to work toward independence from colonial rule.[7]

Scholars in the golden age, almost two thousand years ago, wrote the *Natyasastra,* India's most important early treatise on the performing arts.[8] In it, music is indeed eternal, the creation of *Brahma,* who taught it to the first musician Bharata, who taught it, in turn, to his one hundred sons.[9] Music is also eternal in the resonance of the *damaru* hourglass rattle of dancing Shiva, and in the captivating melodies of Krishna's flute or Saraswati's *veena*.[10] For yogis, "eternal music" is the "unstruck sound" encountered in deep meditation, the product, not of a plucked, struck, or blown instrument, but of a subtle vibration deep within the meditator. Musically speaking, the legacy of this tradition is found in the aura of spirituality surrounding classical music, where the myth of the golden age creates a pervasive nostalgia for a time when music is supposed to have been more profound, more spiritual, and more powerful than it is today.

In *Radio India*, we hear neither the "eternal dream" of the music of the gods nor the unstruck sound of the yogi but, rather, an admixture of the ephemeral creations of the Bollywood film industry and broadcast performances of art song, classical instrumental music, folk songs, recitations, advertisements, and announcements. The "timeless" quality of Indian classical music is heard in places, but it always gives way before long to more contemporary and commercial fare. Listeners are not taxed with the demand of listening to an extended Indian classical performance, which easily could occupy an entire CD. The effect is, indeed, dreamlike—a kaleidoscope of shifting soundscapes—but the sounds themselves originated in particular films and recordings, created for contemporary listeners from the amazingly eclectic tool kit of India's film-music composers: Indian folk and classical instruments, electric and Hawaiian guitars, synthesizers, and orchestral strings. We might *imagine* that this is eternal music, passed down from the gods, but we are really hearing creations of the Bollywood film industry, garnished with a sprinkling of folk and classical music and other broadcast miscellanea. Sublime Frequencies' utilization of the romanticized, Orientalist cliché of the "eternal dream" of Indian music caters to what Gerry Farrell, in *Indian Music and the West*, calls "Western exotic consumerism," in the creation of "a product that can fit neatly into the mass tastes of Western pop fans."[11]

SOUND AND FORM

"Radio India" includes nineteen tracks:

DISC I

Radio Delhi #1
Radio Delhi #2
Radio Varanasi
Radio Transit

Radio Jaipur
Radio Hill Station
Radio Calcutta #1
Radio Bihar
Radio Lowlands

DISC II

Radio Calcutta #2
Deep Disco Drama Diva
Glass Music
Hyderabad Fidelity
Lucknow Explosion/Very Impressed with Calcutta
Spirit of Puja in Bengal/DJ No Home
Trolling the Crossroads of Bliss
Silent or Noisy World?
India's Sound Museum of Oddities
Eternal Finale

The track titles suggest a tour of India, focused on cities north of and including Hyderabad. The audio bears this out: All the songs and announcements are in Hindi, Bengali, or English, and the music is limited to pop, classical, and folk styles from the north, with the exception of a South Indian *nagaswaram* ensemble heard in Track II:7.[12] The two discs have somewhat different complexions. While both employ the technique of serial collage, the second goes farther in exploding musical form, both by utilizing a larger number of excerpts in the individual tracks (Disc I uses 1 to 6 excerpts per track; Disc II, 4 to 17), and by employing more in the way of spoken announcements, static, distortion, and rapid-fire jumps between contrasting selections. This adventurousness is reflected in the track titles. Compare, for example, the prosaic "Radio Calcutta #1" (I:7) with the evocative "Trolling the Crossroads of Bliss" (II:7).

Disc I includes some eight excerpts of popular Hindi songs performed by famous Bollywood vocalists (unnamed in the liner notes) such as Lata Mangeshkar, Asha Bhosle, and Anuradha Paudwal, a handful of instrumental versions of Hindi film songs, five excerpts from classical vocal performances (including one which seems to feature the voice of Ustad Amir Khan), two classical instrumental pieces, two Hindi language announcements, one Urdu *ghazal* by Pankaj Udhas, one Bengali art song composed by Kazi Nazrul Islam, recitation and music from a Bengali mythological drama, and a five-minute informal jam including Hawaiian guitar, piano, tabla, and bamboo flute.[13] Some excerpts seem misattributed; the Bengali drama appears in "Radio Jaipur," but Jaipur is a thousand miles from Bengal. Among the Bollywood and classical selections, some portions are very appealing to Indian music fans, who nevertheless find their brevity and context disappointing (see the section on listener responses below). Track I:9 consists of only one piece, excerpted from a particularly beautiful Hindustani classical violin performance of Rag Kalavati.

Disc II includes a much larger number of short excerpts, a much higher percentage of announcements, and an increased emphasis on Bengali material, both spoken and musical. High-profile Hindi film songs and virtuoso classical instrumental performances continue to be a significant part of the mix, but editor Alan Bishop moves into the foreground, composing collages with much more authority than he exercised on Disc I. His hand is most evident in Track 3, "Glass Music," which includes at least 17 different excerpts, including a high-pitched radio whine that careens wildly up and down in pitch, overlapping signals from competing radio channels, folk songs, *filmi* orchestral music, classical performances on *santur, sarangi,* and tabla, Bengali and Hindi announcements, and other musical snippets from what sound like ocarina, *dholak, sarinda,* and Hawaiian guitar.[14] Subsequent tracks employ somewhat fewer sound sources, but the new, more active compositional aesthetic established in Track 3 continues to predominate.

AESTHETIC APPROACH

From the selection and organization of material in these sonic collages, we can extrapolate several governing principles:

1) Inclusiveness. We hear male and female Bollywood vocalists, male and female classical singers, pop and classical instrumental music, Hindi and Bengali songs both in and out of tune, covers of Western songs (a Bengali version of "Jamaica Farewell" and an instrumental rendition of "El Condor Pasa"), recitations, advertisements, announcements in three languages, interviews, static, and distortion.

2) Roughly proportional representation. The predominant place of Hindi film songs, the relatively lesser roles of classical vocal and instrumental music, and the ratio of various kinds of voices (male, female, Hindi, Bengali, English) all seem to reflect their likely presence in the airwaves at the times and places where these excerpts were recorded.

3) No complete musical items are included. Although other, unnamed artists

created the content, timbre, texture, melody, and rhythm of the recorded items, the editor has taken control of their temporal form. This has a profound effect on the musical message and raises the issue of aesthetic appropriation: Who owns the right to decide what a particular musical performance means? In this regard, *Radio India* treads somewhat perilous ground, caught between two identities: that of musical ethnography and that of experimental composition (see "What Is *Radio India*," below).

4) Contrast. Transitions frequently are designed to catch the listener by surprise, as contrasting genres and voices overlap and/or give way to one another. The opposite principle, by which similarities in pitch, rhythm, timbre, or texture are used to blur the transition between excerpts, is also employed.

5) Celebration of the beautiful, the weird, the silly, and the absurd (see "Very Impressed with Calcutta" and "Sonic Assault," below, for examples).

6) Alienation. By juxtaposing disparate, often opposite, things, the editor prevents the listener from enjoying prolonged immersion in any one item.

7) Sonic value trumps lyrical meaning. In his 2008 interview with *The Believer*, republished in this volume, Bishop explained: "The lyrics are not an important thing to me. In fact, it can be a distraction. If I knew the language enough to know it was a horrible love song with stupid lyrics—like most of the popular songs are today in the English language that I hear—then it would be much more of a turnoff than if it would allow me to interpret it from the expressive capabilities of the vocalizing or of the sound itself, which allow me to work for me."[15]

This discounting of lyrical meaning not only allows the collagist to treat Indian songs as pure sound, it also clears the way for non-Indian listeners to do the same. Discussing the unlikely popularity of *qawwali* music in the West during the 1980s, when the Iranian hostage crisis had provoked a significant occidental anti-Islamic response, Gerry Farrell wrote:

> *Qawwali*'s success lay in the ability of Western audiences to receive only the surface elements of the music and to detach its meaning from its form, lyrical content, and cultural context. This is similar to the reception of elements of Indian classical music by pop musicians in the 1960s. In fact, *qawwali* could not be identified with Islam, either negatively or positively, because its religious roots and cultural milieu were not understood by Western audiences. The vague overtones of Eastern mysticism were an added bonus when *qawwali* was discovered by the West, even though the roots of that mysticism and its cultural meaning were not comprehended.[16]

Radio India seems to rely on the same principle that Farrell outlines: a superficial presentation designed to reach a target audience with only limited knowledge of the music culture being presented.

Here we come up against a crucial dilemma in trying to assess *Radio India*. Although the dismissal of lyrical meaning is designed to give the editor a free hand as a sonic artist, Bishop's inclusion of many fairly lengthy excerpts works against that impulse, and seems to remove the project from the more aggressively experimental tradition of John Cage. As pure sound artifacts, these collages seem somewhat weighed down by a cargo of moods and meanings carried over from the source recordings. At the same time, *Radio India's* ethnographic value is diminished by its rejection of the mission of cultural exegesis. The targeted Western listener is not invited beneath the surface of the music.

SOME LISTENERS RESPOND

Published reviews of *Radio India* reveal a range of responses from that target audience. Reviewer Bill Meyer of Dustedmagazine.com wrote that "the personal touch is what distinguishes the Sublime Frequencies CDs from more conventional world music productions; instead of carefully buffed pop productions targeted at the NPR listening demographic or scrupulously annotated ethnographies packaged with an air of academic distance, you get the odd-ball stuff that commanded the Bishop brothers' attention with minimal explanation."[17]

Meyer praised Alan Bishop's "sharp instincts for dream-like flow and inspired juxtaposition," describing *Radio India* as: "a thoroughly entertaining listen, full of what-the-fuck moments and some flat-out lovely songs which you can savor at length because the dial-spinning is less restless than on earlier radio collage efforts . . . If you're ready to submerge yourself in subcontinental exotica or want to check out some Sublime Frequencies and don't know where to start, this set is your ticket."[18]

While Meyer praises *Radio India* for its lack of "academic distance," he goes on to endorse a less academic brand of distancing: the exoticizing of the cultural "other" (India). His casual use of off-color language establishes his membership in a presumed in-crowd with a shared culture of informal irreverence. Academic ethnography is kept at arm's length—but so is India, which must remain unexplained and unknown to retain its "exotic" status.

This "othering" of India also received praise from the Marmoo.wordpress .com arts blog:

[In *Radio India*] there are no artist names whatsoever, these sounds are only a *document of another world* [italics added]. This in itself is an interesting concept that has been quite controversial for Sublime Frequencies; should world music be presented as a lesson in foreign cultures or should it only be displayed as a document for the listener to "study"? Sublime Frequencies chooses the latter. By only cluing the listener into which city these sounds were recording (directly from the radio), Sublime Frequencies creates a unique listening experience in which the listener is completely unbiased.[19]

The writer assumes that uninformed listeners are by definition "unbiased," but the statement that *Radio India*'s collages are "documents of *another world*" belies that assumption. This perception of otherworldliness confirms a set of widely held preconceptions about India, and the album's lack of contextual commentary does little to dispel such biases. Again, South Asian culture is held at a distance.

Not all Western reviewers embrace *Radio India*'s lack of annotation. Reviewer Ian Mathers wrote on Stylusmagazine.com:

For me, and for an increasing number of people, the music of other countries is no longer something strange or exotic, it's what the guy down the street listens to. Now, this can only be good in my opinion, but it does place projects like this one [*Radio India*] on unsteady ground. I'm already familiar with the cliché of how Indian music is "supposed" to sound, which of course is how it often does sound. I'm even, it's fair to say, interested in getting to know some more of it. But a "radio collage" like this one won't serve my purposes; instead, it only frustrates . . . Everything here is stripped of context . . . I'd be interested in finding out about what names to look for, or in hearing some bombastic choruses; instead I get chopped-up bits.[20]

Mathers dismisses the exoticism that the above reviewers embrace. With that dismissal comes a desire for more information—not about the music of a distant other, but about the music of one's neighbors.

Curious as to how such neighbors—Indian listeners in the West, familiar with the genres, languages, and some of the actual repertoire on *Radio India*—might respond to its manner of presentation, I played selected collages for five South Asians living in the United States. These listeners were not selected at random: all are avid music lovers familiar with Indian film and classical music, and four of the five are serious amateur musicians. Four, ranging in age from their forties to their sixties, grew up during the era when many of the film songs on the album were common fare on the Indian airwaves. The youngest, in her twenties, grew up in America, where her family puts great emphasis on Bengali traditions and Hindustani classical music.

The first of my informants gave a detailed response to track I:6, "Radio Hill Station":

> I identify with many of the songs, because I grew up in that generation, but it leaves me wanting for more, because every song, they've taken just one stanza, and then go on to the next song without any obvious link or explanation or connection to the next song. And so, for me it feels sort of, I'm hearing snippets of music, and it's very dissatisfying, because the way it's structured and connected together, it's not a melodious transition . . . I agree it's like a collage. But the collage also, when you have a collage, there's also some theme to that collage, and I can't figure out what the theme is.[21]

This quotation reveals an aesthetic mismatch between the editor's approach and this audience member. The listener's first problem is "wanting for more." As Hindi film scholar Anna Morcom writes, South Asian listeners incorporate film songs "into the discourses and activities of everyday life, in particular their emotional lives, where they become a means of expressing and constructing feelings."[22] The problem here is, in part, that many of *Radio India's* excerpts are long enough to evoke the desire to hear full songs. Would the listener still "want for more" if the excerpts were shorter and processed to the point of being perceived as pure sound, rather than recognizable song fragments? To an uninitiated Western listener, such excerpts might evoke an "exotic," "other world," but to the Indian ear they signify a familiar soundscape, with specific associations and well-established meanings.

The listener's critique then addresses the lack of "obvious links," "melodious transitions," and a unifying theme. The difficulty is compounded by a clash of values rooted in the culture of Indian radio listeners, for whom broadcasts "would never be a portion of a song. That would be almost criminal, because most of us who listened to radio wanted the entire song, because that was our only way of hearing good music, or some music. Many people didn't have a CD player, or LP, or a cassette recorder, so they would really get their music through radio. Ninety-five percent of the population would actually get all of their music on the radio."[23]

Here, *Radio India* encounters a deeper problem than that of a listener looking for smooth transitions: Sublime Frequencies' compositional principle of excluding complete performances meets head-on with a culture in which the broadcast of excerpts is "almost criminal," an aesthetic value rooted in the habits of generations of Indian listeners. As Bishop explains, his treatment of these materials as pure sound allows him to work for himself, but the approach does not necessarily "work" for an Indian audience, for whom the excerpts are too evocative to function as abstract sonic art.

My second informant, reviewing tracks I:1 and I:2 ("Radio Delhi 1" and "Radio Delhi 2"), echoed the first's discomfort with the lack of a unifying theme. He found the abrupt shifts between genres, and the lack of contextualization, alien to his experience of Indian music. His comments also touch on the problem of how the recordings portray South Asian musical culture:

> I didn't find any theme. I guess I like some theme, and at least some nice transitions, when they go from one song to another. There was nothing, they were kind of mashed together, and the transitions, jumping from one genre to another without any explanations of any kind, it's not very common in Indian concerts or Indian music. Generally there is nice, a little story told before the next song begins . . . you take the audience with you in terms of what the next song is going to say. And that I found missing . . . That doesn't help at all, going through the transitions without having any transitory dialogue or background.[24]

All five informants criticized the collages for featuring abrupt, seemingly illogical transitions that lack flow and a common theme, but they also appreciated the principle of inclusiveness embedded in the recordings:

> If the producer's intent was to juxtapose the very popular, young, youthful Bollywood Hindi movie culture and contrast that to the serious music of India, I think maybe that's a point that they [Sublime Frequencies] want to make, that they all coexist in the same environment. For instance, you might have a young person go for an early morning Indian classical music concert, and then in the evening take friends and go to a movie, and have exposure to this very lighthearted Hindi movie where you have all this light music that is played, and you appreciate both, you appreciate the classical music as well as the Hindi music.[25]

This statement acknowledges that Sublime Frequencies' approach reveals insight into the complex, plural nature of musical taste in modern India. But the speaker goes on to express misgivings about the value of such a presentation to listeners unfamiliar with Indian music. Interestingly, she touches on the very image of a roadmap that we encountered in the liner notes: "But I think, if I had no idea about this music, and I was a noninitiated listener, I wouldn't know what to make of it, because to me there is no connection. And there is no roadmap that the producer's actually giving a new listener, with any kind of a script."[26]

The fifth listener expressed this concern more strongly: "The intellectual, academic, and artistic contribution of this piece is questionable and can definitely mislead the targeted audience who may have a genuine interest in the Indian music."[27]

In these comments, the speakers imagine Western listeners like Mathers, the critic cited above, who expresses a desire to learn more about Indian music and bemoans *Radio India's* lack of contextualization.

It would not be reasonable to expect the aesthetic approach of the collagist to please all listeners, but these anecdotal responses do raise an important issue. *Radio India* purports to represent India, Indian music, and Indian broadcast culture. A century of recording-industry history has taught *all* of us (not only ethnomusicologists) that ethnic representation matters. These South Asian listeners express a legitimate concern about whether *Radio India* is likely to mislead uninitiated listeners who have a real curiosity about Indian music. They, along with some of Sublime Frequencies' targeted Western audience, would like to see that sonic travelers in their radio culture be provided with a map.

"VERY IMPRESSED WITH CALCUTTA"

Radio India's privileging of "the sound itself" over textual meaning is dramatically overturned in Track II:5, "Lucknow Explosion/Very Impressed with Calcutta." This uncharacteristic emphasis on words bursts forth when the first musical excerpt in the track is interrupted by an English-language interview, apparently held in the streets of Calcutta on one of the busy nights of Durga Puja, Bengal's most important religious festival. An interviewer and a tourist struggle to make themselves intelligible over a background of continuous announcements from a public address system, in what sounds like a chaotic street scene:

FOREIGN TRAVELER: I was so glad I came to Calcutta. It was originally going to be Madras.

INTERVIEWER: Why don't you say some words about the country and about the Puja. Please start now.

FOREIGN TRAVELER: I'm very—everything has really taken—it's hard to say what I think about it because you see so many things, and everything is beautiful, every street is lively, and everybody very friendly. It's just so much to take in in one night; it's really so much. Very, very, very nice, yeah, yeah. I'm very impressed with Calcutta.

Both the eager interviewer and the overwhelmed tourist seem in a state of childlike enthusiasm, intoxicated by Calcutta's Puja atmosphere. For a moment, verbal meaning trumps pure sound, as *Radio India* celebrates both beauty (the carnival mood) and the silly, halting speech of interviewer and traveler. At this point, the fact that Bishop highlights an English speaker's exaltation of Calcutta's (as a proxy for all of India's) myriad wonders, suggests that here he has allowed his own intention to come through. The tourist has entered what Richard Bishop has described as "the fourth world," in which "the senses explode on a grand scale, and the unknown, or at least the 'unheard of,' presents itself."[28] If, in "Very Impressed with Calcutta," the traveler speaks as a proxy for the producer, then *Radio India* is Alan Bishop's homage to the complex wonders of the Indian sonic landscape.

But we must return to Earth. As Sublime Frequencies tours the "third world" in search of "fourth world" epiphanies, the traveling, sound-collecting collagist encounters pitfalls met by previous sonic voyagers, and must deal with the legacy of colonial and imperial patterns of thought and behavior. The issues of cultural representation and artistic appropriation have to be addressed. These subjects are the ethnomusicologist's concern, falling squarely into the realm of disciplinary ethics.

WORLD MUSIC GETS A DIVORCE?

The expression "world music" achieved common currency in academia with the founding of Wesleyan University's "Program in World Music" in 1961.[29] The newly coined term denoted three things: the musical subject matter of ethnomusicology, the performance of "non-Western" music, and Wesleyan's approach, which integrated ethnomusicological scholarship with world music performance. This integration extended beyond academia into the recording industry. Record labels such as Topic and Nonesuch, cited today as inspirations by Sublime Frequencies, often worked hand in hand with ethnomusicologists, who provided both sound, in the form of high-quality field recordings, and commentary, in the form of detailed liner notes and printed enclosures. This wedding between academic ethnography and world music recording labels answered several needs.

It provided uninitiated listeners with context and orientation, and it gave record companies access to sound, musicians, and guidance as to appropriate packaging and representation. This collaboration also fulfilled an economic need; specialty recordings unable to attract major record labels needed grant money, and the academic missions of documentation and education provided justification for potential donors.

In 1987, a quarter-century after ethnomusicologists began using the term, a group of record-sellers in London laid claim to "world music" as a "new" commercial category.[30] Farrell writes that the newly appropriated usage jettisoned world music's connection with ethnomusicology:

> Very much a product of 1980s' business awareness, . . . in many ways the idea of World Music is . . . the antithesis of the procedures and methodology of ethnomusicology, the discipline which studies the world's music. The gap between World Music and ethnomusicology may be characterized thus: World Music is fun, colourful, sexy, and saleable, whereas ethnomusicology is serious, rigorous, dull, and academic. The fans of World Music may dip into the music of cultures as they pass through current fashions, for this is where music and the travelogue coalesce. World Music is about a product filled with local colour, exotic and authentic. In many ways the proliferation of World Music represents the aural equivalent of the package holiday.[31]

At the risk of raining on the casual listener's "world music holiday," one wonders if this divergence between world music as a commercial category and ethnomusicology as a discipline is healthy. Ethnomusicology needs to be fun, colorful, sexy, and to some extent saleable, and world music labels require a certain amount of seriousness and rigor—especially when dealing with the sensitive issue of cultural representation. It is difficult to let record companies off the hook for abandoning or minimizing the mission of illumination and education that has long guided labels like Topic and Folkways. *Radio India* undertakes part of that mission, by presenting the listener with an intriguing collection of sounds, but completely sidesteps questions of cultural context and significance.

"ROLLING THE DICE"

The Sublime Frequencies mission statement declares a mandate to acquire and expose "obscure sights and sounds from modern and traditional urban and rural frontiers . . . not documented sufficiently through all channels of academic research, the modern recording industry, media, or corporate foundations."[32] The label thereby joins a long line of musical ethnographers in embracing the mission of rescuing musical traditions from obsolescence. In the case of Sublime Frequencies, the effort is meant in part to save archival recordings from disappearing in obscure academic archives—saving the music from its would-be saviors. The company views academic ethnomusicology with suspicion—a perspective shared, reflexively, by many within the field itself. We are aware that our discipline was born in the age of colonialism, and the effort to move beyond the legacy of European hegemony is ongoing.

Sublime Frequencies' love-hate relationship with ethnomusicology finds colorful expression in Alan Bishop's declaration that "white guys playing the Javanese gamelon [sic] proper . . . are not rolling the dice."[33] Here, Bishop rejects one of the ethnographer's essential research methods: participant-observation. Researchers of all colors play the gamelan, or the sitar—or, for that matter, the piano or violin—in order to gain an insider's experience and understanding.[34] By entering, learning, and practicing within a music culture, one gradually comes to understand the aesthetic and social values that animate the tradition. Bishop's provocative statement evokes the metaphor of playing for stakes, which may be useful in considering the broad enterprise of musical ethnography. Are white guys playing the gamelan—or Ghanaian drums or Turkish dervish music—"rolling the dice"?

It depends on what game is being played. If the game is ethnography, to roll the dice is to penetrate a music culture as deeply as one can, developing an understanding of the music in its cultural context, and documenting, analyzing, and interpreting that music culture, usually via books, articles, lectures, concerts, recordings, and liner notes. If the game is music composition, "rolling the dice" might range from superficial sampling—either figuratively, as a casual listener, or literally, via recording technology—to extended study and total immersion, internalizing a musical genre to the point where it becomes an integral part of one's creative language and approach. The latter seems a more high-stakes endeavor. If the game is performance, then one must play the music. Whether the game is ethnography, composition, or performance, "white guys playing the gamelan" (substitute any color, gender, or musical genre you like) is a legitimate, critical step in coming to understand a music culture.

Radio India's game falls between ethnography and composition, and the two impulses often appear to conflict. The compositions are most interesting when the editor takes a very active hand, creating cuts, transitions, and superimpositions that all but erase the original form and intent of the segments. Ethnography comes to the fore when this same compositor steps back, allowing pieces to retain some of their original form and cultural meaning. In no case, however, does *Radio India's* presentation attempt to translate that meaning, and the "map without a key" manifesto seems totally at odds with the ethnographer's mission of interpretation.

Sublime Frequencies explicitly disavows that mission, but *Radio India* also fails to deliver on a prominent goal in the label's mission statement: bringing to light obscure music and artists underrepresented by academia and the media. The recordings of Asha Bhosle, Pankaj Udhas, and Lata Mangeshkar are not moldering in the forgotten corner of an academic archive, and presenting their songs as if they were obscure field recordings seems disingenuous. One may just as well release a CD of excerpts from the greatest hits of Elvis Presley, Michael Jackson, and the Beatles in order to rescue them from anonymity. *Radio India* does include excerpts from lesser-known artists, but these musicians derive little or no benefit from the exposure because they remain unnamed. I will not go into the question of whether Sublime Frequencies pays its artists, which has been debated elsewhere. Proper attribution, however, is a matter of respect. Appropriation and exploitation are aspects of the colonial heritage that ethnomusicologists have worked hard to overcome, with good reason.

SONIC ASSAULT

Alan Bishop writes in *Radio India's* liner notes that, "Radio stations in India assault the listener," a statement that rings true for a tourist first encountering urban India. The pitch, timbre, and texture of Indian film music seem designed to be audible above street noise, because the street is one of its most common listening venues. On a busy sidewalk, one is likely to meet a sonic barrage, walking past myriad makeshift, plywood stalls where tobacconists, *paan walas*, textile merchants, sweets-sellers, and others each broadcast a favorite radio station or cassette tape, at a volume high enough to compete not only with the neighboring merchants but also with the perpetual roar of traffic, bicycle horns, rickshaw bells, scooter buzzers, and car and truck horns. Wading through this sonic soup, one meets with odd and disjunct transitions not unlike those of selections on *Radio India*. The effect of these overlaps and abrupt changes is rather like that of a scrapbook of snapshots taken on a busy street. The listener remembers that initial confusion, the sense of disorientation that is sometimes disturbing but often intoxicating. Because of the evocative nature of sound, musical collages have the power to return the listener to that "first bloom" of cultural encounter more effectively than do still photos. We are immersed in a somewhat out-of-control ride through the memory of encountering a culture for the first time.

After this initial confusion, the traveler begins to make sense of the cacophony. Anonymous vendors become known, unfamiliar songs are recognized, and a sense of order gradually appears. One learns to block out the noise and focus on a chosen signal—chance disjunctures are ignored while one seeks out intentional meetings, and one slowly sheds the identity of tourist. One enters and attempts to comprehend the culture.

One effect of *Radio India*'s collages is to perpetuate that initial distance—without contextualization and analysis, the jagged transitions and untranslated lyrics create a wall that keeps the listener at arm's length, a tourist in arrested development, never moving beyond that first sense of intoxicating strangeness.

Radio India's ethnographic value suffers because of this distancing. The barrier between the uninitiated listener and the India represented on these CDs is reinforced by the characterization of excerpts (see Track II:9) as pieces in "India's Sound Museum of Oddities." This track title evokes comparison with circus sideshows, in which the foreign, and hence exotic, is presented as the weird, whose oddness is displayed as entertainment. The flaws of colonial ethnomusicology are not corrected, but rather perpetuated, by this distancing of the other.

WHAT IS *RADIO INDIA?*

What, then, is *Radio India*: ethnography or sonic art? What does it seek to convey? Its constant reminders of context—from the CD set's title, to its track titles, to the musical and linguistic markers of Indian-ness in the sound itself—tell us that it is musical ethnography, but its avowed strategy of decontextualizing sound, eschewing the need for mapping and indexing, and the collage form indicate that it is experimental sound art.

There is, however, a third option. In the sonic collages of John Cage, sometimes called "mixes," the composer took control of the *vertical* dimension of sound; they are mixes in the sense that engineers "mix" signals to create textures from several simultaneous sources. The cassette age, from the 1970s through the 1990s, created the amateur "mixtape," in which the compiler, usually a casual listener rather than a sound engineer, mixed sounds *horizontally* by stringing favorite songs from different artists, one after another—the predecessor of the personalized digital playlist. *Radio India* inherits this legacy, in that its "collages" are usually horizontal rather than vertical. Personal mixtapes lack both the ethnographic mission of cultural exegesis and the sonic collagist's preference for decontextualized excerpts; selections usually retain their original forms. Mixtapes also differ from Cage's compositions in that they are compiled by entirely subjective rationale; the "mixer" puts together what she wants to hear. Cage reduced the subjective element by assigning important compositional decisions to chance procedures.

Radio India is in fact a hybrid form, which both suffers from and is enlivened by the conflicting needs of these three, frequently contradictory approaches. The album appears to present ethnographic materials, putting great emphasis on Indian sounds, visual icons, and verbal clichés, but it makes no effort to explain these materials or their cultural significance. It "mixes" sounds from disparate sources in the manner of experimental sonic art, but the excerpts are often too long to be perceived as pure sound, and therefore evoke meanings associated with the original source recordings, though these meanings may remain opaque to listeners unfamiliar with those sources. It consists primarily of horizontal excerpts, heard one at a time, in the manner of a personal mixtape, but no complete selections are included. The rationale for inclusion remains unstated.

In terms of message, *Radio India* is, explicitly, a celebration of "improbable and spectacular audio art" on the Indian airwaves.[35] One thing these collages do well is present the listener with the chaos and random complexity that musical ethnographies often (and of necessity) try to avoid. The arm's-length picture that Bishop presents does not engage deeply with any aspect of Indian music, instead offering a broad sample that steadfastly avoids narrowing its scope to a comprehensible focus. Rejecting the ethnographer's mission of analysis and interpretation, *Radio India* seems to ask: Why would you want to make sense out of this chaos, when it is so beautiful just as it is?

Bishop's use of contrast, juxtaposition, and alienation seems designed to prolong the intoxicating strangeness of a foreigner's first encounter with India. For some listeners, that distancing may enhance the perception of Indian broadcast media as sonic art. For others, it creates an unsatisfying gap between sound and significance: who is singing, what are they singing about, and what is this music for? The danger in ethnographic collage is that one may easily fall into the trap of appropriating and/or misrepresenting culture. The ethnographer's job is to discover meaning; the collage artist's mission is to create it. *Radio India* inhabits the unsettled ground between the two.

NOTES

1. *Filmi geet*: film song; *Junglee*: savage, wild.

2. *Playback singer*: specialist in singing film songs, dubbed over the lip-syncing of the actor. Playback singers dominate Indian popular singing. Mohammed Rafi won numerous awards, including several for "best playback singer of the year."

3. *Alap:* the introductory section in a performance of Indian classical music, usually in slow, free rhythm.

4. *Kathakali* is a South Indian theatrical genre noted for its spectacular costumes, makeup, dance, and music. *Kali,* "the black goddess," and *Shiva,* the god of asceticism, both function as destroyers of ignorance and evil. Shiva is often worshipped in the form of the *lingam,* an erect phallus; he therefore represents creation as well as destruction.

5. Alan Rich, *American Pioneers: Ives to Cage and Beyond* (London: Phaidon, 1995), 159–72.

6. *Raga:* one of the melodic modes of Indian classical music; arguably the defining characteristic which makes music "classical" in the Indian context. Lewis Rowell, *Music and Musical Thought in Early India* (Chicago: University of Chicago Press, 1992), 11–19.

7. David Kopf, *British Orientalism and the Bengal Renaissance: The Dynamics of Indian Modernization 1773–1835* (Berkeley and Los Angeles: University of California Press, 1969).

8. Rowell, *Music and Musical Thought in Early India,* 11–19.

9. *Brahma:* the god of creation.

10. When depicted as Nataraja, the Lord of the Dance, Shiva accompanies his cosmic dance by shaking the *damaru* rattle, which "connotes Sound, the vehicle of speech, the conveyer of revelation, tradition, incantation, magic, and divine truth." Heinrich Zimmer, *Myths and Symbols in Indian Art and Civilization* (Princeton: Princeton University Press, 1974; first pub. 1946), 152. Saraswati, the goddess of music, is often pictured playing the *veena,* an early stringed instrument that is emblematic of Indian classical music.

11. Gerry Farrell, *Indian Music and the West* (New York: Oxford University Press, 1997), 201.

12. *Nagaswaram:* the South Indian counterpart of the double-reed *shehnai,* often played on ceremonial and ritual occasions, in outdoor processions, and in classical music performances.

13. Lata Mangeshkar and her sister Asha Bhosle dominated playback singing for six decades, taking turns being declared the most recorded singer in the world; each has sung in more than a thousand films and more than twenty Indian languages. Their awards are too numerous to list here ("Lata Mangeshkar"; "Asha Bhosle"). Anuradha Paudwal is a prominent film and devotional singer whose career began in the 1970s; she has won five awards for "Best Female Playback Singer" ("Anuradha Paudwal"). Ustad Amir Khan was one of the most influential and respected North Indian classical vocalists from the 1940s

to 1970s ("Amir Khan"). *Ghazals* are Urdu love songs that emphasize elegant poetry and have roots in Persian poetry and Sufi mysticism. Pankaj Udhas is a renowned playback and *ghazal* singer who has received numerous awards, including "Best Ghazal Singer of the Year" in 1985 ("Pankaj Udhas"). Kazi Nazrul Islam, the national poet of Bangladesh, was a prolific songwriter and ardent Indian nationalist in the independence movement of the early twentieth century.

14. *Sarangi* and *sarinda* are bowed instruments with gut strings and membrane-covered resonators. *Dholak* is a two-headed cylindrical drum used in many folk and devotional genres; the paired *tabla* drums are familiar in the West.

15. Alan Bishop, "Alan Bishop," Interview, *Believer*, July/August 2008, believermag. com/issues//200807/?read=interview_bishop (accessed 23 Mar. 2013).

16. Farrell, *Indian Music and the West*, 208–9. *Qawwali* repertoire consists of Islamic mystical songs in the Urdu language. The genre is thought to have originated with Amir Khusrau, who served as court poet in thirteenth-century Delhi.

17. Bill Meyer, "Radio India: The Eternal Dream of Sound," Dusted Reviews, *Dusted magazine.com*, Aug. 22, 2004. www.dustedmagazine.com/reviews/1646 (accessed 2 Nov. 2014).

18. Ibid.

19. "Listen: Sublime Frequencies—Radio India," *Marmoo.wordpress.com*, July 29, 2008 (accessed 2 Nov. 2014). marmoo.wordpress.com/2008/07/listen-sublime-frequencies -radio-india/.

20. Ian Mathers, "Radio India: The Eternal Dream of Sound." *Stylusmagazine.com*. 21 Sep. 2004, www.stylusmagazine.com/reviews/various-artists/radio-india-the-eternal -dream-of-sound.htm (accessed 2 Nov. 2014).

21. Rajani Nadkarni, personal interview, 22 Feb. 2013.

22. Anna Morcom, *Hindi Film Songs and the Cinema* (Burlington, Vt.: Ashgate, 2007), 224.

23. Nadkarni, personal interview, 22 Feb. 2013.

24. Mohan Beltangady, Telephone interview, 24 Feb. 2013.

25. Nadkarni, personal interview, 22 Feb. 2013.

26. Ibid.

27. Azim Fahmi, Email interview, 3 Mar. 2013.

28. Richard Bishop, qtd. in David Novak, "The Sublime Frequencies of New Old Media," *Public Culture* 23, no. 3 (Durham: Duke University Press, 2011), 612.

29. Dorothea E. Hast, "World Music." *Encyclopedia Americana*. Grolier Online, 2013 (accessed 15 Mar. 2013).

30. Farrell, *Indian Music and the West*, 201.

31. Ibid., 202.

32. Sublime Frequencies, www.sublimefrequencies.com (accessed 23 Mar. 2013).

33. Erik Davis, "Cameo Demons: Hanging with the Sun City Girls," http://techgnosis. com/scg.html (accessed 23 Mar. 2013).

34. James B. Spradley, *Participant Observation* (Fort Worth, Texas: Holt, Rinehart and Winston, 1980), 3.

35. Liner notes, *Radio India.*

BIBLIOGRAPHY

"Amir Khan (singer)." *Wikipedia.org.* en.wikipedia.org/wiki/Amir_Khan_(singer) (accessed 23 Mar. 2013).

"Anuradha Paudwal." *Wikipedia.org.* en.wikipedia.org/wiki/Anuradha_Paudwal (accessed 23 Mar. 2013).

"Asha Bhosle." *Wikipedia.org.* en.wikipedia.org/wiki/Asha_Bhosle (accessed 23 Mar. 2013).

Beltangady, Mohan. Telephone interview, 24 Feb. 2013.

Beltangady, Shamal. Telephone interview, 24 Feb. 2013.

Bishop, Alan. "Alan Bishop." Interview. *Believer*, July/August 2008. believermag.com/ issues//200807/?read=interview_bishop (accessed 23 Mar. 2013).

Bishop, Richard. "Travels." *Halana* 1, no. 4 (1999): 7–16, qtd. in Novak, "The Sublime Frequencies of New Old Media."

Davis, Erik. "Cameo Demons: Hanging with the Sun City Girls." http://techgnosis.com/ scg.html (accessed 23 Mar. 2013).

Fahmi, Azim. Email interview, 3 Mar. 2013.

Farrell, Gerry. *Indian Music and the West.* New York: Oxford University Press, 1997.

Hast, Dorothea E. "World Music." *Encyclopedia Americana.* Grolier Online, 2013 (accessed 15 Mar. 2013).

Islam, Rafiqul. "Islam, Kazi Nazrul." *Banglapedia.org.* www.banglapedia.org/HT/I_0109. HTM (accessed 23 Mar. 2013).

Kopf, David. *British Orientalism and the Bengal Renaissance: The Dynamics of Indian Modernization 1773–1835.* Berkeley and Los Angeles: University of California Press, 1969.

"Lata Mangeshkar." *Wikipedia.org.* en.wikipedia.org/wiki/Lata_Mangeshkar (accessed 23 Mar. 2013).

"Listen: Sublime Frequencies—Radio India." *Marmoo.wordpress.com,* July 29, 2008 (accessed 2 Nov. 2014). marmoo.wordpress.com/2008/07/listen-sublime-frequencies-radio-india/.

Mathers, Ian. "Radio India: The Eternal Dream of Sound." *Stylusmagazine.com.* 21 Sep. 2004. www.stylusmagazine.com/reviews/various-artists/radio-india-the-eternal -dream-of-sound.htm (accessed 2 Nov. 2014).

Meyer, Bill. "Radio India: The Eternal Dream of Sound." Dusted Reviews. *Dustedmagazine. com*, Aug. 22, 2004. www.dustedmagazine.com/reviews/1646 (accessed 2 Nov. 2014).

Morcom, Anna. *Hindi Film Songs and the Cinema.* Burlington, Vt.: Ashgate, 2007.

Nadkarni, Rajani. Personal interview, 22 Feb. 2013.

Novak, David. "The Sublime Frequencies of New Old Media." *Public Culture* 23, no. 3. Durham: Duke University Press, 2011.

O'Flaherty, Wendy Doniger. *Hindu Myths.* New York: Penguin, 1984.

"Pankaj Udhas." *Wikipedia.org.* en.wikipedia.org/wiki/Pankaj_Udhas (accessed 23 Mar. 2013).

Ray, Jita. Personal interview, 26 Feb. 2013.

Rich, Alan. *American Pioneers: Ives to Cage and Beyond.* London: Phaidon, 1995.

Rowell, Lewis. *Music and Musical Thought in Early India.* Chicago: University of Chicago Press, 1992.

Spradley, James B. *Participant Observation.* Fort Worth, Texas: Holt, Rinehart and Winston, 1980.

Sublime Frequencies. www.sublimefrequencies.com (accessed 23 Mar. 2013).

Zimmer, Heinrich. *Myths and Symbols in Indian Art and Civilization.* Princeton: Princeton University Press, 1974 (first pub. 1946).

GONÇALO F. CARDOSO,

DISCREPANT.NET

Interview with Laurent Jeanneau

Laurent Jeanneau, aka Kink Gong, is a Frenchman based in Yunnan, southern China, where he specializes in documenting and recording ethnic minority music. He also composes experimental music based on his innumerable field recordings.

From the moment Jeanneau's collage work reached my susceptible ears a couple of years back, on the Touch Records podcast series, my attitude toward traditional "world music" was changed forever. His soundscape approach produced something so unique and captivating that I couldn't stop myself from going back to it for months to come.

Taking the listener to remote regions of our planet and mixing in contemporary electronic sounds, Jeanneau's collage simultaneously presents an old world, an unknown world, and a place so far away from Western cultural references that one has difficulty describing the sounds they hear. For me, repeated listens only reinforced the deep, hypnotic vibes that, in my opinion, are unequalled in the (so-called) genre of "globetrotting psychedelia."

By Googling Jeanneau's name, I quickly found out that, outside his work as a DJ and his occasional contributions to Sublime Frequencies, he spends most of his time recording ethnic minority musics in South Asia—the remote villages of China, Vietnam, Cambodia, and Laos being the main focus of his work. Back at his base in Yunnan, South China, he meticulously compiles the recordings into CDs released on his own label, Kink Gong Records. From recordings of religious ceremonies and gong rituals to compilations of loops coming from "Buddha Machines," Jeanneau creates unique records of the most remote people and tribes on our planet.

DISCREPANT: How long have you been recording ethnic minorities and how did you come to it?

LAURENT JEANNEAU: It's been a long process. I only came to be active in the field in my thirties and became a professional at it in my forties, but I've taken interest in real world music in the early 1980s as a teenager, then started to travel to faraway places in 1990, then did my first recordings in India in 1996 and 1997, mostly in Chennai, former Madras, with the exclusive purpose of remixing it my way, destroying the rigid musical Indian rules. The performers were horrified by the result and it never got anywhere. Then, in 1999 and 2000 in Tanzania, a double CD of the Hadzas Bushmen got released on the French label Musique du Monde. I eventually moved to Cambodia, and never stopped since, going through a lot of music in Cambodia, Laos, Vietnam, and China.

DISCREPANT: Do you see your role as a field-recording documentarian, keeping other people's records for posterity, or as more of a musician?

LJ: I guess those recordings, now 86 CDs, will [extend into] posterity, but let me remind you that the very first and essential impulse is not to pretend to do that work for preserving, but rather for the discovery of an incredible diversity of structures and textures in those unknown music fields that are fast disappearing. That to me has connections to all kinds of different music created in Western contemporary culture—like the first abstract painters of the early twentieth century had been influenced by African art, like pygmies' drawings, as an example. It's about giving a different aesthetic codification of music a chance to be heard, and, in the first place, [letting it] influence me, for my ongoing process of being fed with new things.

DISCREPANT: Name a few of your favorite places and people you've recorded over the years and why?

LJ: In northeast Cambodia and southern Laos I became the specialist of gong ensembles, orchestras of tuned metallic percussions. Hardly anything has been done in terms of recordings. The UNESCO can claim to add this musical culture as one of the masterpieces of intangible patrimony to their list, but they do nothing at all to preserve it. Most gong ensembles are a sociomusical interaction, one gong of different size per person, including nipple gongs, flat gongs, a pair of thick, flat gongs hit with long mallets, . . . different techniques, different tunes, and different occasions [make up] a great diversity of gong playing. Two other major musical expressions attract me very much: the various vocal polyphonies—the Hani of Southern Yunnan in China are an outstanding example—and different mouth organs that I've recorded in northern Vietnam, northern Laos, and southern China.

DISCREPANT: How difficult it is to locate and approach different musicians all over the world?

LJ: Every recording has a different story, according to the country's loose or rigid access, my ability to communicate, the time I spend there, who I'm working with, and lots of other parameters, but usually I know what community I'm targeting, so I get information from locals, mostly, and read all kinds of semi-anthropological content about it, if they exist. Ask me one specific example out of the 86 CDs and I'll tell how I met them.

DISCREPANT: Your work seems to be mostly based in Southeast Asia with some spells in Africa? Have you got projects to record on other continents?

LJ: No, I just wish to continue in the same area. It would be nice to extend further southwest in Myanmar and more eastern parts of India and northern Bangladesh to find about non-Buddhist, non-Muslims, and non-Hindus.

DISCREPANT: Finally, are there any places or people you must record before it's too late?

LJ: [I had] two unfruitful meetings with a French anthropologist in northern Laos—I missed him in June last year and met him in Oudomxai, north Laos last November, when he just got dengue fever, so he could not [get up] from bed. However, we're supposed to get together again to finally reach villages of the small, uncategorized ethnic groups of Phongsaly in north Laos. Basically, there are four big ethnolinguistic families in Southeast Asia . . . , so some [ ] are still not belonging to any category—not that I care, those classifications are actually meaningless to me—but it's just the idea that those outsiders . . . are found in one area where those four ethnic categories all live: Phongsaly. That's pretty unique! And like I've mentioned above, I wish to go to the very northern part of Myanmar, where there's absolutely no information available but it's a dangerous country, home of all kinds of ethnic military oppositions and drug mafias, not to forget a terrible military dictator that's not going to allow me to hang with minorities. At the moment (spring 2012), going there would mean limit[ing] myself to Buddhist temples further south.

NOTE

Sublime Frequencies recordist Laurent Jeanneau has contributed many discs to the label, including *Ethnic Minority Music of Southern China, Ethnic Minority Music of Northwest Xinjiang, Ethnic Minority Music of North Vietnam, Ethnic Minority Music of Southern Laos,* and *Ethnic Minority Music of Northeast Cambodia.* This interview was originally published May 12, 2012, at Discrepant.net and on the webzine *Amour & Discipline,* amour-discipline. org. It is reprinted here, in edited form, with the author's permission.

ANDREW C. MCGRAW

Radio Java

Sublime Frequencies' *Radio Java* is a compilation of Indonesian regional radio broadcasts assembled by Alan Bishop and Manford Cain in 1989. Historically, the majority of Javanese music available in the West has been restricted to the "high art" of Central Javanese court *gamelan*. Despite this form's vigorous preservation by the Indonesian state, it has become largely irrelevant to the daily lives of many working-class Javanese since the introduction of cheap mass media such as cassettes in the 1970s.[1] Sublime Frequencies' interest in noncanonical Indonesian forms is not unprecedented: Previous American albums include the 1989 release by Nonesuch of West Javanese (Sundanese) *jaipongan* music (discussed below), Lyrichord's *New Music Indonesia* series, and Smithsonian Folkways' monumental, twenty-CD series of rare Indonesian musics in the 1990s. Folkways' earlier release of popular forms such as *dangdut* and *kroncong* erodes Sublime Frequencies' claim that the label has rescued "oddities . . . slipping through the cracks."[2] Nevertheless, the idiosyncratic assemblage on *Radio Java* of DJ banter, radio commercials, drama, news broadcasts, hard rock, disco, traditional, and neotraditional musics has no parallel.

In this chapter I first situate *Radio Java* within David Novak's concept of "World Music 2.0."[3] I argue that, while the *Radio* series functioned as a populist response to academic ethnomusicology's historic preference for elite art traditions, Indonesians' current use of digital media as a cultural archive renders a preservationist perspective of the *Radio* series largely irrelevant. I then provide a mini reception study of the album, contrasting the responses of a traditional Javanese musician (Peni Candrarini) and an American experimental musician (Shahzad Ismaily). My main point here is to demonstrate the divergent receptions of the album by its ostensibly intended audience (American experimentalists) versus local musicians. Interpretive divergence is present even at the affective level of distortion.

While an apparently objective acoustical image of Java—freed from academic curatorial practices—is produced through the combination of minimal liner notes and a dense soundscape, I argue that the album represents a carefully manicured montage of sounds intended to encourage new modes of listening.

WORLD MUSIC 2.0

Radio Java is an example of what is sometimes referred to as World Music 2.0. These media are dissociated both from academic (ethnomusicological) field recordings of ostensibly stabilized, learned "traditions" of aged provenance and the hybrid forms (sometimes called "world beat") popular during the 1980s and 1990s—which became the target of a withering, anti-imperialist critique.[4] World Music 2.0, as exemplified by Sublime Frequencies' catalog, involves both the redistribution in the West of locally produced popular recordings as well as the collection of sounds of "everyday life" in the non-West. The latter sometimes are assembled through radio "dial surfing" in foreign broadcast areas. Sublime Frequencies' special focus on dated popular forms, ranging roughly from the 1960s to the late 1980s, responds to a sonic lacuna in the United States. This gap emerged from the overwhelmingly West-to-Rest flow of popular media prior to the Internet, when forms such as Indonesian *dangdut* were largely unavailable in America. World Music 2.0 intends to bring the listener closer to the "reality" of local soundscapes by eschewing Western academic and industrial mediation while simultaneously stimulating listeners' own imaginations through the suspension of exegesis, or even meaning itself, by providing only anemic liner notes.

Within the Western new-music and experimental scene, Sublime Frequencies' releases have often been hailed, as in *The Wire*, for being "a worthy successor to the old school labels like Ocora, Folkways, and Nonesuch Explorer."[5] This is an ironic form of praise considering that Sublime Frequencies, and co-founder Alan Bishop in particular, have expressed a deep ambivalence toward curatorial pretensions and academic ethnomusicology. In Bishop's rather anachronistic view, ethnomusicology reifies notions of tradition and facilitates the transformation of culture into property: "Obviously there's a sense of respect for how to play something like the *gamelon* [*sic*]. But to give in to that respect you don't do right by tradition. Tradition is not about slavish imitation. The last thing I want to see is a bunch of fucking white guys playing Javanese *gamelon* proper. It's disrespectful. . . . because they are not evolving the situation."[6]

Such a view loses sight, as the American *gamelan* subculture often does itself, of the ways in which "bi-musical" performance reflexively creates the very tradition it believes itself to represent. By using *gamelan* toward specific local (American) purposes—as a utopian collectivity apparently disengaged from the law of profit; as a critique of Western musical systems and their often exclusionary associations with gender, class, and race; as a medium for new hybrid composition; as a form of therapy for the enfeebled or incarcerated, etc.—even the most boringly traditionalist American performers of *gamelan* are engaged in innovation through the presentation (and sometimes unintentional transformation) of older Javanese forms within new contexts. Such contexts "evolve the situation," just as Sublime Frequencies' releases also reinstate specific notions of difference and cultural property. As one of *The Wire*'s Best Albums of 2003, *Radio Java* is attributed solely to "traditional musicians," though only a portion of the material could be described as straightforwardly traditional. In this case, tradition serves as a foil for anonymity and a cover for Indonesian copyright infringement.

Some observers have critiqued Sublime Frequencies' and other redistributors' contractual procedures, raising questions regarding ownership, rights, and responsibilities.[7] Indeed, any local analog—*Radio Seattle*—would be prohibited by American copyright laws. Novak describes Sublime Frequencies' *Radio* releases through Jenkins' concept of remediation, a process "in which content is transferred from one media context to another to create new media."[8] While fetishizing local scenes' apparent industrial and aesthetic independence from Western mass mediation, remediation projects such as *Radio Java* risk accusations of appropriation and misuse through the embrace of a global, open-source media culture—an ideal that, if it could ever be fully attained, might potentially erode the very difference valued therein.

In spite of the homage and admiration at their origin, we may question the latent neocolonial potential of such releases, which are centered in and almost completely circulate within the West. The review of Sublime Frequencies' *Radio* series by DJ and scholar Wayne Marshall elides this possibility. He imagines a "production, distribution, representation, etc. [whereby] every corner could offer up its own idea of the sublime frequencies of every other corner. Perspectives could meet and diverge, centers could be decentered, things could fall apart and come together in unimagined ways."[9] But this kind of musical utopia could not be realized until substantial structural inequities are leveled. Western experimentalists can enter Indonesia with a $25 tourist visa and need not register with any governmental agency. They can easily round up a large group of musicians for recordings and pay them low wages by Western standards. On the flip side, innovative Indonesian musicians (often single, young Muslim men) must go through a lengthy visa application process that requires an interview in Jakarta or Surabaya, and must pay a $320 visa fee and another $250 (*fiskal*) simply to leave the country.

CULTURAL LOSS — ETHNOMUSICOLOGY

Clive Bell, writing in *The Wire*, suggests that, "Sublime Frequencies' urgency [in expanding its catalog] is often linked to a sense that [its] favorite music may be on the point of vanishing."[10] In a 2008 interview, Bishop told Novak that: "If I didn't release this music . . . people would never get to hear it."[11] The ambivalent, on-again, off-again anxiety of loss that appears in the label's rhetoric and in reviews of its output appear increasingly ironic in light of the kinds of cultural esoterica, detritus, and miscellanea that are daily uploaded onto YouTube, Facebook, and other sites from all parts of the world.

In 2010, Indonesia became the second largest Facebook community after the United States. Because the infrastructure of that nation's landline telephony is comparatively underdeveloped, much of the population has leapfrogged directly into the smartphone age over the past five years. Many of my Indonesian peers daily upload a bewildering amount of DIY ethnographic material and local media independent of any apparent Western curating or restriction (other than what's imposed by the structures and limits of the Internet and social-media portals). Much of this material is new, though a great deal of the nation's pre-Internet, predigital cultural archive—recordings of 1960s-era bands such as Koes Bersaudura, clips of Benyamin S's many New Order films, etc.—is gradually finding its way online, rendering Sublime Frequencies' ethos of salvage-ethnomusicology increasingly irrelevant.

Sublime Frequencies' focus upon popular media can be seen as a provocative response to the sometimes narrow focus within academic ethnomusicology and the world music industry on classic and revivalist traditions, representations of which have often served the state. Ethnomusicologists studying Indonesia have concerned themselves overwhelmingly with musical analysis of the large *gamelan* ensembles of Central Java and Bali. Scholarly concern with Indonesian popular forms such as *dangdut* and *pop Indonesia* has gained traction only since the release of *Radio Java*, more than a decade after the Bishop brothers first recorded their source material.[12] Sublime Frequencies' interest in the apparently "messy," distorted, popular, and innovative sounds of the late-1980s "Indonesian street" is a response to the rarefied, sometimes exclusionary world of *gamelan*, which for most Americans has long stood as the sole sonic icon of the entire archipelago. Through their dissociation from academic institutions, for which the acquisition of a large set of exotic *gamelan* instruments and faculty trained in its esoteric traditions remains an elite status symbol, the Bishops and their associates in the American experimental underground have become "unlikely ethnomusicologists."[13] Sublime Frequencies is thus able to practice a mode of "subjective ethnomusicology" independent of the multicultural priorities of the university or the trends of academic scholarship.[14] Instead, the label follows the trends and aesthetic priorities of its own subculture.

CONTRASTING IMPRESSIONS

In this section, I unravel *Radio Java* in reference to the responses of two knowledgeable listeners. Shahzad Ismaily (b. 1972) is an American experimentalist, a leading improviser, and a touring musician based in New York who has played extensively with, among other groups, Secret Chiefs 3, a Bay Area experimental ensemble that shares an aesthetic and personal kinship with the Bishops' Sun City Girls and Sublime Frequencies. Peni Candrarini (b. 1983) is a vocalist from central Java who was trained in her youth in the performance of court *gamelan* but has long been engaged in innovative composition.[15]

Radio Java, as its liner notes and reviews of the album imply, is intended for listeners like Ismaily above all. But Sublime Frequencies' recordings can, and do, flow back to the home territories of their musical subjects, where responses can be highly divergent from those of American academia and the experimental underground.

Alexander Provan writes that Sublime Frequencies' approach demonstrates music's dynamism and "capacity to change," and that Alan Bishop "eschews the desire to preserve something in its original state, treating the music as malleable."[16] While *Radio Java* demonstrably achieves this aim for American listeners such as Ismaily, for whom *gamelan* has long stood for Indonesia, the album sounded to Candrarini as a "nostalgic appeal to the past"—a sonic document of her youth in a mountainous, rural village in East Java. Ismaily echoed the album's liner notes, which describe the sounds on *Radio Java* as "random." But Candrarini heard a logical "train ride from Jakarta to Surabaya, down to Yogya and then back again."

Sublime Frequencies has responded to the belabored arguments of folklorists and ethnomusicologists—that music belongs first and foremost to the people who make it—by asserting that it belongs equally to those who hear it. I hope to remind the reader that, in the case of *Radio Java,* the Javanese are also listening. In the following, I include brief descriptions of selections heard on *Radio Java,* alongside Candrarini's and Ismaily's commentary.

Track 1: Radio Jakarta #1

Jakarta, formerly the colonial capital of Batavia, is the desperately overcrowded capital city on the northern coast of West Java. Historically dominated by the Betawi ethnic group, Jakarta is now highly multicultural, attracting migrants from the entire archipelago.

0:00–0:09: The track begins like most releases of traditional Indonesian *gamelan.* We hear a Central Javanese *dalang* (traditional puppeteer) performing in the Solonese style, accompanied by a full *gamelan* orchestra. We hear the highly stylized voice of the *dalang,* who narrates while striking the side of the puppet box with a wooden beater to cue the entrance of the *gamelan.* The broadcast of this regional genre in the metropole is emblematic of the ethnic and political dominance of the Central Javanese in multiethnic Indonesia.

0:09–5:32: Sundanese *jaipongan* music. This form evolved in the 1970s and 1980s from the West Javanese village *ketuk tilu gamelan* and quickly gained national prominence, riding the boom of cassette technology.[17] *Jaipongan* is a rare example of an indigenous popular music that became favored by American audiophiles following the 1987 release of the Nonesuch Elektra album *Tonggeret,* featuring the singer Idjah Hadidjah and arranger Gugum Gumbira.[18] Sublime Frequencies seems to capitalize on the success of that album while demonstrating the national prominence of this regional form. The dense distortion heard is likely a result of both deteriorating tape and poor radio reception. The inclusion of a long, uninterrupted and unattributed track on this U.S. release demonstrates the structural weakness of local musicians within the framework of international copyright. Its opposite, an Indonesian release of American copyrighted material, would be deemed piracy.

7:27–9:31: A gradual, disorienting crossfade into Central Javanese *gamelan* played in a Banyumasan (West-Central) Javanese style. This is likely one of the many hybrid experiments (*kreasi*) composed by Nartosabdho. During the early New Order, many ensembles, the foremost being Nartosabdho's, sought musical catalyst through the adoption and transformation of regional ethnic styles, a development that furthered the New Order's efforts to celebrate signs of a national culture (dominated by the Javanese) while downplaying regional factionalism.

Track 2: Radio Surabaya

Surabaya is a densely populated, heavily industrial port city on the northern coast of East Java that has long been a center of Chinese-Indonesian commercial activity.

0:28–0:40: A jarring fade from *gamelan* to Western-style rock, sung here by Ikang Fauzi (b. 1959), a popular Indonesian rock singer and film star during the 1980s (and now a real estate broker).

0:40–1:57: Candrarini describes this as an example of Javanese *campur sari,* a form of light, neotraditional music typically performed on a reduced set of *gamelan* and keyboards or other Western instruments. It is in the *langgam* style, an older form linking *gamelan* to *kroncong,* an ancient hybrid that incorporates local and Western traditions.[19] Musical clarity is obscured by distortion effects that seem to be produced purposefully, by tuning the radio toward and away from the broadcast frequency.

1:57–2:23: We hear Indonesian *Qiro'at,* a "sung" recitation of the Quran in a style that strongly emulates Saudi (Wahabi) interpretations, according to Candrarini. Islamic fundamentalism, spurred by Arab (primarily Saudi) support of Islamic foundations, grew markedly in Indonesia following the end of dictatorial rule in Indonesia in 1998 and subsequent economic crises in 1997 and 2008. Today, various forms of Quranic recitation are now considerably more popular than they were in the late 1980s.

Track 3: Radio Jakarta #2

0:00–0:13: Brazilian bossa nova. Latin American music, especially rumba and samba, have long been popular in Indonesia. Nartosabdho, among others, frequently incorporated such rhythms into his innovative works for *gamelan.*

0:18–2:54: *Sapu Lidi,* a *kroncong* work that sends Candrarini into nostalgic giggles. The *sapu lidi* is a traditional Indonesian broom made of palm-leaf spines. This recording is performed by the famous Indonesian comic actor and singer Benyamin S. (Benyamin Sueb, 1939–1995). Candrarini describes the genre as *kroncong Betawi,* a national genre localized by the West Javanese Betawi ethnic group. This excerpt could alternately be described as an example of Betawi *gambang kromong.*[20] Benyamin S.'s semi-improvised lyrics (reminiscent of Malay *pantun*) includes thinly veiled sexual references (*sampai pagi!* [until the break of dawn!]) that were rather more common in popular music of the early and mid-New Order. Candrarini finds a sweet nostalgia in this playful, frank sexuality as compared to the simultaneously more puritanical and vulgar sexual semiotics of contemporary Indonesia, influenced by the apparently contradictory poles of Islamic fundamentalism and Western digital media. Ismaily feels this example clearly links bossa nova with "this weirdo Indonesian stuff" and that this track has a clear aesthetic affinity with "reggae/dub."

2:54–3:38: Candrarini, laughing: "What is this?" It's most likely an example of *musikalisasi puesi*, poetry set to music. During and after the New Order, this form was popular among high school and college students who set original poetry to self-composed, sometimes semi-improvised music combining Western and traditional instruments. This example appears manipulated by various effects. For Ismaily, it is "reminiscent of the Lee Hazlewood–Nancy Sinatra collaboration 'Some Velvet Morning.'"

3:38–5:53: Another example of *musikalisisa puesi*; here, an example of *puesi perjuangan*, or poetry inspired by the revolutionary struggle, performed in a deeply overdramatized style. Candrarini laughs uncontrollably, finding it "embarrassingly oversentimental, dated, and naive." Ismaily "loves the distortion" and hears in it the "sentimental phrasing of Bollywood dialog."

5:53–7:30: Sundanese *lagu perjuangan*, patriotic revolutionary songs. These lyrics, Candrarini believes, were likely composed during the Old Order (1945–1965) under General Sukarno. The core lyrics concern Sukarno's concept of *Pancasila*, the five governing principles of the Indonesian state.

Track 4: Radio Republik Indonesia

Radio Republic Indonesia, or RRI, was established as the national, government-controlled radio station in 1945. During the Old and New Orders, it served as the primary source of news and entertainment for most Indonesians. This particular selection is likely from the regional station in Surabaya, which broadcasts news and entertainment produced in Jakarta.

2:02–2:55: East Javanese *ludruk*, a form of theater popular among various ethnic groups in East and Central Java. This program, the announcer tells us, is sponsored by a local pharmaceutical venture.

2:55–3:21: A drum machine playing a hip-hop beat accompanies an ad for *Coklat Top*, an Indonesian candy that one eats, according to the announcer, while listening to "*musik*," a term reserved for Western and modern sounds, as opposed to, say, *gamelan*.

3:21–4:01: A keyboard imitates Balinese *gamelan* and is joined by guitar and saxophone in an ad for Sampoerna clove cigarettes.

4:01–4:56: We hear a quiz show in which contestants send in answers scribbled on a postcard to the central station in Jakarta. The musical cue for each question conjures 1950s American television soundscapes.

6:12–6:47: A jazzy advertisement for Indonesian instant noodles (*mie goreng*). Jazz has a venerable history in the archipelago, emerging within intercultural contexts by at least the mid-1920s. Jazz has long signified upward social mobility and cosmopolitanism in the nation, but is not necessarily felt to be Western.

Track 5: Radio Yogyakarta

Yogyakarta is the largest city in central Java and, along with Surakarta (Solo) to the north, embodies the psychic center of traditional Javanese culture. It is also the largest college town in the nation, attracting students from all over the archipelago.

0:00–2:43: *Jaipongan* (Sundanese contemporary *gamelan*), in this case hybridized with Central Javanese *gamelan* and vocal styles. Candrarini calls this *campur sari* (pop) *jaipongan*. Ismaily focuses again on fidelity, in this case compression, hearing in it the "sound of early Ronnie Spector records."

4:12–5:56: A hybrid of *dangdut* and East Javanese *gamelan* styles. *Dangdut* emerged from the combination of Western, Indonesian, and Bollywood musics, becoming especially popular in the 1970s and 1980s as a form of working-class popular music that occasionally voiced social critique. The form is named after the rolling rhythm of the *takdut* drums, similar to Indian *tabla,* that anchor its beat—here imitated on *gamelan* instruments. This work, entitled "*Rewel,*" exhorts lovers to speak directly ("*ngomong terus terang*") about their feelings. For Candrarini, the tune stirs nostalgic memories of a form highly popular in her rural hometown during her youth.

Track 6: Radio Jakarta #3

0:00–0:52: Indonesian rock band Super Kid, which displays clear AC/DC influences.

0:52–1:57: "Nurlela," an extremely popular *pop Indonesia* tune of the mid-1980s, later re-recorded by various bands in a wide range of styles. The name Nurlela has appeared in several Indonesian popular songs since the 1950s, the most popular being Bing Slamet's cha-cha version, to refer to an attractive young woman. Candrarini laughs at the "stupid, sappy" lyrics about young love. This version adopts a production mode essentially indistinguishable from mid-1980s American Top 40. Ismaily reflects: "Indonesians come across as weirder when they're doing straight Western music than when they are doing their own traditional music."

1:57–4:40: Banter between two young DJs reading listeners' letters and greetings to their friends. The background music seems to be sampled from Cameo's "Word Up" (1986). Candrarini says, "Ah, such a pre-Facebook world! But this must have been only for rich kids; they are telling people to call in and talk about eating pizza and hamburgers. This was the culture of the Jakartan ABG (*anak baru gede,* referring generally to affluent teenagers) at the time." Without being told when this was recorded, she guesses 1988, just one year off.

Track 7: Radio Bandung

The capital of the West Javanese province of Sunda, Bandung is the nation's third-largest city, with a population of nearly 8 million. It has long been a hotbed of *jaipongan* (Sundanese contemporary *gamelan*), jazz, fusion, rock, and various alternative and indie musics.

0:00–1:12: Two ads for the soap brand Give amid radio noise. The distortion, overlapping frequencies, and poor radio reception seem to be manipulated purposefully. (One can't tell if this was achieved "in the field" or through later digital processing; the heavily panned channels suggest post-production.) The segment adheres to the aesthetic preoccupations of the American underground experimental scene. Ismaily "loves its wonderful turning-the-dial quality."

1:22–1:55: *Jaipongan.* Musical developments in Indonesia, be they popular, academic, or experimental, are sometimes theorized as a mimetic, delayed attempt to respond to Western influence—many Indonesian art composers evince an anxious sense of being behind the West. The near-obsession with *jaipongan* on *Radio Java* provides a counterexample of American aesthetic belatedness. By the mid-2000s, *jaipongan* was well past its apex of popularity in Indonesia.

4:55–5:04: Nine seconds of the Rolling Stones' "Sing This All Together." Among the many Western rock bands heard in Indonesia, the Rolling Stones have remained among the most popular. Indonesians appear proud that Mick Jagger has traveled extensively in the nation and maintains a home in Bali.

5:04–5:37: Discussion program in Sundanese. Ismaily says, at this point, that he is beginning to "understand the album's logic and meaning. It began to transfer onto my consciousness the idea that a lot of musics are *related*, not just in obvious ways—i.e., key, tempo—but along more subtle and esoteric axes such as feeling, mood, space, environment, and gesture in a painterly sense. This allows me to consider putting what, on the surface, would seem to be wildly disparate elements together in the same songs, sectionally or as overdubs, listening for whether the parts 'fit' based not on key/rhythm but in other ways of synchronicity."

7:07–7:28: Heavily distorted *pop Indonesia.* Here it sounds as if the tuning needle is being held away from the broadcasting frequency purposefully, transforming the saccharine sounds of Indonesian pop into something much more akin to American industrial music.

7:39–7:40: Big band jazz; saxophone solo.

7:40–8:01: We hear what sounds like a call-in show, where the caller's voice is heavily distorted. Dovetailing with the prior sample, the effect is of a big-band saxophone solo suddenly changed into a squawking, free jazz idiom. Ismaily says simply, "Zorn."

Track 8: Radio Solo / Bandung

0:00–0:45: A hybrid work from Sunda, West Java, entitled "*Malam Minggu*" ("Saturday Night"). In this sample, Sundanese *gamelan* imitates the Western harmonic structure of *kroncong langgam* (hybrid string music). The minor-sounding intonation of the *gamelan* reminds us of the ways in which musical signs can act as homonyms across cultures: While potentially sounding sad to Western listeners, the Indonesian lyrics concern the carefree socializing of young men and women on Saturday night.

0:45–1:05: Classic *dangdut* (Bollywood-inspired pop) likely played by Rhoma Irama, the iconic performer of the form during the 1970s and 1980s. In place of the saccharine lyrics of young love that marked early *dangdut,* Irama's more Islamized version often concerned issues of socioeconomic inequity, sometimes attracting state censure. Ismaily is reminded here of "all of the current fetishizing of 1960s-era production. The sound of the guitar and bass, and the obtuseness of their internal harmonic parts, is brilliant here."

2:57–3:16: Sundanese *kecapi suling* (traditional zither and flute music). Indonesians know very well the Western preference for this genre's calm sounds. *Kecapi suling* permeates the soundscape of Indonesian international airports and expat cafés in Bali. Its repeated appearance on this album undercuts Sublime Frequencies' self-conscious iconoclasm.

3:15–3:53: RRI Bandung marking the 9:00 p.m. hour—just before a reading of the news—sonically heralded by a cuckoo clock and heavily distorted chimes that draw an aesthetic link between the spectra of Western and Indonesian bronze.

5:09–8:46: The album ends with yet another lightly distorted, extended excerpt of *jaipongan*. Ismaily comments, "We are too precious in the Western recording studio; these sounds reminds us that emotion and feeling and space can come through on many kinds of recordings." Candrarini asks, now bored, "Why *jaipongan* again?"

DISTORTION

The prominence of distorted timbres on *Radio Java* reflects an aesthetic affinity with the American experimental underground. There is a preference for the complex, sometimes indeterminate sound of distortion, a sonic sign of independence from both institutional composition and the lossless preoccupations of the recording industry.[21] *Radio Java* presents the overdriven sounds of local low-power stations broadcasting "poorly" recorded live performances of traditional music, the scratchy sounds of old LPs, and the warbling hiss of multi-generation cassettes. This noise reminds us how the signal has been circulated, reproduced, and transformed through various media. To American fans of the experimental, distortion may authenticate these sounds as real, genuine, and raw as compared to the antiseptic, lossless, inauthentic sounds of Western mass culture.

However, according to R. Anderson Sutton, distortion may mean something different to the Javanese ear.[22] The bronze gongs, xylophones, and chimes of the *gamelan* produce complex, inharmonic spectra, and sometimes are designed purposefully to generate buzzing noises and beating, conflicting fundamentals. These instruments, which continue to stand as icons of power, cultural authority, and economic means throughout Java, find a sonic mirror in the complex sounds of the distorted, amplified signal. During the New Order, social prestige and economic status inhered in the traditional instruments of the *gamelan* as well as in large sound systems. The greater a sound system's audible range, the stronger its symbolic power, encouraging users (such as a mosque) to turn them all the way up, often producing distorted timbres. Distortion and disorientation are amplified on *Radio Java* by the apparent placement of the dial between stations, by overlapping original sound files, or by cross-fading.

RESTRICTING INFORMATION — ENCOURAGING
NEW MODES OF LISTENING

Sublime Frequencies' frequent inclusion of only minimal liner notes (*Radio Java* has a 175-word paragraph) has been interpreted as a form of purposeful ambiguation intended to encourage new modes of listening and enliven the sonic imaginations of listeners within the American experimental scene.[23] From an American perspective, Sublime Frequencies' *Radio* releases amplify a sense of serendipitous mystery through the apparently random splicing of old and new, live and recorded, seemingly foreign and local sounds. If we can never put this puzzle back together—or unravel its code—we must relax and luxuriate in endless surprise.

In his review for *Dusted Magazine*, Alexander Provan describes *Radio Java* as a "frustratingly fast train ride through a country you've never seen. Buildings appear and quickly fall back, replaced by villages, deserts, town squares, and bazaars, allowing little time to focus on specifics. Though the rapid cycling of sounds in the 'Radio' recordings makes it difficult for the listener to gain a very concrete conception of the music or the culture itself, the releases are, to some extent, an effort to frustrate the desire to reduce a culture to a single document."[24]

Through frenetic, disorienting channel-surfing, the listener comes ear to ear with the aesthetic heterogeneity of cultures—like Java's—that have, for too long, been boiled down to a single, rarefied, courtly representation.

That Sublime Frequencies does not attempt to label or explain any of the tracks on this disc reminds us of the ways in which ethnomusicologists (and ethnographic filmmakers, art curators, and anthropologists, et al.) consolidate their position through the power to name. Sublime Frequencies chooses not to speak for anyone: It instead publishes sounds unmediated by either academia or the mass music industry.[25] As posted on the blog/zine Blastitude.com:

one of the best things about this label is the way that it removes explanation and agenda and authority so that the music and culture can stand alone . . . Bishop and co. know that you can explain things until you're blue in the face but you'll still never see the whole picture, and who needs to, when the human imagination has so much fun filling in the rest . . . It's been so fresh and exciting, listening to the music of other continents and nations without getting side-tracked by biographical and political detail . . . Instead of reading some white guy's liner notes while I listen, I'm getting out the Rand McNally and opening it to the map of the region I'm listening to, and letting my imagination and sense fill in the rest. Instead of studying and learning minutiae, I'm just FEELING it.[26]

Recalling anthropology's prematurely celebratory embrace of ethnographic film (and Mead and Bateson's earlier interest in ethnographic photography), the *Radio* series permits access to a less biased sampling: a fuller, purer engagement so richly detailed that authority itself appears absent. But *someone's* hand/ear, guided by all the rich complexity of culturally particular taste, assembled this material. This hand/ear decided when to stop the radio dial, how long to leave it there, and how to splice it all together back home—just as Margaret Mead, half a century earlier, decided when and where to open her camera's eye while investigating the "Balinese Personality."[27]

The album arranges side-by-side genres that have evolved through a long historical process in Java. Central Javanese *gamelan* and Sundanese *jaipongan* appear alongside forms more familiar to Western ears, such as *pop Indonesia* and *dangdut*. The former may sound radically different; the latter may only be distinguishable as Indonesian on account of its lyrics. There are many gradations between these two extremes, some of which may sound to Americans like an Indonesian remix of their own culture. To the reviewer Provan: "some of the tracks sound vaguely Hawaiian, some resemble Bollywood soundtracks, some call to mind languorous electrified pop." *Kroncong* and *langgam* evolved from European string instruments and song forms first introduced to the islands by the Portuguese in the sixteenth century. The Hawaiian craze washed over Indonesia in several waves beginning in the late nineteenth century, influencing both these forms as well as Indonesian jazz, light song, and other forms of popular music. Bollywood films were distributed widely through Indonesia beginning in the 1950s; their hybrid soundtracks would influence the development of Indonesian *dangdut*, also heard on *Radio Java*. What appears to be straightforward Western influence on the album is in fact the manifestation of highly complex, circuitous appropriations and feedback loops. Hearing the apparently local as foreign may perform the kind of aesthetic challenge (understood as allegorical) found in the historical avant-garde, the neo-avant-garde (e.g., Fluxus) and its progeny in contemporary American experimentalism.

NOTES

1. Although such preservation efforts can be traced back to the colonial era, they became especially energized during the early New Order (1966–1998), Indonesia's second totalitarian regime led by general Suharto.

2. Sublime Frequencies. *Radio Java,* liner notes, 2003.

3. David Novak, "The Sublime Frequencies of New Old Media," *Public Culture* 23, no. 3 (2011): 603–34.

4. Ibid., 604.

5. Clive Bell, "Sublime Frequencies: The Secret Life," *The Wire* 303 (2009): 28–33.

6. Quoted in Erik Davis, "Cameo Demons: Hanging with the Sun City Girls," www.techgnosis.com/scg.html, 2003 (accessed February 20, 2012).

7. Cf. Novak, "The Sublime Frequencies of New Old Media," 623.

8. Ibid., 604; Henry Jenkins, *Convergence Culture: Where Old and New Media Collide* (New York: New York University Press, 2008).

9. Wayne Marshall, "Whirl-a-whirls." http://wayneandwax.com/?p=146, 2007 (accessed March 10, 2012).

10. Bell, "Sublime Frequencies," 33.

11. Novak, "The Sublime Frequencies of New Old Media," 621.

12. Earlier sources on Indonesian popular music include Peter Manuel and Randall Baier, "Jaipongan: Indigenous Popular Music of West Java," *Asian Music* 18, no. 1 (1986): 91–110; Craig Lockard, *Dance of Life: Popular Music and Politics in Southeast Asia* (Honolulu: University of Hawaii Press, 1998); William Frederick, "Rhoma Irama and the Dangdut Style: Aspects of Contemporary Indonesian Popular Culture," *Indonesia* 34 (1982): 102–30; Phillip Yampolsky, *Lokananta: A Discography of the National Recording Company of Indonesia, 1957–1985* (Madison, Wisc.: Center for Southeast Asian Studies, University of Wisconsin, 1987); Yampolsky, "Hati Yang Luka: an Indonesian Hit," *Indonesia* 47 (1989): 1–17; Judith Becker, "Kroncong, Indonesian Popular Music," *Asian Music* 7, no. 1 (1975): 14–19; and Ernst Heins, "Kroncong and Tanjidor: Two Cases of Urban Folk Music in Jakarta," *Asian Music* 7, no. 1 (1975): 20–32. Important, and more detailed later sources include Emma Baulch, *Making Scenes: Reggae, Punk, and Death Metal in 1990s Bali* (Durham, N.C.: Duke University Press, 2007); Jeremy Wallach, *Modern Noise, Fluid Genre: Popular Music in Indonesia* (Madison: University of Wisconsin Press, 2008); and Andrew Weintraub, *Dangdut Stories: A Social and Musical History of Indonesia's Most Popular Music* (New York: Oxford University Press, 2010).

13. Bell, "Sublime Frequencies."

14. Douglas Wolk, "Invention Shakes," http://www.lacunae.com/archives/2004/01/, 2004 (accessed Feb 25, 2012).

15. Full disclosure: I have known and performed on and off with Ismaily since 1993. I have known Candrarini since 2002, when she and I performed together in an experimental ensemble led by the Balinese composer I Wayan Sadra. Candrarini was interviewed for this chapter on February 8, 2012; her Indonesian commentary was translated by the author. Ismaily was interviewed on February 12, 2012.

16. Alexander Provan, "Pirate Radio International: The Sounds of Sublime Frequencies." http://www.dustedmagazine.com/features/228, 2011 (accessed February 25, 2012).

17. Henry Spiller, *Erotic Triangles: Sundanese Dance and Masculinity in West Java.* Chicago: University of Chicago Press, 2010.

18. Manuel and Baier, "Jaipongan."

19. See R. Anderson Sutton, "Musical Genre and Hybridity in Indonesia: *Simponi Kecapi* and *Campur Sari,*" *Asian Music* 44, no. 2 (2013): 81–94; Yampolsky, "Three Genres of Indonesian Popular Music: Genre, Hybridity, and Globalization, 1960–2012," *Asian Music* 44, no. 2 (2013): 24–80.

20. See Yampolsky, "Three Genres of Indonesian Popular Music."

21. Novak, "The Sublime Frequencies of New Old Media," 608.

22. R. Anderson Sutton, "Interpreting Electronic Sound Technology in the Contemporary Javanese Soundscape," *Ethnomusicology* 40 (1996): 249–68.

23. Cf. Novak, "The Sublime Frequencies of New Old Media"; Provan, "Pirate Radio International"; Marcus Boon, "Sublime Frequencies' Ethnopsychedelic Montages," *Electronic Book Review,* www.electronicbookreview.com/thread/musicsoundnoise/ethnopsyche, 2006 (accessed March 18, 2012); Blastitude.com/SUBLIMEFREQUENCIES.htm (accessed February 20, 2012).

24. Provan, "Pirate Radio International."

25. *Pop Yeh Yeh,* a Sublime Frequencies rerelease of Malaysian pop from 1964 to 1970 (SF079) includes a highly informational 40-page booklet organized by DJ Carl Hamm that approaches Yampolsky's Folkways liner notes in its level of detail. The occasional inclusion of such notes would seem to undercut the impression that the foreshortened notes accompanying most Sublime Frequencies releases are part of a consistent philosophical approach.

26. Blastitude.com.

27. Margaret Mead and Gregory Bateson, *Balinese Character: A Photographic Analysis* (New York: New York Academy of Sciences, 1942).

BIBLIOGRAPHY

Baulch, Emma. *Making Scenes: Reggae, Punk, and Death Metal in 1990s Bali.* Durham, N.C.: Duke University Press, 2007.

Becker, Judith. "Kroncong, Indonesian Popular Music." *Asian Music* 7, no. 1 (1975): 14–19.

Bell, Clive. "Sublime Frequencies: The Secret Life." *The Wire* 303 (2009): 28–33.

Blastitude.com/SUBLIMEFREQUENCIES.htm (accessed February 20, 2012).

Boon, Marcus. "Sublime Frequencies' Ethnopsychedelic Montages." *Electronic Book Review.* www.electronicbookreview.com/thread/musicsoundnoise/ethnopsyche, 2006 (accessed March 18, 2012).

Davis, Erik. "Cameo Demons: Hanging with the Sun City Girls." www.techgnosis.com/scg.html, 2003 (accessed February 20, 2012).

Frederick, William. "Rhoma Irama and the Dangdut Style: Aspects of Contemporary Indonesian Popular Culture." *Indonesia* 34 (1982):102–30.

Heins, Ernst. "Kroncong and Tanjidor: Two Cases of Urban Folk Music in Jakarta." *Asian Music* 7, no. 1 (1975): 20–32.

Jenkins, Henry. *Convergence Culture: Where Old and New Media Collide.* New York: New York University Press, 2008.

Lockard, Craig. *Dance of Life: Popular Music and Politics in Southeast Asia.* Honolulu: University of Hawaii Press, 1998.

Manuel, Peter, and Randall Baier. "Jaipongan: Indigenous Popular Music of West Java." *Asian Music* 18, no. 1 (1986): 91–110.

Marshall, Wayne. "Whirl-a-whirls." http://wayneandwax.com/?p=146, 2007 (accessed March 10, 2012).

Mead, Margaret, and Gregory Bateson. *Balinese Character: A Photographic Analysis.* New York: New York Academy of Sciences, 1942.

Novak, David. "The Sublime Frequencies of New Old Media." *Public Culture* 23, no. 3 (2011): 603–34.

Provan, Alexander. "Pirate Radio International: The Sounds of Sublime Frequencies." http://www.dustedmagazine.com/features/228, 2011 (accessed February 25, 2012).

Spiller, Henry. *Erotic Triangles: Sundanese Dance and Masculinity in West Java.* Chicago: University of Chicago Press, 2010.

Sublime Frequencies. *Radio Java,* liner notes, 2003.

Sutton, R. Anderson. "Interpreting Electronic Sound Technology in the Contemporary Javanese Soundscape." *Ethnomusicology* 40 (1996): 249–68.

———. "Musical Genre and Hybridity in Indonesia: *Simponi Kecapi* and *Campur Sari.*" *Asian Music* 44, no. 2 (2013): 81–94.

Wallach, Jeremy. *Modern Noise, Fluid Genre: Popular Music in Indonesia.* Madison: University of Wisconsin Press, 2008.

Weintraub, Andrew. *Dangdut Stories: A Social and Musical History of Indonesia's Most Popular Music.* New York: Oxford University Press, 2010.

Wolk, Douglas. "Invention Shakes." http://www.lacunae.com/archives/2004/01/, 2004 (accessed Feb 25, 2012).

Yampolsky, Phillip. "Hati Yang Luka: an Indonesian Hit." *Indonesia* 47 (1989): 1–17.

———. *Lokananta: A Discography of the National Recording Company of Indonesia, 1957–1985.* Madison, Wisc.: Center for Southeast Asian Studies, University of Wisconsin, 1987.

———. "Three Genres of Indonesian Popular Music: Genre, Hybridity, and Globalization, 1960–2012." *Asian Music* 44, no. 2 (2013): 24–80.

E. TAMMY KIM

Noraebang with the Dear Leader

Sublime Frequencies' *Radio Pyongyang*

Listening to the CD *Radio Pyongyang*, I find myself in a *karaoke* lounge, subjected to flashing strobes, watered-down whiskey, ear-blasting synth, and brittle falsetto. It's the musical equivalent of fluorescent lighting, illuminating but jarringly artificial. That such exuberance comes from a land of East Bloc grey and scant electricity makes it all more the extraordinary, if ethically dubious. The eight tracks of *Radio Pyongyang* are a time machine back to 1950s Korea, when the nation was freshly divided but still joined by the frenetic pulse of *bbongjjak*-style pop (뽕짝). This dated genre reigns supreme on the album—a sign of decades-long stylistic isolation and a perfect conveyance for propaganda. Consistent with North Korea's state-sponsored visual art, every message, every lyric is multiplied synthetically, as though spoken or sung by an entire people. *Radio Pyongyang*'s collage of shortwave radio emissions, field-recorded performances, television, and archival sounds pays homage to former Supreme Leader Kim Jong-il (김정일) and the *juche* ethnonationalism (주체성) of the Democratic People's Republic of Korea.[1] Aimed at domestic and international audiences, the regime's broadcast network, formerly called "Radio Pyongyang," invokes the language of "Yankee bastards" to brand itself the "Voice of Korea."

In this essay, I analyze Sublime Frequencies' *Radio Pyongyang* in musical and sociopolitical contexts, going beyond its self-description as "Schmaltzy synthpop, Revolutionary rock, Cheeky child rap, and a healthy dose of hagiography for Dear Leader Kim Jong-il."[2] I begin by providing some background on the Korean peninsula—the recent histories of colonization and war, culminating in physical division and the North's alienation from world geopolitics and art—that must

Radio Pyongyang: Commie Funk and Pop from the Hermit Kingdom (SF023) implicitly critiques the Western demonization of North Korea and is one of two Sublime Frequencies albums "from" the Korean peninsula.

frame our understanding of radio and cultural production. Second, I investigate the popular styles and sources of the album, which include *bbongjjak*, karaoke, and patriotic and military anthems. Compared to other Sublime Frequencies radio-collage discs, *Radio Pyongyang* compiles fewer, less readily available materials captured largely outside the DPRK—much of it baffling and ugly but also ripe with musical nostalgia, whimsy, and a certain brand of hope. In the third and final section, I evaluate the fit between radio collage as a form and North Korea as a subject, inquiring whether the album reveals anything new about the cult of Kim and its particular brand of esoteric, ethnonationalist "communism." From my perspective, colored by my Korean-American identity, radio collage gives apt, if inevitably incomplete, expression to the reality of North Korea, short-circuiting judgments too often shaped by Western media pronouncements. *Radio Pyongyang* offers open-textured access to a place we don't and can't really know, provoking equal amounts of wonder and dismay.

THE BLACK BOX OF (NORTH) KOREA

Journalist Barbara Demick's book, *Nothing to Envy*, begins with an inset satellite image of the Korean peninsula.[3] It is night and the northern half is solidly black, save the speck of white light indicating Pyongyang, the capital. Beyond North Korea's arbitrary border, southward into the other Korea, the world's most wired country, black gives way to a confetti saturation of illumination. The perfect literal and figurative representation of a loner nation, shrouded in secrets, a darkness borne of energy shortages and stubborn insularity; so much we do not and care not to know.

Between my first and final drafts of this essay, as revolts and mass protests took place all over the world, North Korea experienced its own change in leadership. It was, of course, anything but revolutionary: The reins were passed from father Kim Jong-il to son Kim Jong-un (김정은), just as they had a generation before. North Korean citizens mourned Kim Jong-il's death as aggressively, and theatrically, as it had his father's in 1994: Thin penitents kept up their wailing and made repeat visits to Kim Il-sung's (김일성) statute "because there were sticky rice cakes handed out after you bowed."[4]

Early on, there were hopes that Kim Jong-un might modernize Pyongyang. Much was made of his youth and the private education he'd received in Switzerland, bastion of liberalism. His body, though, bore its own logic. Tall, barrel-chested, and square-jawed, with severely parted hair and a dark Mao suit, he was his grandfather, Great Leader Kim Il-sung, resurrected and rejuvenated.

A corporeal reprise—and a spiritual one. Kim Jong-un's first months in office were as showy and belligerent as his predecessors'. Nicknamed the "Outstanding Leader," his portrait was hung beside his father's and grandfather's on countless North Korean walls. Since 2012, he has sparred plenty with the United States and South Korea: sharp-tongued ultimatums, UN sanctions, launched missiles, naval exercises, American bomber flights over the Korean peninsula, and imprisoned U.S. citizens paraded on North Korean TV. In February 2013, the same month that Park Geun-hye (박근혜) became the first female president of South Korea, Kim Jong-un stole the show—by hosting former NBA Bulls forward Dennis Rodman on a sensational publicity tour sponsored by the media company VICE.[5] The following year, in an even more bizarre episode, the United States accused North Korea of hacking Sony Entertainment in advance of the company's release of *The Interview*, a comedic film depicting the assassination of Kim Jong-un.[6]

All this has only augmented the image of the DPRK represented by George W. Bush's diatribes, newspaper photos of emaciated children, the satirical marionette film *Team America's* villainous Kim Jong-il, and the once viral Tumblr blog "kim jong-il looking at things," which, until a year after his death, posted photos of the ever-didactic Dear Leader providing "on-site guidance," that is, literally looking and pointing at things, such as ham and bras, while his assistants jotted down notes.[7] Such stereotypical images of North Korea, not dissimilar to those of Stalin and Mao, are entertaining but weak—and easily accessible—versions of reality. For us Americans, despite our country's active role in the making and unmaking of modern Korea, we imagine the North to have emerged from a void: a totalitarian state suddenly, inexplicably thrust onto our geopolitical radar.

The real history is clear enough. In 1905, negotiating the end of a brief war between Japan and Russia, the United States effectively sanctioned colonization of modern Korea. Japan took control in 1910, asserting brutal cultural and political domination, and then, during World War II, mobilizing Koreans as forced laborers, soldiers, and sexual slaves. The war's end brought false liberation, for Korea was immediately divided at the 38th parallel: The United States occupied Seoul and the southern half; the north went to the USSR. But leftist guerrillas remained active in the south, pushing Soviet-backed Pyongyang to decide "to escalate the civil conflict to the level of conventional warfare many months before June 1950," the official start of Korea's civil war.[8] What ensued was arguably the most violent and futile "conflict" of the twentieth century, a three-year war that ended where it began, at the 38th parallel. Called the "demilitarized zone" (DMZ), it is the world's most heavily militarized border.

Out of the Korean War emerged Great Leader Kim Il-sung, freedom fighter and leader of a new, northern communist state. The DPRK developed its *juche* ideology, a brand of anticolonial (anti-U.S., anti-Japanese) self-determination—"a principle of not wanting to be controlled by others"—tinged with the ethnonationalist, imperial cult of Kim.[9] Building on this unifying theory, and with substantial backing by the USSR and China, North Korea fared well until the 1970s, even outpacing the south.[10] The regime grew increasingly insular, however, and lost Soviet and Chinese support—both before and then dramatically after the fall of the USSR. By the time Dear Leader Kim Jong-il succeeded his father in the mid-1990s, North Korea was suffering extreme shortages of fuel, food, and other supplies. These conditions, compounded with national disasters, produced a famine of devastating scale and established the DPRK as an impoverished, bizarre rogue state in the eyes of the world.[11]

CULTURE IN ISOLATION

Little in the way of information or culture, let alone population, has gone in or come out of North Korea for many decades. Even before the Korean War, there were concerns that North Korea had been shut off for too long, prompting the United States to devise a popular-media campaign targeting the rural masses.[12] This "reorientation" plan was never implemented, and citizens of the DPRK still suffer a closed input loop: The country consistently ranks last or second-to-last in Reporters Without Borders' annual Press Freedom Index; it did, however, allow the Associated Press to open a Pyongyang bureau in January 2012.[13] The outside world seeps in, nevertheless, through the erratically porous Chinese border and chaperoned tourism to the capital.

The North Korean arts bear the stamp of isolation. In 1966, Kim Il-sung called for new *juche* art, "a revolutionary and people-oriented art form that is national in form with socialist content," paraphrasing earlier statements by Mao and Stalin.[14] What this has meant in practice is a socialist realist style marked by a "wholesale condemnation of any kind of abstract art."[15] Like that produced under Mao, Stalin, Hitler, and Hussein, North Korean art fits the generic totalitarian mold, reflecting neither left nor right but attempting to consolidate a single vantage point: "the statues looming over every town square, the portraits hung in every office, the wristwatches with the dictator's face on the dial."[16] As art historian Jane Portal observes of the monumental statutes in Pyongyang: They also show that ideas about the purpose of sculptural images have changed little in North Korea since the 1950s. In fact, this is probably true of most forms of art in North Korea, since there is little exposure to any new ideas from outside and little scope for innovative ideas from within.[17]

Not only style but subject matter, too: farming, military campaigns, factories, and schools. Particularly since the fall of the Soviet Union, an event that all but eliminated cultural exchange with Russia, North Korean artists have few opportunities to bring back new forms and notions, and the DPRK repudiates the individual expression so closely associated with art-production in the West. As summed up by Ri Yun Mi, an acting student at Pyongyang's University of Cinematic and Dramatic Arts, "Films made in capitalist countries are commercial products. Movies in our country bring out the idea of the people."[18]

The philosophy of artistic production is, like many things, genetically and mythically linked to the DPRK leadership. Kim Il-sung was reportedly a church organist in his youth—the regime does not like to emphasize that he was born to a practicing Christian mother—and kept an organ in his emergency bunker. Kim Jong-il was a notorious movie fanatic and sometime aesthetician who reportedly authored didactic tracts such as *On the Art of Cinema, On Fine Art,* and *On the Art of Music.*[19] The walls of North Korea's academies feature plaques engraved with his wisdom: for example, "The cultural arts should robustly support *juche* and unwaveringly embody party ideology, the spirit of workers, and humanism."[20] Indeed, the merit of visual and performing arts, TV, and radio is measured by adherence to the regime's party line rather than artistic innovation. Kim Jong-il proclaimed succinctly, "Juche is the life of our music."[21] Current supreme leader Kim Jong-un is married to a former singer and state cheerleader, Ri Sol-ju, who was initially, scandalously, identified as Hyon Song-wol, a married member of the Pochonbo Electronic Ensemble (more on this below).[22] Just six months into his tenure, he had his own national song, "Onwards Toward the Final Victory" ("최후의 승리를 향하여 앞으로").[23]

Most North Korean art is produced by state-sponsored groups, such as the 3,700-person Mansudae (만수대) collective responsible for Pyongyang's monuments, or the popular entertainment groups Wangjaesan Light Music Band (왕재산 경음악단) and Pochonbo Electronic Ensemble (보천보전자악단), named after a raid by Kim Il-sung on the Japanese in 1937.[24] Within the boundaries of the state's ideological and stylistic system—Keith Howard has called this music "authorized pop"—Pochonbo and Wangjaesan have perfected a retrograde kitsch of flashy, sped-up pop-rock (with keyboards, electric guitars, saxophone, vocals, and drum set), conservative choreography, and modestly tailored but fluorescent and sequined costumes.[25] Performers work in this vein at North Korea's state-sanctioned, high-end restaurants abroad, in countries such as Cambodia, Nepal, and Bangladesh, "dressed in *hanbok,* a billowing, traditional Korean dress, wear[ing] permanent smiles as they play a Western-style drum set, electric guitars and accordion—and demurely shuffle across the stage."[26]

There is a remarkable consistency across public speech and vocal music in North Korea, nearly always delivered with uncanny vigor, frozen smiles, heaven-tilted eyes, operatic vibrato, and heavy melisma. Such thoroughgoing kitsch "counteracts the harmful forces that jeopardize the North Korean leaders' hold on power."[27] We hear this unerringly on North Korean radio and on the collaged tracks of *Radio Pyongyang,* the name of the official radio station (평양방송) until 2002, when it was renamed the Voice of Korea.[28] The station plays the national anthem ad nauseam, as well as broadcasts of the Korean Central News Agency, music, and entertainment programs. With a literally captive audience of 25 million residents, Voice of Korea has the world's largest listener base.[29] Every DPRK household and business receives a "government-controlled radio hardwired to [this] central station. The speaker comes with a volume control, but no off switch."[30] In the excellent documentary *A State of Mind*, which traces the lives of two young North Korean gymnasts preparing for the national Mass Games, a little oblong radio blares incessantly from the kitchen wall.[31] And neither are visitors immune: a friend who worked in Pyongyang for several years recalls being able to adjust the volume but not extinguish the radio completely in her Pyongyang hotel room.[32]

Radio has enjoyed a long history on the Korean peninsula. From Japanese rule and the Korean civil war to loudspeakers blaring across the DMZ, government-sponsored radio has served as a vehicle for "public diplomacy."[33] In contemporary North Korean defector narratives, radio figures prominently. Every story of escape, every defiance of the prohibition against out-travel, involves a radio subplot: intercepted South Korean programming that "suggested life there was better," descriptions of the outside world that put life in perspective, or a gradual questioning of propagandistic news.[34] As the primary mass-communication technology in the DPRK, radio takes on exaggerated importance and becomes a critical target of foreign interests (namely South Korean, American, and Christian) wishing to "change the hearts and minds" of the North Korean people. Kim Seong Min, a former defector who has made a name and business of assisting others coming through China, operates Free North Korea Radio, which he sells to donors as a reverse propaganda mechanism.[35] (Critics contend that his emissions, five hours daily, are largely for show and fail to reach listeners inside the DPRK.[36]) Thousands of balloons containing unfixed, freely tuned radios have been flown and dropped across the border in recent years, and humanitarian groups plan to smuggle some 100,000 radios through China in the near future.[37] Persuasive messaging comes in many forms: South Korean soap operas are a popular subversion; and in 2010, following the sinking of the *Cheonan*, a South Korean ship, the South Korean military began blasting musical FM propaganda. "Pop music can be a powerful psychological weapon targeting the oppressed in the North," stated a conservative South Korean activist.[38]

North Korea, too, creates and broadcasts radio programming in nine languages for those outside the DPRK.[39] A fascinating sampling of English-language short-wave is available at northkoreanradio.com, which posts transmissions aimed at and captured by listeners abroad.[40] In addition to the national anthem and some other music, these broadcasts include domestic and international "news" (in accented but sophisticated English) of global conferences devoted to Great Leader Kim Il-sung's *juche* idea and productivity reports from the North Korean manufacturing and agricultural sectors. Reliance on shortwave, a far-floating Cold War technology, seems particularly well-suited to a country politically and physically situated in another time.

STYLE AND SOURCES OF THE ALBUM

It is against this cultural backdrop that I hear *Radio Pyongyang*, one of Sublime Frequencies' hugely popular radio-collage albums and the label's only East Asian pop album.[41] While production and sales figures for the label are unavailable, this 2005 CD-only release, subtitled *Commie Funk and Agit Pop from the Hermit Kingdom*, sold out long ago and is now available via download only—excepting the $90 copy available, as of July 5, 2013, via the amazon.com marketplace.[42]

Radio Pyongyang is the work of recorder-compiler Christiaan Virant, of the Beijing-based FM3 sound duo, who obtained and assembled these snippets over the course of a decade.[43] His liner notes explain that he'd collected pieces for the collage while "sitting in my Hong Kong flat" and "tun[ing] regularly to the Radio Pyongyang short-wave broadcasts," and "while on a short visit to the North." He appears to have culled "excellent archive material" from pyongyang-metro. com as well, and its proprietor Simon Bone is duly thanked. The album's design credit goes to Alexandra Czinczel, a London-based book and multimedia artist (www.thechinchilla.com).

The disc comprises eight tracks of collage, with categories of sources listed as "hypnotic North Korean number lists," "DPRK pop and revolutionary pomp," "live recordings from various performances in North Korea," "People's Army television dramas, captures from Mass Games demonstrations, samples from hard-to-find CD releases obtained in the North and, of course, news reports from the 'real' Radio Pyongyang."[44] In the universe of Sublime Frequencies radio-collage works, *Radio Pyongyang* boasts fewer discrete sound materials and corresponding seams. Each track maintains a relatively smooth skin, with a minimum of rapid, collagist fluctuation. This even aural surface might be explained in two ways: first, due to the difficulty of obtaining North Korean materials, longer stretches of musical works and sound recordings are used; and second, even when shorter sections are collaged and overlaid, their stylistic homogeneity produces a less jagged sound.

Virant's extraterritorial capture of DPRK radio underscores the difficulty of obtaining materials straight from the source.[45] One wonders how much of *Radio*

Pyongyang is the result of actual travel and recording on location in the DPRK. How and when did Virant have occasion to travel to Pyongyang? Was it difficult for him to tape live performances and leave the country with them in hand?[46] These questions of acquisition and geography are not limited to *Radio Pyongyang* either. The materials for *Choubi Choubi! Folk and Pop Sounds from Iraq* are in fact "excerpts from Iraqi cassettes and LPs found in Syria, Europe and the Iraqi neighborhoods of Detroit, Michigan."[47] And the songs for *Cambodian Cassette Archives: Khmer Folk and Pop Music Vol. 1* are "culled from over 150 ravaged cassettes found in Oakland, California, at the public library's Asian branch."[48] The geopolitical upheaval of these locales becomes embodied in the temporal and physical dislocations of form—collage and compilation.

Three musical traditions are prominent on *Radio Pyongyang*: *trot* (트로트) or *bbongjjak* (Virant's "Schmaltzy synthpop"), *noraebang* (노래방) singing ("Tokyo karaoke"), and patriotic song ("Revolutionary rock"). With respect to the first referent, the long, prominent song excerpts on the disc may remind Western listeners of commercial, big-band orchestra and shuffle or swing styles from the interwar period in Europe and America. But it is in fact an East Asian adaptation with roots in the early twentieth century. Koreans call it *trot* (teu-ro-teu), after foxtrot, or, more commonly, *bbongjjak*; in Japan it is known as *enka*. This genre incorporates elements of traditional Korean folk and Western popular musics, especially the romantic ballad. *Bbongjjak* is characterized by sappy lyrics; a brisk, upbeat 4–4; nearly constant melisma and vibrato in the vocals; and loud, oscillating, synthetic instrumentation.

Min-Jung Son has defined *trot* as a "South Korean sentimental love song style performed with an abundance of vocal inflections."[49] In its 1950s' and 1960s' heyday, *trot*—after the couple-style dance the "foxtrot" popular in Asia's mid-century U.S. military clubs—was made to fulfill the dual political agenda of catering to U.S. military tastes and being anti-Japanese/anti-Communist in tonality and lyrics, a rather abstruse requirement.[50] At its core, most *trot* is about love, expressed through the idea of the missing beloved or, in Korean, *nim* (님).[51] Korean *trot* comes in many styles, from Nam Jin's danceable *bbongjjak* to the traditional form practiced by balladeer Na Hoonah, all of which have inspired revivalist attempts by young, new artists.[52] The old classics are still revered, however: In May 2010, after North Korea's sinking of a South Korean naval vessel, Seoul restarted its practice of beaming FM radio propaganda across the DMZ, including songs by Na Hoonah and other trot artists; in September 2011, Nam Jin, age 66, performed to stadium-size crowds in Seoul to celebrate the forty-fifth anniversary of his debut.[53]

The type of *bbongjjak* featured on *Radio Pyongyang* owes much to the "*trot* medley" format whereby individual *trot* songs are linked together and amplified with echo effects, double-tracked vocals, danceable rhythms, and MIDI-instrumentation.[54] In the 1980s, with the advent of cassette and synthesizer technologies, trade in cheaply made *trot*-medley mixtapes became ubiquitous on the streets of South Korea, "commodified as an everyday part of life, particularly for working-class people."[55] These cassettes leaked into North Korea as well via the Chinese border town of Yanbian, which is populated increasingly by ethnic Koreans.[56] As a sentimental yet danceable ballad, *bbongjjak* in general and *trot* medley in particular typically have been associated with lower-class city dwellers or country rubes, and are redolent of seedy postwar nightclubs and open-air markets. It is a popular form to deride, but all Koreans find it familiar and most even like it.

We hear *trot* and *trot* medley throughout *Radio Pyongyang*. At the level of song, the mostly female vocalists inflect pentatonic melodies with generous amounts of melisma and vibrato. This style is not terribly different from indigenous singing traditions, but here, nostalgic odes to one's lover and nation have replaced older songs of work, family, war, and destiny. Likewise, the subtle *changgu* folk-drum accompaniment has given way to hyperactive synthetic accordions, aggressive percussion, laser sounds, and orchestra. *Radio Pyongyang* collages these disparate musical bytes in a manner that echoes the *trot*-medley cassette. Wild sounds and piano riffs act as glue, fusing Virant's collected recordings and musical ideas, like so many *bbongjjak* numbers. These transitions draw our attention all the more to what's between them, paralleling the dried-glue protrusions and paper edges of physical collage.

A second influence on *Radio Pyongyang* is not so much a musical style as a spatially rooted practice of *trot* and other popular music. *Noraebang*, literally "singing rooms" in Korean, are enclosed, rentable rooms equipped with a *karaoke* machine and monitors, a bass-heavy sound system, colorful lighting and strobes, microphones, vinyl booth seats, tambourines, and usually a good amount of booze. They often are staffed by "hostesses," slim, attractive women who pour drinks and sing along with guests. In South Korea and Korean immigrant areas of the United States, *noraebang* exist at all price points and corresponding levels of fanciness. They are a gathering place on dates, post-business meetings, and school reunions for people of all classes—a space to let loose and perform communal catharsis of *han*, that most Korean sentiment of longing and regret. This is no different in Pyongyang's foreigner hotels, upscale bars, and diplomatic enclave, where tourists and foreign workers let loose in *noraebang* featuring dancing hostesses and Western sing-along repertoire.[57] A friend who recently traveled to Pyongyang spent the last day of her journey singing karaoke with her minders. All the South Korean songs had been deleted, but there were songs from Japan, China, and the United States. She sang Frank Sinatra's "Fly Me to the Moon," a rather poignant selection.[58]

Layered atop *noraebang* singing culture and *bbongjjak* is the DPRK's martial music, the third tradition on *Radio Pyongyang*. Marching male choirs, steady snares, cymbals, violins, and brass signal patriotic fervor and recall North Korean military songs and revolutionary opera (혁명가극). As ethnomusicologist Donna Lee Kwon writes: "Certain elements of Western music have been adopted to become symbolic markers for not only modernity but, more important, revolutionary change. For example, leading up to the Korean War and beyond, diatonic choral harmony, military marchlike rhythms and structured, anthemlike melodies signaled revolution and progress; they helped to 'awaken a new political consciousness.'"[59]

The military feel is audible, even in the absence of lexical cues, but there's no lack of direct reference. Most tracks feature spoken praise of the regime, in Korean as well as English. A man's imperfect, radio-intoned English is heard at length on "Arirang" (Track 6), the theme for the 2002 Mass Games, Pyongyang's enormous, celebratory spectacle of music, acrobatics, and visual propaganda. We hear his stilted voice over a symphonically rendered folk melody:

> In this warm and fine season of 2002, Pyongyang will give a mass gymnastic and artistic performance entitled "Arirang." The performance will fill the grand dimensional space of a stadium with 150,000 seats and wonderful kaleidoscopic artistic scenes and ever-changing mysterious pictures of backdrops all combined with a display of super-large screens and the lights of laser illuminations. The applications for audience of this performance are increasing, arousing great interest of foreigners all over the world.[60]

This is typical of the advertisements on Voice of Korea, which emphasize the participatory nature of mass spectacle and take pain to highlight foreign interest in North Korea.

Patriotism is expressed less directly through the album's repetition of the "Song of General Kim Il-sung" (1946). Distinct from the official *Aegukga* national anthem (1947), which references neither the Kim family nor communism, the Great Leader's song is the nation's unofficial, more ubiquitous song.[61] Its first phrase—a repeated, dotted-rhythm C-E-F-G sequence—not only marks the programming transitions on Voice of Korea, but also rings from the bells in Pyongyang's main square.[62] Toward the end of "Motherland Megamix" (Track 1), these notes sound in slow, pulsating, electronic form to interrupt a rapid, ascending C scale. This eerily calming refrain is followed by a male then female voice announcing in English, "This is Radio Pyongyang of the Democratic People's Republic of Korea."

The Korean lyrics to *Radio Pyongyang*'s excerpted tunes reveal the full extent of musical propaganda. The tune dominating "Motherland Megamix" and "Motherland Redux" (Track 8) refrains in Korean: "Comrade Kim Jong-il . . . Without you, we are nothing! Without you, our country is nothing!" A piercing falsetto on "Pride of the Nation" (Track 4) proclaims, "You are our leader. You are our destiny." And the cloying children's chorus on "Start 'Em Young" (Track 5) refers to Kim Il-sung as "father." The first half of "Commie Funk" (Track 7), a *trot* love song entitled "Don't Ask My Name," performed by the state-sponsored Pochonbo Electronic Ensemble, offers only a brief reprieve from homages to the Dear Leader.

In addition to national praise, *Radio Pyongyang* delivers on the fantasy of Korean reunification. "Arirang" (Track 7), which riffs on Korea's most famous folk song, moves from a *garak* (가락) (traditional, scripted rhythm) played on Western instruments but approximating Korean folk percussion into a chorus of "*Reunified* Arirang." "New Model Army" (Track 2) begins with the aspirational song "Reunification Rainbow," whose exuberant Pochonbo sopranos plead: "7,000,000, let's be one again . . . from Baekdu Mountain to Halla Mountain." "Numbers Game" (Track 3), perhaps the album's most sophisticated assemblage, deftly juxtaposes Voice of Korea's enigmatic recitation of numbers against ambient electronic accompaniment, a patriotic *trot* song, spoken reference to the DMZ (*panmunjeom* [판문점]) and historic dates, sounds of exploding bombs, and, to top things off, an electric guitar solo fading into the distance.

STRUGGLING TO REALLY HEAR

On a first listen, Sublime Frequencies' sonically fluorescing, rough-edged *Radio Pyongyang* seems to say nothing new about the DPRK. The music, like the album art composed of monumental works dotting tourist Pyongyang, leave a predictable impression of alienating style and illegible substance, and not merely because of the language barrier. The disc is both over- and underdetermined in meaning. It is overdetermined at the level of its individual components, which, as products of the state, avoid abstraction to speak univocally for the cult of Kim. The repetition, echo effects, and voice multiplication endeavor to convey unanimous support for the regime, as observed by writer Suki Kim, who accompanied the New York Philharmonic on its trip to North Korea in 2007: "The thing about revisiting Pyongyang . . . is that everything is on repeat. The sites one is allowed to see are the same. The images all bear the faces of the father and the son. The songs recycle the same chorus."[63] On *Radio Pyongyang*, proliferating, chronic mention of Kim Jong-il, Kim Il-sung, *juche*, and the DPRK haunt the listener the way Lenin's "omnipresent images" haunted Russian poet Joseph Brodsky: "Whatever there was in plentitude I immediately regarded as some sort of propaganda," he wrote.[64]

For all its relentless emphasis, *Radio Pyongyang* is paradoxically underdetermined in its fragmentary, collagist treatment of language and music. Virant's sonic assemblage defeats any intended monopoly of meaning, for we cannot easily deduce what, if anything, it is trying to "say." How should we feel about radio propaganda? Is the music being critiqued or savored or both? Do Virant and Sublime Frequencies intend to editorialize DPRK politics and culture? The radio-collage format produces a reticence born of chaos. Its failure to speak directly, to articulate a message, forces the listener to dig beyond the music's shimmering surface. *Radio Pyongyang* thereby offers a unique and comparatively unmediated encounter with North Korean cultural products.

At a linguistic level, save the spoken sections in English, the album is impenetrable to most of Sublime Frequencies' European and American listener base. But Virant's decision not to include translations in the liner notes is purposeful and consistent with his desire to compile "my own personal Radio Pyongyang." His choice to leave the material open-ended and individualized accords with Sublime Frequencies' overall approach, as recently explained by co-owner Hisham Mayet: "[Translation]'s an aesthetic decision and a moral one, for me. . . . I've had issues in the past—I really want it to be about the music, I want to hit on that visceral level. And to sit there and have translations of all the lyrics just doesn't quite do it for me on an aesthetic level, and on a kind of musical level. . . . By decoding it, it loses its power. I could have 30 pages of liner notes in every release, but to us that's just a waste of time."[65]

While this curatorial position is controversial, it works well in the case of *Radio Pyongyang*. As a culture, the DPRK is acutely inaccessible to us outsiders, yet the album indeed "hit[s] on that visceral level." Music and sound come straight from the regime to us via shortwave, bypassing stereotyped, Western news-mediated descriptions. We are uncomfortably transported, agitated by unfamiliar styles and left wondering what is being said or sung.

As collage, *Radio Pyongyang* performs a first-order interpretation of sound, speech, music, romantic sentiment, and propaganda. Virant leaves room, however, for listeners to perform our own, second-order interpretation. Some materials are easier on the ears and offer interludes of surprising beauty, like the operatic soprano and male chorus, accompanied by live orchestra, on "Pride of the Nation" (Track 2), or the catchy pop song on "Commie Funk" (Track 7). Other moments demand a repeat listen but still leave questions unresolved: What is the English-speaking announcer saying about the revolutionary museum? How many kids are in the shout-sing chorus of "Start 'Em Young?" Are those land mines exploding? What instrument is that? A further nudge, a more ambitious listen, gets us to important political questions—about Korean division, reunification, artistic expression, and what DPRK residents really believe. Between the overdetermined nature of its parts and the underdetermined assemblage of the whole, Radio Pyongyang offers an opening for us to perceive and contemplate a version of reality in the DPRK.

CONCLUDING THOUGHTS ON "MY OWN *RADIO PYONGYANG*"

Radio Pyongyang reminds me of my parents' music and stories, not those updated on recent visits to Korea, but those from way back when, long before they immigrated to the States. I'm specifically reminded of a sepia photograph I recently found at their home in Tacoma, Washington. My dad, unrecognizably skinny and shaggy-haired, sits at the controls of a Plexiglas DJ booth in an old-style Korean cafe, or *dabang* (다방). He wears oversized headphones and leans toward the camera, a neon "MUSIC" sign animating the scene. Dad, who hardly ever talks about those days, seemed embarrassed by the photo, so I don't know what he was playing or listening to, but I suspect a lot of Motown and Beatles, and probably a good bit of *bbongjjak*. Every so often, he still puts on a *trot* mix-CD, and I catch my mother humming along.

When I played *Radio Pyongyang* for them, they grumbled about my taste in music and inexplicable interest in the DPRK. They found the album jarring and repulsive, mirroring their general reaction to things North Korean. Like most Koreans their age, having lived through the bloody civil war, my parents are fervently anti-Communist, even as they continue to hope for Korean reunification.

Such hoping took place en masse in 2000, when the leaders of North and South Korea—Kim Jong-il and Kim Dae-jung, respectively—met in Pyongyang, in pursuit of a new "Sunshine Policy." I remember compiling a scrapbook of images and articles from those days: the Northerners' grand welcome of their Southern kinfolk, the boulevards of Pyongyang a blur of pink flowers and flags; families wrenched apart by the Korean War, reunited temporarily on one side of the DMZ, now elderly, weeping, embracing at stiff round banquet tables in Pyongyang. It was all a bit of a show, replete with shady corporate dealings and massive wealth transfers to the DPRK; but it was a wonderful show.

In recent years, diplomacy between the United States and North Korea has been cultural at best. There was the New York Philharmonic's trip to Pyongyang in 2008, and, in 2013, a visit by Google executive Eric Schmidt, who tagged along with diplomat and former governor Bill Richardson. Schmidt's daughter Sophie went, too, and later published an absorbing account of their travels. She recalled the toe-numbing cold of public spaces in the fuel-poor state; "sweeping, lamenting orchestral music" in the shared mausoleum of Kim Il-sung and Kim Jong-il; "revolutionary music" echoing through the marble of subway stations; and, strangely enough, "just one song that wasn't patriotic North Korean music . . . first in a promotional video . . . and again over the speakers on our return flight on the national airline, Air Koryo. It was a remastered version of The Cranberries' 'Dreams.'"[66]

According to some North Korea watchers, neither these media events nor the slow creep of popular culture will erode Northern elites' commitment to the regime: "Blue jeans will not bring down *this* dictatorship. Race-based nationalism does not need to fear cultural subversion as much as Marxism-Leninism did. . . . There is little reason, therefore, to believe that smuggled CDs and DVDs will undermine the average North Korean's hostility to the outside world."[67] It's telling, though, that the U.S. government has invested heavily in anti-DPRK radio broadcasts and that humanitarian groups have used South Korean movies and music and old-school balloon drops of Chinese currency and news stories about the Arab Spring as weapons against the regime.[68]

The hope of peaceful reunification makes us do crazy things. In conversation with family, friends, and strangers, I sometimes find myself defending Kim Jong-un. I don't go as far as many Korean-American leftists, whom I've heard make insupportable, ahistorical claims about the regime's social-services framework, respect for workers, belief in gender equality, and enlightened ideology. But I do attempt to explain and contextualize what little we know, not out of love for the Kim regime or an embrace of relativism, but instead as a reaction to demonization—by Bush and the U.S. right, by South Korea at times, and by knee-jerk, Cold War anti-Communism. I'm not so naive as to think that humanizing North Korea will quell geopolitical crisis, but I regard it as a prerequisite for diplomacy.

Whether *Radio Pyongyang* opens up this kind of discourse, I can't say. The open-minded listener, though, will be challenged and edified by the experience. Myriad questions are raised, then left unanswered, pushing the audience to further interrogate the source materials and collaging process, which implicate, in turn, the politicized reality of the DPRK. That the album is able to gather raw materials and then resist editorializing is its greatest virtue, and we all benefit from the encounter that it affords. *Radio Pyongyang* gets us closer to meaningful perception, both confirming and defying aesthetic stereotypes of North Korean art—as propagandistic, cloying, repetitious, démodé, and kitsch. Life in the DPRK surely has little in common with melismatic falsetto or sequined *hanbok* (한복) dresses, but I want to judge for myself what North Koreans see and hear. Despite the state's best attempt to control radio and sound culture, its music veers toward and finally achieves abstraction in Virant's radio collage, which in turn provides a hermeneutic opportunity: For perhaps the first time, no one is telling us how to interpret Kim Jong-un, Kim Jong-il, Kim Il-sung, Pyongyang, or *juche*. The musical fragments speak for themselves.

NOTES

This chapter appeared earlier, in condensed form, as "Not Gangnam's Style: The Kitsch and Soul of Kim Jong-Un Country" in *Salon*, www.salon.com/2012/11/09/radio_pyong yang_the_kitsch_and_soul_of_kim_jong_un_country, November 9, 2012.

1. In his recent book, conservative political scientist Victor Cha argues that Kim Jong-un is practicing "*neojuche* revivalism," "a return to a harder-line, more orthodox *juche* ideology." Victor Cha, *The Impossible State: North Korea, Past and Future* (New York: Harper Collins, 2012), 13.

2. *Radio Pyongyang: Commie Funk and Agit Pop from the Hermit Kingdom,* Sublime Frequencies, www.sublimefrequencies.com/item.asp?Item_id=26&cd=Radio-Pyongyang: -Commie-Funk-and-Agit-Pop-from-the-Hermit-Kingdom.

3. Barbara Demick, *Nothing to Envy: Ordinary Lives in North Korea* (New York: Spiegel & Grau Trade Paperbacks, 2010), 3.

4. Ibid., 101. Keith Howard describes the ritualized visitation of Kim Il-sung's preserved cadaver: "Once on the walkway, passing along endless corridors, it is prohibited to do

anything but stand still. Timing is key to the experience, and in 1995 this was matched to an album of brass band music." Howard, "The People Defeated Will Never Be United: Pop Music and Ideology in North Korea," in *Korean Pop Music: Riding the Wave* (Folkestone, Kent: Global Oriental, 2006), 162.

5. VICE produced a related three-part video, "The VICE guide to North Korea," www.vice.com/video/vice-guide-to-north-korea-1-of-3. Exulting in his self-appointed role as U.S. envoy to the DPRK, Rodman vowed to work out the release of Kenneth Bae, the Korean-American prisoner, writing on Twitter, "I'm calling on the Supreme Leader of North Korea or as I call him 'Kim,' to do me a solid and cut Kenneth Bae loose." Agence France-Presse, "Dennis Rodman Calls on Kim Jong-un 'To Do Me a Solid' and Free Kenneth Bae," *Telegraph*, May 8, 2013, www.telegraph.co.uk/news/worldnews/asia/northkorea/10043537/Dennis-Rodman-calls-on-Kim-Jong-un-to-do-me-a-solid-and-free-Kenneth-Bae.html; Max Fisher, "Dennis Rodman Returning to N. Korea to Free Kenneth Bae: Could It Actually Work?" WorldViews (blog), *The Washington Post*, May 10, 2013, www.washingtonpost.com/blogs/worldviews/wp/2013/05/10/dennis-rodman-returning-to-n-korea-to-free-kenneth-bae-could-it-actually-work/.

6. E. Tammy Kim, "Cold War Imagery and Cyberwarfare in North Korea's Sony Hack," *Al Jazeera America,* December 18, 2014, america.aljazeera.com/articles/2014/12/18/analysis-cold-warimageryandcyberwarfareinnorthkoreassonyhack.html.

7. The puppet version of Kim Jong-il appears in a Sino-fabulous throne room singing "I'm so lonely," except that his "L"s sound like "R"s. He vows to plan an attack like "9-11 times 2356!" *Team America: World Police*, directed by Trey Parker (Los Angeles: Paramount Pictures, 2004), DVD. João Rocha, *kim jong-il looking at things* (Tumblr blog), kimjongillookingatthings.tumblr.com. Rocha went on to publish a collection of his posts in a limited-edition French art book; see www.jean-boite.fr/box/kim_jong_il_looking_at_things_.

8. Bruce Cumings, *The Korean War: A History* (New York: Modern Library, 2011), 9.

9. Christine Ahn, "The Legacy of General Kim Jong Il: An Interview with Professor Han S. Park," Korea Policy Institute, December 28, 2011, www.kpolicy.org/documents/interviews-opeds/111228christineahnhanspark.html. See generally B. R. Myers, *The Cleanest Race: How North Koreans See Themselves and Why It Matters* (New York: Melville House, 2011).

10. Cumings, *The Korean War,* 190; Howard, "The People Defeated Will Never Be United," 161.

11. Cumings, *The Korean War,* 235.

12. Charles Armstrong, "The Cultural Cold War in Korea, 1945–1950," *The Journal of Asian Studies* 62, no. 1 (February 2003): 71–99.

13. Reporters Without Borders, "2013 World Press Freedom Index: Dashed Hopes After Spring," en.rsf.org/press-freedom-index-2013,1054.html; Associated Press, North

Korea Journal, hosted.ap.org/interactives/2011/north-korea-journal/. The Pyongyang bureau chief Jean H. Lee said in August 2012, "I operate under the assumption that everything I say, everything I write, everything I do is being recorded." Hazel Sheffield, "The AP's North Korea Bureau," *Columbia Journalism Review*, August 2, 2012, www.cjr .org/behind_the_news/the_aps_north_korea_bureau.php?page=all.

14. Min-Kyung Yoon, "North Korean Art Works: Historical Paintings and the Cult of Personality," *Korean Histories* 3, no. 1 (2012): 53–72, www.koreanhistories.org/files /Volume_3_1/KH%203.1%20Yoon.pdf.

15. Jane Portal, *Art Under Control in North Korea* (London: Reaktion Books, 2005), 27.

16. Ibid., 27; Demick, *Nothing to Envy,* 45.

17. Portal, *Art Under Control,* 84.

18. *North Korea's Cinema of Dreams: 101 East Gains Rare Insight into the Beating Heart of North Korea's Film Industry,* directed by Lynn Lee and James Leong (Doha, Qatar: Al Jazeera English, 101 East, 2011), web video, www.aljazeera.com/programmes/101e ast/2011/02/2011217113256267999.html.

19. Suki Kim, "Letter from Pyongyang: A Really Big Show: The New York Philharmonic's fantasia in North Korea," *Harper's* (December 2008): 67.

20. *North Korea's Cinema of Dreams.* North Korea conducted purges of musicians and artists in the 1950s and 1960s. Howard, "The People Defeated Will Never Be United," 156, 158.

21. Suki Kim, "Letter from Pyongyang," 67, quoting *Rodong Shinmun,* North Korea's official daily newspaper.

22. Julian Ryall, "North Korea: Kim Jong-un 'Having an Affair with Married Former Singer,'" *Telegraph,* July 10, 2012, www.telegraph.co.uk/news/worldnews/asia/northkorea /9389342/North-Korea-Kim-Jong-un-having-an-affair-with-married-former-singer.html; K. J. Kwon and Alexis Lai, "Kim Jong Un married in 2009, According to Intelligence Service," *CNN.com,* July 26, 2012, www.cnn.com/2012/07/26/world/asia/north-korea -kim-jong-un-wife-identity.

23. "North Korea Releases Kim Jong-un Official Theme Song—Video," *The Guardian,* July 6, 2012, www.guardian.co.uk/world/video/2012/jul/06/north-korea-kim-jong-un -song-video.

24. The Mansudae workshop is reportedly on the itinerary for tours of Pyongyang and includes over 1,000 artists among its stable of 3,700-plus workers. The Korea Society, "Feast or Famine: DPRK Agrarian Posters from the Zellweger Collection," with video of lecture by Katharina Zellweger, August 25, 2012, www.koreasociety.org/arts-culture/gallery-talks /feast_or_famine_dprk_agrarian_posters_from_the_zellweger_collection.html; Bradley K. Martin, *Under the Loving Care of the Fatherly Leader: North Korea and the Kim Dynasty* (New York: Thomas Dunne Books, 2004), 356; generally, Portal, *Art Under Control.*

25. Howard, "The People Defeated Will Never Be United," 159. Lears in this volume

points out the double meaning of "popular" music. A scandal was caused by leaked contraband video of North Korean dancers wearing high heels and mini shorts, doing the splits and other naughty moves to Western music. "Female Dancer Video Circulating in N. Korea: Defector," Yonhap News Agency, November 2, 2009, english.yonhapnews.co.kr/northkorea/2009/11/02/0401000000AEN20091102002500315.HTML. See discussion in Donna Lee Kwon, *Music in Korea: Experiencing Music, Expressing Culture* (Oxford: Oxford University Press, 2012), 159–60.

26. Thomas Fuller, "Where Koreans Go to Reunify (Hint: It's Not the Koreas)," *New York Times*, January 19, 2012, www.nytimes.com/2012/01/19/world/asia/north-and-south -koreans-mix-in-cambodia.html?_r=0; James Pringle, "Meanwhile: A North Korean Pub in the Old Killing Fields," *New York Times*, December 12, 2003, www.nytimes.com/2003/12/12 /opinion/12iht-edpringle_ed3_.html.

27. Yoon, "North Korean Art Works."

28. Tellingly, the direct translation is "Voice of Chosun," the regime's preferred name for Korea, taken after its last dynasty (1392–1897).

29. Robert S. Boynton, "North Korea's Digital Underground," *The Atlantic* (April 2011).

30. Ibid., 55.

31. *A State of Mind*, directed by Daniel Gordon (New York: Kino Lorber Video, 2004), DVD. Myers criticizes the film for inaccurately depicting the mass games as "grim Stalinist exercises" rather than the "joyous celebrations of the pure-bloodedness and homogeneity" that motivate the DPRK. Myers, *The Cleanest Race*, 85.

32. Jane Doe (North Korean relief worker), interview with author, August 23, 2011.

33. By the late 1940s, government radio was a quotidian instructional and propaganda vehicle for the Korean military. Sociological interviews conducted by U.S. military researchers found a North Korean "monopoly of communications sufficient to shut out opposing propaganda and to saturate the people of the state with ideas and attitudes predisposing them to sovietization." Wilbur Schramm and John W. Riley, Jr., "Communication in the Sovietized State, as Demonstrated in Korea," *American Sociological Review* 16, no. 6 (December 1951): 757–66, 758. Martin, *Under the Loving Care of the Fatherly Leader*, 677. For more on technology in North Korea, see the website North Korea Tech, www.northkoreatech.org.

34. Chol-hwan Kang, *The Aquariums of Pyongyang: Ten Years in the North Korean Gulag* (New York: Basic Books, 2005); Ralph Hassig and Kongdan Oh, *The Hidden People of North Korea: Everyday Life in the Hermit Kingdom* (New York: Roman & Littlefield Publishers, 2009). See also Demick, *Nothing to Envy*; and Martin, *Under the Loving Care of the Fatherly Leader*. Young people in North Korea are reported to be devoted fans of South Korean television shows. See Benjamin Ismail, "North Korea: Frontiers of Censorship," *Reporters Without Borders*, October 6, 2011, http://en.rsf.org/IMG/pdf/rsf_north-korea_2011.pdf.

35. Suki Kim, "The System of Defecting: Stories from the North Korean Border," *Harper's* (July 2010).

36. Ibid.

37. Martin, *Under the Loving Care of the Fatherly Leader,* 678; Ismail, "North Korea: Frontiers of Censorship," 7, 8.

38. "Trot Music is S. Korea's Best Propaganda Weapon," *The Chosun Ilbo*, December 30, 2010, english.chosun.com/site/data/html_dir/2010/12/30/2010123000463.html.

39. Ismail, "North Korea: Frontiers of Censorship," 11.

40. North Korean Radio: The Voice of Korea—Recordings of North Korean English Shortwave Radio Broadcasts, northkoreanradio.com. The last posted recording is dated July 9, 2010.

41. Sublime Frequencies' East Asian output (Korea, China, Japan) consists primarily of the traditional folk ethnomusicology of Laurent Jeanneau. See Gonçalo Cardoso's chapter in this volume. *Radio Pyongyang* is one of two Korea albums; the other features traditional zither music. Various artists, *Scattered Melodies: Korean Kayagum Sanjo* SF077, LP, 2013.

42. Lobefood is Sublime Frequencies' authorized online vendor; see lobefood.com /product/sf023-radio-pyongyang-commie-funk-and-agit-pop-from-the-hermit-king dom/; Amazon.com, www.amazon.com/gp/offer-listing/B000AOENGS/ref=dp_olp _new?ie=UTF8&condition=new (last accessed July 5, 2013).

43. *Radio Pyongyang,* SF023, CD booklet.

44. Ibid.

45. Ethnomusicologists of Korea, Keith Howard and Donna Lee Kwon, have observed how difficult it once was to access North Korean music. Kwon recalled when the Sublime Frequencies disc "was one of the only sources I could play of DPRK pop for my classes," pointing to the label's pedagogic uses. Donna Lee Kwon, email to author, August 27, 2012; Howard, "The People Defeated Will Never Be United," 154–55.

46. Virant would not agree to an interview for this volume.

47. CD booklet, *Choubi Choubi! Folk and Pop Sounds from Iraq,* SF025, CD, 2005. CD booklet.

48. CD booklet, *Cambodian Cassette Archives: Khmer Folk and Pop Music Vol. 1.* SF011, CD, 2004.

49. Min-Jung Son, "Regulating and Negotiating in T'urot'u, a Korean Popular Song Style," *Asian Music* 37, no. 1 (Winter/Spring 2006): 51.

50. Ibid., 57–59. The 1930s form, called "new folksong" (신민요), can be seen as a precursor to *trot*. Howard notes that military songs and "mass songs" (대중가요) were the primary popular forms of the 1940s and 1950s. Howard, "The People Defeated Will Never Be United," 157; see also Kwon, *Music in Korea*, 142.

51. In a slightly different context, describing a tradition of Korean women's singing

across the DMZ via PA system, Joshua D. Pilzer writes, "The concept of love is political from the perspective of history." Pilzer, "Sŏdosori (Northwestern Korean Lyric Song) on the Demilitarized Zone: A Study in Music and Teleological Judgment," *Ethnomusicology* 47, no. 1 (Winter 2003): 68–92.

52. Son, "Regulating and Negotiating in T'urot'u," 59.

53. "Trot Music is S. Korea's Best Propaganda Weapon."

54. Son, "Regulating and Negotiating in T'urot'u," 60–61, 64.

55. Ibid., 60–61.

56. Martin, *Under the Loving Care of the Fatherly Leader,* 432. Rowan Pease writes: "By 1990, music shops in most [Chinese] towns stocked not only many kinds of imported music but also home-grown rock, 'urban folksong,' new age music, disco versions of revolutionary classics, and, bigger than any of these, glossy romantic ballads and dance music produced in Taiwan, Hong Kong and China." Pease, "Healthy, National and Up-to-date: Pop Music in the Yanbian Korean Autonomous Prefecture, China," In *Korean Pop Music*, 138.

57. Jane Doe, interview with author, August 23, 2011. Music journalist Alex Hoban wrote a fascinating series of posts, "Pyongyang Goes Pop," for *The Guardian* Music Blog in 2011, www.theguardian.com/music/series/pyongyang-goes-pop.

58. S. Lee, email to author, September 29, 2011.

59. Kwon, *Music in Korea*, 142.

60. Those "Arirang" Mass Games are the setting for the documentary mentioned above, *A State of Mind*, and among the liner note photos shot by Christian Virant. North Korea takes exceptional pride in this national spectacle, which involves tens of thousands of DPRK civilian participants.

61. Both pieces were composed by Kim Wongyun, considered North Korea's premier composer and people's artist. Howard, "The People Defeated Will Never Be United," 156. *Aeguka* means patriotic song; South Korea's national anthem has the same generic name. See discussion in Kwon, *Music in Korea*, 146–47.

62. *Dear Pyongyang*, directed by Yong-hi Yang (2005; Santa Fe, N.M.: Tidepoint Pictures, 2008), DVD.

63. Suki Kim, "Letter from Pyongyang." See also Suki Kim, *Without You, There Is No Us: My Time with the Sons of North Korea's Elite* (New York: Crown, 2014).

64. Joseph Brodsky, "Less Than One," in *Less Than One: Selected Essays* (New York: Farrar, Straus and Giroux: 1986), 6. Interestingly Schramm and Riley observe "a basic difference in soviet terminology between propaganda, which in Leninist terms is the presenting of many ideas about a single subject to a small number of people, and agitation, which is defined as the presentation of a few ideas to the mass of people," "Communication in the Sovietized State," 758.

65. Allan MacInnis, "Sublime Frequencies and Group Doueh: Hisham Mayet and

Doueh interviews!" *The Big Takeover*, July 25, 2011, www.bigtakeover.com/interviews /sublime-frequences-and-group-doueh-hisham-mayet-interview.

66. Sophie Schmidt, "It Might Not Get Weirder Than This" (blog post), January 20, 2013, https://sites.google.com/site/sophieinnorthkorea/home. The lyrics to "Dreams" could not be more fitting: "And oh, my dreams / It's never quite as it seems / 'Cause you're a dream to me / Dream to me."

67. Myers, *The Cleanest Race*, 170. Others observe that the DPRK "lacks the sorts of civil society institutions that could support a sustained challenge to the regime from below." National Bureau of Asian Research, "Political Change in the DPRK: Interview with Stephan Haggard and Daniel Pinkston," *Asia Policy* 12 (July 2011):131–39, nbr.org/ publications/asia_policy/Free/AP12_F_NKoreaQA.pdf.

68. Cha, *The Impossible State,* 204, 415, 441.

BIBLIOGRAPHY

Agence France-Presse, "Dennis Rodman Calls on Kim Jong-un 'To Do Me a Solid' and Free Kenneth Bae." *Telegraph*, May 8, 2013. www.telegraph.co.uk/news/worldnews /asia/northkorea/10043537/Dennis-Rodman-calls-on-Kim-Jong-un-to-do-me-a-solid -and-free-Kenneth-Bae.html.

Ahn, Christine. "The Legacy of General Kim Jong Il: An Interview with Professor Han S. Park." Korea Policy Institute. December 28, 2011. www.kpolicy.org/documents /interviews-opeds/111228christineahnhanspark.html.

Armstrong, Charles. "The Cultural Cold War in Korea, 1945–1950." *The Journal of Asian Studies* 62, no. 1 (February 2003): 71–99.

Associated Press. *North Korea Journal.* hosted.ap.org/interactives/2011/north-korea -journal/.

Boynton, Robert S. "North Korea's Digital Underground." *The Atlantic* (April 2011).

Brodsky, Joseph. "Less Than One." In *Less Than One: Selected Essays.* New York: Farrar, Straus and Giroux, 1986.

Cha, Victor. *The Impossible State: North Korea, Past and Future.* New York: Harper Collins, 2012.

Cumings, Bruce. *The Korean War: A History.* New York: Modern Library, 2011.

Demick, Barbara. *Nothing to Envy: Ordinary Lives in North Korea.* New York: Spiegel & Grau Trade Paperbacks, 2010.

"Female Dancer Video Circulating in N. Korea: Defector." *Yonhap News Agency,* November 2, 2009. english.yonhapnews.co.kr/northkorea/2009/11/02/0401000000 AEN20091102002500315.HTML.

Fisher, Max. "Dennis Rodman Returning to N. Korea to Free Kenneth Bae: Could It Actually Work?" WorldViews (blog). *The Washington Post*, May 10, 2013. www.wash

ingtonpost.com/blogs/worldviews/wp/2013/05/10/dennis-rodman-returning-to-n -korea-to-free-kenneth-bae-could-it-actually-work/.

Fuller, Thomas. "Where Koreans Go to Reunify (Hint: It's Not the Koreas)." *New York Times,* January 19, 2012. www.nytimes.com/2012/01/19/world/asia/north-and-south -koreans-mix-in-cambodia.html?_r=0.

Hassig, Ralph, and Kongdan Oh. *The Hidden People of North Korea: Everyday Life in the Hermit Kingdom* (New York: Roman & Littlefield Publishers, 2009).

Hoban, Alex. "Pyongyang Goes Pop." *Guardian* (music blog), 2011. www.theguardian. com/music/series/pyongyang-goes-pop.

Howard, Keith. "The People Defeated Will Never Be United: Pop Music and Ideology in North Korea." In *Korean Pop Music: Riding the Wave* (Folkestone, Kent: Global Oriental, 2006).

Ismail, Benjamin. "North Korea: Frontiers of Censorship." *Reporters Without Borders,* October 6, 2011. http://en.rsf.org/IMG/pdf/rsf_north-korea_2011.pdf.

Kang, Chol-hwan. *The Aquariums of Pyongyang: Ten Years in the North Korean Gulag.* New York: Basic Books, 2005.

Kim, E. Tammy. "Cold War Imagery and Cyberwarfare in North Korea's Sony Hack." *Al Jazeera America,* December 18, 2014. america.aljazeera.com/articles/2014/12/18 /analysis-cold-warimageryandcyberwarfareinnorthkoreassonyhack.html.

Kim, Suki. "Letter from Pyongyang: A Really Big Show: The New York Philharmonic's fantasia in North Korea." *Harper's* (December 2008).

———. "The System of Defecting: Stories from the North Korean Border." *Harper's* (July 2010).

———. *Without You, There Is No Us: My Time with the Sons of North Korea's Elite.* New York: Crown, 2014.

The Korea Society. "Feast or Famine: DPRK Agrarian Posters from the Zellweger Collec- tion." With video of lecture by Katharina Zellweger, August 25, 2012, www.koreasociety. org/arts-culture/gallery-talks/feast_or_famine_dprk_agrarian_posters_from_the_zell weger_collection.html.

Kwon, Donna Lee. Email to author. August 27, 2012.

———. *Music in Korea: Experiencing Music, Expressing Culture.* Oxford: Oxford Uni- versity Press, 2012.

Kwon, K. J., and Alexis Lai. "Kim Jong Un Married in 2009, According to Intelligence Service." *CNN.com,* July 26, 2012. www.cnn.com/2012/07/26/world/asia/north-korea -kim-jong-un-wife-identity.

Lee, S. Email to author. September 29, 2011.

MacInnis, Allan. "Sublime Frequencies and Group Doueh: Hisham Mayet and Doueh interviews!" *The Big Takeover,* July 25, 2011. www.bigtakeover.com/interviews/sublime -frequences-and-group-doueh-hisham-mayet-interview.

Martin, Bradley K. *Under the Loving Care of the Fatherly Leader: North Korea and the Kim Dynasty*. New York: Thomas Dunne Books, 2004.

Myers, B. R. *The Cleanest Race: How North Koreans See Themselves and Why It Matters*. New York: Melville House, 2011.

National Bureau of Asian Research. "Political Change in the DPRK: Interview with Stephan Haggard and Daniel Pinkston." *Asia Policy* 12 (July 2011): 131–39. nbr.org /publications/asia_policy/Free/AP12_F_NKoreaQA.pdf.

"North Korea Releases Kim Jong-un Official Theme Song—Video," July 6, 2012, www .guardian.co.uk/world/video/2012/jul/06/north-korea-kim-jong-un-song-video.

North Korea Tech. Website. www.northkoreatech.org.

North Korean Radio: The Voice of Korea—Recordings of North Korean English Shortwave Radio Broadcasts. Website. northkoreanradio.com.

Pease, Rowan. "Healthy, National and Up-to-date: Pop Music in the Yanbian Korean Autonomous Prefecture, China." In *Korean Pop Music: Riding the Wave*, edited by Keith Howard (Folkestone, Kent: Global Oriental, 2006).

Pilzer, Joshua D. "Sŏdosori (Northwestern Korean Lyric Song) on the Demilitarized Zone: A Study in Music and Teleological Judgment." *Ethnomusicology* 47, no. 1 (Winter 2003): 68–92.

Portal, Jane. *Art Under Control in North Korea*. London: Reaktion Books, 2005.

Pringle, James. "Meanwhile: A North Korean Pub in the Old Killing Fields." *New York Times*, December 12, 2003. www.nytimes.com/2003/12/12/opinion/12iht-edpringle _ed3_.html.

Reporters Without Borders. "2013 World Press Freedom Index: Dashed Hopes After Spring." en.rsf.org/press-freedom-index-2013,1054.html.

Ryall, Julian. "North Korea: Kim Jong-un 'Having an Affair with Married Former Singer.'" *Telegraph*, July 10, 2012. www.telegraph.co.uk/news/worldnews/asia/northkorea /9389342/North-Korea-Kim-Jong-un-having-an-affair-with-married-former-singer .html.

Schmidt, Sophie. "It Might Not Get Weirder Than This" (blog post). January 20, 2013. https://sites.google.com/site/sophieinnorthkorea/home.

Schramm, Wilbur, and John W. Riley, Jr. "Communication in the Sovietized State, as Demonstrated in Korea." *American Sociological Review* 16, no. 6 (December 1951).

Sheffield, Hazel. "The AP's North Korea Bureau." *Columbia Journalism Review*, August 2, 2012. www.cjr.org/behind_the_news/the_aps_north_korea_bureau.php?page=all.

Son, Min-Jung. "Regulating and Negotiating in T'urot'u, a Korean Popular Song Style." *Asian Music* 37, no. 1 (Winter/Spring 2006): 51.

Sublime Frequencies. Website. www.sublimefrequencies.com.

"Trot Music Is S. Korea's Best Propaganda Weapon." *The Chosun Ilbo*, December 30, 2010. english.chosun.com/site/data/html_dir/2010/12/30/2010123000463.html.

VICE. "The VICE guide to North Korea." www.vice.com/the-vice-guide-to-travel/vice
-guide-to-north-korea-1-of-3.

Yoon, Min-Kyung. "North Korean Art Works: Historical Paintings and the Cult of Personality." *Korean Histories* 3, no. 1 (2012): 53–72. www.koreanhistories.org/files/Volume_3_1
/KH%203.1%20Yoon.pdf.

Blaring Americas

RACHEL LEARS

Collecting the Cultures

of *Latinamericarpet*

Pop Primitivism and

the Shadows of History

In the 1960s and 1970s, while young people in the United States and Europe proclaimed a revolution of values and style to the soundtrack of rock and roll, Latin American youth embraced the sounds of electric guitar as social and political unrest rocked the region. Sublime Frequencies' *Latinamericarpet: Exploring the Vinyl Warp of Latin American Psychedelia* (2007), compiled by Argentine record collector Albano Costillares, unites a determinedly apolitical array of audio oddities from this era into a collage of surf-tinged party songs, children's music, folkloric pop, and spoken excerpts from language-training and self-help records. Taken individually, the recordings point to a wide range of probable intended audiences—from middle-class children to urban migrant workers to aspiring bureaucrats. But the construction of the compilation as a whole subsumes these original social uses into one strange trip for North American and European record collectors.

This essay explores the sounds of *Latinamericarpet* in light of the particular political and cultural histories of Argentina, Mexico, Brazil, Peru, and Chile (the countries represented on the album) as well as the history of the collection of cultural artifacts in the context of ethnographic knowledge-production. As the sheer wackiness (I will return to this word) of the selections and their juxtapositions overshadows these histories, the compilation induces a form of amnesia alongside the attempt to recover "forgotten" sounds. But despite the lack of overt or even coded references on *Latinamericarpet* to the military coups, guerrilla movements, and student massacres that shaped so much popular music and social life in Latin America during this era, political unrest becomes a haunting presence that permeates the record's resignified textures. From a continent where cultural hybridity *avant la lettre* was forged with violence, this postmodern pastiche of playful sounds hints at a complex array of multiple meanings structured by the disparate social contexts of production and reception—and the history of colonial and neocolonial encounters between Latin America, Europe, and the United States.

I. THE MUSIC: GENRES AND GEOGRAPHY

Broadly, the music of *Latinamericarpet* encompasses rock (psychedelic and otherwise), folkloric genres of several nations (including traditional and overtly commercialized performances), music for children (primarily associated with television shows), spoken word (excerpts of instructional recordings about tourism, relaxation techniques, and English-language instruction), and a variety of self-conscious hybrids of folkloric genres and rock, pop, or classical. The title is somewhat misleading in its suggestion that the collection explores Latin American *psychedelia*.[1] Most of the tracks clearly were not conceived to induce or enhance perception and consciousness, and many have little to nothing in common with the sounds most characteristic of psychedelic music, such as delay, fuzz, and wah-wah effects on electric guitars, drone-heavy arrangements, or extended improvisation. It would be more accurate to call the record a "psychedelic collection," since its kaleidoscopic qualities emerge from the compilation itself. Like many Sublime Frequencies releases, the record orients the listener to appreciate a disorienting collage of sounds from a foreign sonic-cultural world as "psychedelic," as though an altered state of consciousness is induced at the moment of reception. Like many cultures of psychedelia in the 1960s and 1970s, this orientation abstains from direct engagement with concrete political language and endeavors, embracing introspection and imagination instead.

I discuss the record's curatorial aspects in detail later on in this essay; I first touch on the musical styles represented and their geographic origins. Although the liner notes and title frame the compilation as a continental voyage on a "magic Latinamericarpet," the record concentrates heavily on Argentina and extends only to several other South American countries and Mexico. The notes credit Argentina as the origin of 16 of the 27 tracks, including some unusual rock and folk tracks (7, 16, 22, 25), much of the children's music (8, 13, 18, 24), and nearly all of the spoken word (1, 4, 6, 15, 19, 26). One supposedly Argentine rock band, however, actually hails from Mexico (10), and one children's song, from Spain (27). Peru provides five tracks (5, 11, 17, 21, 23), two of which are spoken English lessons, but the country's influence is visible on the cover art, as described below. Chile supplies two of the four straight-ahead guitar rock tracks on the collection (2, 20), as well as a Mexican-derived *ranchera* (12). Although Easter Island (Isla de Pascua) furnishes one traditional song, this locale is only connected to Latin America via Chile (which annexed the Polynesian island in 1888). Mexico receives credit for only one folk/pop track (14), but its traditional sounds are heard in the Chilean *ranchera* (12) and versions of folk classics "Cielito Lindo" (22) and "Jarabe Tapatío" (3; also known as "The Mexican Hat Dance"), and one of its classic rock bands appears under an Argentina credit (10). The popular music, rock, and psychedelia of Brazil, as I discuss below, are not present, though the country gets credit for one recording of a Mexican folkloric melody accompanied by birdsong (3).

Rock and roll exploded in many parts of South America with the release of the film *Rock Around the Clock* in 1955–1956, carving a new space for youth culture (Markarian 1998: 238; Cornejo Guinassi 2002: 17). In Mexico, rock and roll grew popular around the same time, though its arrival had less to do with a singular event than the ongoing flows of capital and migration between Mexico and the United States (Zolov 1999: 17).[2] The first waves of Latin American rock and roll were musically "foreign" and socially local. Bands performed both covers and derivative originals in English and Spanish or Portuguese, while integrating themselves into existing infrastructures of cultural production—including record companies and performance venues such as dance halls and theaters (cf. Straw 2000). The Beatles craze had a huge impact on bands throughout the continent (as it did in much of the world) in the early 1960s. Surf rock also spread, though not as widely. By the end of the decade, Latin American rock had metamorphosed along with global trends toward the expansion of youth styles marked by long hair and other "hippie" and countercultural signifiers. In large part, this was due to the uptake of these styles into mainstream US media and advertising over the course of the decade (Frank 1998).

Around this time, Latin American rock music began to reflect the influence of the psychedelic sounds and styles sweeping the United States and Europe. In particular, it was through the experimental impulses associated with psychedelic rock that Latin American bands began self-consciously to fuse rock instrumentation and textures with elements of local folkloric genres. Most of the rock sounds on *Latinamericarpet*, however, appear in rock-tinged songs for children (8, 13, 21, 24, 27) or odd *sui generis* hybrids (7, 25), though the collection includes several examples of early to mid-1960s' instrumental rock from Chile (2, 20), Argentina (16), and Mexico (10).[3] As I will discuss, the record features only one example of the late 1960s'/early 1970s' trend of fusing local sounds with rock: a song by the Peruvian band Los Destellos (5), which pioneered the style known as *chicha*, Peruvian *cumbia*[4] dance music incorporating psychedelic guitar effects and melodic tropes of Andean and Amazonian folklore (cf. Romero 2007).

The compilation also includes more straightforwardly folkloric or traditional styles as well as tracks that push the boundaries between these and other forms of commercial popular music. While in English the word "popular" tends to refer to products of the cultural industries, in Spanish it generally signifies music with direct links to local and national traditions. This ambiguity arises from the relation of both sorts of "popular music" to recording technology: The very notion of musical folklore emerged from practices of collection made possible by the invention of the phonograph (Brady 1999). During the first few decades of the twentieth century, as folklore research and the music industry encoded musical sounds onto recordings, a complex and contradictory set of discourses tied folkloric genres in Latin America to geographies while transporting them to centers of metropolitan taste-making in Paris and New York (Ochoa Gaultier 2006). In particular, between around 1920 and 1940, the sounds of marginalized communities came to symbolize national identities in many countries, including Argentina (tango), Brazil (samba), and Cuba (*son*) (Moore 1997; Vianna 1999; Garramuño 2007). In the 1950s, broader economic shifts sent droves of rural migrants to the capitals of many Latin American nations, where waves of commercially popular folk music saturated media and articulated national identities in new ways. This occurred, for example, with genres like the *chacarera* and the *zamba* from the north of Argentina (Vila 1991) or with the Andean *huayno* in Peru (Romero 2007: 12). It is important to think about the folkloric tracks on *Latinamericarpet* in the context of this long history of the mediation of traditional musical styles through the cultural industries, without assuming false dichotomies between the authentically ethnographic and the commercial.

In fact, the general Sublime Frequencies approach deliberately undermines such dichotomies. *Latinamericarpet* includes two traditional pieces from commercially circulated LPs by folkloric ensembles from Peru (17) and Easter Island (9). In other cases, a Mexican folklore group featuring marimba performs a classic pop song (14), a Chilean group performs Mexican *ranchera* music (12), classi-cized northern Argentine guitar rhythms play quietly beneath spoken words (1, 6), and standardized Mexican folk melodies appear in versions by an Argentine dulcimer trio (22) and a Brazilian ornithologist of Belgian origin who juxtaposes an organ-and-bassoon arrangement with the warbling of canaries (3). The record constructs its peculiar brand of "psychedelia" in part by foregrounding sounds that blur the boundaries between tradition, commerce, and idiosyncrasy.

A great deal of *Latinamericarpet*'s whimsical sensibility also arises from car-toonish voices and effects: 11 of the 27 tracks on the record originally were re-corded for children, and at least seven of these came from television programs. While many renowned composers have created music for children—two excerpts from an Argentine version of Prokofiev's *Peter and the Wolf* appear on the com-pilation (4, 19)—the advent of children's television accelerated the proliferation of commercial releases of music for young audiences. The examples on *Latin-americarpet* show how producers sought to educate and entertain to varying degrees with these recordings. On two tracks (11, 23), beloved Peruvian television personality La Gringa Inga (aka German-born Californian Ingeborg Zwinkel) gives English lessons to a native Peruvian character whose voice is raised to a puppet-like pitch. Most of the other children's songs on the compilation feature rock instrumentation alongside what the liner notes call "weird voices and as-tonishing instrumental arrangements." Two tracks (8, 24) come from the 1975 LP of the animated TV series *Meteoro*, the Argentine version of the American show *Speed Racer*, itself an adaptation of the Japanese *manga* show *Mach Go Go Go*. Three other pieces (15, 21, 27) come from the phonographic releases of Argentine, Peruvian, and Spanish television programs.[5] In one case, the sheer presence of noisy fuzz-guitar effects alongside a children's choir (13) shows how much of rock's countercultural quality had already been subsumed into com-mercial popular culture by the late 1960s, even in Latin America.

Besides the *Peter and the Wolf* and La Gringa Inga tracks, other excerpts of spoken recordings also contribute to the playful, humorous, and collage-like qualities of the compilation. The collection opens with a snippet of a 1970 record entitled *Formosa tiene su hechizo* (*Formosa has its charm*). This LP, apparently pro-duced by a municipal authority in the northern Argentine province of Formosa, presents an informative introduction to the region, guided by a commanding male voice that recounts details of geography and tourist lodging (the capital city has twelve hotels!) while folkloric guitars and concertinas waft through the background. The original album also includes songs in local traditional genres sung by male and female voices, and one orchestral arrangement of a paean to the province, but the brief excerpts sampled on *Latinamericarpet* simply locate the listener between the Paraguay, Pilcomayo, and Bermejo rivers on the "wide plain of Formosa," first in Spanish (1) and then in English (6). Later on in the compilation, two short excerpts appear from an Argentine recording of "techniques of yoga concentration and relaxation." The first (15) alerts listeners, "We will begin with the technique of rapid nervous discharge" ("Comenzaremos con la técnica de descarga nerviosa rápida") before cutting to a song performed in the bizarre, high-pitched voice of Argentine TV cartoon character Calculín (which, for many U.S. audiences, might recall Alvin and the Chipmunks). The second excerpt (26) tells us that, "The entire brain, the entire mind, serves as a resonating box for the sound that arises like a spiral, and like a spiral penetrates the space between our eyebrows directly" ("Todo el cerebro, toda la mente sirve como caja de resonancia para el sonido que surge en forma de espiral, y en forma de espiral, penentra directamente al entrecejo."); this soon unbearable sound (a low synthesizer tone) lasts for nearly two minutes.

The album's pastiche effects happen within tracks as well as between them. The several songs marked in the liner notes as "oddities" involve particularly strange juxtapositions of, for example, the aforementioned classicized folklore and birdsong (3), a bona fide classical piano piece performed by an aged aunt with rock accompaniment by her young nephews (7), or bombastic organ melodies atop a frenetic backbeat (25). In the case of one such oddity, the label's description errs substantially, hailing "Citara Trio's adulterated sitar version of the classic 'Cielito Lindo'" (22). The instrument known in Spanish as the *citara* is not in fact a sitar but a dulcimer or kithara (a harp descended from ancient Greece). Citara Trio united three of these instruments with guitar, bass, and other sounds to perform tango and a variety of other styles of Latin American popular music, including the Mexican melody versioned here.

Beyond these unusual amalgams and articles of ambiguous folklore, the Los Destellos *chicha* song (5) remains the only track that gestures toward the rich array of fusion genres that Latin American musicians began creating in the late 1960s between rock sounds and local forms. Conspicuously absent are examples of the Brazilian *Tropicália* movement, which erupted in 1968 and embraced the psychedelic label along with the sounds and sensibilities of rock, Brazilian popular music, and avant-garde experimentation (cf. Dunn 2001). The *Tropicália* movement included Caetano Veloso and Gilberto Gil, who went on to become luminaries of Brazilian popular music in subsequent decades, as well as the rock band Os Mutantes, whose most significant work appeared between 1968 and 1974, and who became virtually synonymous with psychedelia as a genre in Brazil. Since many of these recordings had already been reissued as North American listeners revived interest in *Tropicália* in the late 1990s (cf. Harvey 2002), it is likely that they were excluded from *Latinamericarpet* due to licensing restrictions, and/ or that the concept of the collection specifically sought to represent sonically related material from beyond Brazil. Given compiler Albano Costillares's base in Argentina, it is also surprising that *Latinamericarpet* excludes psychedelic rock and fusion from neighboring Uruguay, where groups such as El Kinto and Totem combined Afro-Uruguayan carnival rhythms with rock textures and hit songwriting between 1966 and 1973, and Chile, where groups like Los Jaivas, Congreso, and Los Blops combined Chilean folkloric rhythms and instruments with rock around the same time (cf. Trigo 2004; Ponce 2008). Nor does the compilation include the Mexican rock fusion of La Onda Chicana, a movement that arose between 1969 and 1971 and sought to create a new local form combining Mexican and U.S. rhythms and images (cf. Zolov 1999: 167–200).

Although Los Destellos used the term "*sicodélico*" in some of their releases, there are significant differences between the social and discursive domains of *chicha* and those of the psychedelic fusion rock movements of Brazil, Uruguay, Chile, and Mexico. (In Argentina at the time, rock musicians made far fewer attempts to infuse their sounds with elements of Latin American traditional music, which more often appeared as part of acoustic song.) Costillares describes the music of Los Destellos as "unique Amazonic *cumbia*." In fact, the group came from Lima, not from the Amazon region of Peru, and the majority of their work features Andean, rather than Amazonian, sounds. (Other *chicha* groups of the era, such as Los Mirlos, Los Wemblers, and Juaneco y Su Combo, were associated much more closely with the Amazon region.) Also, as Peruvian *cumbia* expanded widely in the 1970s, it would be more accurate to call the sound of Los Destellos innovative or influential, as opposed to unique (cf. Romero 2007: 21–26). *Tropicália*, beyond a style of music, was an intellectual movement that drew inspiration from the 1928 "Cannibalist Manifesto" ("Manifesto Antropófago") by polemical Brazilian poet Osvaldo de Andrade, which exhorted Brazilian artists to "cannibalize" both European and local cultural traditions in order to forge a unique national modernity. Some members of the Uruguayan bands that fused local carnival music with rock in the 1960s and 1970s were similarly oriented toward avant-garde sensibilities. Moreover, musical fusions in Brazil, Uruguay, Chile, and Mexico during this era were associated with middle-class countercultures. Peruvian *chicha*, on the other hand, arose as working-class dance music, and did not achieve wide acceptance by the middle classes until it morphed into *technocumbia* in the 1990s (Romero 2007: 33–42). Despite its scant attention to these sorts of sounds, *Latinamericarpet* asserts a strong affinity with the fusion trend in visual terms, appropriating the fabulous cover photograph of Los Destellos' LP *Mundial* ("Global")[6] as a prominent banner. By choosing for cover art an image of Peruvian musicians posing with electric guitars amid distinctly Mod fashions and backdrop, the collection lays claim to a celebratory vision of "alternative modernities" (cf. Gaonkar 2001) that develop in different ways in different places with the accelerating mediation of intercultural dialogue.

II. THE POLITICS OF COLLECTION

Latinamericarpet selectively subsumes sounds, images, and texts from the 1960s and 1970s into a "vinyl warp" of zany, retro kitsch, omitting any possible reference to the social, political, and economic turmoil that affected the region during this period. Rather than simply dismissing this curatorial strategy as vacuously postmodern, I would like to ask: What sorts of political meanings lie within this depoliticized aggregation? To explore this question, I first examine the politics of the compilation in the context of the relationship of record collecting to the history of taxonomy and modern epistemologies. Then, in the following section, I address the relationship between the collection's curatorial strategy and the historical and cultural contexts of the recordings' creation.

The disc's liner notes strike an oddly ironic tone. The first paragraph reads:

> Historically Latin America was the part of the "new world" that Christopher Columbus "discovered" in 1492, which soon was brutally conquered by the Spanish and Portuguese. Obviously it was only a "discovery" from a Eurocentric perspective because, in fact, on these vast lands there were hundreds of advanced native cultures living for centuries. However after countless years of violent colonization and internal wars, the independence emerged on the whole continent launching a group of new countries with their own and unique identities. But what is Latin America nowadays? A complex answer for a complex puzzle: some people would say it's a huge cocktail that combines—in a more or less chaotic way—the rests (or ruins) of Pre-Columbus Cultures and diverse European traditions mixed with a high dose of pseudo-tropical weathers, Latin manners and unstable economies . . . although that's also a simplification: Latin

America is just Latin America and it deserves to be "rediscovered" . . . But let's go straight to the record.

Who is speaking here and to whom? Compilation author Albano Costillares is from Argentina, but the notes reflect an ambiguous subject position.[7] The first three sentences imply a somewhat indignant voice directed didactically toward an imagined gringo audience that has never cared or thought much about colonialism, or even basic schoolbook histories of the Americas. (Strangely, given this orientation, the notes fail to acknowledge slavery and the contributions of people of African descent to the cultural heritage of the hemisphere.) Following this vague projection of "Eurocentric perspectives," the notes provide a blasé compendium of disparate elements that comprise the "chaotic" cultural life of the continent today. With this move toward unspecific terms and eclecticism, Costillares abandons the possibility of speaking in a first-person voice as an Argentine sharing something of his own personal or social historical memory with U.S. audiences. In the following section, I will discuss the compilation's orientation toward history. Here, I explore what kind of knowledge it produces.

In the liner notes to *Latinamericarpet*, Costillares adopts "insider" and "outsider" positions simultaneously in a way that strongly echoes the classic tropes of ethnography. He offers to guide the listener through the foreign sounds of vintage children's television, partially commercialized folklore, and imitative surf rock—unfamiliar terrain of which he possesses superior knowledge. Words like "forgotten" and "undiscovered" underline the curator's authority and suggest that a collection like this is the only place where a listener could possibly encounter such material. In reality, the album including the Easter Island track was rereleased in 2000 by Ans Records, and tracks by Los Destellos appeared on *The Roots of Chicha*, a compilation released by Barbès Records in 2007, the same year that Sublime Frequencies produced *Latinamericarpet*. More significantly, within a few years of the compilation's release (and possibly even sooner), interested listeners would not have to "wait for further works" to continue exploring this type of material, because a good deal of it would be accessible instantly as full albums for download on blogs such as www.discosdificilesdeconseguir.com.[8] During the 2000s, the explosion of digital piracy transformed and democratized record collecting by accelerating the search process through which consumers come to acquire both what they are looking for and unexpected, unfamiliar treasures. Given the reality of this situation at the time of the collection's release, the knowing tone of the liner notes seems quaintly outdated.[9]

If the text hearkens back to a time when hard-to-find records had not yet become available on the Internet, the compilation's taste world also emerges in part from trends at the turn of the twenty-first century. Will Straw (1997) writes about record collecting as connoisseurship in the "trash fandoms" of the 1990s that revived psychedelia, surf rock, and other genres of the 1960s with "vernacular scholarship" that tied recordings to "an idea of the illicit." He writes, "collecting is refigured as anthropology, an expedition into the natural wilderness of discarded styles and eccentric musical deformations." Unlike other fandoms that are more about ordering, Straw argues, trash fandoms cultivate "the sense that particular moments or spaces of popular culture (the mid-1960s for example) will remain chaotic or unpacified, forever yielding up hitherto unimagined and possibly scandalous artifacts for the adventurer/collector" (Straw 1997: 12–13). These comments strongly prefigure *Latinamericarpet*'s kitschy aural pastiche that revalues the inauthentic, as well as the liner notes' tone of self-styled discernment, which exalts the collector's unique experience with the exploration and acquisition of obscure media artifacts.

In fact, Sublime Frequencies' general mission dovetails fairly explicitly with the notion of adventurer/collector that Straw describes:

> SUBLIME FREQUENCIES is a collective of explorers dedicated to acquiring and exposing obscure sights and sounds from modern and traditional urban and rural frontiers via film and video, field recordings, radio and short wave transmissions, international folk and pop music, sound anomalies, and other forms of human and natural expression not documented sufficiently through all channels of academic research, the modern recording industry, media, or corporate foundations. SUBLIME FREQUENCIES is focused on an aesthetic of extra-geography and soulful experience inspired by music and culture, world travel, research, and the pioneering recording labels of the past [. . .].[10]

These lines indicate substantial shared cultural territory between Straw's collectors, who treated the past as a foreign country, and Sublime Frequencies, which transmutes the pleasures of historical discovery to intercontinental travel, and back again. Moreover, judging by my own experience with collectors, this overlap is social as well as discursive. Many of the same people who revived Anglo-American psychedelia, "Space Age Bachelor Pad Music" (cited by Straw), or Brazilian *Tropicália* in the 1990s have gone on to cultivate interest in Sublime Frequencies releases and their wider "extra-geographic" framework.

Sublime Frequencies is known for refusing to label many of its releases with contextual information about the music, its makers, or the places it comes from. This strategy has been somewhat controversial, as some critics have criticized the label for reproducing colonial fantasies by appropriating and repackaging non-Western products while reducing cultural specificity to a nebulous exotic soup. Yet founders Alan Bishop and Hisham Mayet defend their irreverent, DIY approach against institutional knowledge and forms of appropriation that serve primarily to bolster the authority of traditional experts. (In the words of Barbès Records founder Olivier Conan, "I think they do it just to piss off ethnomusicologists."[11]) Some critics have also pointed out that the fact that Bishop is half-Lebanese and Mayet is Libyan complicates the assertion that their work reproduces clichés of Western exoticism (Boon 2006). With respect to *Latinamericarpet*, the same could be said of Costillares's Argentine identity. To be sure, as all the essays in this volume acknowledge, no simple interpretation captures the ambiguities of the Sublime Frequencies sensibility.

Rather than indict *Latinamericarpet*'s curator or publishers as neocolonial, or defend them as defiant challengers of institutional authority, I argue that the subjective ambiguity of Costillares's liner notes and curatorial strategy, and indeed of the whole Sublime Frequencies approach, arises from the history of the social practice of record collecting itself.[12] Straw's insights use anthropology as a metaphor for all knowledge produced in the West about its internal and external Others. I point out that the discourses and practices of record collecting emerge from the history of the collection, naming, classification, and display of ethnographic art (and by extension musical folklore), which in turn emerged from the natural sciences. Michel Foucault explains how the development of natural history in the seventeenth century enabled Classical thinkers to establish libraries, archives, catalogs, and indexes "as a way of introducing into the language already imprinted on things [. . .] an order of the same type as that which was being established between living creatures" (Foucault 1970: 132). Over the course of the subsequent centuries, the scientific order of biological taxonomy gave rise to the concepts of race and culture as bounded entities akin to species, and to forms of evolutionary thought used to justify social inequality and imperialism. At the same time, museums emerged alongside libraries and archives, material objects circulated through discourses and institutions of classification, and collectors and connoisseurs determined the relative value and authenticity of specimens as art or culture (Clifford 1988). To collect and classify cultural artifacts, then, invokes a history of knowledge produced and embedded within structures of power that consistently transform difference into hierarchy.

I would argue that it is because the social practices of record collecting emerge from this broader modern episteme of taxonomy that Sublime Frequencies' releases invoke a tension between empirical knowledge and imaginative irreverence. Even as the label aims to upend the conventions of ethnomusicological expertise with a focus on the interstices between folklore and pop, records like *Latinamericarpet* reproduce these conventions in unexpected ways. On the one hand, like museums and archives, as well as natural history and early ethnography, record collecting involves classification as knowledge production. Species and tribes become genres and styles, as experts claim the power to order and authenticate sounds. Even if the curator deliberately avoids contextual information and rests this claim only upon unique access to recordings gathered "on location," he positions himself as an authority. In this sense, and this is the most straightforward critique, *Latinamericarpet* and other Sublime Frequencies releases could be said to exoticize urban popular musics in ways reminiscent of "world music" as a marketing category promoting sonic tourism, or traditional ethnography[13] as a discipline for collecting and categorizing the "primitive" expressions of cultural Others.

On the other hand, another impulse in record collecting claims the authority to assert that an album or track exists outside known orders, that it belongs in the cabinet of curiosities, missing links, and unnatural hybrids—from birdsong-folk to children's rock choirs. In the Sublime Frequencies web manifesto quoted earlier, the label uses a position of opposition or indifference to institutions or conventions of knowledge and power ("academic research, the modern recording industry, media, or corporate foundations") to bolster claims to the authority of superior taste. But as Pierre Bourdieu (1984) shows, the relationships among taste, knowledge, and social power are complex. Consumers must incorporate a certain amount of knowledge in order to acquire taste, and this can happen through formal education as well as informal exposure, both of which are (in the realm of "high" culture at least) more accessible to higher classes. Dominant social dynamics, however, actually elevate informal cultural knowledge: "Even in the classroom, the dominant definition of the legitimate way of appropriating culture and works of art favors those who have had early access to legitimate culture, in a cultured household, outside of scholastic disciplines, since even within the educational system it devalues scholarly knowledge and interpretation as 'scholastic' or even 'pedantic' in favor of direct experience and simple delight" (Bourdieu 1984: 2). Even though Sublime Frequencies opposes itself deliberately to what Bourdieu would call "legitimate" taste, the label lays claim to taste in a similar way—by decrying "scholastic" knowledge in favor of aesthetic experience, masking the role of acquired codes in making that experience possible.

Beyond this, the label cultivates "an aesthetic of [. . .] soulful experience inspired by [. . .] research," applauding the work of "pioneering record labels" that produced and classified folkloric recordings in the past. This history of knowledge production at the intersection of ethnography and the music industry (cf. Ochoa Gaultier 2006) is cast as an aesthetic object in itself, in opposition to contemporary academic research and the corporate recording industry. Ultimately, however, I would argue that the power of connoisseurship, however oppositional in tone, has its roots in classificatory practices stretching from early modern natural history through early twentieth century collections of "primitive" art and culture. A collector who snubs conventional taxonomies by constructing kaleidoscopic collages of oddities claims curatorial authority not just through direct aesthetic experience or "simple delight," but also through his specialized knowledge of obscure musical artifacts—and the categories that they defy.

As the collector of *Latinamericarpet* offers, like a seasoned traveler, to guide the casual listener through unfamiliar aural terrain, several shades of primitivism inflect the collection. Children's music, traditional melodies, zany experiments, and artifacts from the childhood of rock appear side by side, with a curatorial approach that seems to suggest a contrast between the collector's worldly knowledge and the naively surreal qualities of the sounds themselves. With such rare specimens, Sublime Frequencies may challenge ethnographic and art-historical conventions of what " 'deserves' to be kept" as authentic art or culture. But *Latinamericarpet*—and in many ways the label in general—reproduces the temporal and spatial dimensions of primitivism, which imply that collections can cultivate opposition to modernity by rescuing objects—especially those gathered in far-off lands—from historical decay or oblivion (cf. Clifford 1988: 231).

III. THE POLITICS OF HISTORICAL AMNESIA

While the "psychedelic" frame of *Latinamericarpet* reflects contemporary reception rather than the ways that the recordings most likely were consumed in the time and place of their production, the glib references in the liner notes to the recovery of "forgotten" sounds erase the actual history of what happened in Latin America during the 1960s and 1970s. The notes go on to bookend a description of the musical selections with these remarks: "This compilation brings together some glittering sounds mainly from 60's/70's Latin American LPs, that have been somehow forgotten over the years. [. . .] For sure these selections are only brief samples of what was done in Latin America in those glorious years, but while we wait for further works that can bring to light more sounds from this 'undiscovered' continent, just relax, turn on your stereo and keep this magic *Latinamericarpet* flying . . . "

It is truly absurd to call these "glorious years." Between 1964 and 1976, military coups brought repressive dictatorial governments to every South American country represented on the record: Brazil (1964), Peru (1968), Chile (1973), and Argentina (1976). As part of the United States' Cold War policy to eradicate left-wing dissent in the region, the CIA's Operation Condor backed the military governments of Argentina, Chile, Brazil, Uruguay, and Paraguay. These regimes coordinated efforts to imprison, torture, and often "disappear" citizens considered subversive, including some armed guerrillas and their sympathizers, but also community and labor leaders as well as anyone associated with the left-wing political parties banned by the dictatorial regimes.

In Peru and Mexico, histories of political repression and violence developed somewhat differently. The military government of Peru participated peripherally in Plan Condor strategy, though that country's worst recent period of political violence would not occur until the 1980s. During the 1950s and 1960s, while economic decline contributed to mounting political unrest and polarization in many of the Southern Cone countries, Mexico witnessed an economic boom later known as the "Mexican Miracle." Its benefits, however, did not extend to most of the working classes. The Mexican government was not the product of a military coup, but it had been controlled by one party since 1929, and left-wing discontent with its anti-democratic policies grew in tandem with global and regional trends. On October 2, 1968, during the lead-up to the Olympic Games in Mexico City, the national army brutally massacred hundreds of university students involved in nonviolent protests for social justice.

During these tumultuous years, political polarization affected popular music in complex ways. Latin American states already had a long history of exalting commercialized musical folklore as iconic of territorial identity. (This practice had begun to approach self-parody by 1970, when the government of Argentina's Formosa province used folkloric guitars to underscore the region's "charm" [Tracks 1 and 6].) Yet beginning in the 1950s, throughout the region, an association had become established between the celebration of national folk traditions and left-wing politics, including revolutionary movements. During the 1960s, popular song movements in many countries united oppositional and progressive messages, acoustic guitar-based songwriting, and indigenous rhythms and instruments. In this context, rock music was associated with *both* oppositional youth counterculture *and* U.S. hegemony, cultural imperialism, and CIA backing of right-wing forces. Debates about the relationship of musical taste to political subjectivity were not always predictable, however, and were complicated further in many cases by the tendency of military governments to appropriate musical folklore as emblematic of right-wing nationalism.

The recordings of *Latinamericarpet* were produced and originally received in this dynamic context. A brief trace of the ideological conflicts surrounding rock music in a number of countries illustrates this complex and ambiguous history, which varied between countries and regions: For example, in Brazil in the late 1960s, the Tropicalists sought to remap ideological conflicts between rockers and cultural nationalist proponents of *música popular brasileira* by combining musical elements of the two; the results antagonized both the left and the right, and members of the movement eventually were imprisoned and exiled by the military government (Dunn 2001; Veloso 2002).

In Mexico, rock music held powerful countercultural associations and links with the student movement for democratization, though some intellectuals decried U.S. influence over fashion. After the massacre of 1968, Eric Zolov argues, "there was, in a fundamental sense, nowhere for youth to turn but La Onda," and the enmeshment of countercultural style, rock rhythms, and left-wing political opposition grew stronger (Zolov 1999: 132).

In Peru, the advent of a nationalistic military dictatorship in 1968 suffocated the vibrant rock scene not because of countercultural associations, which were not as strong as in many other countries, but because of its association with the cultural influence of the United States (Cornejo Guinassi 2002: 33–35).

Uruguay's military dictatorship (1973–1985) also embraced cultural nationalism and eradicated the burgeoning rock scene of the late 1960s. Unlike in Peru, however, rock's disappearance occurred not as a direct result of rising tides of nationalism, but as a consequence of the exile of key figures and the tightening of restrictions on social activity (Trigo 2004).

In Argentina, rock music actually expanded through the late 1960s and 1970s despite censorship and crackdowns on countercultural activity, becoming a central component of cultures of resistance after the coup d'état in 1976 (Vila 1992).

In Chile, on the other hand, although rock musicians suffered curfews and other repressive measures along with the general population, rock music became associated with conservative sectors of society as repression concentrated upon musicians associated with the highly politicized *nueva canción* (new song) movement, many members of which were exiled or murdered by the military regime. At times, the dictatorial government reportedly played rock loudly to mask the cries of prisoners in detainment centers (Ponce 2008).

Given these disparate histories, it is clear that no simple narrative can encapsulate the politics of rock music in Latin America during the 1960s and 1970s. For contemporary audiences in their countries of origin, the electric guitars, fuzz effects, and back beats of *Latinamericarpet* probably held a multitude of social, cultural, and political connotations. But what does it mean to attempt to erase these histories completely, and is it even possible to do so? In rescuing forgotten sounds while actively masking the contexts of their production, the collection replaces one kind of forgetting with another. I do not mean to assert that Costillares should have determined the political orientation of each artist toward the military regime in his or her country and reported it in the liner notes. Rather, I ask what is lost when artifacts of a complex and multifaceted cultural history are reduced to eclecticism and eccentricity.

In the 1990s in North America, the trendy collection of musical oddities dovetailed with a broader commercial celebration of "wackiness" that became so pervasive that National Public Radio's *This American Life* devoted a whole show to it in 1998. As host Ira Glass remarked: "Wacky to me seems to miss the point of everything interesting. Wacky eradicates empathy and thoughtfulness and feeling. [. . .] Wacky is what people say when they don't want to feel anything or think anything. Wacky is what people say when they don't know what else to say. When you call somebody wacky you're ignoring who they are, and painting a big smiley face on top of their real face."[14]

While some Sublime Frequencies releases may seek to impart "soulful experience inspired by music and culture," the framing of *Latinamericarpet* as something akin to "wacky" works against this goal. It would be beyond the scope of this essay to track down the "real face" of all the performers on the compilation and reconstruct how they negotiated personal and aesthetic relationships with the charged debates that undoubtedly surrounded cultural production in their countries at the time these tracks were produced. In my view, however, to become aware of this dark and complicated history adds another layer of meaning to the "soulful experience" of aesthetic appreciation, and allows listeners separated by time, geography, and cultural milieu to cultivate an empathetic and thoughtful relationship to music and history at the same time.

The relationship between the sounds of *Latinamericarpet* and the violence of Latin America's past becomes present in its conspicuous absence from the texts of the liner notes and lyrics. This history haunts the sounds of the record, pushing the past context of production into the present moment of reception, invoking the "ghostly matters" of state terror (not to mention the legacies of slavery and imperialism) that inevitably framed the social lives of musicians and their audiences in Latin America during the 1960s and 1970s (cf. Gordon 1997). How many of the musicians that appear on *Latinamericarpet* (and how many of their relatives, colleagues, and friends) were imprisoned or forced into exile by dictatorial regimes? What was the position of the municipal official who mandated the production of *Formosa tiene su hechizo* toward the increasing surveillance and suspicion of left-wing activists in his region? How many Argentine parents listening to *Peter and the Wolf* with their children in the 1960s would be detained or disappeared by the state a few years later? How many fans of instrumental Mexican surf rock were killed at Tlatelolco in 1968?

While there are many layers of musical experience to appreciate without considering such context, a collector's indifference to these questions reflects privilege: not only the disposable income and time required to sustain the hobby, but also a leisurely disregard for political consciousness and the material conditions that motivate it. Attention to taxonomical knowledge and the experience of disoriented listening replaces acknowledgment of the historical circumstances that produced particular recordings. Audiences can engage with the history that links the sounds of *Latinamericarpet* and other Sublime Frequencies releases to social and political realities, but this requires looking and listening beyond the records themselves. After the initial wackiness subsides, a listener can begin to experience history empathetically as social memory, especially if she seeks out intergenerational and intercultural dialogue with those who witnessed particular times in particular places. In this way, analog vinyl textures become material traces of the social past.

CONCLUSIONS

Instead of seeking to evaluate the relative complicity of *Latinamericarpet* in the colonialist tropes of "discovery" that the liner notes both dismiss and reproduce, I have argued that we can discern political meanings of the compilation in two other ways. First, I argue that the persistence of these tropes in debates surrounding Sublime Frequencies compilations arises because the compilations themselves emerge from the sensibilities, discourses, and practices of record collecting. By considering record collecting as part of the history of the collecting and taxonomy of art objects, ethnographic artifacts, and living things, we can appreciate how the compilations produce a sort of epistemology that simultaneously claims knowledge as power and seeks to challenge this equation by elevating the surreal above the empirical. Second, I argue that, in the case of *Latinamericarpet*, the curatorial strategy of erasing historical and contextual references works against the possibility of empathetic engagement with the musical selections or their creators. Instead, the compilation cultivates an ambivalent relationship to the notion of oppositionality. On the one hand, like many record collectors and Sublime Frequencies as a whole, *Latinamericarpet* cultivates opposition to "mainstream" tastes—and invokes opposition to modernity itself—by championing marginal, forgotten, and eccentric sounds. On the other hand, by completely masking the very real history of high-stakes, socially grounded political opposition and conflict in the times and places where these sounds were produced, the collection reproduces apologist stances of amnesia regarding repressive and violent periods of history. Ultimately, these positions do not have to mutually exclude one another. The impulse to celebrate the rough, analog textures of these recordings and take a semi-illicit pleasure in "discovering" or "exploring" them can derive meaningful strength from a shadowy specter of the countercultural, revolutionary drive that, long ago and in many places, gave rock and roll its edge.

NOTES

Many thanks to Michael E. Veal and E. Tammy Kim for editing feedback, and to Alex Huerta-Mercado, Olivier Conan, and Robin Blotnick for support and references.

1. The notes published with the record on Sublime Frequencies' website acknowledge that very little guitar-based psychedelic rock appears on the compilation; the notes published with the CD have a slightly different text, which refers to all the material as "psychedelia."

2. In Mexico, the first appearances of rock and roll in the mid-1950s were not actually associated with youth culture or rebellion, but appeared alongside mambo and other Caribbean and big band dance musics aimed at adults and youth alike. It wasn't until a few years later that Mexican rock and roll came to represent a youth trend (Zolov 1999: 17–19).

3. Track 10 is credited to an Argentine band called "Los Renos"; it is actually by a Mexican band called Los Reno.

4. *Cumbia* is a genre of traditional popular music that originated on the Caribbean coast of Colombia and Panama through the transculturation of Indigenous, African, and Spanish musical styles. Beginning in the 1940s, Colombia began to export *cumbia* as "tropical" dance music to other parts of Latin America. *Cumbia's* impact on other countries in the region increased particularly after the Cuban revolution of 1959 complicated the import of "tropical" styles from Cuba, which had enjoyed wide popularity during previous decades. Local variants of *cumbia* eventually arose in many different Latin American countries, becoming extremely popular and commercially successful as dance music.

5. Track 27 from *La Familia Telerín* is credited as Argentine and Mexican, but the show actually originated in Spain before being syndicated in Latin America. I was unable to find out whether tracks 13 and 18 were associated with television programs.

6. The *Mundial* LP lists no date, but was probably released in 1970 or 1971 (Olivier Conan, personal communication, October 21, 2011).

7. The notes also reflect translation issues or perhaps Costillares' somewhat limited familiarity with English. For example, "rests" is clearly a bad translation of *"restos"* or remains.

8. The blog's straightforward title means "Hard to Find Records" (accessed November 2011; by November 2015, the site had been taken down). Also, songs by Los Destellos were featured in the soundtrack of the acclaimed 2009 film *La Teta Asustada*, nominated for an Academy Award for Best Foreign Language Film.

9. Digital music piracy actually has declined, however, in recent years, and in 2012 global revenues from recorded music sales rose for the first time since 1999. This is due in large part to the rise of legal downloading through platforms like the Apple iTunes store and inexpensive streaming services like Spotify and Pandora, as well as crackdowns in 2012 on major file-sharing sites and programs by the U.S. government as well as Internet service providers (Kravets 2012; Li 2012; Luckerson 2013). These trends may be making the sort of obscure material represented on *Latinamericarpet* once again less accessible. At the time of this essay's publication, original full albums by the artists on the record were significantly harder to find and download than they were when the essay was first written, in 2011 (though some were still available on music sharing blogs), and very few were available on Spotify (nor was the album itself).

10. http://www.sublimefrequencies.com/ (accessed October 22, 2011).

11. Personal communication, October 21, 2011.

12. Portions of this section's text and argument are reproduced from "Pirate Collections/Virtual Crafts: Visual Mediations of Musical Knowledge in the 'Circuito Cool Montevideano,'" which is chapter 2 of my doctoral dissertation, *Between Two Monsters: Popular Music, Visual Media and the Rise of Global Indie in 21st Century Uruguay* (2012).

13. By "traditional" ethnography, ethnomusicology, and anthropology, I mean the approaches to those disciplines that emerged at the turn of the twentieth century (em-

bedded within colonialism), prevailed through most of the 1970s, and continue to define the fields in popular imagination. Since anthropology embraced self-critique in the 1970s and 1980s, ethnographic scholars increasingly have incorporated critical perspectives on the relationship between knowledge production and power.

14. "Death to Wacky," original air date March 20, 1998. Accessed October 21, 2011 at http://www.thisamericanlife.org/radio-archives/episode/97/death-to-wacky.

BIBLIOGRAPHY

Boon, M. (2006). "Sublime Frequencies' Ethnopsychedelic Montages." *Electronic Book Review*.

Bourdieu, P. (1984). *Distinction: A Social Critique of the Judgment of Taste*. Cambridge, Mass.: Harvard University Press.

Brady, E. (1999). *A Spiral Way: How the Phonograph Changed Ethnography*. Jackson: University of Mississippi Press.

Clifford, J. (1988). "On Collecting Art and Culture." In *The Predicament of Culture: Twentieth-Century Ethnography, Literature and Art*, 215–52. Cambridge, Mass.: Harvard University Press.

Cornejo Guinassi, P. (2002). *Alta Tensión: Los cortocircuitos del rock peruano*. Lima, Emedece Ediciones.

Dunn, C. (2001). *Brutality Garden: Tropicália and the Emergence of a Brazilian Counterculture*. Chapel Hill: University of North Carolina Press.

Foucault, M. (1970). *The Order of Things: An Archaeology of the Human Sciences*. London: Tavistock Publications.

Frank, T. (1998). *The Conquest of Cool: Business Culture, Counterculture, and the Rise of Hip Consumerism*. Chicago: University of Chicago Press.

Gaonkar, D. P. (2001). *Alternative Modernities*. Durham, N.C.: Duke University Press.

Garramuño, F. (2007). *Modernidades primitivas: tango, samba y nación*. Buenos Aires: Fondo de Cultura Económica.

Gordon, A. (1997). *Ghostly Matters: Haunting and the Sociological Imagination*. Minneapolis: University of Minnesota Press.

Harvey, J. J. (2002). "Cannibals, Mutants, and Hipsters: The Tropicalist Revival." In *Brazilian Popular Music and Globalization*, edited by C. A. Perrone and C. Dunn. London: Routledge.

Kravets, D. (2012). "Copyright Scofflaws Beware: ISPs To Begin Monitoring Illicit File Sharing." *Wired*, October 8, 2012. http://www.wired.com/2012/10/isp-file-sharing-monitoring/.

Li, W. (2012). "File-sharing and Online Storage Sites Duck for Cover Following Megaupload Crackdown." *International Business Times*, January 24, 2012. http://www.ibtimes

.com/file-sharing-online-storage-sites-duck-cover-following-megaupload-crack
down-399990.

Luckerson, V. (2013). "Revenue Up, Piracy Down: Has the Music Industry Finally Turned
a Corner?" *Time*, February 28, 2013. http://business.time.com/2013/02/28/revenue-up
-piracy-down-has-the-music-industry-finally-turned-a-corner/.

Markarian, V. (1998). "Al ritmo del reloj: adolescentes uruguayos de los años cincuenta."
Historias de la vida privada en el Uruguay: Tomo 3, Individuo y soledades (1920–1990),
edited by J. P. Barrán, G. Caetano, and T. Porzecanski, 238–65. Montevideo: Taurus.

Moore, R. (1997). *Nationalizing Blackness: Afrocubanism and Artistic Revolution in Havana,
1920–1940*. Pittsburgh: University of Pittsburgh Press.

Ochoa Gaultier, A. M. (2006). "Sonic Transculturation, Epistemologies of Purification,
and the Aural Public Sphere in Latin America." *Social Identities* 12(6): 803–25.

Ponce, D. (2008). *Prueba de sonido: Primeras historias del rock en Chile (1956–1984)*.
Santiago, Ediciones B.

Romero, R. R. (2007). *Andinos y tropicales: La cumbia peruana en la ciudad global*. Lima:
Pontificia Universidad Católica del Perú, Instituto de Etnomusicología.

Straw, W. (1997). "Sizing Up Record Collections: Gender and Connoisseurship in Rock
Music Culture." In *Sexing the Groove: Popular Music and Gender*, edited Sheila Whiteley,
3–16. New York: Routledge.

———. (2000). "Exhausted Commodities: The Material Culture of Music." *Canadian
Journal of Communication* 25(1).

Trigo, A. (2004). "The Politics and Anti-Politics of Uruguayan Rock." In *Rockin' Las
Américas: The Global Politics of Rock in Latin/o America*, edited by D. Pacini Hernan-
dez, H. Fernandez L'Hoeste, and E. Zolov. Pittsburgh: University of Pittsburgh Press.

Veloso, C. (2002). *Tropical Truth: A Story of Music and Revolution in Brazil*. New York:
Alfred A. Knopf; distributed by Random House.

Zolov, E. (1999). *Refried Elvis: The Rise of the Mexican Counterculture*. Berkeley: University
of California Press.

CRISTINA CRUZ-URIBE

Funk Carioca and Urban Informality

Proibidão C.V: Forbidden Gang Funk from Rio de Janeiro (2007) opens with a
slogan reminiscent of that heard before a radio or television news show—but
with a nefarious twist. A heavily altered voice announces "*Frequencia Comando
Vermelho*" (Frequency Red Command), a nod to the criminal faction controlling
the urban shantytowns where the music was recorded in 2003.[1] As this first track
transitions seamlessly into the next, the voice of a news reporter emerges as if
broadcasting from the scene of a crime. Next, through static in the distance, a
rougher voice is heard speaking confidently. Machine-gunshots and sirens follow,
as an MC begins shout-outs to the crowd in a gruff voice. Finally, the shots and
sirens morph into heavy electronic drum-machine beats, while the MC seamlessly
bridges the transition as if there were no difference between the two.

Proibidão C.V contains fourteen musical tracks ranging from one and a half to
five minutes in length. The pieces on the album maintain the barebones texture
heard in this opening rap: one or two vocalists sing in a characteristically rough,
sometimes aggressive, voice over loud electronic beats. Most tracks contain some
form of introduction, including samples of gunshots, sirens, recorded speech,
or the mainstream broadcast media.

Carlos Casas, a filmmaker specializing in documentaries of extreme environments, recorded *Proibidão C.V* in Rio de Janeiro, Brazil, at public dances
during March and April of 2003.[2] The album captures a diverse collection of
funk carioca, funk music produced in Rio de Janeiro since the mid-1980s. As its
name suggests, Rio's funk tradition emerged as a local variant on U.S. hip-hop,
popularized at dances known as *baile funks* throughout the city during the 1970s
and 1980s. *Funk carioca* is also unmistakably Brazilian. The raps are replete with
the imitation and parody of Brazilian pop, samba, and *forró*.[3] In addition, those
attuned to the social and sound environments of Rio's *favelas*, the local name for

The anonymous tracks of *Proibidão C.V: Forbidden Gang Funk from Rio de Janeiro* (SF038) invite the listener into Brazil's *favela* dance parties.

shantytowns, can make out references to individuals, events, and the ambient sounds of the community at large. As the opening moments of *Proibidão C.V* attest, the music heard on the disc is indeed barebones. Yet Casas' collection is also a rich sonic documentary.

Despite the variety of material heard on the *Proibidão C.V* collection, and within *funk carioca* more generally, Sublime Frequencies emphasizes the violence, criminality, and austerity of life in Rio's *favelas* to market the disc. The choice of title and cover images strongly establishes the connection between the music on the album and illegal gang activity. In the liner notes, we see aerial images of bare-chested young men on empty streets and the subtitle *Forbidden Gang Funk from Rio de Janeiro* reinforces the reference to clandestine activity. The word *proibidão* itself can be translated as "extremely prohibited," and C.V, refers to Comando Vermelho, Rio's oldest and most notorious criminal faction. The photo featured on the cover emphasizes an austere and barren image of Rocinha, one of Rio's largest *favelas*.

In a review from 2008, Charlie Bertsch notes that Sublime Frequencies seems to focus on music from the East, particularly from areas strongly influenced by Islam.[4] This is undeniably true, but Sublime Frequencies' eclectic output also prominently features music from burgeoning urban areas of the global South. Both the sound recordings and DVDs include music from some of the world's largest and fastest-growing metropolitan areas, including Delhi, Bangkok, Cairo, and Rio de Janeiro. Since 2004, as Sublime Frequencies has released aural documentaries of these so-called megacities, a noteworthy body of literature studying them has appeared in print.[5] These Southern urban centers are as far apart as their musical traditions are distinct, but they share particular development patterns and challenges increasingly described through the theoretical language of "informality."

The dialogue around informality in Rio and cities across the world focuses on housing, employment, urban planning, and the economy more broadly. Through a case study of *Proibidão C.V,* I explore two questions that connect musical aesthetics with this growing interdisciplinary dialogue: How can informality theory contribute productively to an analysis of cultural production? And how can it shed light on the *Proibidão C.V* disc and on *funk carioca* more generally? I argue that this album exemplifies an aesthetic of informality—an aural rendering of the contrasts between, as well as the juxtaposition and overlap of, the legal and illegal, mainstream and subaltern elements that characterize Rio's urban geography.

These questions differ from those most frequently addressed in the literature on *funk carioca.* In both Portuguese and English-language works, scholars have focused on the lyrical content of funk music, its positive and negative representation in the media, and the ethnography of *bailes funk.*[6] Paul Sneed's work, which consistently challenges the Brazilian and foreign press's connection of funk with Rio's criminal underworld of violence and drug smuggling, has been most influential in criticism of *Proibidão C.V.*[7] Following his lead, Gregory Scruggs harshly criticized Sublime Frequencies in a paper read at the meeting of the Brazilian Studies Association in 2008. His essay decries the disc's cover art, liner notes, and music credits. Moreover, he accuses Sublime Frequencies of exoticizing *funk carioca* and its *favela* context by imposing anonymity on the performers and providing vague or inaccurate information about where the music was recorded and the topics treated therein.[8] I respect Scruggs's criticism but also believe that the fascinating cultural document preserved by Sublime Frequencies in the *Proibidão C.V* recording deserves an analysis that looks beyond the shortcomings of its packaging.

My discussion of the album considers how we can hear the layers and shades of informality in funk carioca and on *Proibidão C.V* in particular. This thesis unfolds in two parts. In the first, I situate the funk music captured by Sublime Frequencies historically, within the gang-led unrest in Rio during the early 2000s as well as in the development of the city's homegrown funk tradition. In the second section, I analyze a series of sonic fragments from the collection containing news clips and song lyrics pertaining to a major gang uprising in Rio during the spring of 2003. I argue that they represent a discourse between Rio's funk artists and the mainstream Brazilian media, and that we can hear the flow, juxtaposition, and rupture in this dialogue as reflections of everyday informality in Rio.

————

During March and April 2003, when Carlos Casas recorded the Sublime Frequencies disc, Rio's *favela* communities were seeing the aftermath of a citywide riot. The unrest had taken place during the third week of February, the week before some 400,000 tourists were set to arrive in Rio for Carnival celebrations. That year, however, Rio made news around the world before Carnival even started. The situation was exceptional enough to inspire one of Rio's most famous authors and music scholars, Ruy Castro, to write a book about that week, set in the history and culture of the city: *Carnival Under Fire.*[9]

As documented in the international press, the conflicts between Comando Vermelho (C.V) gang forces and the government unfolded between Monday and Thursday. Reading the coverage, one cannot help but appreciate the strength of the gang forces—and especially their imprisoned leader Luiz Fernando da Costa, popularly known as Fernandinho Beira-Mar. Following the orders of their imprisoned leader, C.V gang members burned city buses, looted supermarkets, and ordered local businesses to close.[10] In retaliation, police forces detained 22 individuals and occupied nine *favelas*.[11] By Wednesday, the governor had deployed over 30,000 local law-enforcement officials and requested an additional 3,000 federal troops.[12] How had this imprisoned gang leader coordinated a riot of this scale? Although behind bars in Rio's maximum security Bangu-1 prison, Beira-Mar allegedly orchestrated the attacks with a smuggled cellular phone. On Thursday, Beira-Mar was airlifted from his Rio prison to one of the country's most secure facilities in São Paulo. In order to prevent continued telephone communication with his gang, authorities placed him in a facility specially equipped to block the use of cell phones.[13]

In *Carnival Under Fire,* Castro argues that this citywide riot was "one for the record books," but that it also serves to underscore tensions between the legal and illegal, violent and relaxed elements that lurk below the surface of daily life.[14] With increasing frequency, social scientists have applied informality theory to discuss these tensions in megacities like Rio. This same theoretical language is useful in the analysis of cultural production.

Indeed, Castro's thesis aptly applies to *Proibidão C. V.* The contents of this disc reflect the exceptional circumstances in which it was recorded. In *funk carioca*, however, the representation of conflict between criminal factions and authorities, as well as the rough and austere sound quality of the music, are not particularly out of the ordinary.

———

The term "informality" was coined by anthropologist Keith Hart in the early 1970s to describe the market economy in Accra, Ghana. According to his definition, a formal job, such as a government post, is one in which wages are reported to the government and taxed. An informal job, on the other hand—such as that of a domestic worker, street shoeshine "boy," or drug dealer—would go unreported. Informality has also been applied in the realm of housing and urban planning. The *favelas*, for example, are often considered informal settlements, since many of them were built on land to which the residents held no formal title or deed.[15] This dual definition of informality is still in use, although more recent scholars have begun to add nuance to the term. In an introduction to a volume of *Planning Theory* from 2009, Ananya Roy proposes a more dynamic definition: "Inscribed in the ever-shifting relationship between what is legal and illegal, legitimate and illegitimate, authorized and unauthorized, informality is a state of exception and ambiguity such that the ownership, use, and purpose of land cannot be fixed and mapped according to any set of regulations or the law."[16]

This understanding of informality accurately accounts for the complexities of the urban situation in contemporary Brazil, where informality has many layers and shades. We can appreciate the situation in Rio by applying informality to the critical realms of housing and employment.

In Rio, a resident may purchase land, and even a home, yet lack formal paperwork. His neighborhood may be recognized officially as part of the city but be practically governed by a criminal faction. He may pay bills for electricity, Internet, and cable television, or illegally pirate these services. The kinds of employment available to residents lacking work authorization can change over time.[17] Many workers choose to work both formally and informally to make ends meet. The most telling example of this is in Rio's police force, where many officers work for the state and also provide private security services. Officers take these second jobs, at companies that may or may not be legally registered, because state salaries are so low.[18]

The rise of the drug trade in Rio adds a critical facet to informality in Rio. In the 1980s, the city became a major transshipment hub for the trafficking of Colombian cocaine, during the same period when the IMF/World Bank lending policy required borrowing nations to lift economic protections and Latin America's production industries moved overseas.[19] The loss of jobs in manufacturing created an unemployment crisis that the drug trade was able to capitalize on.[20] Rio's *favelas* became centers of international cocaine traffic, and the relative wealth accumulated by criminal factions in the local drug industry fostered the development of the funk tradition heard on *Proibidão C.V.*

Funk carioca has its roots in the music of James Brown. His American hits became popular at large weekend dances in the 1970s, as the *Movimento Black Rio*, the city's Black Power movement, gained momentum.[21] During the 1970s and 1980s, sound artists in Rio began to incorporate Brazilian musical traditions, distinguishing their work from the hip-hop and funk produced in the United States. Hip-hop in an international style remained popular in São Paulo, while a nationalized funk tradition came to dominate the scene in Rio.[22] Starting in the mid-1990s, lyrics were in Portuguese instead of English, and locally produced funk music came into its own, while still clearly referencing its origins in American funk and hip-hop. The most audible stylistic connections was in the beats: from the iconic sound of Afrika Baambaata's drum machine from his hit "Planet Rock" single (1982) to the dance-club feel of the "booty beats" borrowed from Miami bass.[23] Since its inception in Rio, funk was strongly vilified in the press and performed increasingly in the urban periphery, especially the *favelas*, where its association with Rio's drug culture was augmented by its proximity to the traffic.[24] The variant of funk that referenced the *favela* drug culture became known as *proibidão*. This is the illegal, or "forbidden," funk captured on the Sublime Frequencies disc.[25]

Over the same period that funk gained popularity in the *favelas*, locally organized criminal factions established one of the world's largest cocaine-distribution industries in these communities.[26] Initially populated in the late nineteenth century by refugees and freed slaves, Rio's *favelas* have developed into semiautonomous communities.[27] By the 1990s, continual neglect by the city government had left these neighborhoods in dire need of services, leaving an opening for criminal factions. These groups began to attend to the basic needs of residents in return for their tacit support of drug operations. Beyond creating a significant number of jobs, these factions also contributed financially to community projects and organizations.[28] In 2009, according to researcher Janice Perlman, nearly one-fifth of Rio's population lived in some 1,000 *favelas*.[29]

Proibidão funk emerged at the center of one of these social undertakings. In the 1990s, Rio's criminal factions began to organize massive, regularly scheduled dances, called *bailes funk*, or *bailes de comunidade*. The MCs for these events are hired to sing the praises of the reigning criminal faction, while members of the gang appear in person, sporting machine guns, jewelry, and brand-name clothing inaccessible to average members of the community.[30] Based on its frequent references to drug cartels, the music is illegal in Brazil: Two articles of the Penal Code forbid apology for crime.[31] While certainly comparable to the commercially successful subgenre of gangsta rap in the United States, *proibidão* funk has more in common with other Latin American musics associated with the drug trade. These include the folk-derived *narcocorrido* in Mexico and Colombia as well as a subset of Jamaican dancehall music called "gun talk" or "gun business." This variant of dancehall emerged in Kingston in the 1980s, when urban violence increased dramatically and the city preceded Rio as a major transshipment hub for Colombian cocaine.[32] In these dancehall pieces, performers' lyrics, sound effects, and gestures frequently glorified gangsters and guns. On the whole, *proibidão* funk treats a diverse range of topics, but on the *Proibidão C.V* disc, bandits and guns are central.

———

In spite of Comando Vermelho's well-orchestrated riot, Carnival opened the final Friday of February 2003 as planned, the day after Beira-Mar was airlifted to São Paulo. That year, the samba schools' famous parades were accompanied by an equally spectacular display of both municipal and federal security forces.[33] With Beira-Mar imprisoned out of state, the funk performed in Comando Vermelho–controlled *favelas* transformed the gang leader's memory into a call for solidarity. A number of raps on the Sublime Frequencies disc articulate a creative discourse with competitive overtones between funk artists and the mainstream media. Through appropriation, parody, and commentary on the popular media, *Proibidão C.V* exemplifies an aesthetic of informality—an aural rendering of the juxtapositions, contrasts, and overlap of legal and illegal, mainstream and subaltern elements characteristic of contemporary Rio. I elucidate this by analyzing three tracks that specifically reference the city's gang-related tension of 2002 and 2003.

As described in the beginning of this essay, *Proibidão C.V* opens by parodying a news broadcast. Following the first track's announcement of "Frequency Red Command," the second track follows immediately with a series of samples that report and recreate the sound world of events from 2002. The Carnival uprising in February 2003 was strongly reminiscent of a riot orchestrated by Beira-Mar just a few months earlier, in September 2002, just before Brazil's presidential elections. In addition to city riots, that uprising included a prison revolt in which four rival gang members were tortured and executed.[34] At the start of Track 2, we hear a chain of samples that remake this broadcast. The first two sound bites contrast a local news clip from the day after Beira-Mar's prison uprising with another clip—ostensibly of the gang leader himself—separated by an abrupt cut. First, the clear voice of a broadcaster:

> *A Polícia Federal nega ter uma fita na qual o traficante Fernandinho Beira-Mar estaria cantando um funk para comemorar o assasinato de rivais durante a rebelião ontem no presídio Bangu-1.* ("The Federal Police denies having a tape on which the trafficker Fernandinho Beira-Mar is singing a funk to commemorate the assassination of rivals during an uprising yesterday at the Bangu-1 prison.")[35]

Next, Fernandinho Beira-Mar, from behind bars:

> *Quem está no Bangu aí sou eu, mas só tô preso, num tô morto não . . .* ("The one who's in the Bangu is me, but I'm just imprisoned, I'm not dead . . .")[36]

The contrasting narrations of the events are underscored by the sound quality of the samples. The voice of the news broadcaster comes through crisp and clear, while Beira-Mar is difficult to make out in the distance. The poor quality resembles the static of a bad cell-phone connection, as though we are listening in on a smuggled cell-phone call from a jail cell at Bangu-1.

This spoken introduction transitions into the funk proper when Beira-Mar is cut off by machine-gunshots. The crisp timbre of the shots, soon complemented by sirens, cuts through the thick static of the phone call. The MC comes in under the sound of the shots, as if reporting live from the scene of the crime. Then this news broadcast transitions seamlessly into the here and now of the *baile funk*: the MC shouts-out individuals and the various *favelas* represented at the dance, and the mechanical gunshots give way to the beat of an electronic drum machine. For the duration of the rap, the piece assumes the standard texture of *funk carioca* as performed live. The MC sings unaccompanied over the continual and unvaried drum pattern. Echoing the difference in sound quality in the opening samples, the mechanically sharp, clear, and tremendously loud beats contrast with the rough, untrained rasp of the vocalist. The MC's voice explores the grey areas between speaking, shouting, and singing.

We hear a similar procedure in Track 5, where the DJ again samples a clip from the local news. This segment also recalls Beira-Mar's 2002 crime and adds additional details. Taken from the news on September 12, the reporter describes the aftermath of the four assassinations and the citywide closure of schools. She recites the legal names and nicknames of the four rival gang members killed in the Bangu-1 prison:[37]

> *O poder paralelo mantem a cidade sob tensão* [gunfire & sirens], *Quatro presos foram mortos: Ernaldo Pinto de Medeiro, "O Uê"; Elpídio Sabino, "O Robô"; e dois cunhados de Uê: Wanderlei Suares, "o Orelha"; e Carlos Alberto da Costa "O Robertinho do Adeus."* [Gunfire & sirens.] ("The parallel power maintains the city under siege [gunfire & sirens]. Four prisoners were killed: Ernaldo Pinto de Medeiros, Elpídio 'The Robot' Sabino, and two of Uê's brothers-in-law: Wanderlei 'The Ear' Soares and Carlos Alberto 'Bobby Farewell' da Costa." [Gunfire & sirens.])[38]

The crisp sounds of sirens and machine-gunshots punctuate the sample, aurally evoking these killings for the audience.

The discourse with the mainstream media is brought to the fore at another moment in Track 1. The MC does not brag about Beira-Mar's prison uprising and murders or the city riots. Instead, he says these exploits have made Beira-Mar a media sensation, referencing the Globo Network, Brazil's largest media conglomerate:

> *Se liga meus amigos, que não, não vou parar: quem abalou a Rede Globo foi Fernandinho Beira-Mar.* ("Get the picture, my friends. I won't stop: the one who rocked the Globo Network was Fernandinho Beira-Mar.")[39]

While the opening sequence and this subsequent boast evoke memories of the past, the parody of a pop hit by Ivete Sangalo toward the end of Track 1 and in extended form on Track 8 looks to the future, presumably announcing a forth-coming attack. The appropriation of this particular song, "Festa"—from Sangalo's 2001 album of the same title—follows a pattern already established in the news excerpt. In both cases, the funk artists have chosen mainstream sources that make reference to themselves and their world: the news clip mentioned Beira-Mar singing a funk song to commemorate his prison victory, and Sangalo's lyrics invite everyone far and wide to a *favela* party. Rather than alternating between clips from the news and the funk artists' work, the parody of "Festa" retexts the commercially released pop melody with lyrics about a future attack in the *favela*. The original chorus goes:

> *Que vai rolar a festa, vai rolar*
> *O povo do gueto mandou avisar*
> *Que vai rolar a guerra*
> (There is going to be a party, there will be a party.
> The people from the ghetto said to make it known
> that there is going to be a party.)

The *proibidão* parody—performed live at a *favela* dance party—recasts the invitation as a declaration of war. In this new text, the MC sings:

> *E vai rolar a guerra*
> *bonde do M mandou avisar*
> *Que vai rolar a guerra*
> *Bonde do Mineiro mandou avisar*
> (And there is going to be a war
> The M's group said to make it known
> That there is going to be a war
> Mineiro's group said to make it known)

The parody of Sangalo's hit song was popular on the funk scene during the period *Proibidão C.V* was recorded. This short segment on Track 1 is borrowed from a longer funk parody. In Track 8, we hear a retexting of Sangalo's entire song, this time with beats borrowed from the original.[40]

———

By putting gang leader Beira-Mar at the center of the news and reasserting who controls the "party" in Rio, *Proibidão C.V* rewrites the *favela*'s dialogue with the media. The collection consists of a series of parodies or fragments borrowed from mainstream sources, alongside originally produced elements and sound effects. Informality theory provides a productive language and framework for analyzing *funk carioca*. The contrast, juxtaposition, and blurred boundaries between mainstream and *proibidão*, legal and illegal elements reflect the urban geography of Rio's *favelas*, where shades of informality characterize both the physical landscape and many features of residents' everyday lives.

NOTES

I am grateful to André Redwood and Francisco Cornejo de Souza for their generous assistance in the transcription, translation, and interpretation of the lyrics cited and discussed in this essay. All other translations are my own.

1. Sublime Frequencies SF038, November 2007. Recorded by Carlos Casas in Rio de Janeiro, Brazil, in March and April of 2003.

2. Casas specializes in filming documentaries about life in the world's most extreme environments, including Patagonia, Siberia, and the Aral Sea. In 2003, he recorded the music for the Sublime Frequencies collection and also directed a documentary about Rocinha, the *favela* pictured on the *Proibidão C. V* album cover, called "Rocinha: Daylight of a Favela," co-produced by Fabrica (Italy) and Giros (Brazil).

3. Paul Sneed, "*Bandidos de Cristo*: Representations of the Power of Criminal Factions in Rio's *Proibidão* Funk," *Latin American Music Review* 28, no. 2 (December 2007): 221.

4. Charlie Bertsch, "Subverting World Music: The Sublime Frequencies Label," *Tikkun* 2008. www.tikkun.org/bertsch/copy3_of_bertsch (accessed October 29, 2008).

5. This literature notably includes Robert Neuwirth, *Shadow Cities: A Billion Squatters, A New Urban World* (New York: Routledge, 2004); Mike Davis, *Planet of Slums* (New York: Verso, 2006); and Ananya Roy and Nezar AlSayyad, eds. *Urban Informality* (Lanham: Lexington Books, 2004), 171–208.

6. For a concise historiography of literature on Brazilian funk, see Sneed, "*Bandidos de Cristo*," 222–24. See a more recent ethnographic approach to the analysis of funk in Samuel Araújo, "Conflict and Violence as Theoretical Tools in Present-Day Ethnomusicology: Notes on a Dialogic Ethnography of Sound Practices in Rio de Janeiro," *Ethnomusicology* 50, no. 2 (Spring/Summer 2006): 287–313.

7. For a study of the representation of funk in the Brazilian media, see Michael Herschmann, *O funk e o hip-hop invadem a cena* (Rio de Janeiro: UFRJ, 2000).

8. Gregory Scruggs, "Unlabled: The Anonymous as Exotic in Presenting Proibidão," A paper read at the Brazilian Studies Association Annual Conference, New Orleans, 2008. The paper has been republished online: " 'All Artists Are Anonymous': Stolen Gang Funk from Rio," http://www.norient.com/html/print_article.php?ID=117. Scruggs importantly corrects the assertion in the liner notes that the music was all recorded in the *favelas* of Rio's Zona Sul. He points out that significant evidence from the lyrics on the CD suggests that the collection contains pieces recorded elsewhere in the city.

9. Ruy Castro, *Rio de Janeiro: Carnival Under Fire,* translated by John Gledson (London: Bloomsbury, 2004). This book was first published in Brazil as *Carnaval no Fogo* by the Companhia das Letras in 2003.

10. Aldo Gamboa, "A uma semana do carnaval, traficantes mostram sua força no Rio de Janeiro," *Agence France Presse* (Paris), 24 February 2003; "Comando Vermelho assume responsabilidade por atos violentos no Rio," *Agence France Presse* (Paris), 24 February 2003.

11. "Violência no tráfico: 13 feridos, 23 ônibus incendiados e 22 detidos," *Agence France Presse* (Paris), 25 February 2003.

12. Aldo Gamboa, "Governo do Rio de Janeiro lança plano para restaurar tranquilidade" *Agence France Presse* (Paris), 26 February 2003.

13. "Traficante Fernandino Beira-Mar transferido para prisão de São Paulo," *Agence France Presse* (Paris), 27 February 2003' "Beira-Mar é transferido para presídio em São Paulo," *Agence France Presse* (Paris), 27 February 2003.

14. Castro, *Rio de Janeiro,* 3–4.

15. On informal housing in Brazil, see Neuwirth, *Shadow Cities,* and Daniela Fabricious, "Resisting Representation: The Informal Geographies of Rio de Janeiro," *Harvard Design Magazine* 28 (Spring/Summer 2008): 1–8.

16. Ananya Roy, "Strangely Familiar: Planning and the Worlds of Insurgence and Informality," *Planning Theory* 8, no. 1 (2009): 8–9.

17. Janice Perlman offers the most detailed analyses of the lives, housing history, and career paths of *favela* residents: *Favela: Four Decades of Living on the Edge in Rio de Janeiro* (New York: Oxford, 2010). Alan Gilbert considers the multiple facets of the informal sector in Latin American economies in *The Latin American City,* 2nd ed. (London: The Latin American Bureau, 1998), 57–78. For a global perspective, see Ahmed M. Soliman, "Tilting at Sphinxes: Locating Urban Informality in Egyptian Cities," in *Urban Informality,* ed. Roy and AlSayyad, 171–208; Mike Davis, *Planet of Slums* (New York: Verso, 2007), 20–49.

18. Perlman, *Favela,* 182–84; Patrick Neate and Damian Platt, *Culture Is Our Weapon: Making Music and Changing Lives in Rio de Janeiro* (New York: Penguin, 2006), 125–26.

19. For an analysis of the relationship between economic liberalization and the development of the informal economy in Latin America since the 1970s, see Alan Gilbert, "Love in the Time of Enhanced Capital Flows: Reflections on the Links between Liberalization and Informality," in *Urban Informality,* ed. Roy and AlSayyad, 33–66. Gilbert demonstrates that there is not a direct correlation between increased economic liberalization and the growth of the informal sector of the economy, including the drug trade, but that increased liberalization definitely caused changes in the types of work available to residents in Latin American cities.

20. Elizabeth Leeds, "Cocaine and Parallel Polities in the Brazilian Urban Periphery: Constraints on Local Level Democratization," *Latin American Research Review* 31, no. 3 (1996): 48.

21. Silvio Essinger, *Batidão: Uma história do funk* (Rio de Janeiro and São Paulo: Record, 2005), 15–48.

22. Herschmann, *O funk e o hip-hop invadem a cena,* 25–26.

23. Sneed, *"Bandidos de Cristo,"* 221.

24. Ibid., 87–117.

25. For a history of the rise of *proibidão,* see chapter 11, "Rap das Armas," in Essinger, *Batidão,* 229–243.

26. Leeds, "Cocaine and Parallel Polities," 52–58.

27. Ibid., 58.

28. Ibid., 55; Sneed, *"Bandidos de Cristo,"* 224.

29. Perlman, *Favela,* 52.

30. See a fascinating ethnographic consideration of the sounds of violence in *proibidão* funk in the *favela* of Maré in Araújo, "Conflict and Violence."

31. Sneed, *"Bandidos de Cristo,"* 222.

32. Enrique Desmond Arias, *Drugs and Democracy in Rio de Janeiro* (Chapel Hill: The University of North Carolina Press, 2006), 183; Carolyn Cooper, "'Lyrical Gun': Metaphor and Role Play in Jamaican Dancehall Culture," *The Massachusetts Review* 35, nos. 3/4 (Autumn 1994): 429–47. See also Louis Chude-Sokei, "Postnationalist Geographies: Rasta, Ragga, and Reinventing Africa," in *Reggae, Rasta, Revolution: Jamaican Music from Ska to Dub,* ed. Chris Potash (New York: Schirmer, 1997), 218; Norman C. Stolzoff, *Wake the Town and Tell the People: Dancehall Culture in Jamaica* (Durham and London: Duke University Press, 2000), 162–63 and 166.

33. Aldo Gamboa, "Rio de Janeiro abre oficialmente o Carnaval sob segurança máxima," *Agence France Presse* (Paris), 28 February 2003.

34. "Drug Gangs Turn Carnival into a War Zone: Rio's Most Notorious Gang Leader Directs Violence from Jail," Associated Press with files from Reuters. Published in *The National Post* (Canada), 1 March 2003.

35. Track 2: 00:01–00:11.

36. Track 2: 00:11–00:16.

37. An Agence France Presse report announces these names for the first time on September 12, 2002; see "Secretaria de Segurança carioca confirma quatro mortos em rebelião."

38. Track 5: 00:00–00:35.

39. Track 2: 2:34–2:42.

40. On Track 7, *Proibidão C.V* contains another well-known parody of Sangalo's song "Carro Velho." See a transcription and discussion of the *proibidão* parody in Araújo, "Conflict and Violence," 305.

BIBLIOGRAPHY

Araújo, Samuel. "Conflict and Violence as Theoretical Tools in Present-Day Ethnomusicology: Notes on a Dialogic Ethnography of Sound Practices in Rio de Janeiro." *Ethnomusicology* 50, no. 2 (Spring/Summer 2006): 287–313.

Arias, Enrique Desmond. *Drugs and Democracy in Rio de Janeiro.* Chapel Hill: University of North Carolina Press, 2006.

"Beira-Mar é transferido para presídio em São Paulo." *Agence France Presse* (Paris), 27 February 2003.

Bertsch, Charlie. "Subverting World Music: The Sublime Frequencies Label." *Tikkun* 2008. www.tikkun.org/bertsch/copy3_of_bertsch (accessed October 29, 2008).

Castro, Ruy. *Rio de Janeiro: Carnival Under Fire*, translated by John Gledson. London: Bloomsbury, 2004. Originally published as *Carnaval no Fogo.* Brazil: Companhia das Letras, 2003.

Chude-Sokei, Louis. "Postnationalist Geographies: Rasta, Ragga, and Reinventing Africa." In *Reggae, Rasta, Revolution: Jamaican Music from Ska to Dub*, edited by Chris Potash. New York: Schirmer, 1997.

"Comando Vermelho assume responsabilidade por atos violentos no Rio." *Agence France Presse* (Paris), 24 February 2003.

Cooper, Carolyn. "'Lyrical Gun': Metaphor and Role Play in Jamaican Dancehall Culture." *The Massachusetts Review* 35, nos. 3/4 (Autumn 1994): 429–47.

Davis, Mike. *Planet of Slums.* New York: Verso, 2006.

"Drug Gangs Turn Carnival into a War Zone: Rio's Most Notorious Gang Leader Directs Violence from Jail." Associated Press with files from Reuters. Published in *The National Post* (Canada), 1 March 2003.

Essinger, Silvio. *Batidão: Uma história do funk.* Rio de Janiero and São Paulo: Record, 2005.

Fabricious, Daniela. "Resisting Representation: The Informal Geographies of Rio de Janeiro." *Harvard Design Magazine* 28 (Spring/Summer 2008): 1–8.

Gamboa, Aldo. "A uma semana do carnaval, traficantes mostram sua força no Rio de Janeiro." *Agence France Presse* (Paris), 24 February 2003.

———. "Governo do Rio de Janeiro lança plano para restaurar tranquilidade" *Agence France Presse* (Paris), 26 February 2003.

———. "Rio de Janeiro abre oficialmente o Carnaval sob segurança máxima." *Agence France Presse* (Paris), 28 February 2003.

Gilbert, Alan. *The Latin American City*, 2nd ed. London: The Latin American Bureau, 1998.

———. "Love in the Time of Enhanced Capital Flows: Reflections on the Links between Liberalization and Informality." In *Urban Informality*, ed. Ananya Roy and Nezar AlSayyad (Lanham, Md.: Lexington Books, 2004), 33–66.

Herschmann, Michael. *O funk e o hip-hop invadem a cena.* Rio de Janeiro: UFRJ, 2000.

Leeds, Elizabeth. "Cocaine and Parallel Polities in the Brazilian Urban Periphery: Constraints on Local Level Democratization." *Latin American Research Review* 31, no. 3 (1996).

Neate, Patrick, and Damian Platt. *Culture Is Our Weapon: Making Music and Changing Lives in Rio de Janeiro.* New York: Penguin, 2006.

Neuwirth, Robert. *Shadow Cities: A Billion Squatters, A New Urban World.* New York: Routledge, 2004.

Perlman, Janice. *Favela: Four Decades of Living on the Edge in Rio de Janeiro.* New York: Oxford, 2010.

Roy, Ananya. "Strangely Familiar: Planning and the Worlds of Insurgence and Informality." *Planning Theory* 8, no. 1 (2009): 8–9.

Roy, Ananya, and Nezar AlSayyad, eds. *Urban Informality.* Lanham, Md.: Lexington Books, 2004, 171–208.

Scruggs, Gregory. "Unlabled: The Anonymous as Exotic in Presenting Proibidão." A paper read at the Brazilian Studies Association Annual Conference, New Orleans, 2008. Republished online as "'All Artists Are Anonymous': Stolen Gang Funk from Rio," http://www.norient.com/html/print_article.php?ID=117.

Sneed, Paul. "*Bandidos de Cristo:* Representations of the Power of Criminal Factions in Rio's *Proibidão* Funk." *Latin American Music Review* 28, no. 2 (December 2007): 221.

Soliman, Ahmed M. "Tilting at Sphinxes: Locating Urban Informality in Egyptian Cities." In *Urban Informality,* ed. Ananya Roy and Nezar AlSayyad (Lanham, Md.: Lexington Books, 2004), 171–208.

Stolzoff, Norman C. *Wake the Town and Tell the People: Dancehall Culture in Jamaica.* Durham and London: Duke University Press, 2000.

"Traficante Fernandino Beira-Mar transferido para prisão de São Paulo." *Agence France Presse* (Paris), 27 February 2003.

"Violência no tráfico: 13 feridos, 23 ônibus incendiados e 22 detidos." *Agence France Presse* (Paris), 25 February 2003.

Discography

Sublime Frequencies Sound Recordings

(as of May 2015)

Baba Commandant and the Mandingo Band. 2015. *Juguya*. SF097. LP.

Dara Puspita. 2010. *1966—1968*. SF054. CD.

Erkin Koray. 2010. *Mechul (Singles and Rarities)*. SF067. Compilation. CD/LP.

Group Bombino. 2009. *Guitars from Agadez, Volume 2*. SF046. CD/LP.

Group Doueh. 2007. *Guitar Music from the Western Sahara*. SF030. CD/LP.

———. 2009. *Treeg Salaam*. SF048. CD/LP.

———. 2010. *Beatte Harab*. SF063. LP.

———. 2011. *Zayna Jumma*. SF066. CD/LP.

Group Inerane. 2007. *Guitars from Agadez*. SF034. CD/LP.

———. 2010. *Guitars from Agadez, Volume 3*. SF061. CD/LP.

———. 2011. *Guitars from Agadez, Volume 4*. SF069. 7-inch.

Hayvanlar Alemi. 2010. *Guarana Superpower*. SF062. CD/LP.

———. 2012. *Yekermo* Sew. SF070. 7-inch.

Koes Bersaudara. 2010. *1967*. SF053. CD.

Koudede. 2012. *Guitars from Agadez, Volume 5*. SF072. 7-inch.

———. 2012. *Guitars from Agadez, Volume 6*. SF076. 7-inch.

———. 2013. *Guitars from Agadez, Volume 7*. SF084. LP.

Omar Korshid. 2010. *Guitar El Chark (Guitar of the Orient)*. SF052. 2CD/2LP.

———. 2014. *Live in Australia, 1981*. SF091. LP.

Omar Souleyman. 2007. *Highway to Hassake*. SF031. CD/2LP.

———. 2009. *Dabke 2020 (Folk and Pop Sounds of Syria)*. SF049. CD/LP.

———. 2010. *Jazeera Nights*. SF055. CD/LP.

———. 2011. *Haflat Gharbia: The Western Concerts*. SF068. CD/2LP.

Various Artists. 2003. *Folk and Pop Sounds of Sumatra, Volume 1*. SF001. CD/LP. Compiled and edited by Scott Colburn.

———. 2003. *Night Recordings from Bali*. SF003. CD. Compiled and edited by Alan Bishop.

———. 2003. *Radio Java*. SF002. CD/LP. Compiled and edited by Alan Bishop.

———. 2004. *Broken Hearted Dragonflies: Insect Electronica from Southeast Asia*. SF013. CD/LP. Compiled and edited by Tucker Martine.

———. 2004. *Bush Taxi Mali*. SF012. CD/LP. Compiled and edited by Tucker Martine.

———. 2004. *Cambodian Cassette Archives: Khmer Folk and Pop Music*. SF011. CD. Compiled and edited by Mark Gergis.

———. 2004. *I Remember Syria*. SF009. CD. Compiled and edited by Mark Gergis.

———. 2004. *Leaf Music, Drunks, Distant Drums*. ANOM26. CD. Compiled and edited by Robert Millis. (Originally released by Anomalous Records.)

———. 2004. *Princess Nicotine: Folk and Pop Sounds of Myanmar*. SF006. CD/LP. Compiled and edited by Scott Colburn.

———. 2004. *Radio India: The Eternal Dream of Sound*. SF014. 2CD. Compiled and edited by Alan Bishop.

———. 2004. *Radio Morocco*. SF007. CD. Compiled and edited by Alan Bishop.

———. 2004. *Radio Palestine: Sounds of the Eastern Mediterranean*. SF008. CD. Compiled and edited by Alan Bishop.

———. 2005. *Choubi Choubi! Folk and Pop Sounds from Iraq*. SF025. CD / SF085. 2LP. Compiled and edited by Mark Gergis.

———. 2005. *Folk and Pop Sounds of Sumatra, Volume 2*. SF018. CD. Compiled and edited by Alan Bishop.

———. 2005. *Guitars of the Golden Triangle. Folk and Pop Music of Myanmar (Burma), Volume 2*. SF024. CD. Compiled and edited by Alan Bishop.

———. 2005. *Harmike Yab Yum: Folk Sounds from Nepal*. SF017. CD. Compiled and edited by Robert Millis.

———. 2005. *Molam: Thai Country Groove from Isan*. SF019. CD/2LP. Compiled and edited by Mark Gergis.

———. 2005. *Radio Phnom Penh*. SF020. CD. Compiled and edited by Alan Bishop.

———. 2005. *Radio Pyongyang: Commie Funk and Agit Pop from the Hermit Kingdom*. SF023. CD. Compiled and edited by Christiaan Virant.

———. 2005. *Radio Sumatra: The Indonesian FM Experience*. SF021. CD. Compiled and edited by Alan Bishop.

———. 2005. *Streets of Lhasa*. SF016. CD. Compiled and edited by Alan Bishop.

———. 2006. *Ethnic Minority Music of Northeast Cambodia*. SF027. CD. Compiled and edited by Laurent Jeanneau.

———. 2006. *Radio Algeria*. SF029. CD. Compiled and edited by Alan Bishop.

———. 2006. *Radio Thailand: Transmissions from the Tropical Kingdom*. SF028. 2CD. Compiled and edited by Alan Bishop.

———. 2007. *Ethnic Minority Music of North Vietnam*. SF037. CD. Compiled and edited by Laurent Jeanneau.

———. 2007. *Ethnic Minority Music of Southern Laos*. SF036. CD. Compiled and edited by Laurent Jeanneau.

———. 2007. *Latinamericarpet: Exploring the Vinyl Warp of Latin American Psychedelia, Volume 1*. SF039. CD. Compiled by Albano Costillares.

———. 2007. *Molam: Thai Country Groove from Isan, Volume 2*. SF033. CD/LP. Compiled and edited by Alan Bishop.

———. 2007. *Music of Nat Pwe: Folk and Pop Music of Myanmar, Volume 3*. SF035. CD. Compiled and edited by Alan Bishop.

———. 2007. *Proibidão C.V: Forbidden Gang Funk from Rio de Janeiro*. SF038. CD. Compiled and edited by Carlos Casas.

———. 2007. *Thai Pop Spectacular*. SF032. CD. Compiled and edited by Alan Bishop.

———. 2008. *1970's Algerian Proto-Rai Underground*. SF045. CD/LP. Compiled by Hicham Chadly.

———. 2008. *Bollywood Steel Guitar*. SF043 CD/2LP. Compiled by Stuart Ellis.

———. 2008. *Radio Myanmar (Burma)*. SF044. CD. Compiled and edited by Alan Bishop.

———. 2008. *Shadow Music of Thailand*. SF042. CD. Compiled by Mark Gergis.

———. 2009. *Siamese Soul: Thai Pop Spectacular, Volume Two*. SF050. CD. Compiled and edited by Mark Gergis.

———. 2009. *Singapore A-Go-Go*. SF051. CD. Compiled by William Gibson.

———. 2010. *Ecstatic Music of the Jemaa El Fna*. SF056. LP.

———. 2010. *Ethnic Music of Northwest Xinjiang (China)*. SF057. CD. Compiled and edited by Laurent Jeanneau.

———. 2010. *Koes Plus Dheg Dheg Plas and Volume Two*. SF058. CD. Compiled by Alan Bishop.

———. 2010. *Saigon Rock and Soul: Vietnamese Classic Tracks, 1968–1974*. SF060. CD/2LP. Compiled and edited by Mark Gergis.

———. 2011. *Eat the Dream: Gnawa Music from Essaouira*. SF071. LP. Compiled and edited by Tucker Martine.

———. 2011. *Pakistan: Folk and Pop Instrumentals*. SF064. 2LP. Compiled by Stuart Ellis.

———. 2011. *Staring into the Sun: Ethiopian Tribal Music*. SF074. 2LP. Compiled and edited by Olivia Wyatt.

———. 2013. *The Crying Princess: 78 Records from Burma*. SF078. LP. Compiled by Robert Millis.

———. 2013. *Ethnic Minority Music of Southern China*. SF081. CD. Compiled by Laurent Jeanneau.

———. 2013. *Hassaniya Music from the Western Sudan and Mauritania.* SF083. LP. Compiled by Hisham Mayet.

———. 2013. *Pop Yeh Yeh: Psychedelic Rock from Singapore and Malaysia, 1964–1970.* SF079. CD/2LP.

———. 2013. *Scattered Melodies: Korean Kayagum Sanjo.* SF077. LP. Compiled by Robert Millis.

———. 2014. *A Distant Invitation: Ceremonial Street Recordings from Burma, Cambodia, India, Indonesia, Malaysia and Thailand.* SF093. LP. Compiled and edited by Jesse Paul Miller.

———. 2014. *Folk Music of the Sahel, Volume One.* SF090. 2LP. Compiled and edited by Hisham Mayet.

———. 2014. *Radio Niger.* SF086. CD. Compiled and edited by Alan Bishop.

———. 2014. *Rajasthan Street Music.* SF087. 2LP. Compiled and edited by Seb Bassleer.

———. 2014. *The Travelling Archive: Folk Music from Bengal.* SF092. LP. Compiled and edited by Sukanta Majumdar.

———. 2015. *Music of Tanzania.* SF096. 2LP. Compiled and edited by Laurent Jeanneau.

———. 2015. *Radio Vietnam.* SF095. CD. Compiled and edited by Mark Gergis.

SUBLIME FREQUENCIES VIDEO RECORDINGS

Various Artists. 2004. *Folk Music of the Sahara: Among the Tuareg of Libya.* SF010. DVD. Directed by Hisham Mayet.

———. 2004. *Isan: Folk and Pop Music of Northeast Thailand.* SF015. DVD. Directed by Hisham Mayet.

———. 2004. *Jemaa El Fna: Morocco's Rendezvous of the Dead.* SF005. DVD. Directed by Hisham Mayet.

———. 2004. *Nat Pwe: Burma's Carnival of Spirit Soul.* SF004. DVD. Directed by Alan Bishop and Richard Bishop.

———. 2005. *Niger: Magic and Ecstasy in the Sahel.* SF022. DVD. Directed by Hisham Mayet.

———. 2006. *Phi Ta Khon: Ghosts of Isan.* SF026. DVD. Directed by Robert Millis.

———. 2008. *Musical Brotherhoods from the Trans-Saharan Highway.* SF041. DVD. Directed by Hisham Mayet.

———. 2008. *Sumatran Folk Cinema.* SF040. DVD. Directed by Mark Gergis and Alan Bishop.

———. 2009. *Palace of the Winds.* SF047. DVD. Directed by Hisham Mayet.

———. 2012. *The Divine River: Ceremonial Pageantry in the Sahel.* SF075. DVD. Directed by Hisham Mayet.

———. 2012. *Staring into the Sun.* SF065. DVD/CD/Book. Directed by Olivia Wyatt.

———. 2012. *The World Is Unreal Like a Snake in a Rope*. SF073. DVD. Directed by Robert Millis.

———. 2013. *The Pierced Heart and the Machete*. SF80. DVD. Directed by Olivia Wyatt.

———. 2013. *Small Path Music*. SF082. DVD. Directed by David Harris.

———. 2014. *The Stirring of a Thousand Bells*. SF094. DVD. Directed by Matt Dunning.

———. 2014. *Vodoun Gods on the Slave Coast*. SF089. DVD. Directed by Hisham Mayet.

OTHER SOUND RECORDINGS CITED IN TEXT

Amadou & Mariam. 2005. *Dimanche à Bamako*. Nonesuch 79912-2.

Balla et Ses Balladins. 2008. The Syliphone Years. Sterns STCD3035-36.

Beatles. 1967. *Magical Mystery Tour*. Capitol MAL 2835.

Bembeya Jazz National. 2004. *The Syliphone Years*. Sterns STCD 3021-22.

Chadbourne, Euguene with Sun City Girls. 1989. *Country Music in the World of Islam Volume XV*. Save 80.

Coleman, Ornette and Prime Time. 1988. *Virgin Beauty*. Portrait RK 44301.

Davis, Miles. 1970. *Bitches Brew*. Columbia G2K-40577.

Eno, Brian. 1978. *Ambient 1: Music for Airports*. EG Editions. LP.

Frisell, Bill, Matt Chamberlain, Tucker Martine, and Lee Townsend. 2007. *Floratone*. Blue Note B000RPCES4.

Group Bombino, 2013. *Nomad*. Nonesuch 534291.

Hendrix, Jimi. 1967. *Are You Experienced?* Reprise RS 6261.

———. Axis: *Bold as Love*. Reprise RS 6281.

———. 1970. *Band of Gypsys*. Capitol STAO-472.

———. 1999. *Live at Woodstock*. MCA MCA3–11987.

House, Son. 1992. *Father of the Delta Blues: The Complete 1965 Sessions*. Columbia C2K 48867.

King, B.B. 1992. *B. B. King: King of the Blues*. MCA MCAD4–10677.

Konono N° 1. 2004. *Congotronics*. Crammed Discs. CRAW 27.

McLaughlin, John, with Mahavishnu Orchestra. 1971. *The Inner Mounting Flame*. Columbia MAL 2835

Mattalla, Moudou Ould. 2006. *Mauritania—Guitar of the Sands*. Buda Musique.

Santana, Carlos. 2009. *The Woodstock Experience*. Columbia 88697 48242 2.

Schwartz, Tony. 1954. *New York 19*. Folkways FW05558. LP.

———. 1956. *Sounds of My City: The Stories, Music and Sounds of the People of New York*. Folkways FW07341/FR8970. LP.

Stockhausen, Karlheinz. 1969. *Telemusik/Mixtur*. Deutsche Grammophon 643 546.

Sun City Girls. 1987. *Horse Cock Phepner*. Placebo PLA 024.

———. 1990. *Torch of the Mystics*. Tupelo TUPP-44-2.

———. 1993. *Bright Surroundings, Dark Beginnings*. Majora (no release number).

———. 1993. *Kaliflower*. Abduction 001.

———. 1996. *330,003 Crossdressers from Beyond the Rig Veda*. Abduction ABDT 008.

Tinariwen. 2007. *Aman Iman: Water Is Life*. Independiente ISOM 65CD.

Touré, Ali Farka. 1996. *Radio Mali*. World Circuit, Nonesuch 79569-2.

Various Artists. 1951. *Music of the World's People: Vol. 1*. Folkways FW04504. LP. Produced by Henry Cowell.

———. 1952. *Anthology of American Folk Music*. Folkways SFW40090. 6XCD (reissued 1997). Edited by Harry Smith. Smithsonian

———. 1956. *Sounds of a South African Homestead*. Folkways FW06151. LP. Recorded by Raymond B. Cowles.

———. 1958. *Sounds of North American Frogs: The Biological Significance of Voice in Frogs*. Folkways FW6166. LP. Conceived, narrated, and documented by Charles M. Bogert.

———. 1959. *Street and Gangland Rhythms: Beats and Improvisations by Six Boys in Trouble*. Folkways FW05589. LP. Collected and edited by E. Richard Sorenson.

———. 1960. *Sounds of Insects*. Folkways FW06178 / Scholastic SX6178. LP. Recorded and annotated by A. T. Gaul.

———. *Tuareg Music of the Southern Sahara*. Folkways FE 4470.

———. 1961. *Radio Moscow and the Western Hemisphere*. Cook COOK05050. LP.

———. 1962. *The Sounds of Yoga-Vedanta: A Documentary of Life in an Indian Ashram*. Folkways FW08970. LP. Recorded by Leslie Shepard.

———. 1964. *Niger: La Musique des Griots*. Ocora OCR 20.

———. 1965. *Nomades du Niger: Musique des Touareg, Musique des Bororo*. Ocora OCR 29.

———. 1976. *Africa: Drum, Chant and Instrumental Music*. Nonesuch Explorer 9–72073–2.

———. 1976. *Assalam Aleikoum Africa, Volume One*. Antilles 7032.

———. 1987. *Nomades du Désert*. Playasound PS 65009.

———. 1989. *Asmat Dream: New Music Indonesia, Vol. 1*. Lyrichord 7415.

———. 1991. *Masters of the Delta Blues: The Friends of Charlie Patton*. Yazoo 2002. Sony/Legacy CD 48867.

———. 1991. *Music of Indonesia Series, Volumes 1–20*. Smithsonian Folkways.

———. 1993. *Karya: New Music Indonesia, Vol. 3*. Lyrichord 7421.

———. 1993. *Mana 689: New Music Indonesia, Vol. 2*. Lyrichord 7420.

———. 2000. *Cambodia Rocks*. Parallel World CD 6.

———. 2001. *Bosavi: Rainforest Music from Papua New Guinea*. Smithsonian Folkways SFW40487. 3xCD. Recorded and produced by Steven Feld.

———. 2005. *Hunters of the Dallol Mawri*. Ocora C560170.

———. 2006. *The Stuff That Dreams Are Made Of*. Yazoo 2202.

———. 2010. *Les Nomades du Niger: Peuls, Bororos et Tuaregs*. Fremeaux & Associates FA 5290,

Zorn, John. 1986. *The Big Gundown: John Zorn Plays the Music of Ennio Morricone*. Elektra Nonesuch 9 71939–2.

OTHER VIDEO RECORDINGS CITED IN TEXT

1969. *Woodstock*. Directed by Michael Wadleigh. Warner Brothers.

1971. *Soul to Soul*. Directed by Dennis Sanders. Rhino R2 970327.

2002. *City of Ghosts*. Directed by Matt Dillon. Mainline Productions.

2004. *A State of Mind*. Directed by Daniel Gordon. New York: Kino Lorber Video.

2004. *Team America: World Police*. Directed by Trey Parker. Los Angeles: Paramount Pictures.

2004. *Jean Rouch: Screening Room with Robert Gardner*. Directed by Robert Gardner. Watertown, Mass.: Documentary Educational Resources.

2005. *Dear Pyongyang*. Directed by Yong-hi Yang. Cheon, Inc.

2006. *The Golden Voice*. Directed by Greg Cahill. Rising Falcon Cinema.

2007. *Planet Earth: The Complete BBC Series*. Narrated by David Attenborough, BBC/Warner.

2007. *Sleepwalking through the Mekong*. Directed by John Pirozzi. Film 101 Productions.

2011. *North Korea's Cinema of Dreams: 101 East Gains Rare Insight into the Beating Heart of North Korea's Film Industry*. Directed by Lynn Lee and James Leong. Doha, Qatar: Al Jazeera English, 101 East. Web video. www.aljazeera.com/programmes/101east/2011/02/2011217113256267999.html.

2014. *Don't Think I've Forgotten*. Directed by John Pirozzi. New York: Argot Pictures.

CONTRIBUTORS

JONATHAN ANDREWS is a Brooklyn-based writer and film reviewer.

CHRIS BECKER is a composer equally inspired by rock and roll, avant-garde jazz, dub compositional strategies, and *musique concrète*. He has created music for dance, film, and mixed-media installations and received grants from the Louisiana Division of the Arts, Meet the Composer, and the American Music Center. Becker has composed several scores for dance, including choreographer Rachel Cohen's *If the Shoe Fits* (2005), named one of the best dance performances of 2005 by *New York Times* critic John Rockwell. Becker also scored artist Jil Guyon's award-winning video *Widow,* which continues to screen at festivals across the United States. Becker has written about music and the arts for AllAboutJazz.com, Culturemap Houston, and Houston Press, and is completing a book titled *Freedom of Expression: Interviews with Women in Jazz.* He is currently working on a collaboration with choreographer Malcolm Low.

ANDY BETA is a freelance writer based in Brooklyn. He has written extensively about music and art of all stripes and his work has appeared in the *Wall Street Journal,* the *Village Voice, LA Times, Texas Monthly, Wax Poetics, Spin, Pitchfork,* and more. When last Andy Beta spoke with Sublime Frequencies' co-founder Alan Bishop, they discussed the hardships of travel through India and Egypt (Cairo, or "Al Qahira," translates as "the conqueror") and the lesson that, in traversing such foreign land, one must completely "submit to its vast and dizzying realities."

GONÇALO F. CARDOSO aka Gonzo is a Portuguese, London-based DJ and sound artist. He started Discrepant (http://discrepant.net) as a platform to release and diffuse his work and that of like-minded artists. Since 2011, he has released work by Kink Gong (Laurent Jeanneau), Italian outsiders My Cat Is An Alien, Belgian composer Cédric Stevens, and Russian duo Old Komm. Discrepant aims to showcase new, emerging sound techniques from all corners of the world, with a focus on unique styles that defy classification.

CRISTINA CRUZ-URIBE is an independent scholar based in New Haven, Connecticut. Her research focuses on intersections of music, literature, and popular culture in Latin America from the colonial period to the present.

DAVID FONT-NAVARRETE is an artist, musician, and ethnomusicologist. As a compser and performer, his work spans traditional, ritual, and experimental music. He has run the independent label Elegua Records since 1999 and performed with his electro-acoustic "io" project in venues throughout North America and Europe. He has taught at York University, Washington College, and Duke University. His research interests include: African, Latin American, and Caribbean music; music and ritual; multi-stable perception and coordination; applied/public ethnomusicology; archives; documentary arts; electronic, electro-acoustic, and experimental music; and collaborative research.

WILLS GLASSPIEGEL is a multimedia journalist and artist with a background in music management. His work has appeared on NPR, *FADER, VICE, DIS Magazine,* and *Afropop Worldwide.* As a manager, Glasspiegel facilitated the global introduction of two niche electronic music genres: *Shangaan electro* from South Africa and *bubu* from Sierra Leone. He is currently a PhD candidate at Yale in African-American studies/American studies where his work is focused around footwork, a music and dance style from Chicago, Glasspiegel's hometown.

ROBERT HARDIN is a visual artist who started making music in 1997. He co-curated an electronic music/film installation called "The Creamery" at the now-defunct Tonic in 2002 and at Chashama in 2005. He also co-curated "Mending Near the Pole," another electronic music/film installation at Office Ops in 2004. In 2007, he formed a band with Khristian Weeks and Richard Kamerman called Caledonian Laughing Bags—performing at Monkeytown in Brooklyn in 2008. Since 2009, Robert has led the collection of accomplished performing artists/ musicians known as Frogwell, renowned for their extremely conceptual live shows. In 2014, Mr. Hardin performed a spoken word/*musique concrète* piece with Mariette Papic as part of the Paweł Althamer show at the New Museum in New York City.

ETHAN HOLTZMAN is co-founder and keyboardist of the Los Angeles–based rock band Dengue Fever (denguefevermusic.com). The acclaimed band's roots go back to the late 1990s, when Holtzman collected Cambodian cassettes on a long trek through Southeast Asia and his brother Zac fell in love with the same music at a record store in San Francisco. In 2002, Dengue Fever was established officially—with Ethan on keys and Zac on guitar and vocals, plus saxophonist David Ralicke, drummer Paul Dreux Smith, bassist Senon Williams, and, of course, Cambodian chanteuse Chhom Nimol. Known for their trademark blend of 1960s' Cambodian pop and psychedelic rock, Dengue Fever released a fifth, full-length album, *The Deepest Lake,* in 2015.

E. TAMMY KIM is a writer and member of the *New Yorker*'s editorial staff. She previously worked as a staff writer at *Al Jazeera America* and a social justice lawyer. She plays Korean percussion and Western classical music.

RACHEL LEARS is a filmmaker, writer, and musician based in Brooklyn, New York. Her first documentary, *Birds of Passage* (2010), explored the everyday struggles of two Uruguayan songwriters. Her most recent documentary project, *The Hand That Feeds,* follows a historic labor campaign led by undocumented immigrant workers in New York City, and is supported by the Sundance Documentary Program. She has a PhD in Cultural Anthropology from New York University, and her doctoral research on media and cultural policy in Uruguay was supported by grants from Fulbright-Hays and the American Council of Learned Societies/Mellon Foundation. Her ongoing video art collaborations with artist Saya Woolfalk have screened in numerous galleries and museums worldwide.

MARC MASTERS is a freelance journalist currently contributing to *Pitchfork, The Wire,* the *Washington Post,* and the *Independent Weekly.* His work also has appeared in the *Village Voice, Signal to Noise,* the *Baltimore City Paper,* the *New York Sun,* and *Jazz Times.* His book *No Wave,* a history of a radical music and film movement in New York City in the late 1970s, was published by Black Dog in 2008. He lives in Washington, D.C., with his wife, Angela, and son, Max.

ANDREW MCGRAW is an Associate Professor of music at the University of Richmond. He received his PhD in ethnomusicology at Wesleyan University in 2005 and has published extensively on traditional and experimental music in Southeast Asia. As a student and performer of Indonesian musics, McGraw has studied and collaborated with the leading performers of Bali and Central Java during more than five years of research in Indonesia. His current book project, *Radical Traditions: Re-imagining Culture in Balinese New Music*, is forthcoming from Oxford University Press. As a performer and composer, he has appeared on the Tzadik, Sargasso, and Porter record labels.

DAVID NOVAK is Associate Professor of Music at the University of California, Santa Barbara. His work deals with the globalization of popular media, noise, protest culture, and social practices of listening. He is the author of recent essays in *Cultural Anthropology* and *The Wire*, as well as the book *Japanoise: Music at the Edge of Circulation* (Duke University Press, 2013).

LYNDA PAUL is a Postdoctoral Associate in the Integrated Humanities at Yale. Her current research examines the intersections between multimedia and performance, with a focus on the role of music and sound in genres ranging from theater and opera to film and digital media. More broadly, her work raises questions about aesthetics, ideologies, and representations of fantasy, history, myth, and culture as they are manifested through the act and experience of musical performance in diverse societies and historical periods. She holds degrees from Yale University, the University of Chicago, the University of Rochester, and the Eastman School of Music.

ANDRÉ REDWOOD received his PhD from Yale University. In 2012, he joined the faculty of the University of Notre Dame as an assistant professor of music theory. His research focuses chiefly on the history of music theory, music and rhetoric, and the music-theoretical writings of seventeenth-century polymath Marin Mersenne. Additional interests include law and the arts, performance, and music and politics in Brazil.

JOSEPH SALEM's research combines the analysis of musical media (from manuscripts to sound art) with historical theories of music and aesthetics to question the whys and hows of an artist's creative process. While his work has engaged composers from as early as the sixteenth century to as late as the twenty-first (including Cavalli, Rameau, Mozart, Verdi, Wagner, and Yuko Nexus6), his current research examines Pierre Boulez's stylistic development through a detailed study of the composer's manuscript sketches housed at the Paul Sacher Stiftung in Basel, Switzerland.

STANLEY SCOTT teaches Indian music at Yale and Wesleyan universities and directs the Rangila School of Music, serving Connecticut's South Asian community. He received the 2011 Mumbai Music Forum Award for "contribution to the cause of Indian music by an overseas-resident personality," and the 2001 lifetime achievement award from New York's Cultural Association of Bengal. His recordings include *The Weaver's Song: Bhajans of North India* and a major role in Anthony Braxton's opera *Trillium E.* He has performed as a featured artist at Kolkatta's Rabindra Sadhan, Mumbai's NCPA and Bharatiya Vidya Bhavan, Delhi University, and New York's Chhandayan Institute.

BRIAN SHIMKOVITZ started the blog Awesome Tapes from Africa (AFTA) in 2006, and has since played an important role in promoting access to African music outside the continent. In 2011, ATFA developed into a critically acclaimed vinyl label, re-releasing records by artists such as Bola, Dur-Dur Band, Hailu Mergia, and Penny Penny. Drawing on his vast African cassette archive, he DJs on twin tape decks at clubs all over the world.

SHAYNA SILVERSTEIN is an Assistant Professor in Performance Studies at Northwestern University. She was previously a 2013–2014 Mellon Postdoctoral Fellow at the University of Pennsylvania Humanities Forum. Her research examines Syrian popular dance music in relation to body, place, and nation and has received substantial support from Fulbright-IIE, the University of Chicago, and the U.S. Department of Education. Shayna has published in the fields of anthropology, ethnomusicology, and Middle East studies, and serves as an editor for *Norient Journal.* She has taught at Dartmouth College, University of Chicago, and University of Pennsylvania. Shayna received her PhD from the University of Chicago.

JULIE STRAND first traveled to West Africa in 1997 and returns frequently to the region for research and teaching. In 2004, she finished 18 months of field research on xylophone music in Burkina Faso for her PhD in Ethnomusicology, completed at Wesleyan University in 2009. An avid traveler, she has taught for many study abroad programs on music and culture in Ghana, Bali, Indonesia, and has sailed around the world three times with Semester at Sea. Dr. Strand has held teaching positions at Tufts University, MIT, and Brandeis University, and a postdoctoral residency at Northeastern University. She currently resides in Portland, Oregon.

ANDREW R. TONRY is a journalist in the American West. He writes about music, comedy, professional sports, drag queens, drugs, politics, and money.

MICHAEL E. VEAL is Professor of Music in the Departments of Music and African-American Studies at Yale University. He is the author of *Fela: The Life and Times of an African Musical Icon* (Temple University Press, 2000) and *Dub: Soundscapes and Shattered Songs in Jamaican Reggae* (Wesleyan University Press, 2007), as well as several article contributions to the *New York Times*, *The Wire*, *Jazz Perspectives,* and other publications. He is also an active musician.

Index

Page numbers in *italic* refer to illustrations.

collage, 13, 27, 31, 146, 242–45, 349; court cases, 83; Perloff on, 237, 242; Rauschenberg, 161n5. *See also* audio collage; audiovisual collage

collecting, 379. *See also* record collecting

Collins, John, 214

colonization and colonialism, 7–8, 111, 218, 224, 314, 377, 383, 385–86n13; Korea, 343; Mayet view, 158; in radio, 66. *See also* decolonization

Coltrane, John, 60

Comando Vermelho, 388, 389, 391, 394

compensation of musicians. *See* pay, musicians'

compulsory licensing, 82, 89n14

Conan, Olivier, 377

Congo, 43–44, 51n55, 215, 217, 222, 223, 227, 232n38

contracts, 35, 40, 68, 78, 125n8, 210, 325

Cook Records, 156

copyright, 35, 36, 37, 40, 80–91, 325, 328; Hagood on, 38; Harry Smith ploy, 47n8

Copyright Act. *See* U.S. Copyright Act of 1790; U.S. Copyright Act of 1909; U.S. Copyright Act of 1976

Copyright Term Extension Act CTEA, 37, 81, 88n10

Corbett, John, 16

Costa, Luiz Fernando da. *See* Fernandinho Beira-Mar

Costillares, Albano: *Latinamericarpet*, 367–87

country and western music, 69

Country Music in the World of Islam Volume XV, 62

Courlander, Harold, 154

cover art. *See* album art

cover songs, 89n14, 218, 291, 295, 303

Cowell, Henry, 154–55

Cowles, Raymond B., 152–53

Crammed Discs, 43, 51n55

credits, performers', 7, 9, 38, 78, 158, 390; DVDs, 87, 126n9; *Folk and Pop Sounds of Sumatra Vol. 1*, 79, 125n8

Cuba, 76, 154, 215, 218, 370

cubism, 242, 261, 262n10

cultural exploitation, 35, 37, 59, 126n10, 313

Cumbancha (label), 12

cumbia, 370, 373, 374, 385n4

"curiosities." *See* "oddities" and "curiosities"

cut-up technique, 11, 65, 146, 268

cylinder recording, 240

Czinczel, Alexandra, 347

Dabh, Halim El-. *See* El-Dabh, Halim

dabke, 265, 267–79, 288, 289, 290

dancehall music, 274–75, 283n50, 394

dangdut, 323, 324, 326, 331, 333, 336

Dante's Disneyland Inferno (Sun City Girls), 61

Davis, Erik, 125n8

decolonization, 16–17, 124n5, 226, 279

Deep Forest, 26

Deerhoof, 51n55, 65

Demick, Barbara: *Nothing to Envy*, 342

Dengue Fever, 38, 49n35, 65, 174–76

Los Destellos, 370, 372, 373, 374, 375, 385n8

Detroit, 13, 18, 268, 278, 348

Diabate, Sekou, 265

Diabate, Toumani, 200

Diawara, Manthia, 217

Dickinson, Kay, 7

dictatorship: Latin America, 380–83; Myanmar, 322, 329; North Korea, 340–64

digital technology, 14, 19, 27, 32, 36, 39, 40, 42, 228; copyright and, 37, 80, 81, 83, 86, 89n12, 89n14; filmmaking, 140; Indonesia, 323, 330, 332; piracy and, 375, 385n9; Sahel Sounds, 224; Shimkovitz, 98; Wyatt, 140. *See also* DVDs; Internet; iPad apps; samples and sampling

Dimanche à Bamako (Amadou and Mariam), 43

"disorientalism" (Vazquez), 147–48

disorientation, 148, 185, 188, 313, 334

distortion, 42–45, 150, 218, 232n33, 269, 327; in *Radio Java*, 328, 329, 330, 332, 334; in *Radio Palestine*, 248, 249, 250, 251, 252, 257–59

DIY. *See* do-it-yourself aesthetic (DIY)

Djinn Funnel (Sun City Girls), 62

documentaries, nature. *See* nature documentaries

Dogon people, 187, 188–91, 196–97, 198

do-it-yourself aesthetic (DIY), 11, 33, 40, 86, 123, 172, 274, 377

Dolman, Larry, 158

Domino (label), 289

Doueh. *See* Baamar, Salmou "Doueh"; Group Doueh

drug trade, 393, 394

drum machines, 44, 274, 330, 388, 393, 396

drums: African, 182, 186, 189, 196, 198, 200, 232n33; bass, 98; Indian, 303, 317n14; Indonesian, 331; Middle Eastern, 248, 270, 274, 277, 281n21; North Korean, 349; Sun City Girls, 31, 57, 58, 64

"Dry Spell Blues" (House), 210, 212, 229

Dunn, David, 145

Dusted Magazine, 274, 305, 335

DVDs, 14, 45, 74, 390; copyright notices, 87; credits, 126n9; liner notes, 128n15; packaging, *108*

Easter Island. *See* Isla de Pascua (Easter Island)

Edgar, Jacob, 12

Egypt, 74–75, 101–2, 227–28

El-Dabh, Halim, 101–2

Eldred v. Ashcroft, 88–89n10

Electric Cambodia (Dengue Fever), 175, 176

electric guitar, 213; Africa, 30, 214–17, 220, 222, 223, 225–26, 232n33; Latin America, 367, 368, 374, 382; North Korea, 345, 351

Eno, Brian, 161n4, 208

Ethiopia, 135–39, 154

Ethnic Folkways series, 153–54

ethnographic film, 110, 111, 113, 120, 124n5, 125n7, 127n11, 336; Wyatt on, 139–40

ethnographic photography, 183, 336

Evelev, Yale, 12

"exotic" (word), 162n6

exoticism and exoticization, 19, 78, 111, 143–51, 153, 154, 157, 158, 378; African guitar rock, 212, 213, 223, 224; animals, 115; in blurbs, 109; Boon view, 126n10, 377; Brazilian music, 390; *Bush Taxi Mali*, 185, 188, 193, 198, 201; eroticization and, 119; Folkways approach, 154; Gergis view, 131n43; in Hendrix, 228; hybridization and, 131n42; India, 301, 305, 306, 307, 314; Indonesian music, 327; in jazz, 15; Mayet on, 73; *Proibidão C.V*, 389; Smithsonian Folkways, 156, Souleyman, 267–68, 273, 279; Sun City Girls, 59

"experimental ethnography" (Russell), 110–11, 112, 113, 125n7

experimental films, 3, 116, 125n7

exploitation, cultural. *See* cultural exploitation

Facebook, 326

fair use, 82–83

Far Eastern Audio Review, 38

Farrell, Gerry, 301, 304, 305, 311

Feld, Steven, 26, 45

Fernandinho Beira-Mar. *See* Beira-Mar, Fernandinho

file sharing, online. *See* online file sharing

film music, Indian. *See* Bollywood music

films and videos, 14, 29, 38, 45, 61, 72; camera angles, 113–14, 116; close-ups in, 116, 117, 118; digital vs. analog, 140; eroticism in, 117, 119; Gocher's, 62; narration, 112, 128n15, 140; North Korea, 343, 345, 346; rawness (aesthetic) in, 108–31; Souleyman in, 267, 271; violence in, 116, 119; Wyatt's, 135–41; YouTube, 28, 100, 267. *See also* DVDs; ethnographic film; experimental films; Mayet, Hisham; nature documentaries

Folk and Pop Sounds of Sumatra Vol. 1, 78, 79, 125n8

folk music, American, 47n8, 151, 154–55, 196, 211, 213

Folk Music of the Sahel (Mayet), 16

Folkways, 6, 12, 28, 151–56, 160–61, 311, 323, 338n254. *See also* Smithsonian Folkways

Foucault, Michel, 377

found materials, 14, 110, 299–300; cassettes, 13, 39, 348; film footage, 125n7, 188

found sound. *See* ambient sound

Four Tet. *See* Hebden, Kieran (Four Tet)

France, 85, 222, 227, 282. *See also* Ocora

frogs, 142–43, 151, 153

Fula people, 187, 190, 198, 219

funk carioca, 388–402

Gaddafi, Muammar, 221, 225, 226

gamelan, 142–43, 323, 325, 326–29, 331–34, 336; Alan Bishop on, 8, 34, 59, 312, 324

gangsta rap, 394

Garbarek, Jan, 26

Garelick, Jon, 272

Gaul, A. T.: *Sounds of Insects*, 153

Gergis, Mark, 5, 65, 72, 131n43, 174, 226–27; *Cambodian Cassette Archives*, 13, 39, 66, 70, 175; *I Remember Syria*, 18, 268, 278; Souleyman and, 265, 266–67, 268, 269, 275, 278, 289–90; *Sumatran Folk Cinema*, 87, 116, 119, 129n23; *Thai Pop Spectacular*; 70; Yassin and, 269, 280–81n16

Ghana, 98, 99, 216

Ghenea, Serban, 277

Glass, Ira, 382

Glasspiegel, Will, 285n62

Gocher, Charles, 5, 31, 57, 58, 61, 62, 65

Goldsmith, Peter D., 155

gongs, 3, 45, 119, 320, 321, 334. *See also* gamelan

Gossner, Frank "Conakry," 50n40

government-controlled arts, 344, 345–46

government surveillance. *See* surveillance

Graceland (Simon), 16

Great Britain, 73, 255, 257, 267, 300. *See also* Beatles; Rolling Stones

Griaule, Marcel, 160

La Gringa Inga (Ingeborg Zwinkel), 371

griots, 181, 193, 194, 195, 222

Group Bombino, 222, 223

Group Doueh, 17, 30, 50n45, 72, 73, 76–77, 223; *Guitar Music from the Western Sahara*, 87

Group Inerane, 73, 211, 222, 223, 224

Guerewol festival, 219

Guinea, 215, 218

guitar, 195, 210–34. *See also* electric guitar; Hawaii guitar

"guitar heroes," 213, 214, 216, 223

Guitars from Agadez series, 211, 223, 225

Guitars of the Golden Triangle, 29

Gysin, Brion, 65, 146

hackers, 36, 37

Hagood, Mack, 38

Haiti and Haitians, 139, 154

Hamar people, 137, 139

Hamm, Carl, 338n25

The Handsome Stranger (Sun City Girls), 61

Hannerz, Ulf, 124n5

Harbi, Mahmoud, 273, 277, 288, 291

Hardin, Robert, 101–3

Hart, Mickey, 33

Hawaiian guitar, 295, 301, 303

Hawaiian influence on Indonesia, 336

Hebden, Kieran (Four Tet), 279, 280n8, 289

Heider, Karl, 110, 124n5, 127n11

Hendrix, Jimi, 30, 69, 213, 216, 217, 218, 222, 228

Herbert, Matthew, 277

"high" culture, 378

Highway to Hassake (Souleyman), 267, 269, 281n16

hip-hop, 51n55, 69, 97, 224, 330; Brazil, 388, 393; copyright and, 81, 83, 86. *See also* gangsta rap

history, erasure of, 379–83

Holm, Elisabeth, 141

Holtzman, Ethan, 174–76

Holy Warbles, 47

Hong Kong, 347, 360n56

Hood, Mantle, 8

Hooker, John Lee, 222, 224

Horse Cock Phepner (Sun City Girls), 61

House, Son, 210–11, 212, 225, 229, 229–30n7

house music, 99, 266, 273

Howard, Keith, 355–56n4, 359n45, 359n50

hybridity, 25, 27, 33, 324, 325; Alan Bishop view,

South Africa, 15, 99, 152–53

Southeast Asia, 29, 68, 69, 144–45, 207, 320–22. *See also* Cambodia; Indonesia; Malaysia; Thailand

South Korea, 342, 346, 348, 349, 350, 354, 355

Soviet Union, 343, 360n64

spazzcore, 274, 283n42

Stallman, Richard, 36

Staring into the Sun (Wyatt), 135, 138–39, 141

A State of Mind (Gordon), 346, 358n31

Stein, Gertrude, 242

stereotypes, 212, 343, 355

Sterne, Jonathan, 45–46

Stiles, Kristine, 161n5

Stoller, Paul, 160

strangeness, 26, 28, 31, 32, 33, 156, 188, 197; Latinamericarpet, 367, 372; Mathers on, 306; Radio India, 306, 314, 315; Sonneborn on, 157. *See also* exoticism and exoticization; "oddities" and "curiosities"

Straw, Will, 15, 376

Streets of Lhasa (Bishop), 144

stringed instruments, African, 212, 213, 215, 220, 228, 229n6. See also *kora*; *ngoni*

stringed instruments, Indian, 303, 317n14

stringed instruments, Middle Eastern, 270, 277, 281n21. See also *oud*

Stylus Magazine, 306

Sueb, Benyamin. *See* Benyamin S.

Suicide (band), 274

Sukarno, 330

Sumatra, 30, 109. See also *Folk and Pop Sounds of Sumatra Vol. 1*

Sumatran Electric Chair (Sun City Girls), 61

Sumatran Folk Cinema (Gergis and Bishop), 87, 116, 119, 129n23

Sun City Girls, 5, 9, 25, 31, 33, 55–63, 112–13, 128n16; Coley on, 48n25; Martine on, 206; performance art, 113, 128n18; Vazquez on, 147

Sundanese people, 323, 328, 330, 331, 332, 333, 336

Supreme Court cases. *See* U.S. Supreme Court cases

surveillance, 271, 357n13, 383

Sutton, R. Anderson, 45, 334

"Sweet Lullaby," 26

Syliphone (label), 218

Syria, 18, 30–31, 60, 74–75, 223, 227–28, 265–91; instruments, 281n21

tango, 370, 372

Tanzania, 321

Team America: World Police (film), 343, 356n7

"*techno-dabke*," 268, 273, 274, 275, 278–79

television, 103, 146, 182, 189; in audio collage, 138–39, 194, 371, 372; Ethiopia, 138–39

Thailand, 3, 67, 68, 70–71, 87, 97–98, 117–19

Thai Pop Spectacular (Gergis), 70

330,003 Crossdressers from Beyond the Rig Veda (Sun City Girls), 58

Thriller (Jackson), 65

thumb piano. See *likembe* (thumb piano)

Tibet, 144

Tinariwen, 222, 289

Tinder Records, 206–7

Tonggeret, 328

Topic (label), 310, 311

Torch of the Mystics (Sun City Girls), 56, 58

Tosti, Mina, 280n8

Touré, Ali Farka, 222

trademark, 80, 86, 91n40

translation, 16, 100, 281n16; copyright, 84; in liner notes, 3, 281n16, 352; by Mayet, 72; Mayet view, 352

Traoré, Boubacar, 216

Traoré, Lobi Trao, 222

"trash fandoms" (Straw), 376

Tropicália, 49n33, 372–73, 381

trot (North Korea). See *bbongjjak*

Tuareg, 12, 220–25, 227, 289

"Tuareg" (term), 228

Turkey, 270, 271, 278, 281n21, 290

2 Live Crew, 83

Udhas, Pankaj, 302, 313, 317n13

ugliness, 57, 341

Susan D. Crafts, Daniel Cavicchi, Charles
Keil, and the Music in Daily Life Project
*My Music: Explorations of Music
in Daily Life*

Jim Cullen
*Born in the USA: Bruce Springsteen
and the American Tradition*

Anne Danielsen
*Presence and Pleasure: The Funk Grooves
of James Brown and Parliament*

Peter Doyle
*Echo and Reverb: Fabricating
Space in Popular Music Recording,
1900–1960*

Ron Emoff
*Recollecting from the Past: Musical
Practice and Spirit Possession
on the East Coast of Madagascar*

Yayoi Uno Everett and
Frederick Lau, editors
Locating East Asia in Western Art Music

Susan Fast and Kip Pegley, editors
Music, Politics, and Violence

Heidi Feldman
*Black Rhythms of Peru: Reviving African
Musical Heritage in the Black Pacific*

Kai Fikentscher
*"You Better Work!" Underground Dance
Music in New York City*

Ruth Finnegan
*The Hidden Musicians: Music-Making
in an English Town*

Daniel Fischlin and Ajay Heble, editors
*The Other Side of Nowhere: Jazz,
Improvisation, and Communities
in Dialogue*

Wendy Fonarow
*Empire of Dirt: The Aesthetics and
Rituals of British "Indie" Music*

Murray Forman
*The 'Hood Comes First: Race, Space,
and Place in Rap and Hip-Hop*

Lisa Gilman
*My Music, My War: The Listening Habits
of U.S. Troops in Iraq and Afghanistan*

Paul D. Greene and
Thomas Porcello, editors
*Wired for Sound: Engineering and
Technologies in Sonic Cultures*

Tomie Hahn
*Sensational Knowledge: Embodying
Culture through Japanese Dance*

Edward Herbst
*Voices in Bali: Energies and Perceptions
in Vocal Music and Dance Theater*

Deborah Kapchan
*Traveling Spirit Masters:
Moroccan Gnawa Trance and Music
in the Global Marketplace*

Raymond Knapp
*Symphonic Metamorphoses:
Subjectivity and Alienation in Mahler's
Re-Cycled Songs*

Laura Lohman
*Umm Kulthūm: Artistic Agency and the
Shaping of an Arab Legend, 1967–2007*

Helena Simonett
*Banda: Mexican Musical Life
across Borders*

Mark Slobin
*Subcultural Sounds: Micromusics
of the West*

Mark Slobin, editor
Global Soundtracks: Worlds of Film Music

Christopher Small
The Christopher Small Reader

Christopher Small
*Music of the Common Tongue:
Survival and Celebration in African
American Music*

Christopher Small
Music, Society, Education

Christopher Small
*Musicking: The Meanings
of Performing and Listening*

Regina M. Sweeney
*Singing Our Way to Victory:
French Cultural Politics and Music
During the Great War*

Colin Symes
*Setting the Record Straight: A Material
History of Classical Recording*

Steven Taylor
*False Prophet: Fieldnotes
from the Punk Underground*

Paul Théberge
*Any Sound You Can Imagine: Making
Music/Consuming Technology*

Sarah Thornton
*Club Cultures: Music, Media
and Sub-cultural Capital*

Michael E. Veal
*Dub: Songscape and Shattered Songs
in Jamaican Reggae*

Michael E. Veal and
E. Tammy Kim, editors
*Punk Ethnography: Artists and Scholars
Listen to Sublime Frequencies*

Robert Walser
*Running with the Devil: Power, Gender,
and Madness in Heavy Metal Music*

Dennis Waring
*Manufacturing the Muse:
Estey Organs and Consumer Culture
in Victorian America*

Lise A. Waxer
*The City of Musical Memory:
Salsa, Record Grooves, and
Popular Culture in Cali, Colombia*

Mina Yang
*Planet Beethoven: Classical Music
at the Turn of the Millennium*